International Criminal Justice Series

Volume 1

More information about this series at http://www.springer.com/series/13470

Gerhard Werle · Lovell Fernandez
Moritz Vormbaum
Editors

Africa and the International Criminal Court

ASSER PRESS

Springer

Editors
Gerhard Werle
Moritz Vormbaum
Juristische Fakultät Humboldt-Universität
Berlin, Berlin
Germany

Lovell Fernandez
Faculty of Law,
Department for Criminal Law
University of the Western Cape
Bellville, Cape Town
South Africa

ISBN 978-94-6265-028-2 ISBN 978-94-6265-029-9 (eBook)
DOI 10.1007/978-94-6265-029-9

Library of Congress Control Number: 2014945343

Published by T.M.C. ASSER PRESS, The Hague, The Netherlands www.asserpress.nl
Produced and distributed for T.M.C. ASSER PRESS by Springer-Verlag Berlin Heidelberg

Printed on acid-free paper

Springer is part of Springer Science+Business Media (www.springer.com)

Acknowledgments

This book is based on a conference which the South African-German Centre for Transnational Criminal Justice hosted in Cape Town in November 2013; the Centre is run in cooperation between the law faculties of the University of the Western Cape and of Humboldt-Universität zu Berlin. The editors would like to express their gratitude to the German Academic Exchange Service (DAAD) and the German Federal Foreign Office for generously funding the Centre in the framework of the *African Excellence* initiative.

In addition, the editors owe great thanks to *Dr. Horst Freitag* (German Ambassador to the Republic of South Africa), *Prof. Ramesh Bharuthram* (Deputy Vice Chancellor of the University of the Western Cape) and *Dr. Dorothee Weyler* (German Academic Exchange Service, Project Manager Centres of African Excellence) for addressing the audience at the conference. The opening remarks of Ambassador *Freitag* can be accessed under: http://www.southafrica.diplo.de/Vertretung/suedafrika/en/__pr/Speeches-Freitag/2013/11-ICC.html?archive=3519722.

The editors would also like to thank the staff members and Ph.D. students of the Centre who dedicated a lot of their time and energy to help organizing the conference. To be mentioned are, in particular, *Windell Nortje*, *Anja Schepke*, *Marlen Vesper-Gräske*, *Farieda Hendricks*, *Hazel Jeftha*, *Jean Philipo*, *Sosteness Materu*, *Marshet Tessema* and *Thabiso Wiliams.*

The editing of the book was facilitated by the great support of *Prof. Raymond Koen, Dr. Sosteness Materu, Marshet Tessema, Fatuma Silungwe, Aziz Epik, Marlen Vesper-Gräske* and *Janosch Kuner*. *Selemani Kinyunyu* was helpful with the selection of the Decisions by the African Union in the Annex of the book.

Cape Town, March 2014

Gerhard Werle
Lovell Fernandez
Moritz Vormbaum

Contents

Abbreviations

AC	Appeals Chamber
Art(s).	Article(s)
AU	African Union
CIPEV	Commission of Inquiry into Post-Election Violence (Kenya)
DRC	Democratic Republic of the Congo
ed(s).	Editor(s)
edn.	Edition
et al.	And others (*et alii*)
et seq.	And the following (*et sequens; et sequentes*)
FARG	Fund for the Support of Genocide Survivors (*Fonds d'Assistance aux Rescapés du Génocide*)
i.e.	That is (*id est*)
ibid.	In the same place (*ibidem*)
ICC	International Criminal Court
ICJ	International Court of Justice
ICTR	International Criminal Tribunal for Rwanda
ICTY	International Criminal Tribunal for the former Yugoslavia
ISS	Institute for Security Studies
KNCHR	Kenya National Commission on Human Rights
Marg no(s)	Marginal Number(s)
n., nn.	Footnote(s) (*nota, notae*)
NGO	Non-Governmental Organization
no(s).	Number(s)
OTP	Office of the Prosecutor (at the International Criminal Court)
p., pp.	Page(s)
para(s)	Paragraph(s)
PSC	African Union Peace and Security Council
PTC	Pre-Trial Chamber
Res.	Resolution
Rwf	Rwandan Francs
SADC	Southern African Development Community

SALC	Southern Africa Litigation Centre
SCA	Supreme Court of Appeal (South Africa)
TC	Trial Chamber
TIG	Community work (*Travaux d'Interet Général*)
UK	United Kingdom
UN	United Nations
UN Doc.	Documents of the United Nations
UNICEF	United Nations International Children's Emergency Fund
UNTS	United Nations Treaty Series
US	United States of America
VCLT	Vienna Convention on the Law of Treaties of 1969
VWU	Victims and Witnesses Unit

Editors and Contributors

About the Editors

Gerhard Werle is a Professor at Humboldt-Universität zu Berlin, Director of the South African-German Centre for Transnational Criminal Justice and an Extraordinary Professor at the University of the Western Cape. One of his main works, the textbook 'Principles of International Criminal Law', has been published in six languages and in several editions.

Lovell Fernandez is a Professor at the Law Faculty of the University of the Western Cape and Director of the South African-German Centre for Transnational Criminal Justice. Currently, he is a Vice Dean of the Faculty.

Moritz Vormbaum received his Ph.D. at the University of Münster (Germany). He is a Senior Researcher at Humboldt-Universität zu Berlin as well as coordinator and lecturer at the South African-German Centre for Transnational Criminal Justice.

About the Contributors

Temitayo Lucia Akinmuwagun is an alumna of the South African-German Centre for Transnational Criminal Justice. She is currently a Senior State Counsel at the International and Comparative Law Department of the Federal Ministry of Justice, Abuja, Nigeria.

Shamila Batohi is a Senior Legal Advisor to the Prosecutor at the International Criminal Court. Before this position, she worked as a Public Prosecutor in KwaZulu-Natal, South Africa, where she was the Head of the Directorate of Special Operations (also known as the 'Scorpions').

René Blattmann is a former Judge and Second Vice-President of the International Criminal Court, as well as a former Minister of Justice of Bolivia. Currently, he is a visiting Professor at Humboldt-Universität zu Berlin, funded by the German Academic Exchange Service.

Mbacké Fall is the Chief Prosecutor at the Extraordinary African Chambers in the Courts of Senegal. Before this position, he has been a Judge in different courts in Senegal, worked as a Prosecutor and was a counsel to the Criminal Law and Administrative Chambers of the Supreme Court of Senegal.

Florian Jeßberger is a Professor of Criminal Law at the University of Hamburg, Germany. He is also the Director of the Institute of Criminal Justice Studies and a Vice Dean of the Faculty of Law.

Aimé Muyoboke Karimunda is a Senior Lecturer at the University of Rwanda and Advisor to the Deputy Chief Justice. Before this, he has served as a Dean of the Faculty of Law, Campus of Gisenyi, at Kigali Independent University.

Gerhard Kemp is a Professor of International Criminal Law, Criminal Law and Criminal Procedure at Stellenbosch University, South Africa. Among others, he serves on the editorial board of the African Yearbook on International Humanitarian Law.

Sosteness Materu is a Lecturer at the University of Dar es Salaam, Tanzania. He is an alumnus of the South African-German Centre of Transnational Criminal Justice. He has obtained a Ph.D. from Humboldt-Universität zu Berlin in the framework of the Centre.

Sanji Mmasenono Monageng is the First Vice-President and a Judge at the Appeals Division of the International Criminal Court. Before joining the Court, she served as a High Court Judge in the Kingdom of Swaziland, where she was responsible for criminal and civil law as well as constitutional law.

Tim Murithi is the Head of the Justice and Reconciliation in Africa Programme at the Institute for Justice and Reconciliation, Cape Town, and Research Fellow at the African Gender Institute, University of Cape Town.

Juliet Okoth is an alumna of the South African-German Centre of Transnational Criminal Justice. She is the first Ph.D. student, who graduated from the Centre. Following her studies, she worked as a Legal Researcher at the Appeals Court of Kenya and is currently a Lecturer at the University of Nairobi.

Sam Rugege is the Chief Justice of the Supreme Court of Rwanda. Before this position, he was a Professor at the University of the Western Cape and Cornell Law School. He has also been the Principal Judge of the First Instance Division of the Court of Justice of the Common Market for Eastern and Southern Africa (COMESA).

Ekaterina Trendafilova is a Judge at the Pre-Trial Division of the International Criminal Court. Before the Court, she served as an expert to the Ministry of Justice and the Parliament of Bulgaria where she chaired the Criminal Division of the Legislative Consultative Council.

Chapter 1
Introduction: Africa and the International Criminal Court

Gerhard Werle, Lovell Fernandez and Moritz Vormbaum

Contents

This book is based on the conference "Africa and the International Criminal Court" which the South African-German Centre for Transnational Criminal Justice[1] hosted on 22 and 23 November 2013 in Cape Town. The conference brought together eminent experts in the field of international criminal justice at both the international and domestic level, and it was also attended by a large number of young African lawyers from twelve African countries.

At the time of the conference, the tensions between the African Union and the International Criminal Court had reached a new peak, for only a few days prior to the start of the conference the Assembly of the African Union had decided in an

[1] The Centre is a joint project between Humboldt-Universität zu Berlin and the University of the Western Cape, Cape Town. It was founded in 2008 as one of six 'Centres of African Excellence' established on the African continent in cooperation with German partner universities as a teaching and research centre. The Centre is funded by the German Academic Exchange Service (*Deutscher Akademische Austauschdienst*, DAAD) under the auspices of the German Federal Foreign Office (see http://www.transcrim.org). The Centre is located in the Faculty of Law in the University of the Western Cape and also has offices in the Faculty of Law at Humboldt-Universität zu Berlin. The Directors are *Lovell Fernandez* (University of the Western Cape) and *Gerhard Werle* (Humboldt-Universität zu Berlin); the Coordinator is *Moritz Vormbaum* (Humboldt-Universität zu Berlin).

G. Werle (✉) · M. Vormbaum
Faculty of Law, Humboldt-Universität zu Berlin, Unter den Linden 6,
10099 Berlin, Germany
e-mail: gerhard.werle@rewi.hu-berlin.de

M. Vormbaum
e-mail: moritz.vormbaum@rewi.hu-berlin.de

L. Fernandez
Faculty of Law, University of the Western Cape, Bellville 7535, South Africa
e-mail: lfernandez@uwc.co.za

G. Werle et al. (eds.), *Africa and the International Criminal Court*,
International Criminal Justice Series 1, DOI 10.1007/978-94-6265-029-9_1

extraordinary session that no charges should be commenced or continued before any International Court or Tribunal against any serving AU Head of State or Government and that any AU Member State that wished to refer a case to the International Criminal Court "may inform and seek the advice of the African Union".[2] Earlier in 2013, the Ethiopian Prime Minister and then Chairman of the African Union, *Hailemariam Desalegn*, stated during an AU summit that "[t]he intention [of establishing the International Criminal Court] was to avoid any kind of impunity but now the process has degenerated into some kind of race-hunting".[3] At its summit in January 2014 in Ethiopia, the African Union again urged its members to comply with AU Decisions and "to speak with one voice" against criminal proceedings brought against sitting Heads of State.[4]

These developments stand in stark contrast to the instrumental role played by Africa in the creation and the establishment of the International Criminal Court. Today, with 34 members, Africa constitutes the largest regional group of States Parties to the ICC Statute. Furthermore, Africans occupy a number of key positions at the International Criminal Court. At the time of writing, four Judges (including the First Vice President), the Prosecutor, the Head of the Jurisdiction, Complementarity and Cooperation Division, the Principal Counsel for the Defence, among others, are Africans. Moreover, several African States have enacted laws which incorporate the ICC Statute into their domestic legal orders.[5]

However, only a few years into the Court's taking up of its work, this once promising relationship between the International Criminal Court and the African Union has deteriorated. Representatives in the African Union have recently been highly critical of the fact that after more than ten years, all of the eight situations with which the Court is now seized relate to African states. The accusations, coming from a number of African politicians, are that the International Criminal Court is focusing on Africa while, for the sake of political expedience, it overlooks international crimes perpetrated elsewhere. Furthermore, some African leaders are of the view that the UN Security Council's role in the system of the International Criminal Court is partial, in the sense that it uses the Court to prosecute African Heads of State and political leaders of countries that are not States Parties to the ICC Statute. The International Criminal Court came under sharp criticism, in particular, when both the current Kenyan President, *Uhuru Kenyatta,* and his Deputy, *William Ruto,* were indicted. In addition, certain African states have criticized European states, alleging that they are abusing the principle of universality to prosecute Africans.[6]

---

[2] See the Decisions taken at the Extraordinary Session of the Assembly of the African Union on 12 October 2013 in the Annex to this volume.

[3] See Reuters, available at http://www.reuters.com/places/africa/article/2013/05/27/us-africa-icc-idUSBRE94Q0F620130527 (accessed on 3 April 2014).

[4] See the Decision taken at the 22nd Ordinary Session, 30–31 January 2014 in the Annex to this volume.

[5] On the implementation of the ICC Statute in Africa see Chap. 6 of *Kemp* in this book.

[6] See on this matter Chap. 10 by *Jeßberger* in this book.

In their criticism, some African politicians have sought to portray the International Criminal Court as having become a neo-colonial instrument for targeting Africa and its leaders. On the one hand this criticism could be refuted on the ground that it is politically biased. On the other hand it cannot be denied that all eight situations with which the Court is currently dealing are located in Africa. When addressing these issues one must bear in mind that international criminal justice has, since its coming into being, been selective. Prosecutions of international crimes took place only when the political conditions were favorable, as was the case with the Nuremberg and Tokyo trials as well as the Yugoslavia and Rwanda tribunals. Following other situations of human rights atrocities, no courts were created, especially when the interests of political leaders or the military of powerful states where at stake.

Against this background, the following questions arise in the present African context: Why does Africa feature so prominently in the work of the International Criminal Court? Is there a specific bias against Africa? What can be done by African states to avoid impunity and to step up the prosecution of international crimes perpetrated in Africa? And how can the relationship between Africa and the Court be shaped in the future?

These are the questions that the contributors to this book seek to answer from their respective different backgrounds as international or domestic judges and prosecutors, and scholars of international criminal law.

Part I of this book deals with the interface between the International Criminal Court and African states. Accordingly, Judge *Sanji Mmasenono Monageng* (First Vice-President of the International Criminal Court) looks into the relationship between Africa and the Court (Chap. 2). The Judge depicts the Court as a non-political organ whose duty it is to interpret and apply the Rome Statute and to work within this given legal framework. *Monageng* emphasizes that any proceedings before the Court are conducted purely in accordance with the Rome Statute, which, of course, includes any proceedings against sitting Heads of State. It, therefore, surprises her that some African States Parties to the ICC Statute criticize it for doing precisely what it was meant to do by exactly those states. Should there be deficiencies in the Rome Statute, *Monageng* argues, it is not the Court itself, but the Assembly of States Parties which must remedy them. The latter, as a political body, is the competent forum to suggest changes and eventually amend the Statute. *Monageng* leaves little doubt as to her own opinion regarding accusations of racism that have been leveled against the Court, given that there are many Africans employed in various branches of it. As regards the complementarity principle, *Monageng* points to the fact that African states need to take ownership of the justice mechanisms created to deal with human rights atrocities committed on African territory, and that this can be done by implementing the appropriate laws to deal with such crimes. However, notwithstanding the current strained relationship between African states and the International Criminal Court, *Monageng* remains optimistic.

In her chapter on the relation between African states and the International Criminal Court, as seen from a judge's perspective (Chap. 3), *Ekaterina Trendafilova*, an incumbent judge at the Court, analyzes some of the most important legal and practical issues that the Court has to deal with and which have had an impact on the relationship between the International Criminal Court and African states. This includes the admissibility of cases before the Court, the immunity of Heads of State, and the cooperation of African States with the Court. *Trendafilova* points out that where the Court's admission of a case is challenged, the Court looks at the status of the domestic proceedings at the time the challenge is brought. More precisely, the International Criminal Court has to establish whether any concrete steps have been taken to investigate the crimes. She, therefore, argues that the judicial reforms which Kenya had promised, as well as the envisaged institution of criminal investigations, did not meet the standards applied by the Court. The result was that the challenge was rejected. With regard to the issue of immunity for sitting Heads of State, *Trendafilova* cites the *Al Bashir* case and states that in her view there are "convincing arguments" why *Al Bashir* was stripped of immunity by the Security Council's referral in 2005. She argues that the referral not only enabled the International Criminal Court to exercise jurisdiction over *Al Bashir*, but it also activated the entire peace and security mechanisms, which include the deprivation of immunity as contemplated under Article 27(2). *Trendafilova* points to the fact that states such as Chad, Malawi and Nigeria acted contrary to their obligations to cooperate with the Court under Articles 86 and 89 of the Rome Statute when they allowed *Al Bashir* to enter their respective territories without taking any legal steps to arrest him. She adds that as regards *Al Bashir's* envisaged travel plans, it should be noted that countries which are not States Parties are also required to cooperate fully with the Court in the light of the complex Resolution 1593 taken by the UN Security Council under Chapter VII of the UN Charter. *Trendafilova* further expresses her discontent with the UN Security Council for not following up on its referrals to the International Criminal Court and for not giving actual support in such cases.

René Blattmann, former Vice-President and Judge at the International Criminal Court, who is presently a German Academic Exchange Service law professor at Humboldt-Universität zu Berlin, gives an insight into the Court's workings in the *Lubanga* case (Chap. 4), in which the International Criminal Court handed down its first trial judgment. In his introduction, *Blattmann* reflects on the history of international courts by taking us back to the 19th Century Anti-Slavery Courts, which existed, amongst other places, in Freetown and Cape Town. He cites them as an historical example of how international tribunals dealt successfully with violations of human rights in the African context. As regards the *Lubanga* trial itself, *Blattmann* shares some of his experiences as a judge in this trial. He refers, in particular, to the challenging situation in 2008 when the Prosecution, based on agreements it had made with third parties, failed to disclose potentially exculpatory evidence to the accused. *Blattmann* describes this as a decisive moment in the trial, as, in his view, the failure to disclose evidence would have violated the fundamental rights of the accused and furthermore, could have undermined the credibility of the Court as an impartial judicial body. He describes how the Chamber, in reaction to this attitude of the Prosecution, ordered a stay of proceedings—a measure which the Chamber applied two years later for a second time when the Prosecution refused to disclose the identity of intermediaries. Interestingly, *Blattmann* evaluates these incidents positively, as, in his view, they demonstrate that the Trial Chamber was able to react properly to procedural situations that were not foreseen by the Rome Statute.

Shamila Batohi, Senior Legal Advisor to the Prosecutor of the International Criminal Court, gives the Prosecutor's view on the activities of the Court in Africa (Chap. 5). She stresses that many African states were very supportive of the work of the Prosecutor and cooperated in many respects. As regards the perception of an 'African bias' which the Court is confronted with, in her view, this perception is, to a certain extent, understandable. However, as she further argues, the Prosecutor of the International Criminal Court is, unfortunately, not the "world Prosecutor". *Batohi* refers in this connection to the magnitude of human rights violations that were committed in Africa and the huge number of victims who were left without a voice. In her view, the real constituency of the Court are the victims of mass atrocities and the affected communities. International criminal justice, she further contends, was historically developed to fight impunity, a task which the International Criminal Court still strives to fulfill. The Court cannot, therefore, simply ignore the international crimes committed in Africa. *Batohi* describes the work of the Office of the Prosecutor, both in general and especially in relation to African countries by referring to Guinea and Kenya. She underlines that it is important for the Office of the Prosecutor to encourage states to institute their own criminal investigations and to prosecute the alleged perpetrators. Finally, *Batohi* discusses the accusation that the Court's interventions undermine on-going peace processes in Africa. She does this by way of debating the question of 'peace vs. justice'. In her view, justice could create peace that is more stable and long-lasting.

Part II deals with alternative ways of prosecuting international crimes in Africa other than through the International Criminal Court. *Gerhard Kemp*, a law professor at Stellenbosch University, South Africa, regards the domestic implementation of the Rome Statute by African states as key to the enforcement of international criminal law (Chap. 6). He points out several legislative initiatives taken by African states such as South Africa, Mauritius, Kenya, Senegal and Uganda, to incorporate the Rome Statute into their respective domestic legal systems. He analyzes strategies to implement the Rome Statute and refers to the *Windhoek Plan of Action on the ICC Ratification and Implementation in SADC* (*Southern African Development Community*) of 2001, according to which Southern African states agreed to give "priority to the drafting of implementing legislation of the Rome Statute in order to effectively cooperate with the ICC and give effect to the principle of complementarity". However, *Kemp* states that in practice the progressive ideas embodied in the plan did not translate sufficiently into actual collaborative efforts. He cites, as a positive example, the South African ICC Act of 2002, which made South Africa the first country in Africa to incorporate the Rome

Statute fully into its national law. He describes how this Act has in the meantime proved its practical usefulness in a case dealing with allegations of torture committed by Zimbabwean officials against Zimbabwean political activists in Zimbabwe. The North Gauteng High Court in Pretoria had to decide whether the South African criminal justice authorities were under an obligation to investigate this case. The Court held that the ICC Act not only provides for conditional universal jurisdiction, i.e. prosecutions contingent on the presence of the suspect on South African territory, but it also imposes a duty on South African authorities to investigate the allegations before a perpetrator enters the country. This landmark decision was recently affirmed by the Supreme Court of Appeal.

In his wide-ranging contribution (Chap. 7), Chief Justice *Sam Rugege* of the Rwandan Supreme Court, together with *Aimé Muyoboke Karimunda*, analyzes Rwanda's multi-dimensional approach in dealing with the legacy of the 1994 genocide. He states that, in general, the domestic jurisdiction and international jurisdiction must not be regarded as an alternative to the other. He assesses the work of the International Criminal Tribunal for Rwanda (ICTR) positively, referring to the convictions of many *génocidaires*, the establishment of a vast body of jurisprudence on genocide and crimes against humanity, and the useful role played by the ICTR in building the capacity of the Rwandan judiciary. As shortcomings, he points to the fact that the ICTR trials took place far away from where the crimes were committed, which meant that only a few victims, survivors and their relatives could attend the trials. His chapter covers the problems encountered by the Rwandan justice system in handling the genocide cases. He concedes that the Rwandan judicial system was, indeed, overstretched. This resulted in resorting to the traditional Gacaca courts as forums to try the huge number of cases which the ordinary courts were unable to handle. The use of the Gacaca courts has often been referred to as an "African solution to an African problem". *Rugege* argues that this form of participatory justice serves as a reminder that the crimes were committed in public and that there is a "moral obligation to tell the truth" about the crimes witnessed, experienced or perpetrated. *Rugege* contends that the Gacaca courts were successful, as they disposed of 1,958,643 cases through rather informal and less intimidatory judicial procedures which, in turn, encouraged the telling of the truth. In conclusion, *Rugege*, therefore, argues for a multi-dimensional approach in dealing with post-conflict situations.

Mbacké Fall, the Chief Prosecutor at the Extraordinary African Chambers in the Courts of Senegal, depicts another African approach to prosecute international crimes (Chap. 8). He discusses the case of former Chadian president, *Hissène Habré*, who is currently standing trial before the Extraordinary African Chambers in the Courts of Senegal. The Chambers were established by an agreement between the African Union and Senegal on 22 August 2012. As *Fall* argues, the involvement of the African Union in the creation of the Chambers implies that the prosecution of the crimes with which *Habré* is charged, is conducted "on behalf of Africa". He emphasizes the fact that the Chambers are independent and are not in any way linked to either the Senegalese Ministry of Justice or the African Union.

Neither of them monitors the work of the Chambers, nor are the Chambers accountable to either of the two bodies. *Fall* also gives an in-depth insight into the law and procedure applied by the Chambers, which try crimes that were perpetrated in Chad between 7 June 1982 and 1 December 1990. He points out that whenever situations occur for which the Statute does not provide a solution, the Chambers are allowed to resort to Senegalese law as a subsidiary source. Furthermore, the appeal judges may draw upon the jurisprudence of international criminal courts and tribunals, according to Article 25(3) of the Statute. As regards possible alternatives to the interventions of the International Criminal Court in Africa, *Fall* argues in favor of creating temporary ad hoc tribunals. He concludes the chapter with a few remarks on the relationship between the International Criminal Court and the African Union. He suggests that the African Union needs to act ahead of the Court, which means that the African Union should encourage States Parties to fulfill their obligations under the Rome Statute and to try those responsible for international crimes themselves.

While the previous two chapters show proof of 'African success stories' in the fight against impunity, the contribution of *Temitayo Lucia Akinmuwagun* of the Federal Ministry of Justice, Abuja, Nigeria, and *Moritz Vormbaum*, senior researcher in the Faculty of Law at Humboldt-Universität zu Berlin, deals with an on-going African conflict in which the vast majority of the perpetrators have until now not been brought to justice (Chap. 9). In the region of Jos in central Nigeria, communal violence has erupted on a regular basis and has resulted in the deaths of thousands of the region's inhabitants. The authors state that the Nigerian authorities have so far not taken any effective measures to halt the killings. The troops dispatched to the region by the Federal Government of Nigeria have themselves been accused of committing human rights violations in the course of the conflict. There have been only sporadic prosecutions of the planners and perpetrators of the attacks in Jos. This has resulted in the ICC Prosecutor's investigation of the Jos situation as well. However, as *Akinmuwagun* and *Vormbaum* conclude from their legal analysis of the Jos situation, the investigations by the Office of the Prosecutor, too, are irresolute, as the Prosecutor focuses exclusively on the attacks by the Islamist group, *Boko Haram*, which became involved in the conflict a few years ago. The authors argue that there is sufficient evidence pointing to the fact that the planners responsible for most of the international crimes committed in Jos can also be held accountable for crimes against humanity.

Florian Jeßberger, a law professor at the University of Hamburg, Germany, deals with the prosecution of international crimes in Africa by third states, based on the principle of universal jurisdiction (Chap. 10). He analyzes the African position on universal jurisdiction as expressed by the African Union in its extraordinary session on 12 October 2013 at which the Union pointed to the "abuse of universal jurisdiction" while pushing for a Model National Law on universal jurisdiction. Therefore, *Jeßberger* concludes that the African Union generally endorses the principle of universal jurisdiction. However, he finds that although many African states provide for universal jurisdiction in their respective laws, they hardly implement it in practice, unlike in Europe where several trials on the basis of this principle have taken place in countries such as Belgium, France, Germany, the Netherlands, Norway, Spain and Switzerland. As regards the accusation of alleged "abuse" of universal jurisdiction, *Jeßberger* refers to a survey[7] which found that of the total number of cases that were tried worldwide on the basis of universal jurisdiction over the past 25 years, less than five per cent involved Africans. This figure, he infers, does not prove any racial bias against Africans. As a unique instance of the use of universal jurisdiction in Africa, *Jeßberger* singles out the current case of *Hissène Habré*.[8]

Part III focuses on the difficult relationship between the African Union and the International Criminal Court. *Tim Murithi,* who is Head of the Justice and Reconciliation in Africa Programme at the Institute for Justice and Reconciliation, Cape Town, and Research Fellow at the African Gender Institute, University of Cape Town, sketches the relations between African countries, the African Union, and the International Criminal Court from the perspective of a political scientist (Chap. 11). He analyzes the deterioration of this relationship by highlighting the African Union's rationale for criticizing the International Criminal Court. Some of the arguments put forward against the Court, as *Murithi* states, cannot be ignored, for example, the concern that the arrest warrant against *Al Bashir* may run counter to the efforts of the African Union to establish peace in Sudan, or that the Court does not seem to invest the same effort in the prosecution of international crimes in other parts of the world as it does in Africa. Still, he stresses that African states have divergent opinions on the International Criminal Court. *Murithi* then focuses on how the relationship between the Court and the African Union may be improved. His key point is that, on the one hand the International Criminal Court must accept the political dimension of its work and, on the other hand that the African Union must move away from its exclusively political point of view regarding the enforcement of international criminal law. According to him, much will depend on the ICC Prosecutor in the future, but that civil society also has a key role to play in improving the relationship. He stresses the need for the International Criminal Court to communicate politically, an initiative which, in his view, could be bolstered by the appointment of a senior political advisor to the Office of the Prosecutor of the International Criminal Court.

In Chap. 12, *Juliet Okoth*, a law lecturer in the University of Nairobi, Kenya, draws attention to a crucial legal issue complicating the current conflict between the African Union and the International Criminal Court: the question of deferrals of situations before the International Criminal Court on the basis of Article 16 of the Rome Statute. This Article authorizes the UN Security Council to adopt a Resolution under Chapter VII of the UN Charter in which it requests the Court not to commence or proceed with an investigation or prosecution for a renewable period of 12 months. *Okoth* analyzes how the UN Security Council initially

[7] Survey published by Langer (2011).

[8] On the *Habré* case see Chap. 8 of *Fall* in this book.

applied Article 16 in several Resolutions. She argues that Article 16 is a tool that seeks to reconcile the interests of peace and security on the one hand, with the interests of justice and the fight against impunity on the other. Therefore, in her view, a deferral under Article 16 should not happen automatically. Although she identifies shortcomings in the practice initially adopted by the UN Security Council, she assesses the latest Security Council Decisions positively. *Okoth* concludes that the Security Council's turning down of an application by the African Union to have the Kenyan situation deferred has correctly had the effect of setting a high threshold for determining a threat to peace and security as set out under Article 16 of the Rome Statute.

Sosteness Materu, a law lecturer at the University of Dar es Salaam, Tanzania, reflects on the relationship between the African Union and the International Criminal Court against the background of the Kenya situation (Chap. 13). In his view, it is doubtful whether the positions articulated by the African Union in connection with the demand for a deferral of the trials of the Kenyan political leadership are representative for the whole of Africa. He argues that this is especially so because not all Member States of the African Union are States Parties to the ICC Statute. Therefore, the African Union may not adopt a 'common position' on the work of the Court in the same way as, for example, the European Union whose Member States are all signatories to the ICC Statute. In addition, he alludes to the fact that a number of African states, especially those from francophone regions, have expressed their support for the work of the Court. *Materu* further distinguishes between the opinions of leading African politicians and African citizens. He cites, as an example, the findings of a survey conducted in Kenya which showed, inter alia, that 67 percent of the Kenyan population would like to see President *Kenyatta* stand trial at the International Criminal Court. He concludes that, for the victims of international crimes committed in Africa, the Court is still an important institution. *Materu* suggests that in future the opinion of this group should take precedence over that of the political elites.

The book is complemented by an Annex that catalogues Decisions taken by the African Union on the activities of the International Criminal Court relating to African states and on the issue of universal jurisdiction. This compendium of Decisions gives an overview of the controversies dealt with in this book, and affords the reader ready access to important sources referred to by the contributors. In addition, the Annex includes a collection of relevant UN Security Council Resolutions.

After the official closure of the conference, the young African lawyers who had attended expressed their opinions on the theme under discussion. Their statement critiques the position of the African Union as well as the role of the United Nations Security Council in respect of the International Criminal Court. We included the statement in the Annex as we are of the view that the recommendations made will contribute to the debate on the role of international criminal justice in Africa.

Reference

Langer M (2011) The diplomacy of universal jurisdiction: The political branches and the transnational prosecution of international crimes. Am JInt Law 105:1–49

Part I
Prosecutions by the International Criminal Court in Africa

Chapter 2
Africa and the International Criminal Court: Then and Now

Sanji Mmasenono Monageng

Contents

2.1 Introduction

The adoption of the Rome Statute of the International Criminal Court in July 1998 was one of the greatest achievements of the international community in its effort to build a more secure world where peace, security and justice would prevail for all. During the last century, the world witnessed horrible crimes that shocked the conscience of humanity. As we all know, African people have suffered from these mass human rights violations as much as anyone else, and probably more. The long civil war in Sierra Leone, the Apartheid system in South Africa, the genocide in Rwanda and the deadly conflicts in the Great Lakes Region are just some examples. Despite this unspeakable suffering—or perhaps because of it—African people demonstrated great resilience and determination in pursuing peace and reconciliation through justice and accountability. Out of the tragic events that occurred in Africa and elsewhere, a broad global consensus emerged, and it is encapsulated in the Preamble of the Rome Statute, which states that "the most

The views expressed in this chapter are not necessarily those of the International Criminal Court.

S.M. Monageng (✉)
International Criminal Court, The Hague, The Netherlands
e-mail: monagengsanji@yahoo.com

G. Werle et al. (eds.), *Africa and the International Criminal Court*,
International Criminal Justice Series 1, DOI 10.1007/978-94-6265-029-9_2

serious crimes of concern to the international community as a whole must not go unpunished and [that] their effective prosecution must be ensured by taking measures at the national level and by enhancing international cooperation". Africa has been a major actor in creating this consensus which gave life to the International Criminal Court, a permanent and impartial judicial institution designed to prosecute individuals for genocide, crimes against humanity, war crimes and the crime of aggression, when national jurisdictions are unable or unwilling to do so.

Eleven years after its creation, the International Criminal Court is working very actively to fulfil its mandate of investigating and prosecuting grave international crimes. In that regard, the support of African States Parties to the Rome Statute is much appreciated. Unfortunately, there have recently been complications in our continent's relationship with the Court.

2.2 Africa's Active Participation in Establishing the International Criminal Court

The creation of the International Criminal Court was a result of very complex multilateral negotiations which took place from 1995 to 1998, culminating in an international conference held under the auspices of the United Nations in Rome from 16 June to 18 July 1998. African States participated very actively during the whole process.

Prior to the diplomatic conference, African countries made efforts to adopt a common position on the establishment of the International Criminal Court. Those efforts led to different parts of the continent hosting several conferences and workshops. For instance, the Southern African Development Community (SADC) held a Regional Conference on the International Criminal Court in Pretoria in September 1997 and then again in June 1999. Senegal, in West Africa, also hosted an African Conference on the establishment of the International Criminal Court in February 1998 in Dakar, where the participants adopted a declaration in which they affirmed their "commitment to the establishment of the International Criminal Court and underlined the importance that the accomplishment of this Court implies for Africa and the world community as a whole".[1]

At the Rome Conference, African States actively participated in the debates, and African delegations were mainly led by high calibre officials—Ministers of Justice, Ministers of Foreign Affairs, and Attorneys General. Africa was represented in all commissions. Among the 31 Vice-Presidents of the diplomatic conference, eight were from the African continent, namely Algeria, Burkina Faso, Egypt, Gabon, Kenya, Malawi, Nigeria and Sudan, while the Drafting Committee was chaired by Egypt.

---

[1] Dakar Declaration for the establishment of the International Criminal Court in 1998. Available at http://www.iccnow.org/documents/DakarDeclarationFeb98Eng.pdf (accessed on 25 March 2014).

African delegates were at the forefront of pressing for a permanent, impartial and strong International Criminal Court that would address international crimes and help with strengthening national judicial systems. The Head of the South African Delegation, the then Minister of Justice, *Abdula Mohamed Omar*, speaking on behalf of the SADC States, said:

> The establishment of an international criminal court would not only strengthen the arsenal of measures to combat gross human rights violations but would ultimately contribute to the attainment of international peace. In view of the crimes committed under the apartheid system, the International Criminal Court should send a clear message that the international community was resolved that the perpetrators of such gross human rights violations would not go unpunished.[2]

This history demonstrates the active and strong participation of African States in the drafting and adoption of the Rome Statute. The founding document of the International Criminal Court is a result of joint ideas and joint determination to put an end to impunity for the most serious crimes of concern to the international community.

African States were also among the earliest to ratify the Statute, allowing it to enter into force on 1 July 2002. Currently, of the 122 States Parties, 34 are African countries.[3] That makes Africa the biggest regional group in the Assembly of States Parties, the oversight and legislative body of the International Criminal Court.[4] The first and the most recent countries to ratify the Rome Statute are African, that is Senegal and Cote d'Ivoire, respectively.[5]

2.3 Africa and Situations Before the International Criminal Court

States mandated the International Criminal Court to investigate and prosecute the crime of genocide, crimes against humanity, war crimes and the crime of aggression. However, the Rome Statute does not give the Court universal jurisdiction. The Court may only exercise jurisdiction over crimes committed on the territory of a State Party, or by a national of a State Party. The only exception can

---

[2] United Nations Diplomatic Conference of Plenipotentiaries on the Establishment of an International Criminal Court, Rome, 15 June–17 July 1998 Official Records, Volume II, United Nations, New York, 2002, p. 65.

[3] Chronological list of ratifications by African States: Senegal, Ghana, Mali, Lesotho, Botswana, Sierra Leone, Gabon, South Africa, Nigeria, Central African Republic, Benin, Mauritius, Democratic Republic of the Congo, Niger, Uganda, Namibia, Gambia, Tanzania, Malawi, Djibouti, Zambia, Guinea, Burkina Faso, Congo, Burundi, Liberia, Kenya, Comoros, Chad, Madagascar, Seychelles, Tunisia, Cape Verde, Côte d'Ivoire.

[4] States Parties by regional group as at 8 November 2013: 34 African States; 18 Asia-Pacific States; 18 Eastern Europe States; 27 Latin American and Caribbean States; and 25 Western European and other States.

[5] Senegal ratified the Rome Statute on 2 February 1999 and Cote d'Ivoire on 15 February 2013.

be made by the United Nations Security Council, if it uses its powers under Chapter VII of the UN Charter to refer a situation to the Prosecutor of the International Criminal Court.

The Rome Statute also allows a State Party to refer a situation to the Prosecutor, who can also open investigations on his/her own initiative after authorization by a Pre-Trial Chamber. These mechanisms ensure that the Court is accessible in various ways—while also providing a system of checks and balances. Two actors are always required for the opening of an investigation: this can be (1) a State Party and the ICC Prosecutor, or (2) the Security Council and the ICC Prosecutor, or (3) the ICC Prosecutor and the ICC Pre-Trial Chamber.

After eleven years of existence, the International Criminal Court has experienced all three triggering mechanisms:

- Four situations were self-referred by States Parties: Uganda, Democratic Republic of the Congo, Central African Republic and Mali.
- Two situations were referred by the UN Security Council: Darfur (Sudan) and Libya.
- Two investigations were opened by the Prosecutor *proprio motu*: Kenya and Cote d'Ivoire.

These examples demonstrate that diversifying the ways in which a situation can be brought to the Court can help fill the impunity gap. But it also underlines that African States Parties have themselves actively engaged in situations where they found that the International Criminal Court could help them to restore and sustain peace, and provide justice to victims of atrocities. Numerous African States have provided excellent cooperation to the International Criminal Court to assist the investigations and court proceedings.

One must highlight that the Court does not have primacy over national courts, and in this respect it differs from the various *ad hoc* tribunals that were created by or with the support of the United Nations. The relationship between the International Criminal Court and national criminal jurisdictions is based on the complementarity principle that gives States the primary responsibility to prosecute the most serious crimes.[6] In other words, the Court is a court of last resort that should only be relied on when absolutely necessary. Consequently, it is critical for African countries to strengthen their judicial systems so as to address the most serious offenses against international law at the national level, and to ensure that African victims have justice at home.

The complementarity principle offers an opportunity for Africa to take credible ownership of justice for atrocity crimes—by taking legislative measures required to incorporate the Rome Statute provisions into domestic legislation,

---

[6] Preamble (6) of the Rome Statute: "[…] it is the duty of every State to exercise its criminal jurisdiction over those responsible for international crimes".

by strengthening national jurisdictions' capacity to deal effectively with the serious human rights violations on the continent and by supporting the global movement against impunity for the most serious crimes.

2.4 Africa's Support and Criticism of the International Criminal Court

Africa's history is one of incredible human richness, of resilience, strength and unity—but our continent has also experienced bloody conflicts, gross violations of human rights and genocide. By supporting the International Criminal Court, Africa aligns itself with its own values of justice and commitment against oppression and impunity. The concepts of justice and accountability are part of African traditions and cultures. African societies have shown the ability to deal with the legacy of violent conflicts by promoting justice for victims and enabling the restoration of community relations and reconciliation. To this end, we must never forget what the ultimate purpose of the Rome Statute and the International Criminal Court is—to put an end to acts that are destroying humanity. How many more millions have to be killed, deported, tortured and raped before we manage to stop these despicable acts?

Against this background, it is worrisome that some African leaders have started to employ harsh rhetoric about the International Criminal Court, accusing the Court of "targeting Africa"—whereas the reality is that the Court is helping pursue justice for victims in Africa, and is doing so largely at the explicit request of African States.

To state this clearly: the proceedings before the International Criminal Court are fully in conformity with the Rome Statute, including the cases against sitting Heads of State. Article 27 of the Statute explicitly states that the official capacity of any person shall in no case exempt them from criminal responsibility. One cannot help but ask: why should the International Criminal Court be criticized by States for doing exactly what they—the States—created the Court to do?

Of course, if the States Parties to the International Criminal Court identify shortcomings in the Rome Statute or the other legal documents, such as the Rules of Procedure and Evidence, they have every right to propose amendments to these instruments—but in the meantime, the existing legal documents in force should be respected, and the International Criminal Court should not be blamed for applying them. Of course the public is welcome to scrutinize the Court's work and provide constructive criticism—the proceedings and the Court's decisions are transparent and public for anyone to observe and assess. I for one, am fully prepared to recognize that the International Criminal Court is not a perfect institution—there is always room for improvement.

Indeed, the Court is continuously working hard to identify ways to enhance its effectiveness and efficiency in various ways: the Prosecutor has recently adopted a new prosecutorial strategy with the aim of strengthening the process of investigations and prosecutions; the Registrar is re-structuring the various support services of the Court with the aim of improved efficiency, and the Court as a whole is engaged in a Lessons Learned process, in which it aims to identify possible measures to expedite judicial proceedings. I personally have the honour to preside over the Lessons Learned working group, and I am glad to note that two concrete Rule amendment proposals that originated in this working group are on the agenda of the Assembly of States Parties this year, having previously been endorsed by the relevant preparatory bodies of the Assembly.

Despite these various measures to enhance the Court's work, one thing remains clear: the Court cannot cure any defects of the Rome Statute—our job is to interpret and apply the Statute. After all, the International Criminal Court is a court, a judicial body that must respect its legal framework. Anything else would be unthinkable for judges! We have limited room for discretion in the interpretation of the Rome Statute, and the Appeals Chamber, where I sit as a judge, has made clear that this discretion must be exercised with caution.[7]

Let me give you one example: the Court recently considered the request of an accused person to be absent from the courtroom during parts of his trial. The Appeals Chamber had to look at this in light of the Rome Statute's rather explicit provision that "[t]he accused shall be present during the trial". In the end, the Appeals Chamber ruled that the absence of the accused *can* be permissible, but only under exceptional circumstances when strictly necessary.

Whereas the Court is a judicial organ, the Assembly of States Parties, on the other hand, is a political body, consisting of States Parties who effectively constitute the Court's legislature, with the power to amend the Statute and other aspects of the legal framework.

All 122 States Parties are members of the Assembly, with equal rights in the decision-making on various issues such as the adoption of normative texts and of the budget, the election of the judges, the Prosecutor and the Deputy Prosecutor.

Let me reiterate that the States Parties can and indeed should consider ways to enhance and improve the International Criminal Court through amendments to the Court's legal framework. And the correct forum for these discussions is the Assembly of States Parties—ultimately, it is incumbent on the Assembly to identify shortcomings, to find the correct solutions to address them, and in this way shape the future course of the International Criminal Court.

This is why it is positive that African States Parties have brought some concrete proposals to the Assembly of States Parties. I appreciate that the views of African States Parties may be informed by discussions held in the context of the African Union, but ultimately I believe that the States Parties should ensure that they, as the primary stakeholders, founders and owners of the Rome Statute system—as opposed to the countries that have not yet joined the International Criminal Court—will take the collective responsibility for the development of the Court.

---

[7] Cf. Appeals Chamber, Judgment on the appeal of the Prosecutor against the decision of Trial Chamber V(a) of 18 June 2013 entitled "Decision on Mr Ruto's request for excusal from continuous presence at trial", 25 October 2013, ICC-01/09-01/11-1066.

The legal framework of the International Criminal Court is adopted by States Parties that can also amend it, preferably in a way that improves the interests of justice, the needs of victims and the rights of accused persons, in accordance with general principles of international law. I trust that the Assembly will discuss the proposals before it thoroughly and take the necessary time to ensure that any amendments adopted are carefully drafted, do not violate the Statute and are fully considered.

What is important is to retain the division of roles between States, the Assembly and the Court. The Court cannot and must not be drawn into politics. Conversely, States and the Assembly should provide the Court with the required cooperation and give us the necessary space to conduct our judicial mandate without interference.

The relationship between African States and the Court has probably never been as tense and strained as it is today. And this is quite disappointing given the role that African states played in bringing the International Criminal Court to life. A lot of unfortunate statements have been recently made by African leaders, and while I am not going to repeat them, I wish to reject such outrageous accusations in the strongest possible terms.

The staff of the Court is devoted to the mandate that it has been given under the Rome Statute and discharge the mandate professionally and without fear or favour. The Court employs many Africans in top positions, e.g. four Judges, the Prosecutor, the Head of the Jurisdiction, Complementarity and Cooperation Division, the Principal Counsel for the Defence, Ms *Batohi*, Legal Advisor to the Prosecutor, who is here with us, and many others, including myself as a Judge and the First Vice-President. Hundreds of African legal practitioners have made the International Criminal Court what it is. Frankly, it is absolutely ridiculous to accuse the Court of being racist.

The International Criminal Court does not only fight impunity by punishing perpetrators. The Rome Statute also enables the victims to participate actively in the judicial proceedings and to apply for reparations. Victims can lead evidence, question witnesses, challenge admissibility of parties' evidence etc. Furthermore, a Trust Fund for Victims is extending humanitarian assistance to tens of thousands of African victims that have been affected by the crimes under the ICC's jurisdiction. I have often wondered whether anybody has paused to seek the views of the countless victims who have been affected by the alleged mass crimes that the International Criminal Court is trying. Do we ever put ourselves in their shoes? For many of them, the International Criminal Court may be the only viable avenue to see justice done for the wrongs they have suffered.

Africa's commitment to the Court is a crucial aspect of the continent's commitment to the international rule of law. Today, there is widespread conviction that sustainable development and lasting peace are not possible without the rule of law and accountability. It is very important for Africa to take credible ownership of the justice and accountability process in dealing with atrocity crimes in our continent, and to provide strong support for international justice mechanisms.

If Africa wants to take responsibility for its children, its people, and its future, I am deeply convinced that supporting the development of a strong International Criminal Court and playing an active part in States Parties' discussions of the challenges it faces, is absolutely the right thing to do.

2.5 Conclusion

Allow me to tabulate a few challenges the Court faces today:

1. Politicization—This is more pronounced today than at any other time. But regardless of this, the Court is still the best place to be, especially for young professionals.
2. Length of proceedings—Admittedly the Court's proceedings are lengthy, but the Court is presently looking into ways and means of expediting its processes, especially through the "lessons learned" exercise. This will also address the issue of diversity of or plurality of decisions that might lead to uncertainty.

However, there have also been remarkable successes, chief among which so far is that the Court has produced solid jurisprudence and applies high professional standards. At the moment the Court is going through a very stormy period and I am convinced that if it weathers this storm, there is a bright future for it and international criminal justice.

From Rome to The Hague, from Tunis to Cape Town, the spirit of the International Criminal Court remains the same: putting an end to impunity for the most serious crimes that affect the international community as a whole. That is the spirit that should guide our future actions.

Chapter 3
Africa and the International Criminal Court: A Judge's Perspective

Ekaterina Trendafilova

Contents

3.1 Introduction

The purpose of this chapter is to share the author's views on some of the hot issues the International Criminal Court is confronted with in its daily operation. There are, in fact, a number of challenges faced by the Court that one would have to touch upon, but given the space constraints, this chapter will confine to some of the main issues encountered by the Court, in particular, the admissibility of the cases before the Court, the immunity of Heads of State, and the cooperation with the Court in such cases.

The views expressed in this chapter are not necessarily those of the International Criminal Court.

E. Trendafilova (✉)
International Criminal Court, The Hague, The Netherlands
e-mail: admin12@icc-cpi.int

G. Werle et al. (eds.), *Africa and the International Criminal Court*,
International Criminal Justice Series 1, DOI 10.1007/978-94-6265-029-9_3

3.2 Admissibility

The International Criminal Court has been criticized for having before it only situations that spring from the African continent. The tension on this issue has intensified in recent years, provoking legal as well as political debates on the competence of the Court to investigate, prosecute and adjudicate, in particular with regard to some of the cases pending before it.

In this regard, it should be underlined that the proper avenue via which the operation of the International Criminal Court could be contested in the situations before the Court is an admissibility challenge, as enshrined in Article 17 of the Rome Statute. Further, one must recall the complementarity principle,[1] which regulates the relationship between the Court and national jurisdictions by establishing that the jurisdiction of the Court shall be complementary to national criminal jurisdictions. In other words, the primary responsibility to prosecute crimes against humanity, war crimes and the crime of genocide is with the national systems. The International Criminal Court will only step in when the relevant State is inactive, unwilling and/or unable to investigate, prosecute and/or try the alleged perpetrators.

Pursuant to Article 19 of the Rome Statute, admissibility challenges may be brought by States and suspects/accused. The Prosecutor may seek a ruling from the relevant Chamber on a question of admissibility, and the Court may on its own motion determine the admissibility of a case. So far this option has been pursued by States, suspects/accused and the Court.

The discussion below focuses on the admissibility challenges brought by the Governments of Kenya and Libya, which are the only two instances in which the Court's exercise of jurisdiction has been disputed by States.

In their admissibility challenges, both Kenya and Libya submitted that the cases were inadmissible because of ongoing domestic investigations or prosecutions (Article 17(1)(a) of the Rome Statute).[2] Thus, the Court had to consider whether, first, at the time of the admissibility challenge, there was an on-going investigation or prosecution at the national level of the cases pending before the International

---

[1] Rome Statute of the International Criminal Court (1998), 2187 UNTS 3, Preamble, para 10.

[2] *Prosecutor v. William Samoei Ruto, Henry Kiprono Kosgey and Joshua Arap Sang* and *Prosecutor v. Francis Kirimi Muthaura, Uhuru Muigai Kenyatta and Mohammed Hussein Ali,* Application on behalf of the Government of The Republic of Kenya pursuant to Article 19 of the ICC Statute, 31 March 2011, paras 45–79 (hereinafter Application on behalf of the Government of Kenya challenging the admissibility of the Kenya cases); *Prosecutor v. Saif Al-Islam Gaddafi and Abdullah Al-Senussi*, Application on behalf of the Government of Libya pursuant to Article 19 of the ICC Statute, 1 May 2012, paras 1 and 68–75 (hereinafter Application on behalf of the Government of Libya challenging the admissibility of the case against Saif Al-Islam Gaddafi); *Prosecutor v. Saif Al-Islam Gaddafi and Abdullah Al-Senussi,* Application on behalf of the Government of Libya relating to Abdullah Al-Senussi pursuant to Article 19 of the ICC Statute, 2 April 2013, para 1 (hereinafter Application on behalf of the Government of Libya challenging the admissibility of the case against Abdullah Al-Senussi).

Criminal Court (first part of the complementarity test). If the answer is in the affirmative, the Court should consider the second part of the complementarity test, namely whether the State is unwilling or genuinely unable to carry out such an investigation or prosecution.

3.2.1 Admissibility Issues in the Kenya Situation

In the Kenya cases, the Government argued that the State was undertaking constitutional and judicial reforms that would enable it to conduct national criminal proceedings for all crimes arising from the post-election violence.[3] It also submitted that investigative processes were at the time underway, that they would continue over the coming months, and that the investigations would extend up to the highest levels.[4]

Thus, it was evident that Kenya's understanding of the test was that mere preparation to initiate an investigation or prosecution would be sufficient and also that it would also not be necessary to investigate the suspects before the International Criminal Court, but rather only persons at the same level in the hierarchy of State power.

In this regard, the Court has consistently held that the admissibility of a case must be determined on the basis of the facts at the time of the proceedings on the admissibility challenge.[5] Accordingly, the State must demonstrate that it is taking concrete and progressive steps to ascertain whether the individual is responsible for the conduct underlying the warrant of arrest issued by the Court. To this effect, Pre-Trial Chamber II applied the 'same person/same conduct test', namely that the national investigations must cover the same individuals and the same conduct as alleged in the proceedings before the Court.[6]

The Chamber held further that judicial reform actions and promises of future investigative activities, instead of ongoing investigations, do not satisfy the admissibility challenge requirements.[7] Thus, Pre-Trial Chamber II concluded that there remained a situation of inaction and did not proceed to consider whether there was an inability or unwillingness on the part of the State to investigate or

---

[3] Application on behalf of the Government of Kenya challenging the admissibility of the Kenya cases (n. 2 above), paras 2, 5, 12 and 47–66.

[4] Ibid., paras 12–13 and 67–79.

[5] *Prosecutor v. Germain Katanga and Mathieu Ngudjolo Chui*, Appeals Chamber, Judgment on the appeal of Mr Germain Katanga against the oral decision of Trial Chamber II of 12 June 2009 on the admissibility of the case, 25 September 2009, para 56.

[6] *Prosecutor v. William Samoei Ruto, Henry Kiprono Kosgey and Joshua Arap Sang*, Pre-Trial Chamber II, Decision on the application by the Government of Kenya challenging the admissibility of the case pursuant to Article 19(2)(b) of the Statute, 30 May 2011, paras 52 et seq.

[7] Decision on the application by the Government of Kenya challenging the admissibility of the case pursuant to Article 19(2)(b) of the Statute (n. 6 above), paras 64–70.

prosecute the respective cases.[8] On appeal, Kenya's admissibility challenge was likewise rejected by the Appeals Chamber for the same reasons contemplated by Pre-Trial Chamber II.[9]

3.2.2 Admissibility Issues in the Libya Situation

The situation in Libya was referred to the Court by the United Nations Security Council Resolution 1970 (2011). Libya challenged the admissibility of the case before Pre-Trial Chamber I in relation to both Mr *Gaddafi* and Mr *Al-Senussi* on 1 May 2012 and 2 April 2013 respectively.[10] In these cases, the Chamber entered into a "dialogue" with the State in order to gain a full understanding of the steps that were taken domestically and also to acquire knowledge of the challenges encountered by the local authorities so that it could take an informed decision in regard to Libya's sovereign rights to carry out its own domestic proceedings.

In both admissibility challenges Libya submitted that it was conducting active investigations of the two suspects.[11] It indicated that its investigations covered exactly the same incidents and conduct as contained in the International Criminal Court arrest warrants and which were, in fact, broader in terms of time and subject-matter than the ICC investigations.[12]

Pre-Trial Chamber I applied the 'same person/substantially same conduct' test in both its decisions, but arrived at different conclusions with regard to the two admissibility challenges.

In the case against Mr *Gaddafi*, although Pre-Trial Chamber I granted Libya three opportunities to submit evidence on matters relevant to the admissibility of the case, it found that Libya did not satisfy the first part of the complementarity test. The evidence, taken as a whole, fell short of substantiating (due to a lack of

---

[8] Ibid., para 70.

[9] *Prosecutor v. William Samoei Ruto, Henry Kiprono Kosgey and Joshua Arap Sang,* Appeals Chamber, Judgment on the appeal of the Republic of Kenya against the decision of Pre-Trial Chamber II of 30 May 2011 entitled Decision on the application by the Government of Kenya challenging the admissibility of the case pursuant to Article 19(2)(b) of the Statute, 30 August 2011.

[10] Application on behalf of the Government of Libya challenging the admissibility of the case against Saif Al-Islam Gaddafi (n. 2 above); and Application on behalf of the Government of Libya challenging the admissibility of the case against Abdullah Al-Senussi (n. 2 above).

[11] Application on behalf of the Government of Libya challenging the admissibility of the case against Saif Al-Islam Gaddafi (n. 2 above), paras 42–46; Application on behalf of the Government of Libya challenging the admissibility of the case against Abdullah Al-Senussi (n. 2 above), paras 136–138 and 156–179.

[12] Application on behalf of the Government of Libya challenging the admissibility of the case against Saif Al-Islam Gaddafi (n. 2 above), para 46; Application on behalf of the Government of Libya challenging the admissibility of the case against Abdullah Al-Senussi (n. 2 above), paras 156–161.

sufficient degree of specificity and probative value) that the subject-matter of the domestic investigation covered the same case that is before the Court.[13] The submission of additional evidence in support of the first part of the complementarity test was not considered determinative because serious challenges remained concerning due process and sentencing, as well as the relevance of the post-conflict setting, on the second part of the complementarity test, namely Libya's genuine ability to carry out the investigation or prosecution.[14]

In determining Libya's ability to investigate and prosecute Mr *Gaddafi*, Pre-Trial Chamber I acknowledged the significant efforts made by Libya under extremely difficult circumstances to improve security conditions, rebuild institutions and restore the rule of law, as well as to enhance capacity, *inter alia*, with respect to transitional justice.[15] However, without prejudice to the above achievements, the Chamber stressed that the Libyan State continued to face substantial difficulties in exercising fully its judicial powers across the entire territory.[16] Importantly, the Libyan authorities had not been able to secure the transfer of Mr *Gaddafi* (who has been held in Zintan) into State custody, which prevented the case against him from proceedings.[17] There were also impediments to obtaining the necessary evidence (e.g., for lack of control over certain detention facilities), to ensure the protection of witnesses and to secure legal representation for Mr *Gaddafi*.[18] Due to these difficulties the Chamber found that Libya's national judicial system could not yet be applied in full in areas or aspects relevant to the case, thus being "unavailable" within the terms of the Rome Statute (Article 17(3) of the Rome Statute).[19]

The admissibility challenge of the case against Mr *Al-Senussi* took a different turn. The Chamber found, on the basis of a considerable amount of evidence submitted by Libya, that the case was inadmissible before the International Criminal Court. It was satisfied that the evidence provided by the State demonstrated that Libya had taken progressive steps to ascertain the criminal responsibility of Mr *Al-Senussi* for substantially the same conduct as alleged in the proceedings before the Court.[20] The Chamber was also satisfied that Libya was neither unwilling nor genuinely unable to carry out the proceedings against him.[21]

---

[13] *Prosecutor v. Saif Al-Islam Gaddafi and Abdullah Al-Senussi*, Pre-Trial Chamber I, Decision on the admissibility of the case against Saif Al-Islam Gaddafi, 31 May 2013, paras 133–135 and 219.

[14] Decision on the admissibility of the case against Saif Al-Islam Gaddafi (n. 13 above), paras 137 et seq.

[15] Ibid., para 204.

[16] Ibid., para 205.

[17] Ibid., para 208.

[18] Ibid., paras 206–215.

[19] Ibid., para 205.

[20] *Prosecutor v. Saif Al-Islam Gaddafi and Abdullah Al-Senussi*, Pre-Trial Chamber I, Decision on the admissibility of the case against Abdullah Al-Senussi, 11 October 2013, para 167.

[21] Decision on the admissibility of the case against *Abdullah* Al-Senussi (n. 20 above), paras 294–310.

Two significant differences between the case against Mr *Al-Senussi* and Mr *Gaddafi* led to the different outcomes on the question of admissibility. First, the State has custody of Mr *Al-Senussi*, while Mr *Gaddafi* remains in the custody of the Zintan militia. Second, some aspects deemed compelling in the decision on the admissibility of the case against Mr *Gaddafi*, such as the precarious security situation, the absence of effective witness protection programs, or the lack of control over certain detention centers, did not have the same impact on the investigation of Mr *Al-Senussi*.[22]

3.2.3 Conclusion

In conclusion to this part of the chapter, one may emphasize that the admissibility decisions in the Libya situation, as the most recent developments at the Court, stand to counter some fears that the International Criminal Court might step up its mandate, namely depriving domestic jurisdictions of their discretion to exercise their primary jurisdiction, and disregarding the different legal cultures.

First, in regard to the discretion of domestic jurisdictions, Pre-Trial Chamber I found it sufficient that the national case covers substantially the same underlying conduct as that alleged in the ICC arrest warrant.

Second, in respect of the different legal cultures, the Chamber adopted a restrictive interpretation of Article 17 of the Rome Statute and confined itself to assessing due process concerns only to the extent that it affected Libya's ability or willingness to carry out the proceedings. Thus, Pre-Trial Chamber I, mindful of the different legal cultures and respectful of State sovereignty, did not consider that the death penalty, for example, prevented the cases from proceeding at the domestic level.

3.3 Immunity of Heads of State and Cooperation

Having addressed the admissibility challenges brought by Kenya and Libya, what follows is analysis of the issue of immunity of Heads of States that are not Parties to the Rome Statute and the cooperation with the Court in such cases.

3.3.1 Immunity in the ICC Regime

The warrant of arrest for the Sudanese President has raised and continues to raise challenges for the Court, both in terms of the law to be applied and the enforcement

[22] Ibid., paras 297–308.

of the Court's decisions. A diversity of views and positions has arisen in regard of the above issues. It is amidst this diversity of interpretations and the lack of a harmonized approach that the Court has to perform its work.

It is widely accepted that States Parties to the ICC Statute have relinquished the immunities of their senior officials by virtue of Article 27(2) of the Rome Statute.[23] The same cannot be said about non-States Parties since they have not ratified the treaty. A distinction arises, therefore, between the immunities accruing to officials of non-States Parties and those with respect to officials of States Parties of the International Criminal Court. A further distinction needs to be made between the exercise of jurisdiction by an international criminal court and the jurisdiction of national authorities over such officials.

When the first arrest warrant against President *Al-Bashir* was issued in 2009, following a referral by the United Nations Security Council under Chapter VII of the Charter of the United Nations, the Pre-Trial Chamber decided that, in accordance with Article 27 of the Rome Statute, President *Al-Bashir's* position as Head of a State not Party to the Rome Statute had no effect on the Court's jurisdiction over the case.[24]

In this respect, it should be underlined that the question of immunities comes on two levels, and stating that the Court has jurisdiction over a sitting Head of State does not exhaust the issue. In order for the International Criminal Court to exercise jurisdiction in practice, it needs to obtain custody of President *Al-Bashir*, at least during the trial phase. Accordingly, the question of his immunity from arrest by national authorities arises. For that reason, the Chamber directed the Registry to transmit a request for the arrest and surrender of President *Al-Bashir* to all States Parties and also to all United Nations Security Council members that are not States Parties to the Rome Statute.[25]

It appears that the issue of immunity in the case against President *Al-Bashir* is more complex. Two points must be made in this regard. First, the arrest warrant against him was issued by an international tribunal (and not by a domestic court) and second, the jurisdiction of this international court was triggered by the United Nations Security Council, acting under Chapter VII of the United Nations Charter. The following questions arise: (i) Is *Al-Bashir's* immunity affected by the fact that the arrest warrant was issued by the International Criminal Court and that States

[23] *Prosecutor v. Omar Hassan Ahmad Al Bashir*, Pre-Trial Chamber I, Corrigendum to the Decision pursuant to Article 87(7) of the Rome Statute on the failure by the Republic of Malawi to comply with the cooperation requests issued by the Court with respect to the arrest and surrender of Omar Hassan Ahmad Al Bashir, 13 December 2011, para 18; Schabas 2010a, p. 450; Triffterer 2008, pp. 779, 791.

[24] *Prosecutor v. Omar Hassan Ahmad Al Bashir*, Pre-Trial Chamber I, Decision on the Prosecution's application for a warrant of arrest against Omar Hassan Ahmad Al Bashir, 4 March 2009, para 41.

[25] Ibid., p. 93.

would be acting in response to an ICC request? (ii) Does the triggering of the Court's jurisdiction by means of a Security Council referral have any impact on President *Al-Bashir's* immunity?

3.3.2 Lack of Cooperation

At this point one may recall some of the judicial rulings in this case in regard to a number of visits of President *Al-Bashir* to States that are either parties or not parties to the Rome Statute. After the issuance of the Warrant of Arrest, President *Al-Bashir* visited, among other States, Chad (in 2010, 2011, and 2013), Malawi (in 2011), and Nigeria (in 2013). As States Parties to the Rome Statute, each was under an obligation, pursuant to Articles 86 and 89 of the Rome Statute, to execute the Court's cooperation requests for the arrest and surrender of President *Al-Bashir*. They, however, failed to do so.

As a justification for not arresting President *Al-Bashir*, Malawi, for example, invoked the immunities of Heads of State that are not Parties to the Rome Statute, and the position of the African Union towards the arrest warrants issued against the Sudanese President.[26] Malawi argued that Article 27(2) of the Rome Statute is not applicable to officials of States not Parties to the Rome Statute.[27] Furthermore, Malawi implicitly invoked Article 98(1) of the Rome Statute which envisages that the Court may not proceed with a request for surrender or assistance that would require the requested State to act inconsistently with its obligations under international law with respect to the State or diplomatic immunity of a person or property of a third State which is not Party to the Rome Statute.[28]

The Pre-Trial Chambers of the International Criminal Court issued a number of decisions on the visits of the Sudanese President to States Parties or States which are not parties to the Rome Statute. The first decision was issued in 2010 by way of which Pre-Trial Chamber I informed the Assembly of States Parties and the United Nations Security Council of President *Al-Bashir's* 2010 visit to Chad.[29] This decision was followed by two other decisions of 12 and 13 December 2011 respectively, in which the same Chamber found that Malawi and Chad were, first, in breach of their obligations to consult with the Court (Article 97 of the Rome

---

[26] *Prosecutor v. Omar Hassan Ahmad Al Bashir*, Pre-Trial Chamber I, Corrigendum to the Decision pursuant to Article 87(7) of the Rome Statute on the failure by the Republic of Malawi to comply with the cooperation requests issued by the Court with respect to the arrest and surrender of Omar Hassan Ahmad Al Bashir, 13 December 2011, para 8 and Annex 1 (hereinafter Malawi non-compliance Decision).

[27] Malawi non-compliance Decision (n. 26 above), para 8.

[28] Ibid., para 8.

[29] *Prosecutor v. Omar Hassan Ahmad Al Bashir*, Pre-Trial Chamber I, Decision informing the United Nations Security Council and the Assembly of the States Parties to the Rome Statute about Omar Al-Bashir's recent visit to the Republic of Chad, 27 August 2010, p. 4.

Statute) by not bringing the issue of President *Al-Bashir's* immunity to the Chamber for its determination (Article 119(1) of the Rome Statute).[30] Second and most importantly, Pre-Trial Chamber I found that both Malawi and Chad had failed to cooperate with the Court by not arresting and surrendering President *Al-Bashir* to the Court, thus preventing the Court from exercising its functions and powers under its Statute.[31] Accordingly, this time the Pre-Trial Chamber I initiated the non-cooperation procedure and referred the matter to the Assembly of States Parties and the United Nations Security Council. More specifically, in the decision on Malawi's non-cooperation, the Chamber found that the ICC prosecution cannot be opposed on the basis of the immunity principle because the international character of the International Criminal Court makes immunities inapplicable.[32] The Chamber also found that Article 98(1) of the Rome Statute was not applicable.[33]

3.3.3 Head of State Immunity and Security Council Referrals

While one may agree with the view that *Al-Bashir* is not immune from arrest, it could be argued against such a general exception to Head of State immunity in prosecutions before international courts.

An important aspect of the immunities debate that impacts on the analysis of President *Al-Bashir's* immunity is the triggering mechanism in this particular case. One cannot gloss over the fact that the Sudanese President is sought by the Court as a result of a Security Council referral in the exercise of its powers under Chapter VII of the Charter of the United Nations. There are convincing arguments by way of which President *Al-Bashir's* immunity might have been removed despite Sudan not being a States Party to the Rome Statute.

First, when referring the Darfur situation to the International Criminal Court, the Security Council Resolution 1593 (2005) implicitly accepted that the investigations and prosecutions in that situation would take place according to the Court's statutory framework as a whole. This ultimately implies that Sudan, although a non-States Party, has obligations under the Rome Statute, by virtue of the said United Nations Security Council Resolution, as if it were a States Party to the International Criminal Court. In other words, Sudan is subjected indirectly,

---

30 Malawi non-compliance Decision (n. 26 above), p. 21; and *Prosecutor v. Omar Hassan Ahmad Al Bashir*, Pre-Trial Chamber I, Decision pursuant to Article 87(7) of the Rome Statute on the refusal of the Republic of Chad to comply with the cooperation requests issued by the Court with respect to the arrest and surrender of Omar Hassan Ahmad Al Bashir, 13 December 2011, p. 8 (hereinafter Chad non-compliance Decision).

31 Malawi non-compliance Decision (n. 26 above), p. 21; and Chad non-compliance Decision (n. 30 above), p. 8.

32 Malawi non-compliance Decision (n. 26 above), paras 22–36.

33 Ibid., paras 37–43.

by virtue of the Security Council Resolution, to Article 27(2) of the Rome Statute, which waives immunities.[34]

Second, when the Security Council decided that Sudan shall "cooperate fully" with the Court, it implicitly lifted the immunities accruing to President *Al-Bashir*. Sudan is estopped from raising the immunities in this case because of its obligations under the United Nations Charter to comply with the Security Council order to cooperate with the International Criminal Court.[35]

A counter-argument might be put forward, namely that the Security Council could not have stripped President *Al-Bashir* of his immunity because a referral by the Council is simply a mechanism designed to trigger the jurisdiction of the Court.[36] This argument, however, lacks logic and persuasive justification. Its untenability is rooted in the very nature and purpose of the Security Council referral, namely, to activate the mandate of the International Criminal Court. If the Court is prevented from carrying out its functions, the Security Council referrals will not meet their intended purpose either under the Rome Statute or under Chapter VII of the United Nations Charter. One should be mindful that Security Council Resolution 1593 (2005) is not only a triggering mechanism for the jurisdiction of the International Criminal Court, but also a measure for the maintenance of international peace and security. Consequently, as a Chapter VII instrument, the Resolution is binding on all United Nations Member States.

The International Criminal Court has recently emphasized this dimension of Resolution 1593 (2005) as a Chapter VII measure. In two decisions of 18 September and 10 October 2013 respectively, after receiving notifications of President *Al-Bashir's* potential travels to the United States, Ethiopia and Saudi Arabia, Pre-Trial Chamber II invited the three States to arrest him and to surrender him to the Court in the event that he entered their territory.[37] The Chamber acknowledged that, as non-States Parties, the United States, Ethiopia and Saudi Arabia had no obligations *vis-à-vis* the Court arising from the Rome Statute.[38] The Chamber pointed out, however, that Security Council Resolution 1593 (2005) urged all States and the appropriate regional and international organizations to cooperate fully with the Court.

---

[34] Akande 2009, pp. 340–342.

[35] Cryer et al. 2010, pp. 556–557.

[36] Schabas 2010b, p. 7; Gaeta 2009, p. 323.

[37] *Prosecutor v. Omar Hassan Ahmad Al Bashir*, Pre-Trial Chamber II, Decision regarding Omar Al-Bashir's potential travel to the United States of America, 18 September 2013, p. 6; and Decision regarding Omar Al-Bashir's potential travel to the Federal Republic of Ethiopia and the Kingdom of Saudi Arabia, 10 October 2013, p. 6.

[38] Decision regarding Omar Al-Bashir's potential travel to the United States of America (n. 37 above), para 11; Decision regarding Omar Al-Bashir's potential travel to the Federal Republic of Ethiopia and the Kingdom of Saudi Arabia (n. 37 above), para 8.

3.3.4 Following up on Security Council Referrals

Another related problem to the Security Council referrals and the fulfilment of the ICC's mandate is the inactivity of the Council in following up on its referrals. This lack of involvement on the part of the Security Council has been addressed in the recent jurisprudence of the Court. In a decision of 26 March 2013, referring the matter of non-compliance of Chad to the Security Council and the Assembly of States Parties, the Court, for the first time, sent an explicit message to the Security Council, showing its dissatisfaction with the passive position of the Council. Pre-Trial Chamber II stressed that when the Security Council, acting under Chapter VII of the United Nations Charter, refers a situation to the Court as constituting a threat to international peace and security, it is expected to follow-up on its referrals and thus to support the Court in fulfilling its mandate entrusted by the Council.[39] With no follow-up action on the part of the Security Council, any referral by the Council to the International Criminal Court under Chapter VII of the United Nations Charter would never achieve its ultimate goal, namely, to put an end to impunity. Any such referral would become futile.

3.3.5 Conclusion

At this point it should be stressed that the Court has no uniform approach in all cases of non-cooperation. Quite the contrary, the Court carefully analyzes each situation and takes a case-specific approach.

In a recent decision issued by Pre-Trial Chamber II with respect to the visit of President *Al-Bashir* to Nigeria on 3 September 2013, the Chamber received the Government's explanation in good faith and refrained from making a finding on non-compliance with the Court's decisions.[40] The Chamber reminded the competent authorities of their international obligations and requested their cooperation in future cases.[41] The same approach was followed in two more recent decisions of 13 November 2013 concerning the visit of another suspect, Mr *Abdel Raheem Muhammad Hussein*, to Chad and the Central African Republic.[42]

---

[39] *Prosecutor v. Omar Hassan Ahmad Al Bashir*, Pre-Trial Chamber II, Decision on the non-compliance of the Republic of Chad with the cooperation requests issued by the Court regarding the arrest and surrender of Omar Hassan Ahmad Al-Bashir, 26 March 2013, para 22.

[40] *Prosecutor v. Omar Hassan Ahmad Al Bashir*, Pre-Trial Chamber II, Decision on the cooperation of the Federal Republic of Nigeria regarding Omar Al-Bashir's arrest and surrender to the Court, 5 September 2013, paras 10–13.

[41] Decision on the cooperation of the Federal Republic of Nigeria regarding Omar Al-Bashir's arrest and surrender to the Court (n. 40 above), p. 6.

[42] *Prosecutor v. Abdel Raheem Muhammad Hussein*, Pre-Trial Chamber II, Decision on the cooperation of the Republic of Chad regarding Abdel Raheem Muhammad Hussein's arrest and surrender to the Court, 13 November 2013; and Decision on the cooperation of the Central

Thus, to conclude, it has to be emphasized that cooperation is a decisive factor with regard to the execution of arrest warrants. Lacking direct means of enforcement, the International Criminal Court relies on the cooperation of States, the United Nations and on other actors in the international arena, in the absence of which it cannot operate effectively. Challenges to the cooperation regime of the International Criminal Court are some of the most significant obstacles encountered by the Court in carrying out its mandate.

References

Akande D (2009) The legal nature of Security Council referrals to the ICC and its impact on Al Bashir's immunities. J Int Crim Justice 7:333–342

Cryer R, Friman H, Robinson D, Wilmshurst E (2010) An introduction to International Criminal Law and Procedure, 2nd edn. Cambridge University Press, Cambridge

Gaeta P (2009) Does president Al Bashir enjoy immunity from arrest? J Int Crim Justice 7:315–332

Schabas W (2010a) An International Criminal Court and non-party states. Windsor Yearb Access Justice 28:1–21

Schabas W (2010b) The International Criminal Court: a commentary on the Rome Statute. Oxford University Press, Oxford

Triffterer O (2008) Article 27: irrelevance of official capacity. In: Triffterer O (ed) Commentary to the Rome Statute of the International Criminal Court, 2nd edn. C.H.Beck, Munich, pp 779 et seq

Cases

The Prosecutor v. Germain Katanga and Mathieu Ngudjolo Chui, Appeals Chamber, Judgment on the Appeal of Mr Germain Katanga against the oral decision of Trial Chamber II of 12 June 2009 on the admissibility of the case, 25 September 2009, ICC-01/04-01/07-1497.

The Prosecutor v. William Samoei Ruto, Henry Kiprono Kosgey and Joshua Arap Sang and *The Prosecutor v. Francis Kirimi Muthaura, Uhuru Muigai Kenyatta and Mohammed Hussein Ali,* Application on behalf of the Government of The Republic of Kenya pursuant to Article 19 of the ICC Statute, 31 March 2011, ICC-01/09-01/11-19.

The Prosecutor v. William Samoei Ruto, Henry Kiprono Kosgey and Joshua Arap Sang, Pre-Trial Chamber II, Decision on the application by the Government of Kenya challenging the admissibility of the case pursuant to Article 19(2)(b) of the Statute, 30 May 2011, ICC-01/09-01/11-101.

The Prosecutor v. Saif Al-Islam Gaddafi and Abdullah Al-Senussi, Application on behalf of the Government of Libya pursuant to Article 19 of the ICC Statute, 1 May 2012, ICC-01/11-01/11-130-Red.

The Prosecutor v. Saif Al-Islam Gaddafi and Abdullah Al-Senussi, Application on behalf of the Government of Libya relating to Abdullah Al-Senussi pursuant to Article 19 of the ICC Statute, 2 April 2013, ICC-01/11-01/11-307-Red2.

(Footnote 42 continued)
African Republic regarding Abdel Raheem Muhammad Hussein's arrest and surrender to the Court, 13 November 2013.

The Prosecutor v. Saif Al-Islam Gaddafi and Abdullah Al-Senussi, Pre-Trial Chamber I, Decision on the admissibility of the case against Saif Al-Islam Gaddafi, 31 May 2013, ICC-01/11-01/11-344-Red.

The Prosecutor v. Omar Hassan Ahmad Al Bashir, Pre-Trial Chamber II, Decision on the non-compliance of the Republic of Chad with the cooperation requests issued by the Court regarding the arrest and surrender of Omar Hassan Ahmad Al-Bashir, 26 March 2013, ICC-02/05-01/09-151.

The Prosecutor v. Omar Hassan Ahmad Al Bashir, Pre-Trial Chamber II, Decision on the cooperation of the Federal Republic of Nigeria regarding Omar Al-Bashir's arrest and surrender to the Court, 5 September 2013, ICC-02/05-01/09-159.

The Prosecutor v. Omar Hassan Ahmad Al Bashir, Pre-Trial Chamber II, Decision regarding Omar Al-Bashir's potential travel to the United States of America, 18 September 2013, ICC-02/05-01/09-162.

The Prosecutor v. Omar Hassan Ahmad Al Bashir, Pre-Trial Chamber II, Decision regarding Omar Al-Bashir's potential travel to the Federal Republic of Ethiopia and the Kingdom of Saudi Arabia, 10 October 2013, ICC-02/05-01/09-164.

The Prosecutor v. Omar Hassan Ahmad Al Bashir, Pre-Trial Chamber I, Decision pursuant to Article 87(7) of the Rome Statute on the refusal of the Republic of Chad to comply with the cooperation requests issued by the Court with respect to the arrest and surrender of Omar Hassan Ahmad Al Bashir, 13 December 2011, ICC-02/05-01/09-140-tENG.

The Prosecutor v. Omar Hassan Ahmad Al Bashir, Pre-Trial Chamber I, Decision informing the United Nations Security Council and the Assembly of the States Parties to the Rome Statute about Omar Al-Bashir's recent visit to the Republic of Chad, 27 August 2010, ICC-02/05-01/09-109.

The Prosecutor v. Omar Hassan Ahmad Al Bashir, Pre-Trial Chamber I, Corrigendum to the Decision Pursuant to Article 87(7) of the Rome Statute on the failure by the Republic of Malawi to comply with the cooperation requests issued by the Court with respect to the arrest and surrender of Omar Hassan Ahmad Al Bashir, 13 December 2011, ICC-02/05-01/09.

The Prosecutor v. Abdel Raheem Muhammad Hussein, Pre-Trial Chamber II, Decision on the cooperation of the Republic of Chad regarding Abdel Raheem Muhammad Hussein's arrest and surrender to the Court, 13 November 2013, ICC-02/05-01/12-20.

Chapter 4
International Criminal Justice in Africa: Specific Procedural Aspects of the First Trial Judgment of the International Criminal Court

René Blattmann

Contents

4.1 Introduction

The first trial of the International Criminal Court was a significant benchmark in international law. As the first permanent international criminal court, the Court joins an important assembly of international courts which is working to change the global order and provide security and peace in a complex world. Not only did the *Lubanga* case mark the operational beginning of the International Criminal Court; also it highlighted a new and changing international criminal law, focusing attention on the issue of the use and role of children during armed conflict.

The views expressed in this chapter are not necessarily those of the International Criminal Court.

R. Blattmann (✉)
Humboldt-Universität zu Berlin, Berlin, Germany
e-mail: rene.blattmann@rewi.hu-berlin.de

G. Werle et al. (eds.), *Africa and the International Criminal Court*,
International Criminal Justice Series 1, DOI 10.1007/978-94-6265-029-9_4

In order to highlight some of the most important aspects of this time in the history of international justice, one must begin at the beginning—by going backward and providing historical context for the contemporary international courts. History teaches us that Africa was the seat of the first international human rights tribunals. These important early courts were composed of international judges applying international treaty law and serve as a model for the international courts on the rise today. After exploring the roots of international law, this chapter will canvas briefly the significant subject of the crime of using child soldiers in armed conflict—a substantive crime which serves to show the direction in which international criminal law is moving. Finally, this paper will address the *Lubanga* trial, the first trial of the International Criminal Court, by discussing not only the substantive law of child soldiery but also some of the most interesting procedural issues, especially stay of proceedings and how this procedure was used in the first trial before the Chambers of the Court.

However, it is important to note the judgment, sentencing and reparations decisions are all on appeal and, therefore, have not been adjudicated finally. Thus, the exercise which follows will be restrained, referring only to very limited objective issues related to substantial and procedural law.

4.2 The Anti-Slavery Courts

Long before the International Criminal Court was created and long before the Rwanda Tribunal was established, Africa hosted international courts. Africa was a protagonist of international courts in the 19th century already, when mixed courts were created by international treaties of a multilateral nature for the suppression of the transatlantic slave trade.[1]

The concept of mixed commissions to settle disputes goes as far back as the 1794 Jay Treaty between Britain and the United States which allowed their representatives to settle claims arising from the American Revolutionary War.[2] In 1817, after several years of negotiations, Britain reached agreements with the Netherlands, Portugal and Spain to establish mixed courts to prosecute those captured on slave ships.[3] Thus, courts were established in Freetown (Sierra Leone), Havana (Cuba), Rio de Janeiro (Brazil) and Surinam.[4] The US did not ratify the treaty with Britain until 1862. This bilateral agreement opened the door to the establishment of courts in New York, Sierra Leone and Cape Town.[5] The courts were humanitarian in nature, though each treaty was slightly different.[6]

---

[1] Martinez 2008, p. 550.

[2] Nickels 2001, p. 313.

[3] Martinez 2012, p. 34.

[4] Martinez 2012, p. 69.

[5] van Niekerk 2004, p. 432.

[6] Martinez 2012, p. 85.

Annexes to the treaties provided basic procedural rules under which the courts operated. Under the treaties each nation appointed a judge, and the government of the territory in which the court sat appointed a registrar, who acted as the court's chief administrator and assisted in the taking of evidence.[7] Despite their relatively brief existence, these courts adjudicated more than 600 cases, freeing nearly 80,000 slaves.[8]

The court in Sierra Leone was the more active as to both the number of cases heard and the number of slaves freed. Established in 1819, the Sierra Leone court was responsible for the capture of 22 slave-trading ships in 43 years and held hearings in more than 500 cases, with approximately 65,000 slaves been freed during that time.[9] This is a vivid example of how the success of international courts provides hope and promise for the future of international justice.

At the same time it reminds us that Africa not only has played a leading role in the beginnings of international human rights but also has been a target of crimes against humanity. In the 20th century, when the then denominated Congo Free State became the personal property of *King Leopold II of Belgium*, it also became the victim of a regime of brutality, mutilation and mistreatment, causing humanitarian disasters and the decimation of the Congolese population. The scale of killings in the Congo between 1885 and 1908 is terrifying, with the estimated number of victims oscillating between 3 and 13 million.[10]

4.3 The Child Soldiers

As shown above, the International Criminal Court proceeds from the early success of the international courts model as an intervention instrument in human rights. Though the international court as a tool in the fight for justice is not novel to the global order, many of its features, both in respect of substance and structure, are. In the Rome Statute there are several provisions which go beyond the codification of existing international criminal law, including the denunciation of the use of child soldiers as a war crime, codified in Article 8(2)(b)(xxvi) and Article 8(2)(vii) of the Statute. The insertion of this provision in the Rome Statute serves to codify a human rights principle which had not previously entailed criminal liability in international law.

The utilization of child soldiers is not limited to Africa, but has been known to humankind since ancestral times. As an example, children as young as 10 years of

---

[7] Martinez 2008, p. 579.

[8] Ibid. p. 553.

[9] Martinez 2012, p. 79.

[10] See Ewans 2002, Hochschild 1998.

age are documented to have fought in the American Civil War.[11] Today, their recruitment continues in many different parts of the world.[12]

In fact, the use of child soldiers is common practice. Approximately 250,000 children are used in conflicts worldwide.[13] The Human Rights Watch report on child soldiers of March 2012 established that children are involved in fighting in at least fourteen countries, including countries on the continent of Africa as well countries such as Burma, Colombia, the Philippines, Iraq, India and Afghanistan.[14]

In the Democratic Republic of the Congo, where the *Lubanga* case originates, an estimated number of 30,000 children[15] were involved in the conflict, with 8,000–10,000 within the Ituri region.[16] Child soldiers suffer serious harm, from physical injury, through the trauma of separation from family, to the loss of educational opportunities.[17] Such children are robbed of their childhood and exposed to terrible dangers, both psychological and physical. They are placed in combat situations, used as spies, messengers, porters, servants or to lay or clear landmines. Girls, in particular, are at risk of rape and sexual abuse.[18]

Thus, under the Rome Statute, conscripting or enlisting children under the age of 15 years is a war crime. The current global commission of this crime is a clear indication of the necessity of the norm, and so is its immediate application in the Court's first case.

4.4 The *Lubanga* Case

4.4.1 Overview

Trial Chamber I was assigned the case of *Thomas Lubanga Dyilo* upon the Confirmation of Charges as provided by Pre-Trial Chamber I. Trial Chamber I was composed of three judges from diverse backgrounds with experience from both the Romano-Germanic and common law traditions.

The *Lubanga* case had strict jurisdictional parameters, requiring the Court to focus precisely on events that occurred in the territory of the Democratic Republic

---

[11] Rosen 2005, p. 4.

[12] For example, the nineteenth century *Cheyenne* of North America, boys joined their first war parties when they were 14 or 15 years old. The female warriors of Dahomey were recruited between the ages of nine and fifteen. Among the *Yanomamo* of Venezuela and Brazil, children were allowed to determine when they wanted to take up the role of warrior. See ibid. p. 4.

[13] UNICEF 2009.

[14] Human Rights Watch 2012.

[15] Ibid.

[16] Suárez 2009, p. 103 f.

[17] Hausler et al. 2012, p. 175.

[18] Amnesty International. Child Soldiers: From Cradle to War.

of the Congo, and, more specifically, in the District of Ituri, Oriental Province. In addition, the jurisdictional requirements demanded a focus on events which occurred from early September 2002 to 13 August 2003.[19]

The Trial Chamber heard 67 witnesses over 204 days. The prosecution called 36 witnesses, including three experts, and the defence called 24 witnesses. Three victims were called as witnesses following a request from their legal representatives. Additionally, the Chamber called four experts. The prosecution submitted 368 items of evidence, the defence 992, and the legal representatives 13, giving a total of 1,373 items.

Written submissions were supplemented by the oral closing arguments of the parties and participants, heard on 25 and 26 August 2011. Since 6 June 2007, when the record of the case was transmitted to the Trial Chamber, the Chamber delivered 275 written decisions and orders and 347 oral decisions.[20]

On the strength of the evidence before it, the Chamber found Mr *Lubanga* guilty as a co-perpetrator of the crime of conscripting and enlisting children less than 15 years of age into the *Force Patriotique pour la Liberation du Congo* and using them to participate actively in hostilities.[21] In July 2012, he was sentenced to 14 years' imprisonment.[22] In August 2012, the Chamber issued its decision on the principles of reparations to be applied in the case.[23] Both the sentence and the principle of reparations have been taken on appeal.

Thomas Lubanga Dyilo was charged with and convicted of the offence of conscripting and enlisting child soldiers only. The narrow scope of the charge and conviction evoked much commentary and criticism. However, since the Chamber was required to rely upon the charges brought and evidence presented by the Prosecutor, it made no findings of fact or on any other issues.

As the first matter to be tried by the International Criminal Court, the *Lubanga* case had to deal with a host of wide-ranging substantive and procedural issues, such as modes of participation, individual criminal responsibility and the issue of war crimes in international and non-international armed conflict. As regards the characterization of the conflict, the Chamber established the existence of an armed conflict of non-international character and the existence of a nexus between the crimes committed and the armed conflict, which is necessary for any act to

---

[19] *Prosecutor v. Thomas Lubanga Dyilo*, Judgment pursuant to Article 74 of the Statute, 14 March 2012, para 1358.

[20] *Prosecutor v. Thomas Lubanga Dyilo*, Summary of the Judgment pursuant to Article 74 of the Statute, 14 March 2012, p. 5.

[21] *Prosecutor v. Thomas Lubanga Dyilo*, Judgment pursuant to Article 74 of the Statute, 14 March 2012.

[22] *Prosecutor v. Thomas Lubanga Dyilo*, Decision on sentence pursuant to Article 76 of the Statute, 10 July 2012.

[23] *Prosecutor v. Thomas Lubanga Dyilo*, Decision establishing the principles and procedures to be applied to reparations, 7 August 2012.

constitute a war crime.[24] The Trial Chamber recognized that a non-international conflict may become internationalized. Further, with respect to the important issue of individual criminal responsibility and modes of liability, the Chamber confirmed the test of overall control.[25]

With respect to the specific crime, the Chamber did not allow for the child's consent to enlistment to provide a defence for the accused, as posited by the defence. As to the use of children under the age of 15 to participate actively in hostilities, the Chamber applied the criterion that this prohibition was intended to protect children from the risks that are associated with armed conflicts. In the view of the Chamber, the concept of "active participation" had to be extended to encompass the exposure to real danger as a potential target, so that the combination of the child's support and his level of consequential risk becomes decisive.[26]

Other issues dealt with by the Chamber included the legal structure of the crime of conscripting, enlisting or using child soldiers, the issue of disclosure and admissibility of evidence, the stay of proceedings and the release of the accused, the participation of victims, the role of intermediaries, the issue of reparations, asylum, the role of the Trust-Fund, protection of victims and witnesses.

However, a subject of great interest and particular applicability, which may not have been foreseen easily at the beginning of the process, was the use of the stay of proceedings. This issue aroused great interest and triggered considerable debate throughout the *Lubanga* trial and is thus worthy of some effort to understand its use in the case.

The topic involves substantive as well as procedural issues related to the fair trial principle and the doctrine of the abuse of process, which is based on the assumption that certain violations of the accused's rights may be so serious as to render impossible a fair trial.

In the Romano-Germanic systems, courts are very reluctant to stay proceedings on the basis of serious violations of the accused's rights. Thus, it was necessary for the Chamber to engage in an extensive exercise of comparative law, which is a characteristic working methodology at a hybrid or ecumenical court such as the International Criminal Court. The matter of the stay of proceedings in the *Lubanga* case was related closely to the so-called disclosure process, evident in the common law system, which ensures that the accused is entitled to access to the evidence which the prosecution will lead in its case against him or her in a timely and complete fashion. In addition, the accused is entitled to the disclosure of materials of an exculpatory character without regard to whether the materials are admissible at trial.

---

[24] *Prosecutor v. Thomas Lubanga Dyilo*, Judgment pursuant to Article 74 of the Statute, 14 March 2012, para 1358.

[25] Ibid., para 541.

[26] Ibid., para 820.

4.4.2 Disclosure

The issue of disclosure of the prosecutor's evidence to the accused is a fundamental feature of a fair trial in any system. In the Romano-Germanic system (inquisitorial tradition) all the materials collected during the investigation—incriminating or exonerating—are assembled in a "dossier" which, in principle, is available to all parties involved in the trial. In a common law system (adversarial tradition) disclosure is premised on separate prosecution and defence cases, which creates different disclosure obligations. While the prosecutor normally has extensive disclosure obligations, including disclosure of exculpatory materials, defence disclosure is more restricted and often is postponed until the prosecutor has presented his or her evidence at trial.

In the *Lubanga* trial, the challenges of disclosure obligations were apparent already at the Pre-Trial Chamber phase,[27] but due to a lower level of obligation at this phase, the case was able to move to the trial phase. However, both the Trial Chamber and the Appeals Chamber had to deal with the conflicting obligations of the International Criminal Court to ensure disclosure of information to the defence on one side, and the need for confidentiality in respect of information provided by the UN, on the other.[28]

The issue of disclosure is related to the procedural law of the International Criminal Court. Article 67(2) of the Rome Statute and Rule 77 of the Rules of Procedure and Evidence create the basic obligation that the Office of the Prosecutor must disclose exculpatory evidence and material in its possession or control to the defence. At the same time, Article 54(3)(e) provides that the prosecutor may decide not to disclose material obtained on condition of confidentiality and solely for the purpose of generating new evidence, unless the provider of the information consents. Rule 81 places restrictions on disclosure, while Rule 82 provides that if the prosecution has Article 54(3)(e) material in its possession it may not introduce such material into evidence subsequently without prior consent of the information provider.

Finally, reference must be made also to the Relationship Agreement between the Court and the UN,[29] particularly Article 18 which stipulates that:

---

[27] For example, *Prosecutor v. Thomas Lubanga Dyilo*, Decision on the defence request for order to disclose exculpatory materials, 2 November 2006; Decision convening a hearing on the defence request for order to disclosure exculpatory materials, 1 November 2006.

[28] For example, *Prosecutor v. Thomas Lubanga Dyilo*, Decision on the consequences of non-disclosure of exculpatory materials covered by Article 54(3)(e) agreements and the application to stay the prosecution of the accused, together with certain other issues raised at the Status Conference on 10 June 2008, 13 June 2008.

[29] Negotiated Relationship Agreement between the International Criminal Court and the United Nations, available at http://www.icc-cpi.int/nr/rdonlyres/916fc6a2-7846-4177-a5ea-5aa9b6d1e96c/0/iccasp3res1_english.pdf. (All internet resources were accessed on 25 March 2014).

- based on Article 54(3)(e) of the Rome Statute, the sole purpose for providing confidential information should be the generation of new evidence;
- "such information shall not be disclosed to other organs of the Court".

Against this background, the difficulty in the prosecution's ability to disclose came to a head during the spring and summer of 2008 as the Trial Chamber was readying the case for the start of trial.[30] It became apparent that the prosecution, based on the agreements it had made with third party providers of evidence, would not be able to disclose exculpatory evidence. In the process of collecting bulk evidence which would be used to generate new evidence, the prosecution had acquired materials which could be considered exculpatory, but the agreements into which the Prosecutor had entered prohibited their disclosure even to the Chamber. This deprived the judges of the capacity to make a determination as to whether the materials were indeed exculpatory. Following months of orders, negotiations and discussions which proved fruitless, the Chamber had no choice but to stay the proceedings, basing the stay on disclosure violations and fair trial practices.[31] It is important to understand that this decision not only upheld fair trial practices but also expressed the independence of the Court.

4.4.3 First Stay of Proceedings

The first stay of proceedings occurred in June 2008 because the prosecution failed to disclose potentially exculpatory materials to the accused, as a result of agreements with organizations such as the UN, which the prosecution perceived to have restricted its disclosure obligations.

The Trial Chamber determined, among other things, that the disclosure of potentially exculpatory information was a fundamental aspect of the accused's right to a fair trial and that, as a result, the trial process was ruptured to such a degree that it was "impossible to piece together the constituent elements of a fair trial".[32]

---

[30] See, for example, *Prosecutor v. Thomas Lubanga Dyilo*, Order on "Prosecution's application for non-disclosure of information", 9 May 2008.

[31] See, for example, *Prosecutor v. Thomas Lubanga Dyilo*, Decision suspending deadline for final disclosure, 30 January 2008; Decision on the consequences of non-disclosure of exculpatory materials covered by Article 54(3)(e) agreements and the application to stay the prosecution of the accused, together with certain other issues raised at the Status Conference on 10 June 2008, 13 June 2008.

[32] *Prosecutor v. Thomas Lubanga Dyilo*, Decision on the consequences of non-disclosure of exculpatory materials covered by Article 54(3)(e) agreements and the application to stay the prosecution of the accused, together with certain other issues raised at the Status Conference on 10 June 2008, 13 June 2008, para 93.

As a consequence, a stay of the proceedings for abuse of process was imposed by the Trial Chamber and confirmed by the Appeals Chamber, which established unanimously:

1. The Prosecutor may rely only on Article 54(3)(e) for a specific purpose, namely, to generate new evidence.[33]
2. The use of Article 54(3)(e) by the Prosecutor must not lead to breaches of his obligations *vis-á-vis* the suspect or the accused person.[34]
3. The final assessment as to whether the material would have to be disclosed must be made by the Trial Chamber.[35]
4. The Trial Chamber (as well as any other Chamber) must respect the confidentiality agreement and may not order disclosure without prior consent of the information provider.[36]
5. A conditional stay of the proceedings may be the appropriate remedy where a fair trial cannot be held at the time that the stay is imposed, but where the unfairness to the accused person is of such a nature that a fair trial might become possible later were the conditions remedied.[37]

Furthermore, the Appeals Chamber declared:

> The United Nations, from which the Prosecutor had obtained most of the documents in question, had responded negatively to the procedure contemplated at that status conference and to the undertaking of the Trial Chamber. By the time of the Impugned Decision only two of the 156 documents provided by the United Nations had been disclosed to the defence. In relation to 33 other documents, the United Nations had indicated their willingness to consider making available "elements of information" to the Trial Chamber. In relation to 121 documents, however, there were no tangible developments. To the contrary, the submissions of the Prosecutor at the status conference of 10 June 2008 indicated that it might not be possible to find a solution in respect of these documents. Thus, at the time the Trial Chamber rendered the Impugned Decision, and after lengthy discussions between the Prosecutor and the United Nations, it was not even clear that the Trial Chamber would be given access to all or the majority of the documents obtained from the UN, let alone that the documents could be disclosed to the defence. In such a situation, the Appeals Chamber does not consider it erroneous that the Trial Chamber concluded that in spite of the ongoing discussions between the Prosecutor and the United Nations, there was no prospect that the difficulties would be overcome.[38]

---

[33] *Prosecutor v. Thomas Lubanga Dyilo*, Judgment on the appeal of the Prosecutor against the decision in Trial Chamber I entitled "Decision on the consequences of non-disclosure of exculpatory materials covered by Article 54(3) agreements and the application to stay the prosecution of the accused, together with certain other issues raised at the Status Conference on 10 June 2008", 21 October 2008, para 1.

[34] Ibid., para 2.

[35] Ibid., para 3.

[36] Ibid., para 3.

[37] Ibid., para 4.

[38] Ibid., para 91.

Later, a mechanism was developed between the United Nations and the International Criminal Court to deal with the tensions between the conflicting obligations of the International Criminal Court to ensure the disclosure of information to the defence and to maintain confidentiality due to reasons of security and safety. The stay of proceedings could be lifted then and the trial could continue, but this remained an important moment in the *Lubanga* trial and in international justice generally, for it determined that criminal law pillars cannot be bent if legitimate international trials are to be conducted.[39]

4.4.4 Second Stay of Proceedings

The issue of disclosure took a front seat in the *Lubanga* proceedings once again when, on 8 July 2010, a second stay of proceedings was ordered after the prosecution had refused to comply with an order of the Chamber to disclose the identity of an intermediary. The role of the intermediaries had been questioned and thus it was necessary to have their identity disclosed. However, the prosecution argued that its own statutory obligations regarding the safety of its intermediaries take priority over the Chamber's order. In the Chamber's opinion, however, if once seized of the case, it is the only organ of the Court with the power to order and vary protective measures *vis-à-vis* individuals placed at risk because of the Court's work.

It therefore ordered a stay of proceedings for abuse of process, stating that, "no criminal court can operate on the basis that whenever it makes an order in a particular area, it is for the Prosecutor to elect whether or not to implement it, depending on his interpretation of his obligations".[40]

Thereafter, in its judgment on the matter, the Appeals Chamber confirmed that "under the Statute, the Trial Chamber, subject only to the powers of the Appeals Chamber, is the ultimate guardian of a fair and expeditious trial".[41] The Appeals Chamber also made it clear that a stay of proceedings for abuse of process can be

---

[39] Of further interest but less relevant for this paper, is the parallel issue of the release of the accused during a conditional stay of proceedings. See the Trial Chamber's position at *Prosecutor v. Thomas Lubanga Dyilo*, Decision on the release of Thomas Lubanga Dyilo, 2 July 2008. See also the Appeals Chamber's position at *Prosecutor v. Thomas Lubanga Dyilo*, Judgment on the appeal of the Prosecutor against the decision of Trial Chamber I entitled "Decision on the release of Thomas *Lubanga* Dyilo", 21 October 2008. See also Judge *Pikis'* dissent from the Appeals Chamber Decision, ibid., p. 19.

[40] *Prosecutor v. Thomas Lubanga Dyilo*, Redacted decision on the prosecution's urgent request for variation of the time-limit to disclose the identity of intermediary 143 or alternatively to stay proceedings pending further consultations with the VWU, 8 July 2010, para 27.

[41] *Prosecutor v. Thomas Lubanga Dyilo*, Judgment on the appeal of the Prosecutor against the decision of Trial Chamber I of 8 July 2010 entitled "Decision on the prosecution's urgent request for variation of the time-limit to disclose the identity of intermediary 143 or alternatively to stay proceedings pending further consultations with the VWU", 8 October 2010, para 47.

ordered only as an *ultima ratio*, stating that a Trial Chamber, to the extent possible, should impose sanctions before ordering a stay of proceedings because of a party's refusal to comply with its orders.[42]

To ensure fair proceedings in exceptional circumstances, the Chamber has an important power to stay proceedings. Thus, even though the international community and even the Chamber itself expected that the *Lubanga* trial would be adjudicated in a quick and clinical manner, the decisions of the Trial Chamber and the Appeals Chamber exemplify the importance of the principle of judicial independence and respect for the integrity of international criminal proceedings. The credibility of the International Criminal Court in practice will depend predominately on the fairness and integrity of its proceedings.

The importance of the incorporation of the stay of the proceedings, as an element of last resort, is shown by decisions in other cases, and particularly by the decision of 26 April 2013 in the *Kenyatta* case when the defence asked to terminate proceedings against the accused, or remit the case to the Pre-Trial Chamber for consideration because the Prosecutor neglected to disclose potentially exculpatory information.[43]

4.5 Conclusion

The use of Anti-Slavery Courts to curtail the worst human rights abuses provides us with an early example of a functioning and truly international court system. These courts established a necessary system of procedures and rules to maintain the proper functioning of the courts and to ensure their success against human rights abuses in Africa. This practice is analogous to modern international criminal courts.

Today, 16 years after the adoption of the Rome Statute, the International Criminal Court operates in a system of international justice by working not only with States in Africa and around the world, but also with international organizations. By operating on a global scale, the goal of ending impunity, and thereby deterring the commission of the most serious international crimes of concern to the world community, may come closer to fruition.

Of course, in many respects the International Criminal Court is still in the early stages of its development. For example, it is waiting still to exercise jurisdiction over the crime of aggression, as provided for in Article 5 of the Statute. The review conference in Kampala advanced the debate on aggression and provided, through

---

[42] Ibid., para 3.

[43] *Prosecutor v. Uhuru Muigai Kenyatta,* Decision on defence application pursuant to Article 64(4) and related requests, 26 April 2013. See also *Prosecutor v. Uhuru Muigai Kenyatta,* Decision on Defence application for a permanent stay of the proceedings due to abuse of process, 5 December 2013.

the amendment process, a definition of the crime, but it will be several years before this crime is fully incorporated into the jurisdiction of the Court.[44]

Despite the fact that the Court is in its early stages and it has advanced proceedings related to situations in Africa only, we have started to grasp the full potential of the International Criminal Court. In order to continue down this path, it is necessary that certain principles continue to be highlighted, namely, the Court's permanent role, its push toward universality, and its mandate to conduct just, independent and impartial investigations and proceedings in strict conformity with the Rome Statute.

Over the years, a body of jurisprudence will be formed which will resolve pending questions about the definitions in the Rome Statute and will increase the efficiency of proceedings. The doctrine of the abuse of process and the stay of proceedings, although not mentioned in the Statute, now are integrated completely in the procedural praxis of the Court, as a guarantee of a due process.

From Anti-Slavery Courts to upholding and advancing human rights norms against the use of children as soldiers in war, international law continues to advance a civil society which respects fundamental human rights norms and the importance of these norms in the global order. The ability to take procedural steps to uphold fair trial practices enhances the legitimacy of international courts and thus plays an important part in advancing substantive human rights norms. The *Lubanga* decision on child soldiers has been a pivotal moment in advancing these norms and the Court is on course to continue the important work begun by the Anti-Slavery Courts so many years ago.

References

Ewans M (2002) European atrocity, African catastrophe: Leopold II, the Congo Free State and its aftermath. Routledge Curzon, New York

Hausler K, Urban N, McCorquodale R (2012) Protecting education in insecurity and armed conflict: an international law handbook. British Institute of International and Comparative Law/Education Above All, London

Hochschild A (1998) King Leopold's Ghost: a story of greed, terror and heroism in colonial Africa. Houghton Mifflin Company, Boston

Martinez J (2008) Antislavery courts and the dawn of international human rights law. Yale Law J 117:550–641

Martinez J (2012) The slave trade and the origins of international human rights law. Oxford University Press, Oxford

Nickels B (2001) Native American free passage rights under the 1794 Jay Treaty: survival under United States statutory law and Canadian common law. Boston Coll Int Comp Law Rev 24:313–340

[44] See Resolution RC/Res.6, Adopted at the 13th Plenary meeting on 11 June 2010 by consensus, available at http://www.icc-cpi.int/iccdocs/asp_docs/Resolutions/RC-Res.6-ENG.pdf

Rosen D (2005) Armies of the young: child soldiers in war and terrorism. Rutgers University Press, Piscataway
Suárez GP (2009) Kindersoldaten und Völkerstrafrecht. Die Strafbarkeit der Rekrutierung und Verwendung von Kindersoldaten nach Völkerrecht. Berliner Wissenschafts-Verlag, Berlin
van Niekerk JP (2004) British, Portuguese, and American judges in Adderley Street: the international legal background to and some judicial aspects of the Cape Town Mixed Commissions for the suppression of the transatlantic slave trade in the nineteenth century. Comp Int Law J South Afr 37:1–39, 197–225, 404–435

Cases

The Prosecutor v. Thomas Lubanga Dyilo, Decision convening a hearing on the defence request for order to disclosure exculpatory materials, 1 November 2006, ICC-01/04-01/06-640.
The Prosecutor v. Thomas Lubanga Dyilo, Decision on the defence request for order to disclose exculpatory materials, 2 November 2006, ICC-01/04-01/06-649.
The Prosecutor v. Thomas Lubanga Dyilo, Decision suspending deadline for final disclosure, 30 January 2008, ICC-01/04-01/06-1141.
The Prosecutor v. Thomas Lubanga Dyilo, Order on "Prosecution's application for non-disclosure of information", 9 May 2008, ICC-01/04-01/-06-1316.
The Prosecutor v. Thomas Lubanga Dyilo, Decision on the consequences of non-disclosure of exculpatory materials covered by Article 54(3)(e) agreements and the application to stay the prosecution of the accused, together with certain other issues raised at the Status Conference on 10 June 2008, 13 June 2008, ICC-01/04-01/06-1401.
The Prosecutor v. Thomas Lubanga Dyilo, Decision on the release of Thomas Lubanga Dyilo, 2 July 2008, ICC-01/04-01/06-1418.
The Prosecutor v. Thomas Lubanga Dyilo, Judgment on the appeal of the Prosecutor against the Decision in Trial Chamber I entitled "Decision on the consequences of non-disclosure of exculpatory materials covered by Article 54(3) agreements and the application to stay the prosecution of the accused, together with certain other issues raised at the Status Conference on 10 June 2008", 21 October 2008, ICC-01/04-01/06-1486.
The Prosecutor v. Thomas Lubanga Dyilo, Judgment on the appeal of the Prosecutor against the decision of Trial Chamber I entitled "Decision on the release of Thomas Lubanga Dyilo", 21 October 2008, ICC-01/04-01/06-1487.
The Prosecutor v. Thomas Lubanga Dyilo, Redacted decision on the prosecution's urgent request for variation of the time-limit to disclose the identity of intermediary 143 or alternatively to stay proceedings pending further consultations with the VWU, 8 July 2010, ICC-01/04-01/06-2517-Red.
The Prosecutor v. Thomas Lubanga Dyilo, Judgment on the appeal of the Prosecutor against the decision of Trial Chamber I of 8 July 2010 entitled "Decision on the prosecution's urgent request for variation of the time-limit to disclose the identity of intermediary 143 or alternatively to stay proceedings pending further consultations with the VWU", 8 October 2010, ICC-01/04-01/06-2582.
The Prosecutor v. Thomas Lubanga Dyilo, Judgment pursuant to Article 74 of the Statute, 14 March 2012, ICC-01/04-01/06-2842.
The Prosecutor v. Thomas Lubanga Dyilo, Decision on Sentence pursuant to Article 76 of the Statute, 10 July 2012, ICC-01/04-01/06-2901.
The Prosecutor v. Thomas Lubanga Dyilo, Decision establishing the principles and procedures to be applied to reparations, 7 August 2012, ICC-01/04-01/06-2904.
The Prosecutor v. Uhuru Muigai Kenyatta, Decision on defence application pursuant to Article 64(4) and related requests, 26 April 2013, ICC-01/09-02/11.
The Prosecutor v. Uhuru Muigai Kenyatta, Decision on Defence application for a permanent stay of the proceedings due to abuse of process, 5 December 2013, ICC-01/09-02/11.

Other Documents

Amnesty International. Child Soldiers: From Cradle to War. http://www.amnestyusa.org/our-work/issues/children-s-rights/child-soldiers
Human Rights Watch, Child Soldiers Worldwide, 12 March 2012. http://www.hrw.org/news/2012/03/12/child-soldiers-worldwide
UNICEF, Press Release, 23 June 2009. http://www.unicef.org/media/media-50066.html

Chapter 5
Africa and the International Criminal Court: A Prosecutor's Perspective

Shamila Batohi

Contents

5.1 Involvement of African States in the Rome Statute System

The topic for discussion is 'Africa and the International Criminal Court', which comes at a very opportune time when the relationship between African States and the Court has been somewhat tense, amongst others as a result of the Kenya trials. At some stage, there was even talk of a possible withdrawal of African States from the Rome Statute.

Let us first look at the involvement of African States in the Rome Statute system. I purposely say "system" because the Rome Statute created a comprehensive system—not just the Court, as is sometimes misunderstood—whereby the International Criminal Court complements domestic systems and acts *only* if Member States fail to act (which I will deal with later). The majority of African states (34) have ratified the Rome Statute, Africa is the most represented region of

---

This contribution is based on a presentation made by the author at the conference "Africa and the International Criminal Court". The format of direct speech has been retained.
The views expressed in this chapter are not necessarily those of the Court.

S. Batohi (✉)
International Criminal Court, The Hague, The Nederlands

G. Werle et al. (eds.), *Africa and the International Criminal Court*,
International Criminal Justice Series 1, DOI 10.1007/978-94-6265-029-9_5

the world in the Rome Statute system (23 % of all States Parties). A number of African states have also adopted implementing legislation, incorporating, in whole or in part, aspects of the Rome Statute into domestic criminal codes.

In addition let me highlight the following:

- *Kofi Annan* convened the Rome Conference;
- African States led the ratification process, with Senegal as the first States Party;
- The Prosecutor is an African woman from The Gambia; she was presented as sole candidate by the African Union, and elected by consensus of States Parties;
- African judges make up 25 % of the bench;
- Approximately half of the Office of the Prosecutor's requests for assistance go to African States and around 70 % are responded to positively;
- African countries surrendered a large percentage of the suspects currently before the Court;
- UN Security Council Resolution 1593, which referred the situation of Darfur to the Court, included the positive votes of Benin and Tanzania and an abstention of Algeria; and
- UN Security Council Resolution 1970, which referred the situation of Libya unanimously to the Court, included the positive votes of Gabon, Nigeria and South Africa.

It was not until the request by the Office of the Prosecutor for an arrest warrant for President *Al Bashir* of the Sudan, in July 2008, that a controversy first arose about an alleged 'African bias', which was promoted by President *Al Bashir* himself and supported by some leaders. The confirmation of charges against the current Kenyan leaders—at the time they were not in the positions that they are in today—raised this perception of a bias against Africa to new heights, with the African Union convening a special meeting to discuss the issue and talk of a mass withdrawal of African States which, fortunately, did not materialize. Such action would have been disastrous for international justice and for Africa for many reasons, the key ones being a demonstration of a lack of commitment by African States to taking action against human rights abuses and to ending impunity for atrocities and to bringing justice for victims.

5.2 The Perception of 'African Bias'

So let us deal with the perception of 'African bias' which is an important issue that we cannot ignore. About targeting Africa: All the 32 persons who are or have been the subject of a Summons or Warrant of Arrest (public) are Africans. However, there are also more than 5 million African victims displaced, more than 40,000 African victims killed, thousands of African victims raped, and hundreds of thousands of African children transformed into killers and rapists. All victims are Africans.

Is this not a factor to be considered? There are so many voices in this debate, but where are the voices of the victims? We must never forget our real constituency. The constituency that the Court ultimately serves is comprised of the victims and communities affected by the massive crimes we investigate and prosecute.

About ignoring 'bigger criminals', in particular from the West: Africans are tired of double standards and justifiably so. It is, indeed, an imperfect system. But how can we try to do the best with what we have? How do we collectively try to move this to a more equitable system? The ICC Prosecutor is unfortunately not the world Prosecutor. She is the Prosecutor of 122 States Parties. The lack of universal jurisdiction is a challenge that I will touch on later.

Let us recall why the International Criminal Court was created. It was in response to a recognition that there was, and still is, a need in the world to do all we can to prevent massive crimes, to bring the perpetrators to account, and to offer some measure of justice to the victims and communities affected. Its creation was rooted in the desire to prevent a repeat of the human suffering triggered through decades of massive crimes. The Rome Statute was adopted under the leadership of *Kofi Annan*, the then Secretary General of the UN, and is largely the product of the commitment of Africa, Europe and Latin America, three regions which suffered massive crimes during the last century.

Fifty years earlier, British Prime Minister, *Winston Churchill*, referring to the Nazis' deliberate and systematic extermination of as many as six million Jews, called it a "crime that has no name". But a name was soon found: genocide—literally, the killing of a people or nation. After World War II, the Genocide Convention, adopted by the United Nations in 1948, was meant as a pledge by States to ensure that the horrors of the Holocaust would never again be repeated. But sadly, since then, the world community has consistently failed to prevent the occurrence of genocide in places like Cambodia, Rwanda, and the Former Yugoslavia. The Nazi trials and the 1948 Genocide Convention reflected a determination in the world community to prevent a recurrence of the Holocaust. But it was not enough. Thirty years after the Holocaust, the international community had no effective policy to stop the *Khmer Rouge*. Twenty years later, it could not prevent the cold-blooded executions of more than 7,000 Muslim men and boys in Srebrenica, and it neglected the *Hutu* machete-and-rape-driven killing of thousands of the *Tutsi* minority in the Rwandan genocide.

'Never again' was an unfulfilled promise. Why and how did it happen that mass murder of national, ethnic, and tribal groups continued with depressing frequency? Why did the international community fail to prevent the recurrence of crimes that shock the conscience of humanity? The hope, commitment and rhetoric after the horrors of World War II were sadly not supported by a willingness to stop or even condemn the crime itself.

The world would wait for almost half a century after Nuremberg, before the UN Security Council decided to create the International Criminal Tribunal for the former Yugoslavia and the International Criminal Tribunal for Rwanda, thus making the connection between peace and international justice again.

The creation of the International Criminal Court was rooted in a strong desire to prevent a repeat of the human suffering, triggered through decades of massive crimes, a desire and commitment shared by the many African States that participated in the Rome Conference, and even more so by those that ratified the Statute. We now have the opportunity to give it meaning, if we work together, and if that commitment is still there. In 1998, in Rome, the majority view of the international community was to establish an innovative and unprecedented institution, beholden to no single State, but to humanity as a whole. Its sole purpose: to hold individuals accountable for the crimes they commit, irrespective of the individual's status, and by so doing, to prevent them happening again. Delegates at the Rome Conference recognized that accountability and the respect for the rule of law are fundamental preconditions to provide the framework to protect individuals and nations against massive atrocities, to promote peace and international security, and to manage conflicts.

The framework of the Rome Statute has created an opportunity to realize international justice by applying one standard to all its States Parties and the people that are under its protection: a framework to help societies come to terms with the past and to move forward together in peace. As a permanent, independent, judicial institution of last resort, the International Criminal Court is at the heart of a new system of international criminal justice. To achieve its goal, no more impunity for the perpetrators of massive crimes, the Rome Statute, therefore, built an interdependent, mutually reinforcing system of justice. The Statute, in its Preamble, recalls "the duty of every State to exercise its criminal jurisdiction over those responsible for international crimes", thereby giving States the primary responsibility for investigating and punishing atrocities. The legal framework of the Rome Statute is predicated upon national courts, in the first instance, holding perpetrators to account, and if not, to cooperate with the International Criminal Court in investigating and holding perpetrators to account. It is only when national courts are unable or unwilling to act that the Court, as a court of last resort, can assert jurisdiction.

5.3 The Work of the Prosecutor of the International Criminal Court in Africa

The creation of the International Criminal Court responded to a need of combating the most serious crimes of concern to the international community which often remained unpunished, as national systems did not always deal adequately with such crimes, either because of a lack of investigative, prosecutorial or normative capacities, or because of a lack of a political will to do so. The system was created in this way because it recognizes the principle of primacy of states over their nationals, with the International Criminal Court serving as the court of last resort.

Complementarity is a crucial factor that is taken into consideration in determining whether to open investigations.

Let me explain how this works in practice by describing the example of Guinea, as it shows the impact of the Office's preliminary examinations activities in triggering national proceedings in accordance with the Rome Statute. As a core activity of the Office, we conduct such preliminary examinations to determine independently whether or not to open an investigation in any given situation, irrespective of how that situation has come to the attention of the Office, and by following clear and sound legal criteria established by the Rome Statute, relating to jurisdiction, admissibility and the interests of justice. They are explained in great detail in our prosecutorial strategies and our policy papers, which are public.

After the Office publicly announced that it was monitoring the serious allegations surrounding the events of 28 September 2009 in Conakry, the Office sent various, regular missions to Guinea to enquire and confirm that a national investigation had been opened into the September events, and to assess the progress. The Office has, in so doing, sought to encourage and cooperate with national and international efforts to conduct genuine national proceedings, thereby ensuring justice for victims of alleged crimes without the need for the Office to intervene, and also with a view to preventing further crimes. The judicial authorities in Guinea have indicted several officials for the alleged crimes committed on 28 September 2009, including the former Minister of Health and the current head of presidential security. A similar approach is taken in all our situations under preliminary examination, including in situations such as Colombia, Georgia, and Afghanistan, to highlight a few examples of activities outside the African continent. Once again, a key factor is whether local authorities are willing or able to pursue the matters of concern, in line with the guiding principle of complementarity that governs the Court's operations.

Wherever possible we encourage States to investigate and prosecute in situations where grave and serious crimes under international law have been committed. This is what is referred to as positive approach to complementarity, meaning that the Office encourages genuine national proceedings where possible, through publication of periodic reports, dialogue with States, support for national proceedings, etc. We monitor such situations closely. The Office of the Prosecutor has opened investigations in eight situations: the Democratic Republic of the Congo, Uganda, Central African Republic, Darfur, Kenya, Libya, Côte d'Ivoire and, most recently, Mali. In none of these countries were there ongoing national investigations at the time that these situations were brought to the attention of the Prosecutor.

The African continent has been supporting and assisting the Office at each step of its activities: in referring situations to the Office for investigation, in cooperating with the Office by facilitating investigative missions and responding to other requests for assistance, in pursuing and arresting individuals sought by the Court, and in protecting witnesses.

As previously mentioned, we must never forget our real constituency. The constituency that the Court ultimately serves comprises the victims and communities affected by the massive crimes we investigate and prosecute. In the African situations that are before the Court, innocent people have been killed, large numbers of people have been displaced, and children's lives have been destroyed as they have been recruited or forced into becoming child soldiers. Men and women have been the victims of horrific, sexual and gender-based violence. I believe that these victims of massive crimes deserve whatever measure of justice we can bring them through our investigations and prosecutions. The lack of universal jurisdiction of the Court remains a challenge.

The Rome Statute is merely an extension of national judicial systems in the fight to end impunity. Indeed, as an institution founded on the principle of complementarity that recognizes the primary responsibility of states to protect their citizens, the true relevance of the International Criminal Court will depend on the consistent efforts of national authorities to conduct genuine investigations into massive crimes and to prosecute them, or, in the alternative, the extent to which national prosecutorial authorities support the activities of the Office. All actors have a role to play in this regard, from political leaders to civil society. In 1998, the idea of a permanent International Court was just an idea on paper. Now, the system is in motion.

5.4 The International Criminal Court as an Obstruction to African Peace Processes?

Let me turn to the issue of peace and justice, an apparent tension that those against interventions by the International Criminal Court have often cited in their contention that the activities of the Court are obstructive in peace processes.

Can there be peace without justice? Perhaps for a while. But peace with justice is surely a more stable and lasting peaceful solution. They are not mutually exclusive. Justice and accountability are necessary to achieve regional, national, and international peace. Above all, justice creates a global environment in which perpetrators of the gravest crimes find no safe haven and are held to account. Justice ensures that no one, irrespective of status, can resort to violence, rapes, and killings to gain power or maintain power, and that those who do resort to such criminal violence will be investigated and prosecuted.

The International Criminal Court is a judicial institution; it promotes lasting peace through its judicial mandate. If its activities jeopardize peace-making efforts, it would be the responsibility of the UN Security Council to ask for a temporary suspension of the Court's proceedings, as it is allowed to do under the Rome Statute.[1]

The relationship between the Court and Africa continues to engage the interest of many around us. It is no secret that during recent African Union summits,

[1] On this issue, see Chap. 12 by *Okoth* in this volume.

international criminal justice has been regularly put to the test. AU Decisions included the refusal to cooperate with the International Criminal Court in the arrest and surrender of President *Al Bashir*, the refusal for the setting up of an ICC liaison office at the African Union in Addis Ababa, and the request that the Kenya cases be handed back to national authorities. Anti-ICC elements worked to discredit the Court and to lobby for non-support.

The International Criminal Court is, however, an African court, as much as it is a court of any other region in the world. It would not exist without the support of African States Parties to the ICC Statute. Notwithstanding the public controversies, our Office continues to receive support from African governments, NGOs, and civil society, and we serve in a very real way African victims and communities affected by the crimes we prosecute.

In five situations (if one includes the situation in Côte d'Ivoire) on the African continent in which the Court has become involved, African States themselves referred the situations to the Court. In two situations the referrals came from the UN Security Council. It has only been very rarely that the Office of the Prosecutor has moved on its own motion to investigate and prosecute in situations where the State itself has been unable or unwilling to act, despite the situation crying out for a response.

One of those is Kenya, which is *sub-judice*, so I will not mention anything about the case, but it is important to understand how the Office of the Prosecutor became involved. Following the post-election violence in 2007 and 2008, pursuant to the *Waki* Commission report, the Kenyan Government was given one year, beginning July 2009, to set up a national tribunal to deal with the issue. Failure to do this would see the jurisdiction of the International Criminal Court triggered. The primary responsibility, however, lay with Kenya. Despite several attempts in 2009, Kenya's Parliament did not pass the legislation required to establish a special tribunal. On 5 November 2009, the (former) Prosecutor of the Court, *Luis Moreno Ocampo*, met with President *Mwai Kibaki* and Prime Minister *Raila Odinga* in Nairobi. He informed them that since all the statutory criteria were fulfilled, he would be seeking authorization from the Chamber to proceed with an investigation into the situation in Kenya in relation to the post-election violence of 2007–2008. At that time, the President and Prime Minister issued a joint statement in which they reiterated their constructive meeting with the Prosecutor of the International Criminal Court, stating that Kenya was fully committed to cooperating with the Court within the framework of the Rome Statute. The investigation in Kenya was thus initiated with a strong Kenyan commitment to it. A poll in early 2012 indicated that a majority of Kenya's population (over 60 %) were in favor of the Court's intervention in Kenya.[2]

In Northern Uganda, to mention as second example, the international community was for a long time keen to appease *Joseph Kony*, both before and after the

---

[2] See Chap. 13 by *Materu* in this book. See also the forthcoming book of *Materu* on the international and domestic responses to the 2007 post-election violence in Kenya.

ICC warrant. *Kony*, however, was only interested in impunity and repeatedly took advantage of peace talks to re-group and re-arm his forces. He expanded his activities and intensified his campaign of rapes, abductions and killings. And he still remains at large.

The principles of the Rome Statute are contained in African seminal norms. The Constitutive Act of the African Union provides that the organization shall function consistently with the "condemnation and rejection of impunity", among other principles. It also provides, quite extraordinarily, for the right of the African Union to intervene in a Member State in the event that war crimes, genocide and crimes against humanity are committed. This is a unique provision in the founding document of an inter-governmental organization. An end to impunity should not be an academic, abstract notion.

5.5 Conclusion

To be effective in our work, we must learn from experiences and constantly re-examine our strategies. We also need the assistance and support of States Parties to the Rome Statute and the international community as a whole, including NGOs and civil society. We must make common cause in the fight against impunity.

As difficult as the challenges we face may be, I believe we can succeed in our mission. No matter who it is, the states in Africa, the ordinary people of Africa or the International Criminal Court, we all want the same things—peace, stability, security, respect for the rule of law and democratic values, and justice for the victims of massive atrocities. I believe that there is sufficient commitment in Africa to ensure that we can work together at closing the impunity gap.

We cannot pretend that the world we live in today is one in which genocide, crimes against humanity and war crimes are no longer committed. But we can say most emphatically that it is a world in which we no longer expect perpetrators of such crimes to escape being held accountable. In 1998, at the Rome Conference, we turned our backs on impunity. We said "no more" to crimes without accountability. We dared to believe that a new international system, backed up by a strong court of last resort, could provide for criminal responsibility where impunity once reigned—acting for victims of past crimes while serving as a deterrent to future ones. The Court has justified those original hopes. Five of the eight situations before the Court today were the result of either a direct States Party referral or an invitation to the Prosecutor to investigate. States have given unfettered access to the Prosecutor while fully acknowledging that the person who holds that office has a duty to investigate all sides of a conflict. Not so many years ago, such steps would have been unthinkable.

Africa's cooperative efforts should be directed at strengthening national law enforcement and judicial systems to be able to deal genuinely and effectively with massive crimes and thus exclude ICC 'interference'. We must stand united to ensure that this powerful tool that we all believe in, the rule of law, can serve humankind equally and consistently to redress the imbalance between the criminals who wield power and the victims who suffer at their hands. This is the only way to ensure durable and lasting peace in our societies.

Part II
African Prosecutions of International Crimes

Chapter 6
The Implementation of the Rome Statute in Africa

Gerhard Kemp

Contents

6.1 Introduction

This chapter focuses on the implementation of the Rome Statute of the International Criminal Court in selected African countries. It will therefore not deal with the domestic application of international criminal law in a more general sense. Other papers in this volume deal with various aspects of domestic application of international criminal law and with the impact of universal jurisdiction.

By way of introduction, a few preliminary remarks on the role of the Rome Statute as a blueprint, or at least, a normative framework, for the domestication of international criminal justice:

G. Kemp (✉)
University of Stellenbosch, Stellenbosch, South Africa
e-mail: gkemp@sun.ac.za

G. Werle et al. (eds.), *Africa and the International Criminal Court*,
International Criminal Justice Series 1, DOI 10.1007/978-94-6265-029-9_6

- The *principle of complementarity*, as a foundational principle underlying the international criminal justice project as envisioned in the Rome Statute, is premised on the ability of national criminal justice systems to investigate and prosecute crimes under international law.
- States Parties to the Rome Statute are not obliged to incorporate the *substantive criminal law* of the Rome Statute into domestic law. In this regard, the Rome Statute seems to be a weaker international criminal law treaty compared to others, for instance the UN Torture Convention or relevant parts of the Geneva Conventions.[1]
- Article 70(4) of the Rome Statute provides that a States Party must provide in its domestic criminal law for the *offences against the administration of justice* referred to in Article 70. These include offences like the giving of false testimony, as well as bribery and corruption, in the context of the administration of justice.
- Part 9 of the Rome Statute provides for certain *obligations regarding co-operation and legal assistance to the International Criminal Court.* The key provision in this regard is Article 88, which provides that "States Parties shall ensure that there are procedures available under their national law for all of the forms of co-operation which are specified under this Part".[2]
- Although the letter and spirit of the Rome Statute provides for *some flexibility in terms of the domestication* of the various aspects of the Statute, a number of commentators agree that the Rome Statute, as a whole, certainly encourages States Parties to enact domestic legislation[3] as the best way to implement fully the various obligations under the Rome Statute, and to give effect to the principle of complementarity.

The author agrees fully with *Werle's* very apt description of the Rome Statute's central message, namely that "states should be both willing and able (through their domestic legislation) to prosecute genocide, crimes against humanity, and war crimes in a capacity similar to that of the International Criminal Court".[4] Whether we should add the crime of aggression to this list is perhaps a debate for another day, but it is added here for the sake of completeness and in light of the prognostications of the Kampala Resolution on Aggression.[5] It is at any rate assumed that the domestic implementation of the crime of aggression will be influenced by the complex nature of the crime and the underlying reluctance to provide for the crime at domestic level—a reluctance reflected in the Understandings adopted at the Kampala Review Conference.[6]

---

[1] Werle 2009, p. 118.

[2] For a brief discussion see Kemp et al. 2012, pp. 575–578.

[3] Werle 2009, p. 118 (as well as the authors cited).

[4] Werle 2009, p 119.

[5] At present nine states have ratified the amendments pertaining to the crime of aggression. Botswana is thus far the only African State to ratify the amendments.

[6] Kemp 2012, p. 55.

6.2 Implementation Typologies

In terms of *method of incorporation* of substantive international criminal law, *Werle* points out that states have broad discretion.[7] *Werle* identifies the following methods[8]:

6.2.1 Complete Incorporation

Complete incorporation in this context normally entails three possibilities: The direct application of customary international criminal law; reference to relevant provisions in the Rome Statute in conjunction with domestic law; and adoption of the ICC crimes *verbatim* into domestic law. The latter simply involves a method of copying of the relevant provisions of the Rome Statute. These possibilities are also considered below, in the context of national case studies.

6.2.2 Non-incorporation or Application of 'Ordinary' Criminal Law

Although national criminal courts could, in theory, be able to punish perpetrators of genocide, war crimes and crimes against humanity under the rubric of 'ordinary crimes' like murder, or assault with intent to do grievous bodily harm, this is obviously not a sustainable solution from an international criminal justice perspective. To massage domestic criminal law in order to enforce international criminal law has very limited utility—as we have experienced in South Africa with failed attempts to prosecute alleged apartheid-era war crimes.[9] In the absence of domestic criminal law incorporating international criminal law, the prospects of success will always remain slim. In addition, and from an ICC perspective, commentators pointed out that despite the absence of explicit legal obligations in the Rome Statute to incorporate substantive international criminal law into domestic law, the non-incorporation of international criminal law is not in conformity with the spirit and broad aim of the Rome Statute, namely to end impunity for the most serious crimes under international law.[10]

---

[7] Werle 2009, p. 119.

[8] Ibid., pp. 119–121.

[9] See, for instance, the failed attempt to prosecute Dr *Wouter Basson* for alleged war crimes committed during the apartheid era, *State v. Basson* 2005 (1) SA 171 (CC). See remarks by Chief Justice Chaskalson, paras 84 and 97.

[10] Werle 2009, pp. 120–121.

6.2.3 Modified Incorporation

Modified incorporation means that the substance of international criminal law is integrated into domestic criminal law,[11] while providing for distinctive national features or doctrinal characteristics. This method is often found in jurisdictions in which provision for crimes under international law pre-dates the Rome Statute of the International Criminal Court.[12]

6.3 A Brief Remark About Incorporation, Transformation and Implementation

This chapter is not primarily concerned with the theoretical differences between incorporation and transformation of international law. However, given Africa's diverse legal landscape, any discussion about the implementation of a multilateral treaty such as the Rome Statute of the International Criminal Court, might be in need of some theoretical context, where appropriate.

For purposes of this brief discussion, incorporation of international law into national law means international law becomes part of national law because it is international law. Sometimes this view of international law is also equated with the monist view of international law, namely that international law is automatically incorporated into national law by virtue of the fact that international law and national law are part of the "same unified system".[13] Transformation means that international law becomes part of national law because of a "deliberate act on the part of the state concerned".[14] It is said that the theory of transformation corresponds with dualism; the latter being the idea that international law and national law "operat[e] in [their] own area[s] of competence [...] and rules of international law can operate in national law only if they are deliberately transformed into that system by the appropriate national process".[15]

Many factors—historical, legal-cultural, and, arguably most importantly, constitutional—will inform any particular national treatment of international law. Therefore, the concept of implementation can be viewed as a pragmatic approach, namely to answer the question "how does a national system implement the rules of international law?" The *origin* of the international rule is, in terms of this empirical approach, less important than the *likely impact* on the national legal system.[16]

---

[11] Ibid., p. 121.

[12] Notably war crimes, as incorporated via national legislation on the Geneva Conventions.

[13] Dixon 2013, p. 98; Dugard 2011, pp. 42–43; Cassese 1986, pp. 17–22.

[14] Dixon 2013, p. 98.

[15] Ibid., pp. 98–99.

[16] Ibid., p. 100.

This chapter focuses on the implementation of the Rome Statute of the International Criminal Court in Africa: The African case studies will thus be examined in light of the various theoretical dimensions identified above, with the ultimate aim of answering the question: What is the (likely) impact of the Rome Statute of the ICC on the selected national systems?

6.4 Strategies for Implementation in African States

This chapter does not deal with the role of African States Parties and their relationship with the International Criminal Court in the more general sense. The negotiating history of the Rome Statute and the role of African states[17] are, of course, issues of interest for the broad theme of this volume. The focus here is on specific strategies for purposes of the implementation of the Rome Statute. One such strategy was the so-called Windhoek Plan of Action on ICC Ratification and Implementation in SADC.[18]

The Windhoek Plan of Action followed the earlier so-called Pretoria Statement on the Common Understanding on the ICC[19] adopted by the SADC delegates in 1999. This Statement recommended the expeditious ratification of the Rome Statute by the SADC States. The Windhoek Plan was therefore intended to take the matter of ratification by the SADC States further, and to "give priority to the drafting of implementing legislation of the Rome Statute in order to effectively co-operate with the International Criminal Court and give effect to the principle of complementarity".[20] Participants at the Windhoek conference also agreed on the need to establish capacity building programmes in order to assist the SADC members in the process of ratification and implementation of the Rome Statute. It should be noted that there was—following on the Windhoek Conference—anecdotal evidence of capacity building linked to ICC ratification and implementation, but not much in terms of a concerted SADC (government) effort.

It must be said that, apart from regional (governmental) efforts like the SADC conferences mentioned above, various non-governmental organisations also tried to move African states towards ratification and eventual implementation of the Rome Statute.[21]

---

[17] For a regional perspective, see Maqungo 2000.

[18] The Final Document was adopted at the "Conference on International Criminal Court (ICC) Ratification and Implementation for the Southern African Development Community (SADC) Region", 28–30 May 2001, Windhoek, Namibia. The conference was hosted by the Government of Namibia and co-organised by the International Criminal Court Technical Assistance Program as well as the Parliamentarians for Global Action.

[19] For the full statement, see The International Criminal Court Monitor, Issue 12 (August 1999) 3.

[20] Windhoek Plan, para 4.

[21] Civil society organisations like the Institute for Security Studies should be mentioned in this regard. During the past few years the Institute has done valuable work in terms of awareness,

The discussion now turns to a few case studies to illustrate the various levels of progress in the implementation of the Rome Statute in Africa. It starts with two examples from SADC, namely South Africa and Mauritius. Both jurisdictions have adopted fairly comprehensive implementation legislation.

6.5 South Africa and Mauritius: Acts of Transformation

6.5.1 South Africa

The Implementation of the Rome Statute of the International Criminal Court Act 27 of 2002 ('the ICC Act') is an act of transformation.[22] It was enacted on 18 July 2002, shortly after the entry into force of the Rome Statute. The ICC Act came into operation on 16 August 2002. South Africa became the first state to fully implement the Rome Statute in Africa.[23]

The ICC Act essentially does two things: It provides for the domestic criminalisation of the most serious crimes of international concern (genocide, war crimes, and crimes against humanity) as set out in the Rome Statute; and it provides for a comprehensive framework for co-operation between South Africa and the International Criminal Court.[24] The ICC Act incorporates the substantive criminal law of the Rome Statute with direct reference, via a Schedule appended to the ICC Act, of the definitions of the crimes provided for in the Rome Statute. There is no specific reference to the Rome Statute's Elements of Crimes, but it is suggested that nothing would prevent a South African court from taking note of the Elements of Crimes if a domestic prosecution of one of the ICC crimes would come before a South African court.[25]

The ICC Act provides for four grounds upon which jurisdiction may be exercised by a South African court over the crimes of genocide, crimes against humanity and war crimes:

- Territorial jurisdiction
- Nationality
- Active personality
- Universal jurisdiction

(Footnote 21 continued)
advocacy, and capacity building with respect to international criminal justice in Africa. Various workshops and conferences resulted in useful frameworks and texts aimed at the practical realisation of international criminal justice in Africa, including the implementation of the Rome Statute. See, for example, Du Plessis 2008.

[22] Katz 2003, pp. 25–30.

[23] Du Plessis 2007, p. 461.

[24] Du Toit et al. 2013, App B57.

[25] Kemp et al. 2012, p. 561.

Contributions elsewhere in this volume deal with jurisdiction, and universal jurisdiction in particular. It is, therefore, not necessary to expand on this issue, save for a few comments on the jurisprudential consequences of implementation of the Rome Statute in South Africa.

In *Southern Africa Litigation Centre and others v National Director of Public Prosecutions and others*[26] some of the important implications of the ICC Act, notably the provision on universal jurisdiction, are considered by the North Gauteng High Court in Pretoria, South Africa.[27] In this case, the High Court was asked by the applicants to set aside the decision by South African government agencies not to open an investigation into allegations of torture as a crime against humanity, involving Zimbabwean officials.

The judgment by the High Court is remarkable, since it is the first time that a court in South Africa considered the duties of South Africa in terms of the ICC Act. It is also one of the first judgments of its kind by a national court in Africa. *Gevers* identified a number of important implications of the judgment by the High Court. First, the High Court held that the Rome Statute's evidential threshold (namely, a "reasonable basis to believe crimes have been committed") should also apply to decisions by South African authorities of whether or not to prosecute under the ICC Act. It is thus a clear illustration of the value and importance of implementing the Rome Statute, also from an investigative and prosecutorial perspective. Second, the High Court rejected the submission that the ICC Act only provides for a so-called conditional universal jurisdiction. The Court correctly held that it would be absurd for an investigation into crimes under the ICC Act to be conditional on the presence of the accused on South African soil—and that jurisdiction would end the moment the suspect would leave South Africa. Although the High Court's decision is not very clear on the distinction between enforcement jurisdiction and prescriptive jurisdiction, *Gevers* suggests that the practical implication is clear: South African authorities have, as a consequence of the ICC Act, a duty, irrespective of the location of the accused, to investigate international crimes under certain circumstances.[28] It should be mentioned that the ICC Act does not provide for criteria or mechanisms to determine which crimes (i.e. crimes within its substantive ambit) should be selected for investigation and prosecution. The High Court in the SALC-case also did not give much guidance on the direction. Perhaps the most useful mechanism will be the suggestion by the applicants, namely that crimes for investigation and prosecution should be selected on the basis of "anticipated presence" of a suspect or suspects. Ultimately, this is something that the relevant authorities, especially the National Prosecuting

---

[26] *Southern Africa Litigation Centre and Anther v. National Director of Public Prosecutions and Others*, [2012] ZAGPPHC 61 (8 May 2012).

[27] For a discussion of the case, see Werle and Bornkamm 2013, pp. 659–675; Kemp et al. 2012, pp. 561–564.

[28] Kemp et al. 2012, p. 563.

Authority, will have to determine in policy directives, as is the case with other categories of crimes. Third, the High Court quite correctly rejected the proposition that the so-called political implications of the proposed investigation and possible prosecution in terms of the ICC Act were relevant factors to be considered and entertained.

Because of the above-mentioned implications, the police and the National Prosecuting Authority took the SALC-matter on appeal to the Supreme Court of Appeal. Argument was heard on 1 November 2013 and judgment was delivered on 27 November 2013.[29] The Supreme Court of Appeal essentially agreed with the High Court and declared that the decision of the South African police (a decision of June 2009) not to investigate the complaints laid by SALC that certain named Zimbabwean officials had committed crimes against humanity[30] against Zimbabwean nationals in Zimbabwe, is set aside.[31] Furthermore, the Supreme Court declared (with reference to the facts of the case) that the police are empowered to investigate the alleged crimes irrespective of whether or not the alleged perpetrators are present in South Africa. The police are required to initiate an investigation under the ICC Act into the alleged crimes. It must be noted that the Supreme Court of Appeal order is not as extensive as the High Court order and is clearly focussed on the obligations of the *police* in terms of the ICC Act.

The Supreme Court of Appeal viewed its task as an interpretation of the ICC Act, and in particular, the "exercise of jurisdiction by a domestic court (and the logically antecedent exercise of investigative powers by the relevant authorities) over allegations of crimes against humanity—in particular, the crime of torture—committed in another country".[32] Of course, the Supreme Court of Appeal analysed the provisions of the ICC Act within the context of developments in international criminal law, notably developments surrounding the notion of universal jurisdiction. The Court understood the idea of universality as a basis for prescriptive jurisdiction as the idea that "states are empowered to proscribe conduct that is recognised as [threatening] the good order not only of particular states but of the international community as a whole". Furthermore, international crimes are "crimes in whose suppression all states have an interest as they violate values that constitute the foundation of the world public order". Universality as a basis for jurisdiction "is not tied to the state's territory or some other traditional connecting

---

[29] *National Commissioner of the South African Police and another v. Southern Africa Litigation Centre and others* (485/2012) [2013] ZASCA 168 (27 November 2013). Hereafter referred to as *SALC* case (SCA).

[30] The allegations contained in the victims' affidavits describe "severe physical assaults being perpetrated, which included the use of truncheons, baseball bats, fan-belts and booted feet." Furthermore, there are also allegations of victims being "suspended by a metal rod between two tables; of being subjected to water boarding; and of electrical shocks being applied to the genitals of some of them". *SALC* case (SCA), para 11.

[31] It is necessary to recall that the case before the High Court was an administrative review of the decision of the police not to investigate the allegations of torture (crimes against humanity).

[32] *SALC* case (SCA), para 5.

factor, but is rather grounded in the universal nature of the offence committed".[33] The Supreme Court of Appeal then proceeded to link these developments with the establishment of the International Criminal Court under the Rome Statute of 1998. The Supreme Court regarded the Rome Statute as a "codification of sorts" of developments in customary international law, including developments regarding the notion of universal jurisdiction.[34]

The Supreme Court of Appeal stated clearly that the enactment of the ICC Act by South Africa was in fulfilment of its obligations as a State Party to the Rome Statute. It is interesting to note that the Court regarded the criminalisation at national level of the ICC crimes to be part of the obligations of a States Party.[35]

With reference to the allegations of torture which formed the basis for the initial application before the High Court, the Supreme Court of Appeal considered the definition of crimes against humanity in South Africa's ICC Act and held that, in relation to this case, "the acts complained of, if established, would amount to punishable offences in terms of the ICC Act".[36]

Having established that the relevant acts of torture would fall under the rubric of crimes against humanity as defined in the ICC Act, the Supreme Court of Appeal next dealt with the Commissioner of Police's contention that the conduct complained of is only deemed to have been committed upon the perpetrator's arrival in South Africa. The Court noted that the logical corollary of this submission is that once the alleged perpetrator departs South Africa the conduct complained of ceases to be a crime. It quite correctly called these submissions to be "patently fallacious".[37] Indeed, the substantive provisions of South Africa's ICC Act criminalise the relevant conduct "at the time of its commission, regardless of where and by whom it was committed".[38]

The more difficult part of the judgment, at least from an international criminal law perspective, is the issue of the investigative authority of South African agencies flowing from the provisions of the ICC Act. The general framework in terms of which the South African police can conduct criminal investigations basically consists of the relevant Constitutional provision, as well as provisions contained in the South African Police Service Act (as amended). Section 205(3) of South African Constitution, 1996 provides: "The objects of the police service are to prevent, combat and investigate crime, to maintain public order, to protect and secure the inhabitants of the republic and their property, and to uphold and enforce the law". In addition, the South African Police Service Act provides that the police may exercise such powers and shall perform such duties and functions as are by law conferred on or assigned to a police official. A Schedule to the Police Act

[33] Ibid., para 39.
[34] Ibid., para 40.
[35] Ibid., para 43.
[36] Ibid., para 46.
[37] Ibid., para 51.
[38] Ibid., para 51.

classifies all crimes under the ICC Act as "national priority offences".[39] Thus, the South African police are quite clearly empowered by the Constitution and relevant legislation (including the ICC Act) to investigate the commission of any crimes criminalised by the ICC Act. This includes crimes committed extra-territorially, since these crimes are crimes under South African law.[40]

To establish that the police have, in principle, the power to investigate crimes committed abroad is one thing; to find that the circumstances of any given case warrant an investigation, is quite another. The Supreme Court of Appeal considered the principles of general international law as well as comparative law. The Court also considered some regional instruments, including the African Union Model Law on Universal Jurisdiction over International Crimes, which contains no presence requirement of the suspect for the commencement of investigations. The Court concluded that "there is no universal rule or practice against the initiation of investigations in the absence of alleged perpetrators." The Court held:

> In some jurisdictions anticipated presence is sufficient. Adopting a strict presence requirement defeats the wide manner in which our legislation is framed, and does violence to the fight against impunity. Conversely, adopting a policy that calls for investigations, despite the absence of any effective connecting factor, is similarly destructive in wasting precious time and resources that could otherwise be employed in the equally important fight against crime domestically. I can understand that, if there is no prospect of a perpetrator ever being within the country, no purpose would be served by initiating an investigation. If there is a prospect of a perpetrator's presence, I can see no reason, particularly having regard to the executive and legislature's earnest assumption of South Africa's obligations in terms of the Rome Statute [...] why an investigation should not be initiated.[41]

Having established the police's duties and powers under the various statutes (including the ICC Act), the Supreme Court of Appeal proceeded to confirm that it did not see it as its task to prescribe to the police how the investigation is to be conducted.[42]

Given South Africa's position as a regional power and South Africa's early ratification and implementation of the Rome Statute, the judgment of the Supreme Court of Appeal will no doubt have implications beyond South Africa's borders. Not only did the Court interpret the meaning of substantive (or prescriptive) jurisdiction under the ICC Act, it also provided a clear path forward to the police when the police are next confronted by similar situations. The police, quite simply, have the power under the South African ICC Act to investigate crimes against humanity, war crimes and genocide regardless of where these crimes were committed. The pragmatic qualification that there should be a prospect of the suspect being present in South Africa, seems to be a realistic qualification—at least in terms of the realities of limited resources and the general crime situation in South

[39] Ibid., para 54.
[40] Ibid., paras 55–56.
[41] Ibid., para 66.
[42] Ibid., para 68.

Africa. Of course, the Supreme Court of Appeal is not the last stop—there is also the possibility that the matter can go to the Constitutional Court. For now, the Supreme Court's interpretation of South Africa's implementation legislation with regard to the investigation of crimes under the Act stands as the authoritative interpretation.

The ICC Act also provides for co-operation between South Africa and the International Criminal Court, in line with South Africa's obligations under the Rome Statute. The key provisions are contained in Chapters 4 and 5 of the ICC Act.[43] Chapter 4 of the ICC Act provides for a comprehensive co-operation regime between South Africa and the International Criminal Court. This regime includes the arrest and surrender of individuals, as well as general judicial assistance to the Court. Chapter 5 provides for miscellaneous matters, such as the admissibility of documents, offences against the administration of justice and agreements between South Africa and the International Criminal Court relating to other forms of assistance to the Court.

It should be noted that Section 14 of the ICC Act provides for the utilisation of relevant domestic statutory frameworks in order to complement the mutual legal assistance methods provided for in the ICC Act. This is very sensible, and unnecessary duplication is thus avoided. Section 31 of the ICC Act designates South Africa as a state in which sentences of imprisonment imposed by the International Criminal Court may be served.

An important part of the co-operation regime between South Africa and the Court, is the arrest and surrender of individuals. The ICC Act provides for two types of arrest:

- Arrest based on an existing ICC warrant (Section 8).
- Arrest in terms of a warrant issued by a magistrate upon request from the National director of Public Prosecutions (Section 9).

Regardless of the type of arrest, the form and manner of execution of the arrest warrant must be "as near as possible to what may be prescribed in respect of warrants of arrest in general by or under the laws of the Republic relating to criminal procedure". Again, this is a very sensible harmonisation between and utilisation of the different domestic legal regimes, including the ICC Act.

Initially the ICC Act was deficient as regards co-operation with the International Criminal Court. The ICC Act did not provide for an effective order of surrender to the Court of a suspect after arrest. This was rectified in 2005 with an amendment. The ICC Act currently provides that a magistrate must order that an arrested individual be surrendered to the International Criminal Court "and that he or she be committed to prison pending such surrender". The ICC Act, together with other relevant statutory frameworks, now provides for co-operation, mutual legal assistance, arrest and surrender, every step of the way, thus fulfilling South Africa's legal obligations under the Rome Statute.

---

[43] For a discussion, see Du Toit et al. 2013, App B43–B59.

6.5.2 Mauritius

The International Criminal Court Act 27 of 2011 implements the Rome Statute with respect to Mauritius.[44] Like its South African counterpart, the Mauritius ICC Act also provides for the incorporation of substantive international criminal law, jurisdiction of national courts over the ICC crimes, as well as for co-operation between the Court and Mauritius.

In terms of substantive criminal law, Section 4 of the ICC Act provides for the criminalisation of crimes against humanity, genocide and war crimes under Mauritius national law. It also provides for a maximum prison sentence of 45 years for these crimes. Section 4 also provides for the separate crime of incitement to commit genocide, and for criminal liability for the three international crimes based on common purpose. In terms of the jurisdiction of the national courts of Mauritius, Section 4(3) provides as follows:

> Where a person commits an international crime outside Mauritius, he shall be deemed to have committed the crime in Mauritius if he—
>
> (a) is a citizen of Mauritius;
> (b) is not a citizen of Mauritius but is ordinarily resident in Mauritius;
> (c) is present in Mauritius after the commission of the crime; or
> (d) has committed the crime against a citizen of Mauritius or against a person who is ordinarily resident in Mauritius.

In line with the Rome Statute, the ICC Act of Mauritius also provides for the criminal responsibility of commanders and superiors, and for the position that official capacity (including status of an individual as Head of State) shall not be a defence to any of the ICC crimes. Section 7 of the ICC Act provides for the separate crime of contempt of the International Criminal Court, which includes corruption-related offences, thus giving effect to Section 70(4) of the Rome Statute.

Part IV of the Mauritian ICC Act provides for the arrest and surrender of persons. The detailed provisions contained in this Part of the Act are clearly aimed at effective co-operation with the International Criminal Court and the protection of procedural safeguards under Mauritian national law. Section 16 of the Act provides for the interim release of an individual arrested under the Act, and Section 18 provides for the procedure of removal of a person surrendered to the Court. Part V of the Act provides for general judicial assistance and other forms of co-operation with the International Criminal Court. Section 21 contains a list of areas of assistance in relation to investigations and prosecutions, for instance: the taking of evidence; questioning of persons; service of documents; execution of searches and seizures; identification, tracing and freezing or seizure of proceeds, property and assets and instrumentalities of international crimes. The Section also contains a generic, open-ended reference to "any other type of assistance which is

---

[44] Mauritius ratified the Rome Statute on 5 March 2002.

not prohibited by law, with the view to facilitating the investigation and prosecution of crimes within the jurisdiction of the International Criminal Court."

Part VII of the ICC Act provides for the enforcement of a sentence of imprisonment in cases where the International Criminal Court has designated Mauritius as a State in which a person upon whom the Court has imposed a sentence of imprisonment shall serve that sentence.

The definitions of crimes against humanity, genocide, and war crimes provided for in the Schedule to the ICC Act, largely and substantially correspond with the Rome Statute definitions, although the definitions are not verbatim copies of the relevant articles in the Rome Statute.

6.6 Other African Jurisdictions

6.6.1 Kenya

The International Crimes Act of 2008, like the two SADC counterparts discussed above, provides for the incorporation of substantive international criminal law (the three Rome Statute crimes of genocide, war crimes, and crimes against humanity), as well as for co-operation between Kenya and the International Criminal Court, and judicial and legal assistance. It also provides for the offences against the administration of justice, as per Article 70(4) of the Rome Statute.

In terms of substantive criminal law, it should be noted that the International Crimes Act provides for the three ICC crimes by reference to the relevant provisions of the Rome Statute (the Rome Statute is also attached as a Schedule to the Act[45]). 'Crime against humanity' is defined as having the same meaning as Article 7 of the Rome Statute and "includes an act defined as a crime against humanity in conventional international law or customary international law that is not otherwise dealt with in the Rome Statute or in[the International Crimes] Act".

An interesting feature of the International Crimes Act is Part IX, which provides for investigations or sittings of the International Criminal Court in Kenya. Given the current processes before the Court, involving senior government officials of Kenya (including the president), some have argued that it would be better for the International Criminal Court to sit in Kenya so that the government of Kenya can keep functioning as best it could, given the fact that the President (and Deputy-President) may have to spend some time away from the seat of government for the duration of the trial. The mechanisms, at least in terms of the International Crimes Act, seem to be provided for. The Act provides that the ICC Prosecutor may conduct investigations on the territory of Kenya. It further provides that the International Criminal Court as an institution with judicial powers may sit in Kenya. In order for the Court to perform its judicial functions, it may

[45] Compare also with the South African Implementation Act, 2002.

administer oaths in Kenya. However, the Act is also clear that there is no formal link between the International Criminal Court and the courts of Kenya. It is therefore not possible to take orders issued by the Court on review to the courts of Kenya. From a practical point of view, the Act provides that the Kenyan authorities have the power to detain ICC prisoners in Kenyan prisons if the International Criminal Court holds a sitting in Kenya. The Act also provides for the removal of ICC prisoners from Kenya.

6.6.2 Senegal

Senegal has the historic distinction of being the first country to ratify the Rome Statute of the International Criminal Court (on 2 February 1999). It signed the Rome Statute on 18 July 1998. Senegal does not have comprehensive implementation legislation comparable to South Africa, Mauritius or Kenya (discussed above) but does provide for substantive jurisdiction over the ICC crimes (genocide, crimes against humanity, and war crimes) in its Criminal Code (*Loi 2007 02 du fevrier 2007 modifiant le Code pénal*). The Code of Criminal Procedure was amended (*Loi 2007 05 du 12 fevrier 2007 modifiant le Code de Procedure penale*) in order to provide for co-operation with the International Criminal Court.

Commentators have noted that the adoption by Senegal of some implementation legislative measures underscores the fact that Senegal, in this regard at least, moved away from the 'monist' tradition and recognised that legislative measures implementing the Rome Statute (or at least the most important obligations contained therein) are desirable.[46]

6.6.3 Uganda

The International Criminal Court Act, 2010, entered into force on 25 June 2010.[47] The Act incorporates the relevant parts of the Rome Statute into Ugandan law. Since the ICC Act provides for both substantive issues and co-operation with the International Criminal Court, one can compare this Act to the models of incorporation discussed above with reference to South Africa, Mauritius and Kenya.

Although the ICC Act, 2010, does not mention the International Crimes Division of the High Court (previously known as the War Crimes Division), it does provide for the jurisdiction of the High Court to hear cases of genocide, crimes against humanity and war crimes. The International Crimes Division is, of course, part of the High Court structure.

---

[46] Du Plessis and Stone 2008.

[47] The Uganda Gazette No 39, Vol CIII dated 25 June 2010.

It is important to mention that the ICC Act, 2010, provides for jurisdiction over the three core crimes committed from 2002. Since the atrocities in Northern Uganda mostly occurred from 1986 to 2002, the ICC Act is structured in such a way as to link the relevant parts of substantive law of the Penal Code as well as the Geneva Conventions Act with the ICC Act, 2010.

A possible bone of contention is the apparent conflict between Article 98(4) of the Constitution of Uganda, and Section 25 of the ICC Act. The former provides for the immunity from criminal proceedings of the President of Uganda (for as long as he or she holds office). The latter provides for the non-applicability of immunity in the context of surrender of individuals to the International Criminal Court. It thus seems unlikely that Uganda would be able to arrest and transfer its own President to The Hague, or prosecute him in Uganda for one or more of the ICC crimes. Of course, this hypothetical situation could still be clarified by the courts in a real case.

6.7 Concluding Remarks

There are 34 African States Parties to the Rome Statute of the International Criminal Court. There are, however, only a small number of states with implementation legislation—either in a comprehensive form or more limited. The early drive for implementation as reflected by initiatives such as the "SADC Plan of Action" turned out to be rather disappointing in terms of real legislative action.

The aim of this chapter was to provide some overview and some thoughts on implementation of the Rome Statute as a strategy to combat impunity and as a legal obligation. Both aspects are premised on the rather ubiquitous concept of 'political will'. Of course, the Rome Statute and its domestic implementation are not the only possible strategies to combat impunity. The activities of various ad hoc tribunals, or domestic trials in terms of other legal mechanisms (Geneva Conventions or the Torture Convention, for instance) must obviously also be viewed as part of the international criminal justice project's primary aim, namely to end impunity for the worst crimes under international law. Therefore, the observations and remarks in this chapter should not be viewed in isolation, but rather as complementary to other aspects of international criminal justice and the operation of the International Criminal Court itself, as addressed elsewhere in this volume. Not least of these contextual matters is the current debate surrounding the relationship between Africa and the Court. It is not inconceivable that the outcome of the debates, or even the political trends that feed into the debates, might have a real impact on the way in which African States Parties to the Rome Statute adopt national implementing legislation.

Case law is always helpful in bringing issues into crisp focus, and also in exposing flaws in legal frameworks. There are not many domestic cases in Africa concerning direct interpretation and application of the Rome Statute and relevant implementing legislation. In fact, up till now, the so-called Zimbabwe Torture

Docket Case brought before the High Court and eventually the Supreme Court of Appeal in South Africa, might be the first of its kind in Africa. The fact that a court (or, rather, two courts) have had the opportunity to interpret the relevant provisions of domestic implementation legislation is to be welcomed as such. The merits of the judgments are self-evidently open to further debate and analyses. The future effect of the judgment by the Supreme Court of Appeal of South Africa is contingent upon future events, not least of which is the presence of suspects in South Africa. But, apart from the obvious important legal consequences flowing from the judgment (notably the powers and duties of the South African police in terms of the ICC Implementation Act), the practical reality is that, as a consequence of this judgment (and the judgment of the High Court preceding the Supreme Court of Appeal judgment), it is safe to say that the world had become a little bit smaller and a slightly more inconvenient to travel in for some Zimbabwean officials suspected of having committed crimes against humanity. If this can be replicated throughout the continent of Africa, ICC sceptics and critics might just find that there is, ultimately, less of a need for the Court. That would, of course, be the best illustration of complementarity in action, thus fulfilling the ultimate goal of the Rome Statute, namely to make international criminal justice a domestic affair.

References

Cassese A (1986) International Law in a divided world. Clarendon Press, Oxford

Dixon M (2013) International Law, 7th edn. Oxford University Press, Oxford

Du Plessis M (2007) South Africa's implementation of the ICC Statute. J Int Crim Justice 5:460–479

Du Plessis M (2008) African guide to international criminal justice. Institute for Security Studies, Pretoria

Du Plessis M, Stone L (2008) Implementation of the Rome Statute of the International Criminal Court (ICC) in African countries. Institute for Security Studies, Pretoria

Dugard J (2011) International Law—a South African perspective, 4th edn. Juta, Cape Town

Du Toit E, De Jager F, Paizes A, Skeen A, Van der Merwe S (2013) Commentary on the Criminal Procedure Act. Juta, Cape Town

Katz A (2003) An act of transformation: the incorporation of the Rome Statute of the ICC into national law in South Africa. Afr Secur Rev 12:25–30

Kemp G (2012) Implementing at national level the amendments to the Rome Statute of the International Criminal Court with respect to the crime of aggression: a South African perspective. In: Ambos K, Maunganidze OA (eds) Power and prosecution—challenges and opportunities for international criminal justice in sub-Saharan Africa. Universitätsverlag Göttingen, Göttingen, pp 39–56

Kemp G, Walker S, Palmer R, Baqwa D, Gevers C, Leslie B, Steynberg A (2012) Criminal Law in South Africa. Oxford University Press, Cape Town

Maqungo S (2000) The establishment of the International Criminal Court: SADC's participation in the negotiations. Afr Secur Rev 9(1):42–53

http://www.issafrica.org/Pubs/ASR/9No1/InCriminalCourt.html

Werle G (2009) Principles of International Criminal Law, 2nd edn. T.M.C Asser Press, The Hague
Werle G, Bornkamm PC (2013) Torture in Zimbabwe under scrutiny in South Africa. J Int Crim Justice 11:659–675

Cases

State v Basson, Constitutional Court of South Africa, 9 September 2005 (1) SA 171 (CC).
SALC and Another v. National Director for Public Prosecutions and Others, High Court of South Africa (North Gauteng High Court), Judgment of 8 May 2012, Case No. 77150/09.
National Commissioner of the South African Police Service and Another v. Southern African Human Rights Litigation Centre and Another, Supreme Court of Appeal of South Africa, Judgment of 27 November 2013, Case No. 485/2012.

Chapter 7
Domestic Prosecution of International Crimes: The Case of Rwanda

Sam Rugege and Aimé M. Karimunda

Contents

The views expressed in this chapter are not necessarily those of the Supreme Court of Rwanda.

S. Rugege (✉)
The Supreme Court of Rwanda, Kigali, Rwanda
e-mail: sam.rugege@judiciary.gov.rw

A.M. Karimunda
University of Rwanda, Butare, Rwanda

G. Werle et al. (eds.), *Africa and the International Criminal Court*,
International Criminal Justice Series 1, DOI 10.1007/978-94-6265-029-9_7

7.1 General Introduction

The need to combat impunity for gross violations of human rights in breach of national and international laws has led to the pursuit of different approaches to the prosecution of crimes under international law involving international courts and tribunals, hybrid courts and national courts. At the same time, as such violations are committed during widespread conflict, there is often the need for national reconciliation, the pursuit of strategies for national unity and for reconstruction and development; hence the resort to truth commissions or certain neo-traditional justice initiatives.

There have been debates as to which approach is best suited to the African context; whether to go for international courts or domestic jurisdictions. In many situations, however, the two are not mutually exclusive alternatives. Domestic mechanisms of justice should be the default form of justice in any situation. Only where the concerned state is unable or unwilling to prosecute, should an international or regional court or tribunal be set up to supplement domestic justice systems. This is indeed the position taken in the Statute of the International Criminal Court on the basis of complementarity.[1] This may be because the country emerging from conflict does not have the capacity in terms of human and material resources to conduct credible prosecutions; it may be unwilling to prosecute because those who perpetrated the atrocities are too powerful to handle or the perpetrators may have fled the country and are out of reach of the national authorities. Moreover, for practical reasons, domestic jurisdictions are better suited to prosecute where large numbers of perpetrators are involved. They are able to prosecute more easily, cheaply and quickly than international courts and tribunals could.[2] In some situations, post-conflict regimes have opted for amnesty for those who committed crimes in return for truth about how and why the crimes were committed and the fate of the victims. Truth in such cases is seen as necessary for healing and reconciliation. In some cases amnesty is a result of a compromise reached during negotiations for regime change whereby the outgoing leaders make their departure conditional on being granted immunity from prosecution.

In Rwanda, given the decades of impunity for gross violations of human rights, post-genocide Rwanda as well as the international community opted for prosecutions of those who had committed crimes during the genocide in order to bring justice to victims and to put an end to the culture of impunity. However, as will be shown below, the need for reconciliation and nation-building was not ignored.

---

[1] The Preamble to the Rome Statute recalls that "it is the duty of every State to exercise its criminal jurisdiction over those responsible for international crimes" and emphasizes "that the International Criminal Court established under this Statute shall be complementary to national criminal jurisdictions". Article 17 of the Statute further states that a case is inadmissible where "[t]he case is being investigated or prosecuted by a State, unless the State is unwilling or unable to genuinely carry out the investigation or prosecution".

[2] Werle 2009, p. 82 (marg no 229).

The administration of justice in post-genocide Rwanda has been a combination of judicial systems with the dual purpose of rendering justice for victims and combating impunity by punishing perpetrators, while at the same time incorporating mechanisms for forging healing, reconciliation, national unity and reconstruction. Prosecutions were carried out at the international level by the International Tribunal for Rwanda (ICTR), by Rwandan conventional courts and by neo-traditional Gacaca courts.

The ICTR was created by the United Nations Security Council in November 1994, a few months after the Rwandan genocide. It was set up to prosecute persons responsible for genocide and other serious violations of human rights under international humanitarian law. It was a stated objective of the United Nations that the prosecutions would be part of the effort of ensuring that impunity for perpetrators of genocide and crimes against humanity would no longer be tolerated. Importantly, it was also stated that the Tribunal was to contribute to the process of national reconciliation and the restoration of peace in Rwanda and the Great Lakes Region.

How has the ICTR performed in these two aspects? There is no doubt that the ICTR has played an important role in the area of international justice and in demonstrating that impunity should not be tolerated. First, the ICTR has tried, convicted and punished a number of high profile leaders of the genocide, including a former prime minister, other high government officials, military leaders and even religious leaders, for their involvement in the genocide. The exposure of the evidence against these *génocidaires* has drawn the world's attention to the brutality of the crimes committed. The prosecutions have also demonstrated that, however powerful, the long arm of the law catches up with one wherever one hides, thus significantly contributing to the war against impunity and in favor of accountability for serious violations of human rights and humanitarian law.

Secondly, through its detailed and well-researched judgments and interlocutory decisions, the ICTR has built up a body of jurisprudence on international criminal law relating to the crimes of genocide and crimes against humanity, as well as defining the elements of the crimes hitherto not well understood. A notable case is that of *Jean Paul Akayesu* in which the ICTR decided that rape can constitute an act of genocide.[3] Another ground-breaking case was the so-called *Media case* in which both the Trial Chamber and the Appeals Chamber laid out principles relating to hate speech and direct and public incitement to commit genocide, and spelled out the differences between the two.[4] The jurisprudence will assist other

---

[3] Ibid., p. 75 (marg no 227–229 and sources quoted therein).

[4] *Prosecutor v Nahimana, Barayagwiza and Ngeze*, Judgment and Sentence of 3 December 2003, Trial Chamber I and *Prosecutor v Nahimana, Barayagwiza and Ngeze*, Judgment of 28 November 2007, Appeals Chamber. In this case the defendants were accused of genocide and incitement to commit genocide based on their role in the broadcast and publication of hate propaganda against the Tutsi before and during the genocide. *Ferdinand Nahimana* was the founder and ideologist of Radio Television Libre de Mille Collines, *Jean Bosco Barayagwiza* was its Board member and founder of the extremist Hutu political party, Coalition for the Defence of the Republic, and *Hassan Ngeze* was the Editor-in Chief of the extremist newspaper Kangura.

courts, as well as researchers and students who are concerned with genocide and crimes against humanity.

Thirdly, in accordance with its mandate of assisting the domestic justice system to improve its capacity to deliver justice fairly and efficiently, the ICTR has assisted in the capacity building of the Rwandan judiciary and the prosecution service through workshops in Rwanda and study visits to the Tribunal in Arusha. The ICTR also has important outreach programmes in Rwanda, such as the documentation centers established around the country.

These are all important achievements for which the ICTR must be applauded. However, as far as contributing to peace building and national reconciliation in Rwanda and the Great Lakes region, which was also part of its mandate, is concerned, the impact of the ICTR is not so clear. International courts and tribunals, including the ICTR, have the major limitation of prosecuting those in leadership positions. Only a tiny fraction of those who have committed crimes under international law are dealt with by these tribunals. In the case of the ICTR, it has tried only 75 defendants in nearly 19 years, at a huge financial cost. The vast majority of those cases have involved some of the top leadership. The vast majority of suspects, however, had to be tried in the domestic courts.

Another issue is that international courts are seen as too remote and foreign to the communities concerned. The process happens far away from the victims and survivors of the crimes committed. There is not sufficient publicity of the proceedings of these tribunals reaching those most closely concerned—namely the victims and relatives of victims. Because of the distance, expense, visa requirements and other logistics involved in travelling to another country for a trial, only a handful could travel to Tanzania to attend the ICTR trials. There is no opportunity for victims to come face to face with the perpetrators and there is no chance to ask for forgiveness and reconcile between perpetrators and victims/survivors. Of those who have been tried by the ICTR, only nine have pleaded guilty and even in those cases it is not clear that the perpetrators had acknowledged of wrongdoing. Many continue to deny that genocide ever took place in Rwanda even after the Tribunal took judicial notice of the fact that genocide of the Tutsi had taken place in Rwanda in 1994. There is no expression of remorse by those convicted of genocide or crimes against humanity. There is therefore little chance that these proceedings can, in a significant way, contribute to reconciliation and national unity in Rwanda, except perhaps in the sense that the process has made it difficult for such former leaders to engage in politics and destabilize the recovery of Rwanda and nation-building efforts.

Given the limited mandate of the ICTR, it was always clear that it would not handle the bulk of the genocide perpetrators. However, even within the limited mandate, the ICTR was not able to prosecute all the masterminds, planners and organizers of the genocide. Many genocide fugitives are still at large, walking the streets of world capitals and are in some African countries. The hope to see them face justice was diminished by the United Nations Security Council's decision to close the ICTR in addition to the lack of political will of some host states to exercise their international obligations to either exercise their universal jurisdiction over the genocide fugitives or extradite them to Rwanda for prosecution. In

Rwanda, in order to prosecute any remaining genocide suspects that may be arrested and those that are transferred from the ICTR or from other countries, provision has been made for the former to be tried by the Intermediate Courts, while the latter are tried by a Special Chamber of the High Court dealing with international crimes. The rest of this chapter analyses the merits, challenges and the way forward of the domestic prosecution of the crime of genocide and crimes against humanity before Rwandan courts.

7.2 Prosecutions in Rwandan Specialized Chambers

After the genocide, there was a determination that those who had committed the horrendous crimes should not again enjoy impunity but should be brought to account for their actions. Hundreds of thousands of suspects were detained and awaited trial. Yet since the ICTR was only mandated to try the lead-planners and organizers of the genocide, the bulk of suspects had to be dealt with domestically. An attempt was made by setting up specialized chambers to prosecute the suspects despite the meagre human and material resources available. The shortage was not mitigated by the fact that prior to the genocide the judiciary was neglected as a public institution and not properly staffed with qualified judicial officers. As *William Schabas* has said: "The Rwanda judicial system had never been more than a corrupt caricature of justice [...]."[5]

When the genocide against the Tutsi occurred in 1994, Rwanda had not yet enacted legislation giving effect to the Genocide Convention[6] that it had ratified two decades before.[7] The Genocide Convention is one of the international treaties that cannot effectively be applied without additional legislation. It is not a pure self-executing treaty. Article VI provides that the crime of genocide shall be tried before an international criminal court or by domestic courts of the country where the crime was perpetrated, although the provision is now interpreted as giving a subsidiary jurisdiction to countries with no territorial or personal jurisdiction.[8] The Convention does not prescribe punishments for acts of genocide it describes in its Articles II and III either. It leaves the obligation to States to take measures that will ensure its effective enforcement within the internal legal order.

Article V of the Genocide Convention calls on States "to undertake to enact, in accordance with their respective Constitutions, the necessary legislation to give effect to the provisions of the [...] convention and, in particular, to provide

---

[5] Schabas 2008, p. 212.

[6] The Convention on the Prevention and Punishment of the Crime of Genocide, Paris, 9 December 1948 (entered into force 12 January 1951), 78 UNTS 277.

[7] Ratified by the Presidential Decree No 8/75 of 12 February 1975, Journal Officiel, 1975, at p. 230.

[8] Ruling of the National Audience on Jurisdiction of Spanish Justice to Pursue Crimes of Genocide in Chile, *Augusto Pinochet* of 5 November 1998.

effective penalties for persons guilty of genocide or any of the other acts enumerated in Article III". For diverse reasons that may be political, constitutional, legal or technical, countries, including Rwanda, evaded for a long time their obligations to domesticate the Genocide Convention. The then Government of Rwanda did not forget to pass legislation enforcing the Genocide Convention. It rather concluded that there was no need to legislate crimes under the Genocide Convention. *Nicodème Ruhashyankiko*, a Rwandan scholar who was in the 1970s the United Nations Special Rapporteur on the Prevention and Punishment of the Crime of Genocide, argued that there was no need for such legislation as the requirement of Article V of the Genocide Convention was implicit in the Convention "in accordance with a well-established practice in the field of conventions concerning international penal law"[9] and that "ordinary laws in force are sufficient to prevent and punish genocide".[10]

The determination not to pass a law on genocide became obvious with the enactment of the Penal Code in 1977. The Code that was passed only two years after the ratification of the Genocide Convention made no reference whatsoever to the word genocide. The Government was aware that the Convention was not a pure self-executing treaty. Contrary to *Ruhashyankiko*'s view, some of its provisions cannot be enforced without domestic legislation. By not enacting an enforcing legislation and avoiding reference to the word "genocide" in the Penal Code, *Habyarimana*'s regime maintained the politics of impunity that had characterized Rwanda since 1959, and this deliberately created a legal gap that left Rwandan courts with no appropriate piece of legislation to try and punish genocide perpetrators. This was in addition to the problem of staff shortage, institutional obstacles and logistical problems.

Experts advised the Rwandan government to rely on international law in considering that the 1946 Resolution of the United Nations' General Assembly[11] called for states to directly apply international norms that resulted from the Nuremberg principles. The formula would have resulted in what *Daniel de Beer* calls "dual indictment" where the criminal act would constitute a breach of international law and a violation of the 1977 Penal Code, which at the same time provided for punishments for some of the crimes.[12] Although the argument appeared seductive, the government cautiously chose to address the issue of the legal gap by enacting the Organic Law no 08/96 of 30 August 1996[13] which, in addition to the principle of dual indictment, introduced other innovations that

[9] UN Doc E/CN.4/Sub.2/L/597 (1974), para 11.

[10] UN Doc E/CN.4/Sub.2/L/623, (1975), para 39.

[11] UN Doc, Res/GA 95 (I), 11 December 1946.

[12] De Beer 1997, p. 19.

[13] Organic Law No 08/96 of 30 August 1996 on the organisation of prosecution for offences constituting the crime of genocide or crimes against humanity committed since 1 October 1990, in Official Gazette No 17 of 1 September 1996.

would help Rwandan courts to bring to justice genocide suspects that numbered approximately 100,000 in December 1996. The number of suspects had increased to 125,000 in 2000.[14]

7.3 The Organic Law of 30 August 1996: Rationale, Merits and Difficulties

The Rwandan lawmaker enacted this law as the first step in domesticating the Genocide Convention. The purpose of the law was to incorporate international customary law into domestic law and enable domestic courts to apply international norms. It was a situation-inspired legislation, enacted to provide responses to a particular situation.

7.3.1 Background and Rationale of the Organic Law of 30 August 1996

The genocide against the Tutsi had put the entire world before an atypical situation. Its complexity and immensity derive from the number of victims, the scale of mass participation, the choice of weapons and the process of executing the crime. In only three months more than one million people were cruelly killed by a population gone mad, including friends, relatives and neighbors.[15] The country had become a society of hunters and hunted. A correct and restrictive application of the Rwandan Penal Code would have found that there was no bystander. Those who did not kill could still be prosecuted for direct incitement, assault, rape, theft or destruction of property, or for refusing to assist victims or abstaining from assisting them.

Judges and prosecutors who had not been killed had fled the country. Only 37 % of the judges were available in November 1994. There were altogether 14 prosecutors for the entire country, compared to 158 before the genocide.[16] The newly established Bar of 1997[17] consisted of only 35 lawyers and 18 interns. All these made the prosecution of the crime of genocide against the Tutsi a defying process.

In 1995, Rwandan leaders invited international experts, researchers and activists to reflect on strategies that would enable Rwanda to try genocide suspects and simultaneously constitute mechanisms for unity and reconciliation. The

---

14 UN DOC A/55/269, p. 26, para 102.

15 Ministère de l'Administration Locale, du Développement Communautaire et des Affaires Sociales, Dénombrement des Victimes du Génocide, Rapport final, Kigali, 2004, p. 21.

16 Réseau des Citoyens, Extrait du Rapport, Aperçu du Système judiciaire au Rwanda, Décembre 1995.

17 Law No 03/97 of 19 March 1997 establishing the Kigali Bar Association.

colloquium on *La Lutte Contre l'Impunité: Dialogue pour une Réconciliation Nationale* of 31 October–3 November 1995[18] recommended the establishment of special chambers in charge of genocide cases within ordinary courts and tribunals, the categorization of offenders based on the seriousness of their involvement in the crime of genocide, the introduction of a procedure of guilty plea and confession in the criminal procedure as a mitigating circumstance to speed up the trials and the exclusion of capital punishment for genocide convicts other than those from the first category of masterminds, planners and organizers.

These strategies were included in the Organic Law of 30 August 1996. Its Preamble stresses that the law is aimed at eradicating the culture of impunity forever as a prerequisite for unity and national reconciliation.

By providing for the prosecution and adjudication of the perpetrators and accomplices of the crimes of genocide and crimes against humanity, the Organic Law of 30 August 1996 was intended to halt cycles of violence and the impunity of perpetrators that accompanied them and to satisfy the need for justice. It needs to be stated here that after the 1994 genocide against the Tutsi, any legislative initiative leading to the creation of new crimes or the provision for new penalties for existing crimes could not avoid the challenge posed by the principle of non-retrospectivity of criminal law. This principle is provided for in the Constitution and in the International Covenant on Civil and Political Rights that Rwanda ratified in 1975.[19]

However, that was not the only concern presenting itself to the lawmaker for a solution. The new legislation was expected to domesticate the international law of genocide and crimes against humanity, to foster truth through confessions, to distinguish criminal responsibilities of offenders, to differentiate particular responsibilities of masterminds, to take into account the rights of victims and to lay the basis for the process of unity and national reconciliation. The legislator was faced with an arduous task. The result was a complex piece of legislation, but which had the chance of providing answers to all these concerns.

7.3.2 Dual Incrimination

The law addresses first the issue of domestication of international norms criminalizing genocide and crimes against humanity. The Genocide Convention had been duly ratified and its ratifying instrument published in the Official Gazette.[20] Rwanda was then a monist state. Monism postulates that international law and

[18] République Rwandaise, Bureau du Président, Rapport du Colloque International sur La Lutte Contre l'Impunité: Dialogue pour une Réconciliation Nationale, Kigali, Décembre 1995.

[19] Article 12 of the Constitution of the Republic of Rwanda of 10 June 1991, Journal Officiel, 1991, p. 615 and Article 15.1 of the International Covenant on Civil and Political Rights Ratified by the Decree Law No 8/75 of 12 February 1975.

[20] Ratified by the Presidential Decree No 08/75 of 12 February 1975, Journal Officiel, 1975, p. 230.

national law constitute one single legal system.[21] For a monist state, the procedure was sufficient to empower Rwandan judges to rely on the Convention directly.

However, not all provisions of the Genocide Convention could be directly invoked before national courts without the support of domestic legislation. *William Schabas* reminds that "the Genocide Convention provisions cannot easily be applied within domestic law without some additional legislation and are therefore, in a general sense, not self-executing".[22] Indeed, as noted earlier, there is an obligation in Article V of the Genocide Convention to enact domestic legislation providing for effective penalties.

Before the enactment of the Organic Law of 30 August 1996, the existing legal gap had left Rwanda with the simple option of relying on the Penal Code. Yet the Code contained no reference to genocide. Prosecuting the crime of genocide on the basis of the Penal Code would mean that perpetrators of genocide could only be charged with murder, rape, assault, destruction of property etc. as domestic crimes. Most of these crimes were subjected to ten years' prescription. Article 111 of the Penal Code read as follow: "L'action publique résultat d'une infraction se prescrit: 1° par dix années révolues pour les crimes [...]."[23] In other words, prosecutions would have become illegal by 2004 for the majority of offenders.

One of the important innovations of the Organic Law of 30 August 1996 was the introduction of the principle of dual incrimination. The first stage of this principle consisted in checking whether a specific offence in the Penal Code was perpetrated by the suspect. The second stage was for the judge to verify whether the offence constitutes simultaneously a crime of genocide or a crime against humanity. The approach allowed a court to rely at the same time on the domestic law and on the Genocide Convention, the four Geneva Conventions of 1949 and their Additional Protocols and on the Convention on the Non-Applicability of Statutory Limitations to War Crimes and Crimes against Humanity of 26 November 1968.[24]

In practice, applying the principle of dual incrimination proved not to be an easy task for Rwandan judges. In criminal matters, judges were used to finding offences and their punishments in a single book, namely the Penal Code. Moreover, the majority of the judicial personnel in charge of implementing the Organic Law of 30 August 1996 were not professional lawyers. They had undergone accelerated training sessions on substantive and procedural laws in order to deal with the unprecedented situation that the country faced.

---

[21] Ferdinandusse 2005, p. 137.

[22] Schabas 2009, p. 405.

[23] "A criminal action shall lapse after: 1° a period of 10 years for felonies." Articles 111 of the Decree Law No 21/77 of 18 August 1977 instituting the Penal Code, Official Gazette, No 13*bis*, 1978, p. 1.

[24] See the Preamble of the Organic Law No 08/96 of 30 August 1996 on the organization of prosecution for offences constituting the crime of genocide or crimes against humanity committed since 1 October 1990, in Official Gazette No 17 of 1 September 1996. De Beer 1997, pp. 31–32.

There are judges who reached sound findings by effectively referring to both international criminal law and domestic criminal law. For instance, in the case of *Prosecutor v. Banzi Wellars and Others*, the Court recalled that each of the 54 co-accused had breached international law. In the findings, the judges carefully based their ruling on international law and on the above-mentioned Organic Law.[25] There are judges who based their findings on both international law and the Penal Code. In the case of *Prosecutor v. Ukezimpfura Jean and Others*,[26] the court first listed international law, including the Statute of the ICTR, before listing domestic sources. In the case *Prosecutor v. Mvumbahe Denys and Others*,[27] the Court relied first on the Constitution and other relevant domestic provisions before referring to the Genocide Convention of 1948.

However, not all judges effectively relied on international norms. For example, in the case of *Prosecutor v. Hanyurwimfura Epaphrodite*,[28] the judge simply recalled the Preamble of the Organic Law of 30 August 1996 that mentions the international convention above, to constitute the basis of the charge. The development of the judgment that followed, including the decision, did not refer at all to international law. In the case of *Prosecutor v. Karorero Charles and Others*, the First Instance Tribunal of Cyangugu also stated that the accused were prosecuted for "acts of genocide provided for in the International Convention on the Prevention and Punishment of the Crime of Genocide of 09/12/1948, the International Convention on the Non-Applicability of Statutory Limitations on war crimes and crimes against humanity".[29] This, however, was the only reference to international law in this judgment. The judge's ruling was instead based on domestic law. Relying exclusively on domestic law indicates that judges had not understood the purpose of the principle of dual incrimination. Since a prescribed offence is considered as an offence which has no legal standing,[30] judges run the risk of delivering judgments that could be challenged for violation of the principle of legality.

---

[25] *Prosecutor v. Banzi Wellars*, Tribunal de Premiere Instance de Gisenyi, Judgement of 25 May 2001, p. 52.

[26] *Prosecutor v. Ukezimpfura Jean and Others*, Tribunal de Premiere Instance de Kibungo, Judgment of 29 September 2000.

[27] *Prosecutor v. Mvumbahe Denys and Others*, Tribunal de Premiere Instance de Kibuye, Judgment of 16 July 2000.

[28] *Prosecutor v. Hanyurwimfura Epaphrodite*, Tribunal de Premiere Instance de Butare, Judgment of 8 August 2001.

[29] *Prosecutor v. Karorero Charles and Others*, Tribunal de Premiere Instance de Cyangungu, Judgment of 31 March 2000.

[30] French Court of Cassation, Criminal Chamber, Judgment of 19 April 1995, Case No 94-83519.

7.3.3 Categorization of Offenders

During the drafting process of the Organic Law, there was a debate on whether the law should provide for collective criminal responsibility for political parties and militias that planned and executed the genocide. Another view was that if members of political parties or militias could not bear collective criminal responsibility they should at least be presumed guilty until they reverse the onus of proof.[31] The two proposals did not find favor with the legislature. It was decided neither to criminalize groups and associations nor to replace the presumption of innocence by a presumption of guilt. The law maintained the principle of individual criminal responsibility but introduced the categorization of offenders.

According to Article 2 of the Organic Law of 30 August 1996, categorization is done after examining each offender's criminal responsibility.

- In the first category belong masterminds of the genocide. They are people who planned, organized, and supervised the genocide. The category also includes notorious murderers and persons who committed acts of sexual torture.
- The second category consists of group perpetrators, conspirators and accomplices to murders other than those who were zealous in the perpetration of the crime. Offenders who seriously assaulted victims with intent to kill but did not accomplish their objective are placed in this category.
- The third category is meant for perpetrators who were involved in other serious attempts against bodily integrity without necessarily intending to kill the victim.
- The fourth category relates to people who committed offences in respect of property.

Judges retained the discretionary power to move an offender from one category to another. The effect of categorization was that offenders from the first and second categories were liable to be sentenced to death or to life imprisonment, respectively, while offenders from the third category received punishments that corresponded to their criminal responsibility under the Penal Code. Article 14(d) of the Organic Law specifically states that persons convicted of offences against property are liable to civil damages in compliance with the law of damages. The provision was intended simultaneously to decongest the prisons and to lay down the basis of unity and reconciliation. However, offenders from the second and third category who confessed were also eligible for lenient punishments. This mechanism was also new in the Rwandan legal system.

[31] De Beer 1997, p. 27.

7.3.4 Confession and Guilty Plea

A confession, as evidence, was not regulated in the Organic Law of 30 August 1996. The ordinary criminal procedure provided and still provides for a confession as an element of evidence whose weight is assessed according to the discretion of the judge. At present, it would be dangerous to rely on the offender's confession only as if it remains the queen of evidence (*regina probatia*) as it was before the Enlightenment. Confession must be corroborated by other evidence as there are laudable and not so laudable reasons that might lead any suspect to confess.

In genocide cases, a confession was intended to be a factor contributing to unity and reconciliation. Offenders were encouraged to confess and to enter a guilty plea in exchange for lenient punishments. A confession and expression of remorse served at the same time as an acknowledgement by the wrongdoer for having violated the victim's humanity and dignity. Genocide and crimes against humanity constitute the denial of human dignity, even before they take away the right to life. Both the right to dignity and the right to life are fundamental human rights.

Offenders from the Second Category would normally have been liable for capital punishment under the Penal Code. They were spared the death penalty and this led to offenders from other categories also being spared the death penalty. Sentencing robbers to death whereas Second Category *génocidaires* had escaped it would have defied the logic of justice. Second Category offenders who took advantage of the procedure of confession and guilty plea and were found to be sincere, received a maximum of 11 years in custody instead of life imprisonment if they took the initiative before prosecution. Offenders from the Third Category whose confessions and guilty plea were found to be sincere and complete received a third of the punishment that the judge would normally have imposed.[32]

The procedure of confession and guilty plea was a mitigating excuse. Only mitigating excuses are provided for by the law whereas mitigating circumstances are left to judicial discretion. Judges read provisions on confessions and guilty plea as non-exclusive of mitigating circumstances. The punishment was further reduced where, in addition to confession and guilty plea, there were mitigating circumstances. The silence of the law on mitigating circumstances meant that the lawmaker did not encroach upon judicial discretion to decide on mitigating circumstances. Although, it is submitted, the lawmaker had gone beyond the necessary in mitigating the punishment for genocide. Judges imposed 2 years,[33]

---

[32] Article 15, para 1(a) and (b) of the Organic Law No 08/96 of 30 August 1996 on the organization of prosecution for offences constituting the crime of genocide or crimes against humanity committed since 1 October 1990, in Official Gazette No 17 of 1 September 1996.

[33] *Prosecutor v Kanyabugande and Others*, Tribunal de Première Instance de Byumba, Judgment of 2 May 1997 and *Prosecutor v. Mahirane alias Kagina*, Tribunal de Première Instance de Kibungo, Judgment of 21 October 1998.

4 years,[34] 5 years,[35] 7 years,[36] 8 years,[37] 10 years,[38] 12 years,[39] 13 years,[40] 14 years[41] and 15 years imprisonment.[42]

This practice, it is further submitted, is evidence that Rwandan judges were too lenient in handling cases of genocide. They considered mostly the good faith of the accused in helping the court to discover and understand the way crimes were perpetrated without giving sufficient weight to the gravity of the offence. There are convicts who received lenient sentences even though they had not strictly complied with the confession and guilty plea procedure. In the case of *Prosecutor v. Nzabonimpa Kajabo and Others*, the judge stated, for example, that although the accused had partially confessed his crimes, he assisted the court in discovering the truth.[43] Other judges would simply consider the remorse that the accused showed during the trial.[44]

Rwandan judges are said to have been too soft on criminals who committed heinous crimes. *Nzakunda* argues that judges should not have imposed sentences below the minimum of punishments provided for under the Organic Law of 30 August 1996. He argues that genocide is an abominable crime that destroyed the Rwandan society and for which only exemplary punishments should be imposed. Only juvenile offenders should escape these exemplary punishments, *Nzakunda* contends.[45] In 1995, it was suggested that in the case of Rwanda "justice means [...] blood".[46] The demand for so-called exemplary punishments

34 *Prosecutor v. Byiringiro J.P. and Others*, Tribunal de Premiere Instance de Kibungo, Judgment of 21 October 1998.

35 *Prosecutor v. Nshogoza Anastase and Others*, Tribunal de Première Instance de Byumba, Judgment of 30 November 1999.

36 *Prosecutor v. Hakizimana Appolinaire and Others*, Tribunal de Première Instance de Gitarama, Judgment of 24 August 1998.

37 *Prosecutor v. Semukanya Vincent and Others*, Tribunal de Première Instance de Kibungo, Judgment of 17 July 1998.

38 *Prosecutor v. Munyangabo and Others*, Tribunal de Premiere Instance de Gikongoro, Judgment of 10 June 1998.

39 *Prosecutor v. Nsabimana and Others*, Tribunal de Première Instance de Cyangugu, Jugdment of 5 June 1997.

40 *Prosecutor v Gatsimbanyi and Others*, Tribunal de Première Instance de Nyamata, Judgment of 13 November 1998.

41 *Prosecutor v. Musangwa and Others*, Tribunal de Première Instance de Kibungo, Judgment of 18 June 1997.

42 *Prosecutor v. Murangira Jean Baptiste*, Tribunal de Première Instance de Nyamata, Judgment of 30 March 1998.

43 *Prosecutor v. Nzabonimpa Kajabo and Others*, Tribunal de Première Instance de Nyamata, Judgment of 8 September 1999.

44 *Prosecutor v. Kabiligi Athanase and Others*, Tribunal de Première Instance de Kibuye, Judgment of 10 December 1998.

45 Nzakunda 2005.

46 Prunier 1995, p. 355.

for heinous and mass crimes such as terrorism, crimes against humanity and genocide is said to be justified by the need for proportionality.[47]

The Rwandan lawmaker did not fully embrace this principle of proportionality between the gravity of the crime and its punishment. The judges were expected to use their discretion to arrive at the appropriate sentence in line with the goal of justice as conceived through the Organic Law of 30 August 1996. Adjudicating the crime of genocide had to be done in the context of horrendous crimes committed but also the need to promote reconciliation in order to weld again the Rwandan social fabric that genocide had torn apart. The latter is not normally a concern of classical tribunals that are often indifferent to the effect of their rulings on the social cohesion of the parties before them. Nevertheless, it is apparent that in some cases the discretion was either misused or even abused in meting out overly lenient sentences for those convicted of genocide and crimes against humanity.

7.3.5 The Inadequacy of the Organic Law of 30 August 1996

It was clear that, by 2000, the laudable objectives of this law had not been translated into tangible results. It had been expected that the law would speed up trials and reduce the prison congestion, that suspects would in large numbers and sincerely embrace the confession and guilty plea opportunity and that the accompanying lenient sentences would speed up the process of unity and reconciliation. An assessment of the implementation of the Organic Law in 2000 was not encouraging. The number of suspects rose to 125,000.[48] The figure included 4,454 juvenile offenders and 7,176 women, all of whom were dispersed in the 19 prisons and detention centers.[49]

Rwandan prisons and detention facilities, already inadequate before 1994, were occupied far beyond their capacities. The overpopulation of prisons made the hygiene conditions of detainees very difficult. In such a context the question of genocide detainees quickly monopolized the debate on justice in Rwanda. In 1998, the international community was already very critical of the situation. Not only were overcrowded prisons a concern for human rights organizations but also the turn that justice took when the government carried out executions of 22 persons convicted of the genocide. At the local level, judges and prosecutors were deemed to be very slow in handling genocide cases. Only 2,580 cases out of 124,800 detainees were completed by December 1999.[50] Genocide suspects were suspicious about the procedure of confession and guilty plea while the survivors were

[47] Ohlin 2005.

[48] UN DOC A/55/269, p. 26, para 102.

[49] Karekezi 2001, p. 22.

[50] Ibid., p. 22.

unhappy about sentences handed down. By August 2000, courts had registered 3,751 instances of recourse to the procedure of confession and guilty plea.[51]

The Organic Law of 30 August of 1996 did not properly address the issue of compensation for victims. Judges relied on the law of damages and especially on Article 258 of the Civil Code, Book III. However, it quickly became apparent that assessing damages for genocide victims was not an easy task for judges. Judgments were condemning peasant suspects to pay compensation of millions of Rwandan Francs (Rwf) with no reasonable expectation that payment would materialize. For example, in the case of *Prosecutor v. Karorero and Others*, the Court imposed compensation of 212,155,000 Rwf.[52] In the case of *Banzi Wellars and Others*, the Court imposed compensation of 219,500,000 Rwf.[53]

A study of the cases conducted between 1997 and 1999 also revealed that compensation was only awarded to one out of two victims. This resulted from the fact that most victims were not aware of their rights to compensation, or failed to prove their relationship with their deceased relatives.[54] To resolve the issue of unrecovered damages, the victims' advocates started suing the suspect and the State of Rwanda simultaneously. The records of proceedings show that the State never appeared before the courts in these cases. Judges were obliged to condemn the State to pay damages by default judgment. In the year 2000, the Government declared that it owed 37,000,000 Rwf in judicial damages to victims.[55]

On the whole, the Special Chambers did a commendable job of prosecuting genocide crimes with the minimum resources. As *William Schabas* observed:

> Considering the impoverishment of Rwanda's justice system prior to the genocide, and the resource problems that continue to confront development in that country, 10,000 trials is an impressive figure by any standards [...]. Arguably, Rwanda has done more in this respect in ten years than did the national jurisdictions of Germany, Italy and Austria from 1945–1955.[56]

Despite the commendable work of the Special Chambers trying genocide cases, Rwanda realized that strategies it had formulated in the Organic Law of 30 August 1996 were not realizing the results hoped for. It became apparent that the Rwandan judicial system was overwhelmed. At the rate at which it was going, trying all the genocide suspects before regular courts would have taken about 200 years. The failure of the judicial system to reduce the volume of pending cases significantly and the pressure on the prisons and other resources, led to the need to find an alternative way of dealing with genocide cases. Various discussions led to the

---

[51] Ibid.

[52] *Prosecutor v. Karorero Charles and Others*, Tribunal de Première Instance de Cyangungu, Judgment of 31 March 2000.

[53] *Prosecutor v. Banzi Wellars and Others*, Tribunal de Premiere Instance de Gisenyi, Judgment of 25 May 2001.

[54] Karekezi 2001, p. 24.

[55] Le Verdict, No 01, 15 April 1999, p. 15.

[56] Schabas 2008, p. 218; Bornkamm 2012, pp. 24–25 and sources cited there.

rejuvenation of the Gacaca courts, a traditional method of conflict resolution, as a forum for prosecuting and punishing crimes committed during the genocide.

7.4 The Legacy of Gacaca Courts

Gacaca courts are neo-traditional courts that involve local communities. In 2001, it became compelling to resort to this heritage of Rwandan culture as a response to the challenge of the large number of genocide suspects awaiting trial who could not be tried in the conventional courts within a reasonable period of time. They were specifically inducted and empowered to hear and decide genocide cases.

7.4.1 Traditional Gacaca Courts and Neo-traditional Gacaca Courts

Traditionally, Gacaca, or lawn, is a metonym referring to a physical space where men of a certain age gathered to debate and resolve conflicts among members of the community. Members of the assembly that formed the Council of Elders were selected among men known for their integrity (*inyangamugayo*) in the village. The test of suitability for the position was the elder's reputation for wisdom, erudition, probity and impartiality in taking a decision. The chief of the family or clan led the gathering, with the assistance of the Council of Elders. The role of a judge was a sacred matter.

During the gathering, parties were invited to defend their cases before the assembly. Gacaca resolved all conflicts in the interest of the family and the community. The decision was taken immediately and publicly. Gacaca imposed fines, compensation, restitution and damages. The sanction was often immediately executed. When one of the parties was condemned to pay a fine of pitchers of beer, judges shared the contents with parties, witnesses and the assembly as a sign of reconciliation. Some offences were, however, so serious that they sullied the entire family. In such cases, the family resorted to collective purification, which then closed the matter.[57]

The concept of justice under traditional Gacaca courts was distinct. Judges did not focus on looking for truth as understood by modern courts. Elders were first and foremost concerned with social harmony in which the losing party participated. The goal of justice was to reconcile the parties and not to humiliate the offender. However, efforts at reconciliation were not synonymous with impunity for serious crimes for which a heavy punishment was justified. Incorrigible and dangerous criminals were punished by ostracism. The convicted person ceased to

[57] Ntampaka 2005, p. 53.

enjoy social status within the community, which withdrew its support. The individual became a pariah for all intents and purposes, and was forbidden from taking part in social activities. This was the most feared punishment, because in traditional societies reciprocity played a vital role in everyone's life.[58] Crimes against the State and crimes that threatened human lives were tried by the Mwami's (King's) Bench itself and the death penalty was among possible punishments that the court could impose.[59]

Gacaca justice was thus built on the premise that punishment and reconciliation were not contradictory or mutually exclusive objectives. Eventually colonization refashioned traditional Gacaca courts. They first lost jurisdiction over petty criminal offences and retained jurisdiction over civil disputes only. Later, colonial authorities replaced clan chiefs with people who owed allegiance to the colonial regime, without paying attention to whether or not they were persons of integrity, who were fit to be Gacaca judges. After independence, Rwandan authorities maintained the Gacaca courts, granting them authority again to hear cases involving petty offences in order to decongest prisons. The Government, however, selected members of Gacaca courts from among local administrative authorities.[60] Before 1994, Gacaca tribunals had become pre-trial instances where persons prosecuted for theft, assault and destruction of properties would be heard before being tried by the *Tribunal de Canton*. It was no longer a forum for debating social cohesion but rather a political institution parallel to courts.[61]

In the post-1994 period, Gacaca courts were created in order to establish the real truth of what happened, to punish perpetrators of the crimes committed during the genocide and thus to end impunity as well as to promote unity and reconciliation. The Organic Law No 40/2000 of 26 January 2001 that set up Gacaca courts recalled that since genocide crimes were perpetrated publicly, the population had a moral obligation to tell the truth about what happened as witnesses, victims or offenders.[62] Therefore the choice was not between truth and justice. In transitional justice, there are policy-makers who choose to create some types of truth commissions which often trade amnesty in exchange for the full disclosure of the truth. There are others who opt for judicial mechanisms without necessarily demanding that the offender gives a complete account of the past.[63]

The Rwandan model was truth and reconciliation through justice. The country did not favor purely retributive justice that would widen the rupture between Rwandan communities. It also rejected a truth commission solution that would

---

[58] Ibid., p. 54.

[59] Bourgeois 1954, p. 397.

[60] Karekezi 2001, p. 32.

[61] Ntampaka 2005, p. 55.

[62] Preamble of the Organic Law No 40/2000 of 2 January 2001 setting up Gacaca jurisdictions and organizing prosecutions of offences constituting the crime of genocide or crimes against humanity committed between 1 October 1990 and 31 December 1994, Official Gazette No 6, of 15 March 2001.

[63] For details see Clark 2010, pp. 33–35.

lead to a blanket amnesty, synonymous with impunity.[64] The government intended to get rid of the policy and practice of amnesty that had become inseparable with crimes perpetrated against the Tutsi. As far back as 1961, by a Resolution on crimes perpetrated against the Tutsi minority, the United Nations recommended to Belgium to release Hutu extremists it had imprisoned and to grant "full and unconditional amnesty".[65] After independence, all those who committed crimes against the Tutsi and their sympathizing Hutu between 1959 and 1963, in 1974 and in 1991 were subsequently granted amnesty by the Government.[66] Thus, until the 1994 genocide against Tutsi, "there was total impunity for the perpetrator" as *Gérard Prunier* reminds us.[67]

By establishing Gacaca courts through a law, extending their jurisdiction over life-threatening crimes and constituting them with elected judges, including women, on their benches, the lawmaker gave a modern character to this traditional institution. This modernized Gacaca should not be confused with the conventional system of prosecuting offences. It was rather an institution aimed at re-establishing the social concord and to put genocide convicts on the right path as citizens. The population was therefore invited to participate actively in this new form of participatory justice.

7.4.2 Goals Assigned to Gacaca and the Assessment of Its Achievements

Much has been written about Gacaca courts and it is not possible to do justice to the subject of assessing the achievements and challenges in this chapter. What is intended here is to give an overview of the role of Gacaca in prosecuting international crimes in order to present a comprehensive picture of domestic prosecutions of international crimes in post-genocide Rwanda.

The procedure followed by Gacaca Courts was simplified to ensure that cases were processed rapidly. The purpose was to have as many suspects as possible answer to the charges against them and for victims or survivors to see justice dispensed in their lifetime. The proceedings excluded lawyers and as a result there

---

[64] Jones 2010, p. 51.

[65] UN Doc A/1605 (XV), 21 April 1961, para 9.

[66] Loi du 20 Mai 1963 portant amnistie générale des infractions politiques commises entre le 1er Octobre 1959 et le 1er Juillet 1962, Official Gazette, 1963, p. 299; Décret-Loi du 30 Novembre 1974 portant amnistie de certaines infractions politiques, Official Gazette, 1974, p. 626 ; Loi no 60/91 du 13 Décembre 1991 portant amnistie générale et voie de solution au problème des refugies, Official Gazette, 1991, p. 1930.

[67] Prunier 1995, p. 31.

were no objections on minor points of law or procedure. Judgments were delivered on the day that all arguments were concluded or on the next day. The judicial process, including the suspect's responses to the charges, the assembly's public discussion of the evidence, and the judges' decision on the guilt or innocence of the accused was expected not to take more than three weeks. Gacaca laws permitted the bench to hear different witnesses in the same hearing.[68]

To illustrate how rapidly cases were processed, some figures may be cited. The pilot phase in 2002 started with 751 Gacaca courts at the Cell level in 118 Sectors.[69] This phase was primarily for conducting investigations. Given the challenges that this pilot phase faced, the law governing Gacaca courts was modified in 2004.[70] The trial of the cases completed in the 118 sectors started in 2005. Then only 118 Gacaca courts at the Sector level out of 1,545 and 118 Gacaca courts of appeal out of 1,545 started hearing cases.[71] Already by July 2006, Gacaca courts at the Cell level had gathered information on 717,942 persons of whom 63,000 belonged to the Category One, 335,000 to the Category Two and the others to Categories Three and Four. By 2006, Gacaca courts at the Sector level had already delivered 20,957 judgments out of the 23,423 cases heard.[72] Although figures do not mean justice, the results speak for themselves, having regard to the modest resources invested in these courts.

Gacaca courts also had the merit of being less formal. There were no strict procedures, no robing, no Latin formula, no French or English principles cited and no exceptions, etc. The court was user-friendly and less intimidating to witnesses. The relaxed environment encouraged everyone to say what he or she knew or saw. People attending the courts were neighbors who shared the same culture, and who were used to the metaphors of their language. Most modern courts lack a relaxed ambience, so witnesses can feel intimidated. On 31 October 2001, ICTR judges *William Sekule* (Tanzania), *Winston Maqutu* (Lesotho) and *Arlette Ramaroson* (Madagascar) suddenly burst out laughing when a Rwandan woman victim of genocide and who had been raped nine times by different men was asked, during cross-examination, to describe the genital parts of her rapists and the feeling she had during rape.[73] According to the Prosecutor in the case, witness *T.A.* had

---

[68] Clark 2010, p. 172.

[69] Avocats Sans Frontières, Monitoring des Juridictions Gacaca, Octobre 2005–Septembre 2006, Kigali, Palloti Press 2006, p. 7.

[70] Organic Law No 16/2004 of 19 June 2004 establishing the Organization, Competence and Functioning of Gacaca courts charged with prosecuting and trying the perpetrators of the crime of genocide and other crimes against humanity, committed between 1 October 1990 and 31 December 1994, Official Gazette, No Special of 19 June 2004.

[71] Avocats Sans Frontières 2006, p. 7.

[72] Ibid., p. 8.

[73] *Prosecutor v. Pauline Nyiramasuhuko* et al. Transcripts of October 2001, pp. 67–100.

repeated 1,194 times that she had been raped.[74] Such an atmosphere can only discourage witnesses.

Testimonies submitted to Gacaca courts had practical effects for survivors. Genocide survivors were not interested in symbolic justice. They simply wanted to know when, where and how their loved ones died. Gacaca hearings permitted victims to learn how their loved ones were killed, locate their remains and have them reburied in dignity.[75] The offender was also given an opportunity to acknowledge what he did, show remorse and ask for forgiveness in exchange for a lenient sentence. To encourage reintegration, the convicts were given an opportunity to influence the determination of their sentence by confessing and showing remorse. This procedure gave them the choice between remaining behind bars in prison or having half of their prison sentence converted into community work, also known as TIG (*Travaux d'Interet Général*).[76] By 2010, at least 90,000 persons, mostly second category perpetrators, co-perpetrators and accomplices, had chosen to take advantage of the guilty plea and confession procedure, which resulted in community work instead of long-term imprisonment.[77] At the same time, the community work performed by genocide convicts contributed to the reconstruction of the country. The interaction between the offender and the victim created chances for healing, reconciliation and ultimately, recreation of social cohesion.

A further advantage of Gacaca courts was that they were cost-effective for the State, victims and witnesses. Court proceedings took place where the crime was perpetrated. Witnesses did not need to travel far to attend court sessions.

In sum, Gacaca courts were a unique Rwandan solution to a unique Rwandan problem. They closed on 18 June 2012 after clearing nearly all genocide cases and helping establish the truth about what happened during the genocide. Gacaca courts tried 1,958,634 cases.[78] The figure proves that this is an unprecedented judicial experiment. The institution of Gacaca provided justice and constituted a basis for unity and reconciliation. Reconciliation is, however, a slow and gradual process. It involves emotional and interpersonal dynamics. As Archbishop *Desmond Tutu* rightly puts it, reconciliation can only be promoted.[79] Engaging the entire population in the process of justice, as well as a continuing dialogue has provided an important step towards a more sustainable reconciliation and harmony in the Rwandese society.

---

[74] Quoted in Nowrojee 2005, p. 23.

[75] See African Rights and Redress 2008, p. 31. Available at http://www.redress.org/downloads/publications/Rwanda%20Survivors%2031%20Oct%2008.pdf (All internet resources were accessed on 28 March 2014).

[76] Presidential Decree No 26/01 of 10 December 2001 relating to the Substitution of the penalty of imprisonment for community service, Official Gazette, No. 3 of 1 February 2002.

[77] Penal Reform International 2010, p. 29.

[78] National Service of Gacaca Courts 2012, p. 34.

[79] Tutu 1999, p. 274.

7.5 Criticisms and Challenges of Gacaca

7.5.1 Some Criticisms of the Gacaca Process

7.5.1.1 Lack of Legal Representation

The Gacaca system has been criticized for not permitting the accused a right to legal representation. For instance, *Nicholas Jones* has argued that "the absence of legal representation in the process may undermine the guarantee for a fair trial in that the accused is not presented with legal advice in preparation for their defence and during the process".[80] However, there was no inequality of arms since there was no prosecutor either. The court took on the role of the prosecutor by reading out the charges and questioning the accused and the witnesses, assisted in this by members of the community present (the general assembly of the Gacaca court). Since the events in question took place in public view, it is argued that all that needs to be known is the truth about what happened and that, furthermore, determining the veracity of eye witnesses can be done by lay persons as well as lawyers. With reference to the Gacaca process, it has been said that

> fairness is ensured through the presence of a whole range of witnesses, which allows an instant oral reconstruction of all the facts relevant to the case. The general assembly acts as prosecution and defence at the same time and thus ensures equality between the two parties. The presence of a professional in a Gacaca court would jeopardise this balance, confuse the witnesses, and contravene the spirit of the Gacaca system.[81]

This view conforms with a position held that "the General Assembly should engage in a largely open discussion at Gacaca hearings, in which judges act as mediators to help the community achieve certain legal and social objectives".[82] Moreover, permitting legal representation would have changed the whole character of the court and would have turned it into a regular court. It would have involved elaborate, formal legal procedures and consequent delays. It would also have meant bringing in legally qualified judges who would understand the legal jargon and technicalities so well-loved by lawyers. It would have brought in the almost hostile atmosphere of cross-examination, all kinds of preliminary objections, adjournments, etc. Moreover, even if the system were designed to accommodate lawyers, there were not enough in the country to represent hundreds of thousands of suspects scattered in villages around the country. Before 1994, the law school produced not more than ten law graduates a year. This was part of the control system of the State that did not encourage a rights discourse.

[80] Jones 2010, p. 95.

[81] This is a summary by Bornkamm of arguments that explain the absence of legal representation in the Gacaca process, see Bornkamm 2012, p. 110.

[82] Clark 2008, p. 312.

It is also noteworthy that traditional courts in other African countries do not permit legal representation, the idea being to keep proceedings simple, people-friendly and to ensure a speedy resolution of disputes. Once again, it was a matter of weighing the pros and cons and in the Rwandan case the country chose to capitalize on the many advantages of Gacaca and live with the possible disadvantage of not having professional legal representation. At the same time, the accused had enough time to challenge whatever was said by the complainant or witness, and to call witnesses willing to testify on his or her behalf. Moreover, the accused person could be assisted by another person to present the defence and there was nothing in the law prohibiting a lawyer not claiming the prerogatives of defence counsel to come to the assistance of the accused.

7.5.1.2 No Appeals to Regular Courts

Appeals were only allowed from the village Gacaca court to the ward or sector Gacaca court. Cases heard by the sector Gacaca courts at first instance could be appealed to the Gacaca court of appeal. However, there were no appeals to the regular courts. In the regular courts, convictions and sentences of imprisonment are appealable at least up to the High Court and in some cases up to the Supreme Court. For the reasons given regarding delays in regular courts, it was considered prudent to limit appeals to the system of Gacaca in the interest of fast-tracking genocide cases, getting convicted persons back into normal society as soon as possible and hence promoting reconciliation. Permitting appeals to regular courts would have meant following the usual procedures in those courts with the inevitable delays. That would have defeated the whole idea of taking the cases to Gacaca in the first place.

7.5.2 *Challenges*

7.5.2.1 Intimidation and Killing of Witnesses in Genocide Cases

Despite the obvious successes of the Gacaca system, there were challenges. One of the most serious ones was the intimidation and in a number of cases the killing of witnesses to dissuade them from testifying against suspects. Acts of intimidation included setting houses of survivors ablaze, sending them anonymous letters, uprooting their crops and killing their animals. There are also other acts of intimidation such as throwing stones on roofs of houses.[83] Witnesses have been killed; some after testifying, others before they were due to testify. This became a source of bitterness for some survivors who thought that the State was not doing

[83] African Rights and Redress 2008, p. 6. See also Redress 2012, pp. 23–29.

enough to protect them and a number became discouraged from participating in the process. Some Gacaca judges have also been intimidated, assaulted or killed.[84]

7.5.2.2 Incomplete or Fake Confessions

As indicated, the law allowed suspects who confessed, told the truth and asked for forgiveness to get lighter sentences and to serve half of their sentence in community service. It was also the practice to identify those who had confessed and asked for forgiveness to be released from prison and await their trial in Gacaca from their homes. However, it turned out that quite a number did not tell the whole truth and just said enough to get them out of prison or to get them a light sentence, or even lied.[85] Some even mocked the Gacaca process once they were out and threatened to finish the job they started when the time is right.[86] This did not advance the cause of reconciliation. The whole philosophy of reconciliation was that truth and justice must precede reconciliation and not the other way round. Otherwise the survivors had no incentive in participating in reconciliation processes. They could only forgive when forgiveness was genuinely sought.

7.5.2.3 Cases of Judges and Witnesses Succumbing to Corruption

There have been a few cases of Gacaca judges who were discovered to have been involved in genocide and other crimes against humanity. They were removed and prosecuted. Some Gacaca judges have also been prosecuted for corruption.[87] The National Gacaca Service acknowledged corruption as having been a challenge but also pointed out that the vice had been fought.[88] Some witnesses also succumbed to accepting bribes not to testify or even to change their testimonies at the appeal level, partly because of their impoverished living conditions and seeing no likelihood of improvement after the conviction of the accused. In other cases they

[84] African Rights and Redress 2008, pp. 7–8 for testimonies on killing of Gacaca judges and witnesses.

[85] Ibid., p. 119. See also De Brouwer and Ruvebana 2013, p. 947.

[86] African Rights and Redress 2008, pp. 123–124.

[87] Hirondelle News of 6 October 2008, where it is reported that a Gacaca court judge was prosecuted and sentenced to five years imprisonment for attempting to bribe fellow judges so they could free his brother-in-law. www.hirondellenews.com/ictr-rwanda/411-rwanda-gacaca/22354.

[88] See "Interview with the Executive Secretary of the National Gacaca Service, Domithile Mukantaganzwa, on the eve of Closing of Gacaca Courts" (no date indicated, but presumed to be in June 2012), available at http://www.gov.rw/Interview-with-the-Executive-Secretary-of-National-Gacaca-Service-Domithile-Mukantaganzwa-at-the-eve-of-closing-of-Gacaca-Courts. See also Republic of Rwanda National Service of Gacaca Courts, Summary of the Report Presented at the Closing of Gacaca Courts Activities, Kigali, June 2012.

succumbed to the threat that they either accept the money or be killed.[89] However, most of the Gacaca judges were honest and committed to the cause of justice and reconciliation.

7.5.2.4 Escaping from Community Service

Not all persons sentenced to TIG showed up for the community service. Because they perform it in camps close to communities and because of a lack of supervision, a number manages to escape and disappear. They change their identities and resettle in places far from their former communities or leave the country. These are, of course, those who were not sincere in their pleas for forgiveness in the first place. This still poses a serious challenge to the search for maximum reconciliation, especially given the fact that there are known perpetrators who escaped unpunished.[90]

7.5.2.5 Lack of Reparations and Insufficient Material Support for Survivors

Most survivors lost family members and all the property they had in the genocide. They did not obtain any compensation, even in cases where perpetrators were convicted. The Gacaca Law only provided for reparation in respect of cases relating to destruction or damage to property, that is Category Three crimes.[91] Initially, it was envisaged that a State fund would be established, largely funded by contributions from the international community, to take care of non-property reparations to victims and survivors of the genocide.[92] However, the fund has not materialized due to a lack of contributions to it. At the same time, even the limited scope of reparation for property looted or damaged has not been enforced, not only because the convicted persons lack the means to pay, but also because some who have the means are reluctant to pay and find ways of evading the obligation. This state of affairs hurts survivors especially as they see those who were not affected by the genocide living comfortably. Although the State has acknowledged responsibility for reparations to survivors under the state succession doctrine, it has

[89] African Rights and Redress 2008, pp. 47–49.

[90] "Bacitse Imirimo Nsimburagifungo Bavuga ko Bashaj", Kigali Today, 2 January 2014, TIG: 151 "Batorotse Ingando", Imvaho Nshya, No 2007.

[91] Article 95 of Organic Law establishing the organization, competence and functioning of Gacaca Courts charged with prosecuting and trying the perpetrators of the Crime of genocide and other crimes against humanity, committed between 1 October 1990 and 31 December 1994, Law No. 16/2004 of 19 June 2004.

[92] Ibid., Article 96.

so far only been able to help those who are destitute or very poor through a special State fund.[93] It would be difficult for a country like Rwanda, at its level of development, to compensate victims of the Genocide for their losses and pain.

The Fund for the Support of Genocide Survivors popularly known as FARG or *Fonds d'Assistance aux Rescapés du Génocide* is a state fund established in 1998.[94] The 1998 law setting up the fund was replaced by a more comprehensive law of 2008.[95] The State contributes six percent of the national budget to this fund which provides assistance for housing, the medical treatment of needy survivors and school expenses for their children as well as to orphans.[96] The fund also assists needy survivors to engage in beneficial self-help, economic and social programs. The fund administrators also have the responsibility of supervising and coordinating activities relating to the collection of contributions intended for survivors. The fund may raise money from any source, including charities. It may also take action against or seek indemnity for those convicted of genocide. However, there has not been much in terms of contributions from international sources.

7.6 Post-Gacaca Justice for the Genocide Cases

The eradication of impunity requires maximum accountability. Many of the masterminds of the genocide are still at large. Victims are still waiting to see host countries activate their universal jurisdiction to try genocide fugitives. Although there are a number of national foreign courts that have tried suspects of genocide against the Tutsi, two decades have now elapsed without witnessing any investigation into genocide cases in some countries. The concern that genocide suspects are escaping justice became greater when the United Nations' Security Council decided to terminate the activities of the ICTR.[97] The Rwandan legislature reacted to these concerns by establishing a special chamber within the High Court and reintroducing the jurisdiction of the Intermediate Courts to try genocide cases. The

[93] For a general discussion see, Ibuka and others 2012.

[94] Law No 02/98 of 22 January 1998 creating the National Fund for Assistance to Victims of Genocide and Massacres perpetrated in Rwanda from 1 October 1991 to 31 December 1994.

[95] Law No 69/2008 of 30 December 2008 relating to the establishment of the Fund for the Support and Assistance to the Survivors of the Tutsi Genocide and Crimes Against Humanity committed between 1 October 1990 and 31 December 1994, and determining its organization, competence and functioning, Official Gazette, No Special of 14 April 2009.

[96] Article 22(1) of the Law No 69/2008 of 30 December 2008 relating to the establishment of the Fund for the Support and Assistance to the Survivors of the Tutsi Genocide and Crimes Against Humanity committed between 1 October 1990 and 31 December 1994, and determining its organization, competence and functioning, Official Gazette, No Special of 14 April 2009.

[97] UN Doc S/RES/1966 (2010).

High Court Chamber deals with cases of persons extradited from abroad or transferred from the ICTR, while the Intermediate Courts deal domestically with First Category offenders who were not tried before or who came to light only after the Gacaca hearings came to an end.

Post-Gacaca justice has involved trials of: cases which should have been tried by these courts but which for one or another reason were not; some Category One cases which are still pending; and cases transferred from the ICTR, or cases of suspects extradited from other countries. Genocide suspects within the country who, for one reason or another, were not tried by Gacaca courts fall under the jurisdiction of the Primary Court or the Intermediate Court.[98] Other genocide cases, including those transferred and extradited, are tried by a specialized Chamber of the High Court in charge of international crimes. At first instance the case is tried by a single judge. The law, however, provides for the possibility of having a bench of three judges, depending on the complexity of the case. So far all the cases in this Chamber are being handled by panels of three judges.

For several years, the ICTR and foreign courts turned down all requests to transfer cases for trial in Rwanda. The reluctance was based on complaints related to the legal framework for the prosecution of suspects, the nature of punishments provided for the crime of genocide and crimes against humanity in Rwanda, and the ability of the Rwandan judiciary to conduct a fair trial. Rwanda addressed these concerns progressively by amending its laws and effecting reforms in the judicial system, as discussed below.

*7.6.1 Legal and Institutional Reforms Related to Rule 11*bis *of the ICTR Rules of Procedure and Evidence*

In light of the call by the Security Council on the Ad Hoc Tribunals, the ICTY and ICTR, for a completion strategy,[99] Rule 11*bis* was introduced into the Rules of Procedure and Evidence, thus making it possible for low-level and medium-level cases to be transferred to national jurisdictions. The ICTR made its first transfer order on 13 April 2007 when it ordered the case of *Michel Bagaragaza*,[100] former head of the tea authority in Rwanda, to be transferred to The Netherlands for trial. This was followed in November 2007 by the decisions to transfer the cases of the

[98] Organic Law No 04/2012/OL of 15 June 2012 abolishing Gacaca Courts. See especially Articles 8 and 10 of the Organic Law No 02/2013/OL of 16 June 2013 modifying and complementing Organic Law No 51/2008 of 9 September 2008 determining the organization, functioning and jurisdiction of courts as modified and complemented to date, Official Gazette, No Special *Bis*, 16 June 2013.

[99] UN Doc S/RES 1503 (2003).

[100] *Prosecutor v. Michel Bagaragaza*, ICTR Trial Chamber III, Decision on Prosecutor's Request for Referral of the Indictment to the Kingdom of The Netherlands, Rule 11*bis* of the Rules of Procedure and Evidence of 13 April 2007.

former Kigali priest, *Wenceslas Munyeshyaka*,[101] and former prefect of *Gikongoro*, *Laurent Bucyibaruta*,[102] to France. Rwanda was naturally a candidate for such transfers as the crimes had been committed in Rwanda by its own citizens. It therefore prepared itself for transfers by enacting an appropriate legal framework, namely the Transfer Law.[103] The law designated the competent court as the High Court, the Supreme Court as the appellate court. It also provided for guarantees of the rights of accused persons, the production of evidence, and the security of witnesses and defence lawyers. The law further provided that the ICTR could revoke a referral if it was not satisfied with the way in which the case was conducted.

At the time, Rwanda had the death penalty on its statute books although there had been a moratorium since 1998 when the last executions were carried out. At the same time, Rule 11*bis* (C) stipulated that a transfer could not be made to a country with capital punishment in its law. For this reason, the Transfer Law provided that the heaviest penalty to be applied in cases transferred from the ICTR, or to cases of persons extradited from other states, was life imprisonment. However, the death penalty remained applicable to other cases such as ordinary cases of murder, armed robbery, rape of children, etc. It was subsequently considered to be unfair and probably contrary to the Constitution for those transferred from the ICTR or extradited from other countries to be treated differently from those arrested and prosecuted in Rwanda. Moreover, the issue of the abolition of the death penalty had been debated in Rwanda for a long time and it was therefore decided to abolish the death penalty altogether in 2007.[104] The death sentence was substituted with life imprisonment or life imprisonment with special provisions, including solitary confinement.

7.6.1.1 Life Imprisonment with Special Provisions

Following the passing of the Transfer Law and the abolition of the death penalty, it seemed all clear for cases to be transferred to Rwanda. However, questions continued to be raised in all applications lodged by the ICTR Prosecutor for referrals on various grounds, including the argument that although the death penalty had

---

[101] *Prosecutor v. Wenceslas Munyeshyaka*, ICTR Trial Chamber III, Decision on Prosecutor's Request for Referral of Wenceslas Munyeshyaka's Indictment to France, Rule 11*bis* of the Rules of Procedure and Evidence of 20 November 2007.

[102] *Prosecutor v. Laurent Bucyibaruta*, ICTR Trial Chamber III, Decision on Prosecutor's Request for Referral of Laurent Bucyibaruta's Indictement to France, Rule 11*bis* of the Rules of Procedure and Evidence of 20 November 2007.

[103] Organic Law No 11/2007 of 16 March 2007 concerning the transfer of cases to the Republic of Rwanda from the International Criminal Tribunal for Rwanda and from other states, Official Gazette, Special Issue, 19 March 2007.

[104] Organic Law No 31/2007 of 25 July 2007 relating to the Abolition of Death Penalty, Official Gazette, Special Issue, 25 July 2007.

been abolished, there was a risk of suspects convicted in Rwandan courts being sentenced to life imprisonment with special provisions and thus to life in solitary confinement. Defence lawyers argued that solitary confinement was contrary to Article 7 of the International Covenant on Civil and Political Rights to which Rwanda is a party and which prohibits the use of torture, and that there was no assurance that accused persons transferred to Rwanda would not be subject to the sentence of life imprisonment with special provisions. In the *Munyakazi* referral decision,[105] the Trial Chamber held that although the Transfer Law stated that the maximum sentence for persons transferred from the ICTR was life imprisonment, it was not clear that the Rwandan courts would not apply the later Abolition of the Death Penalty Law, which replaced the death penalty with life imprisonment or life imprisonment with special conditions, and which in its Article 9 declared all previous provisions on the matter inconsistent with it repealed. The Appeals Chamber upheld the decision of the Trial Chamber, dismissing the application for transfer. It argued that although the Transfer Law was the *lex specialis* and therefore to be construed to prevail over general laws, the Abolition of the Death Penalty Law was the *lex posterior* and therefore could be construed as prevailing over the Transfer Law, thus as allowing the possibility of imposing life imprisonment with isolation in transfer cases. It further argued that, although the Abolition of the Death Penalty Law did not explicitly mention the Transfer Law, it provided in Article 9 that "all legal provisions contrary to this Organic Law are hereby repealed", which could be interpreted as including those provisions in the Transfer Law that are inconsistent with it. Similar decisions were made in the Prosecutor's application for the transfer of *Ildephonse Hategekimana*.[106]

In 2008, the Supreme Court was called upon to rule on the constitutionality of the sentence of solitary confinement in the *Tubarimo Aloys* case.[107] In that case, the argument was that solitary confinement amounted to torture, which is prohibited by the Constitution and by international conventions. The Court dismissed this argument. The ruling of the Court, however, appeared not to have reassured the ICTR, and foreign states requested the extradition of genocide fugitives from Rwanda. The same year the Abolition of the Death Penalty Law was amended to provide that life imprisonment in solitary confinement was not applicable to transferred or extradited cases.[108] Furthermore, to put the matter beyond doubt, in

[105] *Prosecutor v. Yussuf Munyakazi*, ICTR Trial Chamber III, Decision on Prosecutor's Request for Referral of the Indictment to the Republic of Rwanda, Rule 11*bis* of the Rules of Procedure and Evidence of 28 May 2008, paras 22–32.

[106] *Prosecutor v. Ildephonse Hategekimana*, ICTR Trial Chamber, Decision on the Prosecutor's Request for the Referral of the Case of Ildephonse Hategekimana to Rwanda, Rules 11*bis* of the Rules of Procedure and Evidence of 19 June 2008.

[107] Re Tubarimo Aloys, Supreme Court of Rwanda, 29 August 2008.

[108] Organic Law No 66/2008 of 21 November 2008 modifying and completing the Organic Law No 31/2007 of 25 July 2007 relating to the Abolition of the Death Penalty, Official Gazette, No. 23, 1 December 2008.

2010, Parliament passed an interpretive law that confirmed that life imprisonment per se did not amount to torture and spelt out conditions regulating its implementation.[109]

Another issue that delayed the transfer of cases from the ICTR and extraditions from other countries is that of 'fair trial'. Rule 11*bis* (D) requires that in deciding whether to order the transfer of a case to a national jurisdiction, the Trial Chamber seized of the matter shall satisfy itself that the accused will receive a fair trial in the courts of the state concerned. In every case in which the Prosecutor has sought transfer of the suspect to Rwanda the defence and some NGOs have argued that that the accused would not be guaranteed a fair trial. Fair trial, according to the ICTR, includes being tried before an independent and impartial tribunal. For instance, in the *Munyakazi* case,[110] it was alleged by the defence that the fact that at the first instance the transferred accused would be tried by a single judge would not guarantee a fair trial as such a judge would be liable to influence by the Executive. The Chamber found that, while Rwandan legislation enshrines the principle of judicial independence, which by definition includes guarantees against outside pressures, it was not satisfied that the practice accorded with the theory. It found that a judge sitting alone would be particularly susceptible to pressure. Furthermore, the Chamber was not convinced that the accused's fair trial right to obtain the attendance of, and to examine, defence witnesses under the same conditions as witnesses called by the prosecution, could be guaranteed at that time in Rwanda.

However, in the subsequent case of *Hategekimana*, the Trial Chamber dismissed the argument on single judge trials, saying none of the submissions had provided evidence that single judge trials in Rwanda, which commenced with the judicial reforms of 2004, have been more open to outside influence than previous trials involving panels of judges.[111] Nevertheless, the Chamber declined the application for transfer on the grounds that it was not satisfied that Rwanda could ensure *Hategekimana*'s right to obtain the attendance and examination of witnesses on his behalf under the same conditions as the witnesses against him; and that, pursuant to Rwandan law, *Hategekimana* might face life imprisonment in isolation without adequate safeguards in violation of his right not to be subjected to cruel, inhuman or degrading punishment.[112]

---

[109] Organic Law No 32/2010 of 22 September 2010 relating to Serving Life Imprisonment with Special Provisions, Official Gazette, No Special, 14 October 2010.

[110] *Prosecutor v. Yussuf Munyakazi*, ICTR Trial Chamber III, Decision on Request for Referral of 28 May 2008, para 48 and paras 67–70.

[111] *Prosecutor v. Ildephonse Hategekimana*, ICTR Trial Chamber, Decision on Request for Referral of 19 June 2008, para 41.

[112] *Prosecutor v. Ildephonse Hategekimana*, ICTR Trial Chamber, Decision on Request for Referral of 19 June 2008, para 78.

7.6.1.2 Witness Protection

Another issue raised by some *amicus curiae* in the various referral application cases was that witnesses could not be guaranteed safety and could be charged with the offence of genocide ideology for what they said in their testimonies. For this reason it was argued that defence witnesses, whether from inside or outside Rwanda, would be reluctant to come forward and testify. The Chamber in *Kanyarukiga* accepted that the "defence may face problems in obtaining witnesses residing in Rwanda because they will be afraid to testify. This may affect the fairness of the trial."[113] The Chamber went on to say that despite the presence of video link facilities in Rwanda, it was not satisfied that *Kanyarukiga* would be able to call witnesses residing outside Rwanda to the extent and in the manner which will ensure a fair trial if the case is transferred.[114] To put it beyond doubt that witnesses would not be prosecuted for what they said in court, the Transfer Law was amended in 2009 to read as follows: "Without prejudice to the relevant laws on contempt of court and perjury, no person shall be criminally liable for anything said or done in the course of a trial."[115] Thus even if an accused or his/her counsel makes a statement during proceedings denying the genocide against Tutsi or trivializing it (which are offences under Rwandan law) he or she will not be prosecuted for that.

Much was said in the various cases of referral about the safety of defence witnesses. The Transfer Law provides for witness protection for both prosecution and defence witnesses. Article 15 of that law states that in cases transferred from the ICTR and other states, the High Court shall provide appropriate protection for witnesses and shall have the power to order protective measures similar to those set forth in Rules 53, 69 and 75 of the ICTR Rules of Procedure and Evidence. Article 15 further protects witnesses who travel to Rwanda to testify in transfer cases against search, seizure, arrest or detention during their testimony and during their travel to and from trials. Moreover, the Chief Justice issued an order creating the Witness Protection Unit within the judiciary to meet the criticism that the Victim and Witness Services Unit based in the Prosecutor General's office was inadequate to protect witnesses for the defence and that such witnesses would be afraid to come forward and testify.

---

[113] *Prosecutor v. Kanyarukiga*, ICTR Trial Chamber, Decision on Request for Referral of 6 June 2008, para 73.

[114] *Prosecutor v. Kanyarukiga*, ICTR trial Chamber, Decision on Request for Referral of 6 June 2008, paras 77–81.

[115] Article 2, para 2 of the Organic Law No 03/2009/OL of 26 May 2009 modifying and completing the Organic Law No 011/2007 of 16 March 2007 concerning the transfer of cases to the Republic of Rwanda from the International Criminal Tribunal for Rwanda and from other states, Official Gazette, Special Issue, 26 May 2009.

7.6.1.3 Alternative Ways to Obtain Testimony

The Transfer Law sets out in detail guarantees of rights of the accused person and deals with alternative ways of obtaining testimonies from persons residing abroad, including video link and rogatory missions by judges to take *viva voce* evidence. Article 14*bis* of the Transfer Law, inserted in 2009, provides that upon request of a party the judge may, in a transferred case in which a witness is unable or for good reason unwilling to appear before the High Court, order that the testimony of such witness be taken in any of three ways:[116]

1. By deposition in Rwanda or in a foreign jurisdiction before a competent authority authorized by the judge for that purpose;
2. By video-link hearing taken by the judge at the trial;
3. By a judge sitting in a foreign jurisdiction for the purpose of recording such *viva voce* testimony.

Testimony given in any of these ways must be transcribed so it can be made part of the trial record. The law specifies that such evidence shall carry the same weight as testimony given in court. The order must designate the date, time and place where such testimony will be taken, requiring the parties to be present to examine and cross-examine the witness.

While in the previous cases of *Kanyarukiga*, *Munyakazi* and *Hategekimana* the Appeals Chamber had found the use of video-link testimony inadequate to ensure fairness in the trial in that there would be inequality of arms between the prosecution and the defence, the Trial Chamber in *Uwinkindi* found the addition of the option of taking of testimony by a judge sitting in a foreign jurisdiction with the possibility of the presence of the accused by video-link to examine or cross-examine witnesses, to be adequate guarantees of equality between the parties.[117]

7.6.1.4 Independence of the Judiciary

During Rule 11*bis* hearings at the ICTR and during extradition hearings in foreign courts, such as those in the UK and Sweden, the issue of independence of the judiciary in Rwanda has been raised since it is one of the criteria for an accused to have a fair trial. It was argued by Human Rights Watch and the Association of Defence Lawyers that there can be no fair trial in a case transferred under Rule 11*bis* or in case of extradition because the judges in Rwanda are not independent of the Executive. However, this argument was rejected by the Chamber in the

---

[116] Article 3 of the Organic Law No 03/2009/OL of 26 May 2009 modifying and completing the Organic Law No 011/2007 of 16 March 2007 concerning the transfer of cases to the Republic of Rwanda from the International Criminal Tribunal for Rwanda and from other states, Official Gazette, Special Issue, 26 May 2009.

[117] *Prosecutor v. Jean Uwinkindi*, ICTR Referral Chamber, Decision on Request for Referral of 28 June 2011, para 106.

Uwinkindi case. The Chamber was satisfied that there has been a rigorous reform process in the judiciary since 2003 to enshrine and protect the independence of the judiciary in Rwandan laws.[118] Article 140 of the Constitution provides that the judiciary shall be independent from other branches of the Government and shall have administrative and financial autonomy.[119] The Law on the Statutes of Judges,[120] as well as the Law on the Code of Ethics for the Judiciary,[121] require the independence and impartiality of judges.

The appointment and termination of judges is a transparent process which is done through the High Council of the Judiciary which consists of a majority of judges with only one representative from the executive. There is security of tenure for all judges. Except for the President and Vice President of the Supreme Court who have limited terms of 8 years each, all other judges have an unlimited tenure. This is in accordance with Article 23, Para 4 of the Law on the Statutes of Judges and Judicial Personnel which states that judges who have been confirmed in their posts are irremovable. The provision in the 2008 amendment of the Constitution[122] introducing limited tenure for judges was removed in the 2010 Amended Constitution[123] which, therefore, restores the *status quo ante* of unlimited tenure until retirement or removal for serious misconduct or serious incompetence or incapacity.

The Penal Code also provides an incentive for the impartiality of judges in that it provides for stiff sentences for judges found to engage in corruption either by soliciting or accepting bribes or by using other forms of corruption.[124]

7.6.1.5 Participation of Foreign Judges

In the context of Rule 11*bis* on transfer and extradition cases, the possibility of participation of foreign judges in trials may be said to enhance the assurance of independence. Under Rwanda's law on the Organization, Functioning and Jurisdiction of Courts, foreign judges may be requested to sit with their Rwandan counterparts to hear a case involving international crimes or cross-border crimes.

---

[118] *Prosecutor v. Jean Uwinkindi*, ICTR Referral Chamber Decision on Request for Referral of 28 June 2011, para 51.

[119] Constitution of the Republic of Rwanda of 4 June 2003 as amended to date, Official Gazette No Special, 4 June 2003.

[120] The latest legislation is the Law No 10/2013 of 8 March 2013 governing the statutes of judges and judicial personnel, Official Gazette No 15 of 15 April 2013.

[121] Law No 09/2004 of 29 April 2004 relating to the code of ethics of for the Judiciary, Official Gazette, No 11 of 1 June 2004.

[122] Revision No 03 of 13 August 2008.

[123] Revision No 04 of 17 June 2010.

[124] Article 639 of the Organic Law No 01/2012/OL of 2 May 2012 instituting the Penal Code, Official Gazette, No Special of 14 June 2012.

In addition, the law governing the Supreme Court[125] gives powers to the Chief Justice to request the United Nations, other international organizations or a foreign country, to provide foreign judges to sit with Rwandan judges in cases transferred to Rwanda involving international crimes or transnational crimes committed in Rwanda or in a foreign country. The power may be exercised at the request of the accused, his/her advocate or by the prosecutor or by an international prosecution authority. However, this has not been requested or considered necessary so far.

7.6.2 Current and Pending Prosecutions

So far Rwanda has received seven files from the ICTR. These are files of *Jean Uwinkindi*, *Bernard Munyagishali*, *Charles Sikubwabo*, *Ladislas Ntaganzwa*, *Aloys Ndimbati*, *Ryandikayo*, *Fulgence Kayishema* and *Pheneas Munyarugarama*. The two first accused persons were transferred from the ICTR's detention center to Rwanda. Others are still at large.[126] *Charles Bandora* is the only suspect extradited from Norway. *Leon Mugesera* was not extradited but deported from Canada for infringing Canadian domestic law. *Emmanuel Mbarushimana* is still fighting an extradition ruling by Norwegian courts before the European Court for Human Rights.

It is expected that this Court will follow its previous ruling in the *Ahorugeze* case where it stated that it was satisfied that suspects extradited to Rwanda received fair trials and had no ground to doubt about the independence of the Rwandan judicial system.[127] The court systematically rejected the defence counsel's allegations of persecution to which the suspect would be subjected once in Rwanda and concluded that on the basis of previous decisions by the ICTR and other domestic courts such as those of The Netherlands or the Court of Oslo, there was evidence that in Rwanda prisoners are detained in good conditions.[128]

Two other genocide fugitives in France, *Innocent Musabyimana* and *Claude Muhayimana*, have requested the French *Cour de Cassation* to overrule the decision of the Paris Court of Appeal on their extradition to Rwanda. The French highest court has so far rejected extradition requests on the grounds that laws regulating and punishing the crime of genocide in Rwanda were *ex post facto* laws. *Libération*, a French Newspaper, alleges that in Rwanda the crime of genocide is prosecuted on the basis of a law of 19 June 1994 whereas the acts it criminalizes

[125] Organic Law No 03/2012/OL of 13 June 2012 determining the organization, functioning and jurisdiction of the Supreme Court, Official Gazette, No 28 of 9 July 2012.

[126] "Transfer of Bernard Munyagishari to Rwanda", available at http://www.nppa.gov.rw/component/content/article/54-top/708-transfer-of-bernard-munyagishari-to-rwanda.html.

[127] *Ahorugeze v. Sweden*, European Court of Human Rights, Final Judgment of 4 June 2012.

[128] Ibid.

started in April 1994.[129] It is not known, where *Libération* found reference for this statement.

Most international crimes, and particularly genocide, are already criminalized by customary international law. The *nullum crimen sine lege* rule can no longer be a barrier for the prosecution of international crimes of the magnitude of genocide. Article II(2) of the Universal Declaration of Human Rights declares that the principle of legality in criminal matters is interpreted as having codified that principle for all nations. The Declaration itself is widely viewed as a codification of customary international law.[130] Other genocide fugitives are still fighting their extradition before domestic courts of some European or North American countries.[131]

In Rwanda, the judicial process for the extradited or transferred persons has not been rapid. None was expecting, however, those trials to follow an easy process. Cases are very complex. Countries that extradited genocide fugitives to Rwanda as well as the ICTR's Mechanism continue to make a direct or remote follow up, including monitoring by the representatives of the ICTR Prosecutor and Registrar. Accused persons are aware of the guarantees that the Government has pledged before their extradition or their transfer and which are largely reflected in the Transfer Law. They do invoke these guarantees but also appear to abuse the procedure.

For instance, *Leon Mugesera* challenged first the legality of his detention from the lower courts to the High Court. The High Court found that *Mugesera*'s arguments that he could not be detained before Canada sent his file to Rwanda were baseless. *Mugesera* lodged an appeal before the Supreme Court. He was later informed that his appeal before the Supreme Court did not comply with Article 162 of the Civil Procedure Code on the admissibility of appeals against interlocutory judgments. Such appeals are only admissible after and jointly with the final judgment.[132] *Mugesera* immediately challenged the constitutionality of the legal provision prohibiting an appeal against interlocutory judgments. A few days before the delivery of the Supreme Court's judgment on the constitutionality or unconstitutionality of Article 162 of the Civil Procedure Code, *Mugesera* withdrew his request.[133] The process on preventive detention took up to 4 months. When the trial was about to start the accused alleged that he was unable to plead in

---

[129] Génocide: la Justice Francaise Favorable à l'Extradition des Rwandais, Libération, 13 November 2013.

[130] Schabas 2013, p. 681.

[131] See for example, *Vincent Brown and Others v. The Government of Rwanda and Another* [2009] EWHC 770 Admin, United Kingdom High Court (England and Wales), Judgment of 8 April 2009; "Rwanda: Genocide Suspects in UK set for Extradition Hearing" available at http://allafrica.com/stories/201309040096.html.

[132] Article 162, para 2 of the Law No 18/2004 of 20 June 2004 relating to the Civil, Commercial, Labour and Administrative Procedure, Official Gazette, No Special *Bis* of 30 July 2004.

[133] *Ex Parte Leon Mugesera*, Supreme Court of Rwanda, 28 September 2012.

his mother tongue. The objection followed again the same process until the highest court decides on that matter.

Accused persons have also resorted to all kinds of procedural and legal technicalities as a way of getting away with the charges they are prosecuted for or adjourning and prolonging the trial. The plea of unconstitutionality of procedural laws has been used in other cases.[134] The Rwandan judiciary remains firm and determined to see the cases proceed and conclude in accordance with international standards.

7.7 General Conclusion

Rwanda has come a long way. It has not been easy to try genocide cases. Committed to eradicating the culture of impunity in the country, hundreds of thousands of perpetrators of genocide and other crimes against humanity had to be prosecuted. The International Criminal Tribunal for Rwanda was neither mandated, nor could it possibly have had the capacity to prosecute all perpetrators. It fell on national courts to carry the major burden. Against all odds, Rwanda has succeeded in bringing to justice to the majority of perpetrators. More than that, she opted to handle the perpetrators in a multi-faceted approach, focusing on fighting impunity but also on national unity and reconciliation through the neo-traditional Gacaca courts and innovative forms of punishment. The Rwanda experiment is likely to be adopted by other post-conflict societies if one considers the number of country delegations coming to Rwanda to learn how Gacaca operated. At the same time, international tribunals are important in using the available human and material resources to produce reference judgments for generations of scholars, students and other jurisdictions. Post-conflict justice, it appears, is best served by a multi-dimensional approach.

References

Bornkamm PC (2012) Rwanda's Gacaca Courts: between retribution and reparation. Oxford University Press, Oxford

Bourgeois R (1954) Banyarwanda et Barundi: La coutume. Institut Royal Colonial Belge, Brussels

Clark P (2008) The rules (and politics) of engagement: The Gacaca Courts and post-genocide justice, healing and reconciliation in Rwanda. In: Clark P, Kaufman ZD (eds) After genocide,

[134] See, for example, *Prosecutor v. Umuhoza Victoire and Others*, Judgment of 13 October 2011; *Prosecutor v. Nditurende Tharcisse and Another*, Judgment of 28 March 2013. *Ex Parte Uwinkindi Jean*, Supreme Court of Rwanda, *Ex Parte Ingabire Umuhoza Victoire*, Supreme Court of Rwanda, in Urukiko rw'Ikirenga, Icyegeranyo cy'Ibyemezo by'Inkiko, Igitabo cya 2, No 17, 2013, pp. 3–27.

transitional justice, post-conflict reconstruction and reconciliation in Rwanda and beyond. Hurst & Company, London
Clark P (2010) The Gacaca Courts, post-genocide justice and reconciliation in Rwanda. Cambridge University Press, Cambridge
De Beer D (1997) The Organic Law of 30 August 1996 on the organisation of the prosecution of offences constituting the crime of genocide or crimes against humanity: commentary. Alter Egaux Editions, Kigali
De Brouwer AA, Ruvebana E (2013) The legacy of Gacaca Courts in Rwanda: survivors' views. Int Crim Law Rev 13:937–976
Ferdinandusse W (2005) Direct application of International Criminal Law in National Courts. T.M.C. Asser Press, The Hague
Jones NA (2010) The courts of genocide: politics and the rule of law in Rwanda and Arusha. Routledge, New York
Karekezi UA (2001) Juridictions Gacaca, Lutte contre l'Impunité et Promotion de la Réconciliation Nationale. Cahiers du Centre de Gestion des Conflits, Les Juridictions Gacaca et les Processus de Réconciliation Nationale. Editions de l'Université Nationale du Rwanda, Kigali
Nowrojee B (2005) Your justice is too slow: will the ICTR fail Rwanda's rape victims? United Nations Research Institute for Social Development, Occasional Paper, No 10, 2005
Ntampaka C (2005) Introduction aux Systèmes Juridiques Africains. Presse Universitaire de Namur, Namur
Nzakunda J (2005) Les circonstances attenuantes et les causes legales de reduction des peines en droit Rwandais. Rwanda Law Rev 2:58
Ohlin JD (2005) Applying the death penalty to crime of genocide. Am J Int Law 99:747–778
Prunier G (1995) The Rwanda crisis: history of genocide. Columbia University Press, New York
Schabas WA (2008) Post-genocide justice in Rwanda. In: Clark P, Kaufman ZD (eds) After genocide, transitional justice, post-conflict reconstruction and reconciliation in Rwanda and Beyond. Hurst & Company, London
Schabas WA (2009) Genocide in international law, 2nd edn. Cambridge University Press, Cambridge
Schabas WA (2013) The contribution of the Eichmann trial to international law. Leiden J Int Law 26:667–699
Tutu D (1999) No future without forgiveness. Doubleday, New York
Werle G (2009) Principles of International Criminal Law, 2nd edn. T.M.C. Asser Press, The Hague

Cases

The Prosecutor v. Pauline Nyiramasuhuko et al., ICTR Trial Chamber II, Transcripts of October 2001, Case No ICTR-98-42-7-31.
The Prosecutor v. Nahimana, Barayagwiza and Ngeze, ICTR Trial Chamber I, Judgment and Sentence of 3 December 2003, Case No. ICTR 99-52-T.
The Prosecutor v. Nahimana, Barayagwiza and Ngeze, ICTR Appeals Chamber, Judgment of 28 November 2007, Case No. ICTR 99-52-A.
The Prosecutor v. Michel Bagaragaza, ICTR Trial Chamber III, Decision on Prosecutor's Request for Referral of the Indictment to the Kingdom of The Netherlands, Rule 11bis of the Rules of Procedure and Evidence of 13 April 2007, Case No ICTR-2005-86-11bis.
The Prosecutor v. Laurent Bucyibaruta, ICTR Trial Chamber III, Decision on Prosecutor's Request for Referral of Laurent Bucyibaruta's Indictement to France of 20 November 2007, Case No ICTR-2005-85-I.

The Prosecutor v. Wenceslas Munyeshyaka, ICTR Trial Chamber III, Decision on Prosecutor's Request for Referral of Wenceslas Munyeshyaka's Indictement to France, Rule 11bis of the Rules of Procedure and Evidence of 20 November 2007, Case No ICTR-2005-87-I.
The Prosecutor v. Yussuf Munyakazi, ICTR Trial Chamber III, Decision on Request for Referral of 28 May 2008, Case No ICTR-97-36-R11bis.
The Prosecutor v. Kanyarukiga, ICTR Trial Chamber, Decision on Request for Referral of 6 June 2008, Case No ICTR-2002-78-R11bis.
The Prosecutor v. Ildephonse Hategekimana, ICTR Trial Chamber, Decision on Request for Referral of 19 June 2008, Case No ICTR-00-55B-R11bis.
The Prosecutor v. Jean Uwinkindi, ICTR Referral Chamber, Decision on Request for Referral of 28 June 2011, Case No ICTR-2001-75-R11bis.
Ahorugeze v. Sweden, European Court of Human Rights, Final Judgment of 4 June 2012, Application No 37075/09.
The Prosecutor v. Kanyabugande and Others, Tribunal de Première Instance de Byumba, Judgment of 2 May 1997, RMP10529/S3/ND/KB.
The Prosecutor v. Nsabimana and Others, Tribunal de Première Instance de Cyangugu, Jugdment of 5 June 1997 RMP 78764/S2/ KRL.
The Prosecutor v. Musangwa and Others, Tribunal de Première Instance de Kibungo, Judgment of 18 June 1997, RMP 85743/S3/ND/JMR.
The Prosecutor v. Murangira Jean Baptiste, Tribunal de Première Instance de Nyamata, Judgment of 30 March 1998, RMP 101893/S1/BA/NMTA.
The Prosecutor v. Munyangabo and Others, Tribunal de Premiere Instance de Gikongoro, Judgment of 10 June 1998, RMP 98909/S2/MP.
The Prosecutor v. Semukanya Vincent and Others, Tribunal de Première Instance de Kibungo, Judgment of 17 July 1998, RMP 89295/S3/ND.
The Prosecutor v. Hakizimana Appolinaire and Others, Tribunal de Première Instance de Gitarama, Judgment of 24 August 1998, RMP 24778/S4/MBF.
The Prosecutor v. Byiringiro J.P. and Others, Tribunal de Premiere Instance de Kibungo, Judgment of 21 October 1998, RMP82011/S4/ND.
The Prosecutor v. Mahirane alias Kagina, Tribunal de Première Instance de Kibungo, Judgment of 21 October 1998, RMP 82127/S11/NS.
The Prosecutor v. Gatsimbanyi and Others, Tribunal de Première Instance de Nyamata, Judgment of 13 November 1998, RMP102065/S1/BA.
The Prosecutor v. Kabiligi Athanase and Others, Tribunal de Première Instance de Kibuye, Judgment of 10 December 1998, RMP 51498/S4/CM/KB/97.
The Prosecutor v. Nshogoza Anastase and Others, Tribunal de Première Instance de Byumba, Judgment of 30 November 1999, RP 040/1/Ch. Sp./98/BY.
The Prosecutor v. Karorero Charles and Others, Tribunal de Premiere Instance de Cyangungu, Judgment of 31 March 2000, RP 26/99.
The Prosecutor v. Karorero Charles and Others, Tribunal de Première Instance de Cyangungu, Judgment of 31 March 2000, RMP 78752/S2/KRL.
The Prosecutor v. Mvumbahe Denys and Others, Tribunal de Premiere Instance de Kibuye, Judgment of 16 July 2000, RP Ch. Sp. 005/01/2000.
The Prosecutor v. Ukezimpfura Jean and Others, Tribunal de Premiere Instance de Kibungo, Judgment of 29 September 2000, RP 0139/EX/R3/99/KGO.
The Prosecutor v. Banzi Wellars and Others, Tribunal de Premiere Instance de Gisenyi, Judgment of 25 May 2001, RP221/R2/2000.
The Prosecutor v. Banzi Wellars, Tribunal de Premiere Instance de Gisenyi, Judgement of 25 May 2001, RP 35/1/99.
The Prosecutor v. Hanyurwimfura Epaphrodite, Tribunal de Premiere Instance de Butare, Judgment of 8 August 2001, RP 52/2/2000.
Re Tubarimo Aloys, Supreme Court of Rwanda, Judgment of 29 August 2008, Case No RS/INCONST/PEN0002/08/CS.

The Prosecutor v. Umuhoza Victoire and Others, High Court Kigali, Judgment of 30 October 2012, RP 0081-0110/10/HC/KIG.
Ex Parte Ingabire Umuhoza Victoire, Supreme Court of Rwanda, Judgment of 18 December 2012, RS/INCONST/PEN0002/12/CS.
Ex Parte Uwinkindi Jean, Supreme Court of Rwanda, Judgment of 22 February 2013, RS/INCONST/PEN0005/12/CS.
The Prosecutor v. Nditurende Tharcisse and Another, Supreme Court of Rwanda, Judgment of 28 March 2013, RPA 0255/12/CS.
French Court of Cassation, Criminal Chamber, Judgment of 19 April 1995, Case No 94-83519.
Augusto Pinochet, National Audience on Jurisdiction of Spanish Justice to Pursue Crimes of Genocide in Chile of 5 November 1998, Case No1/98.
Vincent Brown and Others v. The Government of Rwanda and Another [2009] EWHC 770 Admin, United Kingdom High Court (England and Wales), Judgment of 8 April 2009, Case No CO/8862/2008.

Documents

African Rights and Redress (2008) Survivors and Post-Genocide Justice in Rwanda, Their Experiences, Perspectives and Hopes. http://www.redress.org/downloads/publications/Rwanda%20Survivors%2031%20Oct%2008.pdf.
Avocats Sans Frontières (2006) Monitoring des Juridictions Gacaca, Octobre 2005—Septembre 2006, Palloti Press, Kigali.
Ibuka (2012) Right to Reparation for Survivors: Recommendations for Reparation for Survivors of the 1994 Genocide Against Tutsi. http://www.redress.org/downloads/publications/121031right_to_rep.pdf.
National Service of Gacaca Courts (2012) Summary of the Report Presented at the Closing of Gacaca Courts' Activities, Kigali.
Penal Reform International (2010) The Contributions of Gacaca Courts to Resolving Cases Arising from Genocide, London.
Redress (2012) Testifying to Genocide: Victim and Witness Protection in Rwanda, Redress Trust, London.

Chapter 8
The Extraordinary African Chambers: The Case of *Hissène Habré*

Mbacké Fall

Contents

8.1 Introduction

It is not hard to trace the history of the case of *Hissène Habré*, the former president of Chad from 1982 to 1990. One needs only visit the websites of the big human rights NGOs, such as Human Rights Watch,[1] to find detailed information about

The views expressed in this chapter are not necessarily those of the Extraordinary Chambers in the Courts of Senegal.

[1] For more details, see: http://www.hrw.org/habre-case (all internet sources in this chapter were accessed on 18 March 2014).

M. Fall (✉)
Courts of Senegal, Dakar, Senegal
e-mail: fallmbacke@hotmail.com

G. Werle et al. (eds.), *Africa and the International Criminal Court*,
International Criminal Justice Series 1, DOI 10.1007/978-94-6265-029-9_8

him and the various attempts to bring him to justice until he was finally arrested and brought before the Extraordinary African Chambers.[2] For this reason, this chapter will focus on the law and procedures applied by the Extraordinary African Chambers. Then it examines the extent to which the creation of the Chambers by the African Union may serve as an alternative model to the International Criminal Court for trying Africans accused of serious violations of international law.

8.2 The Law and Procedures Applied by the Extraordinary African Chambers

Following the ruling by the International Court of Justice of 20 July 2012,[3] that Senegal must prosecute or extradite *Habré*, Senegal and the African Union signed an agreement on 22 August 2012 creating the Extraordinary African Chambers within the courts of Senegal.[4]

The Statute of the Chambers included as an annex to the agreement is comprised of 37 Articles. It is titled "Statute of the Extraordinary African Chambers within the courts of Senegal created to prosecute international crimes committed by Chad between 7 June 1982 and 1 December 1990."[5]

Four chambers were created:[6]

- One Investigative Chamber within the *Tribunal Régional Hors Classe de Dakar* composed of four investigative judges and two alternate investigative judges. The Investigative Chamber is responsible for investigating the '*Habré* affair' and its decisions may be appealed.
- One Indicting Chamber within the Dakar Court of Appeals before which the acts of the Investigative Chamber may be challenged. The Indicting Chamber is composed of three judges and one alternate judge. The judges of the Indicting Chamber convene and rule on all appeals lodged, and its decisions are final and unappealable.

---

[2] Statute of the Extraordinary African Chambers, unofficial translation to English available at http://www.hrw.org/news/2013/09/02/statute-extraordinary-african-chambers. The website of the Extraordinary African Chambers is available at http://www.chambresafricaines.org/.

[3] *Belgium v. Senegal*, ICJ, judgment of 20 July 2012 (Questions relating to the obligation to prosecute or extradite).

[4] Accord entre le gouvernement de la République du Sénégal et l'Union africaine sur la création des Chambres africaines extraordinaires au sein des juridictions sénégalaises, August 22, 2012. See also, Human Rights Watch 2012.

[5] Statute of the Extraordinary African Chambers, unofficial translation by Human Rights Watch, available at http://www.hrw.org/news/2013/09/02/statute-extraordinary-african-chambers. For the official text in French, see: http://www.chambresafricaines.org/pdf/Projet%20Statut%20chambres%20africaines_tel%20que%20Finalis+%C2%AE%2024%20Juillet%202012.pdf.

[6] Article 11 of the Statute of the Extraordinary African Chambers.

- One Trial Chamber within the Dakar Court of Appeals responsible for trying those persons indicted by the Investigative Chamber. The Trial Chamber is composed of three judges and two alternate judges, and is presided over by a non-Senegalese judge from another African Union Member State.
- One Appeals Chamber attached to the Dakar Court of Appeals, whose decisions are final and unappealable. The Appeals Chamber is composed of three judges and two alternate judges, and is presided over by a non-Senegalese judge from another African Union Member State.

All judges are nominated by the African Union.[7]

For reasons linked to the safeguarding of the presumption of innocence, only the Investigative and Indicting Chambers have as yet been set up. The Trial Chamber will be set up once the investigative phase has been completed and a committal order is issued and the case is referred to the Trial Chamber. The Appeals Chamber will be set up when and if an appeal has been lodged against the decision rendered in the first instance by the Trial Chamber.

The Office of the Prosecutor for the Extraordinary African Chambers is represented by the Chief Prosecutor nominated by the African Union, along with his three deputy prosecutors.[8] The Office of the Prosecutor is the only body that may initiate prosecutions and may do so until the end of the entire procedure, which is expected to last 27 months, including an investigative phase lasting 15 months, the trial lasting seven months and an appeal lasting five months.

The Registry is composed of one or several clerks who will assist the Extraordinary African Chambers and whose duties are determined pursuant to the Senegalese Code of Criminal Procedure.[9] The clerks are nominated by the Minister of Justice of Senegal.[10]

The Administrator of the Chambers is nominated by the Minister of Justice of Senegal and is responsible for the non-judicial aspects of the administration and the servicing of the Extraordinary African Chambers.[11] The Administrator is also responsible for the Chambers' public relations with the international community and enters into agreements to carry out the outreach program activities and to raise public awareness both in Africa and globally about the work of the Extraordinary African Chambers.[12] The Administrator is also responsible for directing and assisting the witnesses and victims who appear before the Chambers, in addition to providing for the necessary measures and arrangements to ensure their protection and security.[13]

---

7 Idem.

8 Ibid., Article 12.

9 Ibid., Article 13(1).

10 Ibid., Article 13.

11 See generally, ibid., Article 15.

12 Ibid., Article 15(3).

13 Ibid., Article 15(4).

8.2.1 The Applicable Law

According to Article 16 of the Statute, the Extraordinary African Chambers apply the Statute, and for those cases not provided for in the Statute, the Chambers apply Senegalese law.

8.2.1.1 The Statute

The Statute defines the jurisdiction of the Chambers:

- Jurisdiction *ratione loci*: the Chambers have jurisdiction over crimes committed in the territory of Chad.[14]
- Jurisdiction *ratione temporis*: the Chambers have jurisdiction over crimes committed during the period from 7 June 1982 and 1 December 1990.[15]
- Jurisdiction *ratione materiae*: The Chambers have subject matter jurisdiction over four types of crimes defined in Articles 5–8 of the Statute: the crime of genocide, crimes against humanity, war crimes and torture.[16]
- According to Article 24, the Chambers may impose a penalty of imprisonment for 30 years or more, or a term of life imprisonment, when justified by the extreme gravity of the crimes and the individual circumstances of the convicted person.
- In addition to imprisonment, the Chambers may order a fine under the criteria provided for in Senegalese law, and the forfeiture of proceeds, property and assets derived directly or indirectly from the crime, without prejudice to the rights of third parties acting in good faith.[17]
- Torture is listed as a stand-alone crime in addition to being included among the acts that may constitute a crime against humanity or war crime.[18]
- The Chambers also have jurisdiction to try persons who have committed grave breaches of Common Article 3 of the Geneva Conventions of 12 August 1949 relating to the Protection of Victims of Armed Conflicts and of the Second Additional Protocol to the Geneva Conventions of 12 August 1949, and relating to the Protection of Victims of Non-International Armed Conflicts, of 8 June 1977.[19]

The Statute also defines the prosecution strategy, both in terms of which persons and which crimes are targeted.

---

[14] Ibid., Article 3.

[15] Idem.

[16] Ibid., Articles 4–8.

[17] Ibid., Article 24(2).

[18] See, ibid., Articles 4 and 8.

[19] Ibid., Article 7(2).

- The Chambers have the power to prosecute and try the person or persons most responsible for crimes and serious violations of international law, customary international law and international conventions ratified by Chad, committed in the territory of Chad during the period from 7 June 1982 to 1 December 1990.[20]
- Within this frame, the Chief Prosecutor initiated an investigation pursuant to Article 17(4) of the Statute which states that "the Prosecutor may initiate investigations *proprio motu* or on the basis of information obtained from any source, particularly from governments, international organizations and non-governmental organizations, or on the basis of complaints filed by victims notwithstanding their place of domicile".
- The work of the Prosecution has been facilitated by cooperation with the Belgian judicial authorities, who agreed to a visit by the Prosecution to Belgium and transmitted the files of their still open case against *Habré*;[21] as well as other information and evidence gathered by such international organizations as Human Rights Watch and Amnesty International.[22] During a mission to Chad, we visited former detention centers and the sites of mass graves.[23]
- This preliminary investigative work allowed the Prosecution to gather the serious and corroborative evidence it needed to demand the indictment of *Hissène Habré*, *Saleh Younouss*, *Mahamat Djibrine*, *Guihini Koreï*, *Abakar Torbo* and *Zakaria Berdeï* as those alleged to be most responsible for grave violations of international law committed in Chad between 7 June 1982–1 December 1990.[24]

The Extraordinary African Chambers may choose to prosecute the most serious crimes within their jurisdiction.[25]

- *Hissène Habré* was charged with crimes against humanity, war crimes and torture,[26] while the others are being investigated for torture and crimes against humanity.

---

[20] Ibid., Article 3.

[21] See "Mission Parquet général en Belgique" from the Extraordinary African Chambers, 12 June, 2013, http://www.chambresafricaines.org/index.php/le-coin-des-medias/communiqu%C3%A9-de-presse/496-mission-parquet-general-en-belgique.html.

[22] See for example Human Rights Watch 2013b.

[23] See "Mission Parquet general au TCHAD" from the Extraordinary African Chamber, 12 June, 2013, http://www.chambresafricaines.org/index.php/le-coin-des-medias/communiqu%C3%A9-de-presse/495-mission-parquet-general-au-tchad.html.

[24] See "Communiqué de presse du 11 novembre 2013" from the Extraordinary African Chambers, 11 November, 2013, http://www.chambresafricaines.org/index.php/le-coin-des-medias/communiqué-de-presse/551-communiqué-de-presse-du-11-novembre-2013.html.

[25] Article 3(2) of the Statute of the Extraordinary African Chambers.

[26] See "Communiqué de Presse du Mardi 02 Juillet 2013" from the Extraordinary African Chambers, 13 August, 2013, http://www.chambresafricaines.org/index.php/le-coin-des-medias/communiqu%C3%A9-de-presse/505-communiqu%C3%A9-de-presse-du-mardi-02-juillet-2013.html.

- Arrest warrants were issued against all five, and *Habré* has been held in detention since 2 July 2013,[27] after being kept in police custody for 48 hours.[28]
- Two are currently being held in detention in Chad within the frame of a domestic procedure and are expected to be transferred to the Extraordinary African Chambers pursuant to the judicial cooperation agreement between Chad and Senegal provided for in the Statute of the Chambers.[29]
- Because the investigative phase is subject to confidentiality and in full respect of the rights of the defense, the work of the Investigative Chambers is not presently subject to disclosure.

8.2.1.2 Senegalese Law

The Chambers may only apply Senegalese law subsidiarily in those cases not provided for in the Statute.[30] "Senegalese law" refers to the Senegalese Code of Criminal Procedure, general principles and all international conventions ratified by Senegal.

8.2.2 The Procedures Applied by the Extraordinary African Chambers

Pursuant to Article 17(1) of the Statute, "the Extraordinary African Chambers shall apply, in the first place, [the] Statute, and, for those cases not provided for in [the] Statute, the Code of Senegalese Criminal Procedure".

---

[27] Human Rights Watch 2013a.

[28] See "Interpellation de *Habré*" from the Extraordinary African Chambers 2013; AFP, "Sénégal: première nuit en garde à vue pour *Hissène Habré*", 1 July, 2013, http://www.jeuneafrique.com/actu/20130701T110258Z20130701T110250Z/.

[29] A number of former agents of the "Documentation and Security Directorate" (a secret police force) have been arrested in Chad since April 2013, pursuant to criminal complaints for torture, murder, and "disappearance", filed by victims in October 2000. See, e.g. Radio France Internationale, "Tchad: 'El Djonto', tortionnaire sous le régime d'*Hissène Habré*, a été arrêté", 15 May, 2013, www.bbc.co.uk/afrique/region/2013/05/130515_chad_tchad_arrest_habre.shtml; Radio France Internationale, "Tchad: trois personnalités du régime *Habré* arrêtées", 5 July, 2013, http://www.rfi.fr/afrique/20130705-tchad-trois-personnalites-regime-habre-arretees.

[30] Article 16(2) of the Statute of the Extraordinary African Chambers.

8.2.2.1 The Code of Senegalese Criminal Procedure to Fill in the Absence of Special Rules of Procedure and Evidence

The ad hoc international criminal tribunals and the International Criminal Court adopted special rules of procedure and evidence regarding the admission of evidence, the conduct of investigations and trial proceedings.

In contrast, the Extraordinary African Chambers apply the rules of the Senegalese Code of Criminal Procedure.[31] This is because the Chambers are not an ad hoc international criminal tribunal, but an internationalized tribunal located *within* the courts of Senegal, which were created by an international agreement.

- In this way, the Office of the Prosecutor carries out prosecutions with the powers as provided for by the Senegalese Code of Criminal Procedure;[32]
- the duties of the Registry are determined pursuant to the Senegalese Code;[33] and
- the manner in which the investigation and hearings are carried out is governed by the Senegalese Code of Criminal Procedure.[34]

8.2.2.2 The Senegalese Code of Criminal Procedure and the Provisions of the Statute Together Guarantee a Fair Trial

It is important to remember that Senegalese procedure is based on the Romano-Germanic inquisitorial legal system, and not the Anglo-Saxon adversarial system, which more closely resembles that of the international criminal tribunals.

In the Romano-Germanic system, the judges do not play the role of an arbiter. Rather,—take for example the investigative judges—they are investigators who take all measures deemed useful to uncover the truth, investigating and examining both incriminating and exonerating evidence.

The same can be said for the President of the Trial Chamber, who is responsible for the proper conduct of the hearings and oral proceedings, and who decides when the prosecution, civil parties and defence shall speak, with the defence always having the last word.

The underlying principles of criminal law are always respected, from the investigation phase to the proceedings before the courts. These apply to the four main actors in the proceedings: the prosecution, the accused, the victims and the judges.

---

[31] Ibid., Article 17(1).

[32] Ibid., Article 12(3).

[33] Ibid., Article 13(1).

[34] Ibid., Article 22.

8.2.2.2.1 The Prosecution: The Rules Governing Prosecution

- Structure: The Office of the Prosecutor is represented by the Chief Prosecutor or his or her deputy prosecutors.[35] The requirements of impartiality and integrity required by Article 12 of the Statute mirror Article 16 of the ICTY Statute and Article 15 of the ICTR Statute.
- Independence: The Office of the Prosecutor has no relationship or link to the Ministry of Justice or the African Union.[36] It receives no instructions from them and does not report to them.
- Exclusive Power to Initiate Prosecutions: The Office of the Prosecutor is the only body that may initiate prosecutions, and may do so by initiating investigations *proprio motu* or on the basis of information obtained from any source. The relevant Article 17 of the Statute mirrors Article 18 of the ICTY Statute and Article 17 of the ICTR Statute.
- The Office of the Prosecutor also has certain powers as provided by the Senegalese Code of Criminal Procedure.[37]

8.2.2.2.2 The Rights of the Accused in the Proceedings

Article 21 of the Statute lists the rights of the accused, and mirrors Article 21 of the ICTY Statute and Article 20 of the ICTR Statute. The "accused" means not only the person before the court, but also anyone who has been charged with crimes and serious violations of international law.

The investigative phase is confidential and the rights of the defence feature prominently in the process.

- The accused has a right to counsel of his or her own choosing and cannot be forced to appear without his attorney or if his counsel has not been duly summoned.[38]
- While in detention, the accused has a right at all stages of the proceedings to provisional release.[39] The Chamber must issue a decision within five days of receiving the response of the Prosecution, which must be submitted within ten days of receiving the request.
- If the accused believes that a mistake has been made in the investigation, he or she has—pursuant to Article 165 of the Senegalese Code of Criminal Procedure—a right to file a motion requesting that the decision be reversed.
- The accused has the right to a fair and speedy trial.[40]

---

[35] Ibid., Article 12(1).

[36] Ibid., Article 12(2).

[37] Ibid., Article 17(1).

[38] Ibid., Article 21(4)(b).

[39] Article 130 of the Senegalese Code of Criminal Procedure.

[40] Article 21(4)(c) of the Statute of the Extraordinary African Chambers.

- The sentence shall be in writing and must state the reasons on which it is based, as per Article 23 of the Statute, which mirrors Article 23 of the ICTR Statute.
- The accused has a right to appeal orders issued by the investigating judges (as per the Senegalese Code of Criminal Procedure) as well as the decisions of the Chambers on the grounds recognized by most jurisdictions, such as: procedural errors; an error concerning a material question of law invalidating the decision, including an error relating to the Chamber's exercise of jurisdiction; and an error of fact which has occasioned a miscarriage of justice.[41]

The Statute also gives the Appeals Judges the capacity to draw upon the jurisprudence of international criminal courts and tribunals.[42]

The Statute also specifies that all prison sentences shall be served in accordance with international standards.[43]

8.2.2.2.3 The Victims

- The Formation of Civil Parties: As per Article 14 of the Statute, Civil Parties may be formed at any stage during the investigative phase by submitting a request in writing to the Registry, either by a victim or by his or her beneficiary. Victims may choose to form groups and may decide to be represented by a joint representative of their choice. The exact legal personality of these groups is not laid out in the Statute in detail. If a group of victims does not have the means to pay a joint representative, it may request assistance from the Administrator who shall rule on the request.
- Right to Reparations: The Extraordinary African Chambers may order that a reparations award in the form of compensation be made to a Trust Fund established for the benefit of the victims.[44] The Trust Fund shall be financed by voluntary contributions from foreign governments, international institutions, NGOs, or other interested persons or States.[45] The approach of the Extraordinary African Chambers is original in that reparations are open to all victims, individually or collectively, whether or not they participated in the proceedings before the Chambers.[46]
- Right to Protection: The victims have a right to protection that is equal to that of witnesses and experts. The Government of Senegal is responsible for ensuring the protection of all parties and witnesses to the trial for the entire duration of the proceedings.[47]

---

[41] Ibid., Article 25.

[42] Ibid., Article 25(3).

[43] Ibid., Article 26(2).

[44] Ibid., Article 27(2).

[45] Ibid., Article 28(1).

[46] Ibid., Article 28(2).

[47] Ibid., Articles 34 and 35.

8.2.2.2.4 The Judge

The functions of investigation and trial are kept separate in the Extraordinary African Chambers.[48] The investigation may end with the dismissal of the case stating the reasons in fact and in law, a committal order, or a decision (in the case of an appeal referring the case to the Trial Chamber). The Trial Chamber is presided over by a non-Senegalese judge from another African Union Member State, two judges of Senegalese nationality and two alternate judges of Senegalese nationality.[49]

Hearings shall be held in public and questions concerning the manner in which they are carried out shall be governed by the Senegalese Code of Criminal Procedure.[50]

The trial court is governed by Articles 218 and 367-13 of the Senegalese Code of Criminal Procedure.

Specific provisions also govern the taking of evidence,[51] the appearance of the accused before the court,[52] the taking of witness testimonies,[53] civil parties and the role and responsibilities of the Office of the Prosecutor.[54]

Pursuant to Article 290 of the Senegalese Code of Criminal Procedure, the President is responsible for the proper conduct of hearings and oral proceedings. He can take all reasonable measures to ensure the dignity of the hearings, and must remain impartial.

The Chamber makes a ruling first on the prosecution, and then the civil parties, and finally on all the points raised by the defence.

The Trial Chamber will impose a sentence in the form of a judgment and shall state the reasons on which it is based so that it may be appealed to the Appeals Chamber.[55] The Trial Chamber shall be presided over by a non-Senegalese judge from another African Union Member State, two judges of Senegalese nationality and two alternate judges of Senegalese nationality.[56]

The judgment may be challenged on appeal within 15 days by all parties to the trial:[57] the accused, the prosecution and the civil parties with respect to their civil interests, on the following grounds:[58]

---

[48] Ibid., Article 2.

[49] Ibid., Article 11(3).

[50] Ibid., Article 22.

[51] Articles 305 et seq. of the Senegalese Code of Criminal Procedure.

[52] Ibid., Articles 298 et seq.

[53] Ibid., Articles 291 et seq. and 305 et seq.

[54] Ibid., Articles 23 et seq.

[55] Ibid., Article 23(2).

[56] Ibid., Article 11(3).

[57] Ibid., Article 367-6.

[58] Ibid., Article 25(1).

- Procedural error;
- An error concerning a material question of law invalidating the decision, including an error relating to the Chambers' exercise of jurisdiction;
- An error of fact which has occasioned a miscarriage of justice.

The judgments rendered by the Appeals Chamber are final and unappealable,[59] as compared to normal criminal cases falling under the Senegalese Code of Criminal Procedure, which may be appealed to the *Cour de Cassation*.

8.3 The Extraordinary African Chambers: An Alternative to the International Criminal Court?

Before addressing the current debate on relations between Africa and the International Criminal Court with regard to the ongoing proceedings against certain Heads of State on the continent, it is useful to stress the key distinction between international crimes committed before and after the entry into force of the Treaty of Rome, as well as crimes committed in states which are Party to the Rome Statute as opposed to those which are not.

8.3.1 International Crimes Committed Before the Entry into Force of the Rome Statute: The Example of the Extraordinary African Chambers and Their International Legitimacy

There is a difference between an international criminal tribunal and an *internationalized* tribunal. An *international criminal tribunal* is created by the Security Council under Chapter VII of the UN Charter. Examples include the ICTY[60] and the ICTR.[61] The second type, *an internationalized tribunal*, includes special or hybrid courts. These tribunals may be created by an agreement between a State or States and the United Nations, and are part of national judicial systems, while integrating international norms into their structure and set-up.[62]

---

[59] Ibid., Article 25(4).

[60] United Nations Security Council, Resolution 827 (1993), 25 May, 1993, S/RES/827 (1993).

[61] United Nations Security Council, Resolution 955 (1994), 8 November, 1994, S/RES/955 (1994).

[62] This is the case, for example, for the Extraordinary Chambers in the Courts of Cambodia, established as part of an agreement between Cambodia and the United Nations, or the Special Court for Sierra Leone, which was set up by the government of Sierra Leone and the United Nations.

The authority of the African Union to create an ad hoc tribunal finds its legal basis in the Constitutive Act of the African Union and customary international law.

8.3.1.1 The Constitutive Act of the African Union

As has been underscored by the Group of African Experts, the authority of the African Union to create special courts is derived from the power of the Assembly as defined in Articles 3(h), 4(h)&(o), 9(1)(d) and 5(1)(d) of the Constitutive Act of the African Union.[63] The Extraordinary African Chambers constitute the first internationalized tribunal ever established by agreement between the African Union and an AU Member State.

It is thus that on 1 and 2 July 2006, the Assembly of Heads of State and Government of the African Union mandated the Republic of Senegal to prosecute and ensure that *Hissène Habré* is tried on behalf of Africa by a competent Senegalese court with guarantees for fair trial.[64] By the decision of the Assembly/AU/DEC.401(XVII) adopted on 31 January 2012, the Assembly of Heads of State and Government requested the Commission of the African Union and the Republic of Senegal to consider the practical modalities as well as the legal and financial implications of the prosecution of international crimes committed on the territory of Chad during the period from 7 June 1982 to 1 December 1990.[65] On 22 August 2012, Senegal and the African Union, represented by the President of the Commission, signed an agreement creating the Extraordinary African Chambers within the courts of Senegal.

8.3.1.2 Customary International Law

As was noted by the Court of Justice of the Economic Community of West African States (ECOWAS) in its ruling of 18 November 2010 in the case of *Hissène Habré v. Senegal* (No. ECW/CC/JUD06/10),[66]

> the implementation of the mandate of the African Union should follow the international practice which has become customary in such situations to create ad hoc or special courts. The phrase '[…] jurisdiction' contained in this term means nothing other than the establishment of a judicial ad hoc creation and powers find their low relief in the provisions of Article 15.2 of the International Covenant on Civil and Political Rights and that

[63] Constitutive Act of the African Union adopted by the 36th ordinary session of the Assembly of Heads of State and Government in Lomé, Togo, 11 July, 2000, http://www.africa-union.org/root/au/aboutau/constitutive_act_en.htm.

[64] Assembly of Heads of States of the African Union 2006.

[65] Assembly of Heads of States of the African Union 2012, p. 20 (in French).

[66] *Hissène Habré v. République du Sénégal*, ECOWAS Court of Justice, 18 November 2010, para 58 (in French).

> Senegal is responsible for proposing the principal forms and modalities of implementation of such a structure.

In its most recent ruling of 5 November 2013 in a case between the same parties (No. ECW/CCJ/RUL/05/13) the ECOWAS Court of Justice[67] pointed out as follows:

> The Extraordinary African Chambers, even if they were created within the courts of Senegal, do not thereby have any less of an international character due on the one hand to the manner in which they were created (by international agreement) and on the other hand, to their rules and regulations (the Statute of the Chambers), which differ from those applied in the national courts of Senegal; that the existence on a national territory; that the location of the Chambers in a national territory (in this case, Senegal) and the make up of these chambers- at least in part- of national judges (here, Senegalese) does not in any way detract from the international character of these chambers.

The Court then goes on to conclude that: "the agreement that created the Extraordinary African Chambers and their special rules as laid out in the Statute give the Chambers an international character".[68]

As discussed, the AU's authority to create special courts is derived from international custom and the Constitutive Act of the African Union which reject impunity. This principle must form the basis of the African Union's political will to move toward more prosecutions by Africa of international crimes committed by nationals of the respective African countries, no matter their rank or status within the State apparatus.

8.3.2 International Crimes Committed After the Entry into Force of Rome Statute

8.3.2.1 Crimes Committed in States that Are Not Parties or Signatories to the Rome Statute

In the name of the fight against impunity and the protection of human rights, the African Union can find a legitimate means of becoming involved in the prosecution of serious violations of international law which are ongoing in one of its Member States.

The African Union could issue a Resolution calling on the State to institute criminal proceedings or to have the African Union launch legal proceedings through the creation of an external ad hoc court or a court created with the cooperation of the State at issue.

---

[67] *Hissène Habré v. République du Sénégal*, ECOWAS Court of Justice, 5 November 2013, para 47.

[68] Idem.

8.3.2.2 Crimes Committed in States Parties to the Rome Statute

The Preamble to the Rome Statute clearly states that it is the duty of every State to exercise its criminal jurisdiction over those responsible for international crimes. It also underscores that the International Criminal Court is *complementary* to national criminal jurisdictions.[69]

In light of the principle of *pacta sunt servanda,* States Parties must respect the obligations arising from their international commitments under the treaties they have signed and ratified. Even if the Rome Statute allows for withdrawal, such withdrawal only comes into force after one year and has no suspensive effect on proceedings which have already commenced.[70]

If the UN Security Council implements Article 16 of the Rome Statute as the African Union has requested, then it must only do so if it is necessary for the protection of the national security of the States and only if it is severely threatened by proceedings initiated by the International Criminal Court. Article 16 must be used only very rarely and when certain objective criteria are met so that it does not become an open door to impunity and set risky judicial precedents.

Another possible alternative to prosecution of African leaders by the International Criminal Court would be to expand the jurisdiction of the Court of Justice of the African Union so that it could prosecute international crimes itself. However, this would involve the revision and modification of fundamental instruments regarding the setup and structure of the Court so that a special criminal chamber could be established. While such an endeavor would require a permanent budget and staff, temporary ad hoc courts might provide a more economical alternative for countries whose budgets are already very tight and already have trouble paying their dues.

8.4 Conclusion

The recent outcry among certain Member States of the African Union arises within the context of the 'Kenyan affair'. Access to power is an insufficient ground for exoneration or the suspension of proceedings by the International Criminal Court. Any procedure commenced and pending before the Court must proceed in accordance with the Rome Statute, unless Article 16 is applied by the UN Security Council.

For international crimes committed in States which are parties to the Rome Statute and for which no proceedings have begun, the African Union should act prior to any action by the International Criminal Court. The African Union must encourage such States to respect their obligations under the Rome State to exercise criminal jurisdiction over those responsible for the crimes. Only in the case of failure should the Court's complementary jurisdiction be applied.

---

[69] Rome Statute of the International Criminal Court, Preamble (10).

[70] Ibid., Article 127.

References

Cases

Belgium v. Senegal, ICJ, Judgment of 20 July 2012 (Questions Relating to the Obligation to Prosecute or Extradite), ICJ Reports 2012, pp 422 et seq.

Hissène Habré v. République du Sénégal, ECOWAS Court of Justice, 18 November 2010, ECW/CCJ/JUD/06/10. http://www.hrw.org/fr/news/2010/11/18/arr-t-cedeaoecowas-ruling-hissein-habr-c-r-publique-du-s-n-gal.

Hissène Habré v. République du Sénégal, ECOWAS Court of Justice, 5 November 2013, ECW/CCJ/RUL/05/13. http://www.courtecowas.org/site2012/pdf_files/decisions/judgements/2013/HISSEIN%20HABRE_c_REPUBLIC_OF_SENEGAL2013.pdf.

Documents

Assembly of Heads of States of the African Union, July 1 &2, 2006, ASSEMBLY/AU/Dec. 127(VII). http://www.hrw.org/en/news/2006/08/02/decision-hiss-ne-habr-case-and-african-union.

Human Rights Watch 2012, Senegal: New Court to Try Chad Ex-Dictator in Senegal (22 August 2012). http://www.hrw.org/news/2012/08/22/senegal-new-court-try-chad-ex-dictator-senegal.

Human Rights Watch (2013a), Sénégal: Hissène Habré inculpé, 2 July 2013. http://www.hrw.org/fr/news/2013/07/02/senegal-hissene-habre-inculpe.

Human Rights Watch (2013b), "La Plaine des Morts", published in December 2013. http://www.hrw.org/sites/default/files/reports/chad1013frwebwcover_0.pdf.

Interpellation de Habré from the Extraordinary African Chambers, 13 August 2013. http://www.chambresafricaines.org/index.php/le-coin-des-medias/communiqu%C3%A9-de-presse/511-interpellation-de-habr%C3%A9.html.

Chapter 9
The Nigerian 'Jos Crisis' from the Perspective of International Criminal Law

Temitayo Lucia Akinmuwagun and Moritz Vormbaum

Contents

This chapter is based on a study by Ms. *Akinmuwagun* conducted at the South African-German Centre for Transnational Criminal Justice (University of the Western Cape, South Africa). The authors would like to thank the Directors of the Centre, Professor *Fernandez* and Professor *Werle*, for their guidance and useful comments.

T.L. Akinmuwagun (✉)
Federal Ministry of Justice, Abuja, Nigeria
e-mail: luciatee@yahoo.co.uk

M. Vormbaum
Humboldt Universität zu Berlin, Berlin, Gemany
e-mail: moritz.vormbaum@rewi.hu-berlin.de

G. Werle et al. (eds.), *Africa and the International Criminal Court*,
International Criminal Justice Series 1, DOI 10.1007/978-94-6265-029-9_9

9.1 Factual Background to the 'Jos Crisis'

9.1.1 The Violence in the Jos Area

In recent years, Nigeria has been in the headlines for repeated acts of violence and terrorism committed on its territory and leading to the deaths of thousands of people.[1] The geographical center of these attacks is Jos, the capital city of Plateau State, situated in North-Central Nigeria. The term 'Jos crisis', therefore, refers to the series of attacks that has taken place there.[2]

In this region tensions have existed for over a century between the local ethnic groups, namely, the *Berom*, *Anaguta* and *Afizere* ethnic groups, on the one hand, and the *Hausa/Fulani* ethnic groups,[3] on the other hand. Despite the fact that the conflict in the Jos area has a long history, the situation has not been one of continuous strife. However, in 1994 a major outbreak of violence occurred; between 2001 and 2008 the violence was sporadic; since 2010 it has increased again. The incidents of brute force entail gross violations of human rights such as mass-murders, bombings, arson, looting and the destruction of public and private property. Victims, including children, women and the aged, have been hacked to death, burned alive or murdered in a chain of cruel and indiscriminate killings. Others have "disappeared", never to be found.[4] The organized manner in which most of these attacks were executed indicates that they were well-planned and sponsored.[5]

Records show that the alleged crimes were perpetrated repeatedly, resulting in the deaths of several thousands in the last few years. The figures range between 3,800 and 10,000 deaths, depending on the time frame used by authors and

---

[1] For a summary of the violence in Nigeria see Amnesty International 2013, pp. 196 et seq. See also International Criminal Court Report on Situation in Nigeria, 5 August 2013, pp. 5, 10.

[2] Theoretically, one could speak also of 'Jos-*violence*' or 'Jos-*conflict*', terms that would probably capture the situation in Jos even better. However, the most common description in Nigeria has been 'Jos crisis'. Therefore, this article will use this terminology. The term does not include a strict geographical ambit, but also refers to the violence which occurred in the neighboring towns and villages to the city of Jos.

[3] The *Hausa* and the *Fulani* are two distinct ethnic groups, but are mostly associated together because they share culture and religion and are the two dominant ethnic groups in North-West and North-East Nigeria. They constitute other groups such as the *Jasawa* and the "*Miyetti* Cattle Rearers Associations".

[4] See e.g. Human Rights Watch 2011. See also the Government of Nigeria's "Whitepaper [sic] on the Report of the Commission of Inquiry into the Riots of 12 April 1994 in Jos Metropolis" (Fiberesima Report), 2004, pp. 7 et seq.; the "White Paper on the Report of the Judicial Commission of Inquiry into the Civil Disturbances in Jos and its Environs" (Niki Tobi Report), 2002; as well as "The Report of the Commission of Inquiry into the Unrest of 28th November 2008 in Jos North Local Government area of Plateau State" (Ajibola Report), 2009, pp. 25 et seq.

[5] See Human Rights Watch 2005, pp. 6 et seq.

experts.[6] Groups other than those mentioned above, including the *Yorubas*, *Igbos* and people from the Niger-Delta region, have also become involved in the conflict and have suffered serious losses. From available statistics, by the end of 2011, 630 *Yoruba*, 604 *Igbo* and 430 Niger-Delta people had lost their lives to the violence.[7] Thousands of people have been wounded and hundreds of thousands have been displaced. In addition, it has been estimated that public and private properties worth about 180 billion Nairas (over one billion USD) have been destroyed in the course of the conflict.[8]

Although there has been no major outbreak of violence in recent years, the systematic killing of civilians by armed groups is far from over in Jos.[9] This is especially true since *Boko Haram*, an Islamist terrorist group in Northern Nigeria, has become involved prominently in the conflict. *Boko Haram* has claimed responsibility for numerous attacks in Jos which have resulted in the death of hundreds of people.[10]

It comes, therefore, as no surprise that the Jos crisis has been described by a Nigerian politician as having caused more damage to the country than the bloody Biafra War in the late 1960s.[11]

9.1.2 Reasons for the Conflict

The recurrent violence in Jos is attributable to a number of immediate and remote, direct and indirect causes, chief among which are the dispute over the ownership of Jos and the issue of "indigenship". The latter has manifested itself in a long-standing communal suspicion, distrust and bitterness among the original inhabitants and the *Hausa/Fulani* community in Jos.[12] Although not addressed expressly in the 1999 Constitution of Nigeria, the divide between "indigene" and

---

[6] See International Crisis Group 2012, p. 2; Kalu 2011; Higazi 2011, pp. 18, 23. See also Danfulani 2006, p. 3.

[7] See Kalu 2011.

[8] International Crisis Group 2012, p. 2.

[9] To give some examples of the current violent attacks in Jos as reflected in the Nigerian media: An attack by persons alleged to be *Fulani* herdsmen carried out on 30 March 2013 led to the death of 19 persons and led 4,500 persons to flee their homes, available at http://news.naij.com/29736.html (all internet sources cited in this chapter were accessed on 20 March 2014). Clashes between *Tarok* Christians and *Hausa/Fulani* Muslims resulted in the death of 11 persons, see Niger Reporters, 7 April 2013 http://www.nigerreporters.com/nigeria-11-killed-in-tarok-village-attacks. Between 15 and 19 April 2013, over 17 persons were killed in Riyom and Barkin Ladi Local Government, Area of Plateau State, see Adinoyi, This Day, 19 April 2013, available at http://allafrica.com/stories/201304200130.html. The list of incidents could be easily amended.

[10] International Crisis Group 2012, pp. 13 et seq.; Williams 2013.

[11] Article available at http://thenationonlineng.net/new/jos-crisis-worse-than-biafra-war-says-senator.

[12] See Solomon Lar Report 2010, p. 2.

"non-indigene" is embedded in the policy and administration of virtually every Federal State in Nigeria. It is a source of discrimination which determines distribution of a State's resources, including political appointments, elections to office, job opportunities, awarding of scholarships and, most importantly, the allocation of land at the local and community level in a State.[13] The indigenes of a State invariably are the primary beneficiaries of its limited resources, thus making indigenship a covetous status.[14] Notwithstanding their claims, the *Hausa/Fulani* groups thus far have not been awarded indigenship status in Jos. Instead, ownership and indigenship of Jos have been assigned to the *Berom*, *Anaguta*, and *Afizere* ethnic groups exclusively.[15] This inequity has caused distrust and rivalry between the ethnic groups, sparking violent attacks and counter-attacks.

The ethnic struggle has been magnified by religious differences amongst the inhabitants of the Jos area, as the *Berom*, *Anaguta*, and *Afizere* groups are Christians, whereas the *Hausa/Fulani* are mostly Muslims.[16] Religion also constitutes the background to the involvement of *Boko Haram* in the conflict. Claiming vengeance for the death of its *Hausa/Fulani* Muslim brothers who were killed in the crisis, it has carried out series of suicide bomb attacks in Jos, killing and injuring many. This, in turn, has led to further clashes between indigene Christians and *Hausa/Fulani* Muslims.

9.2 Nigeria's Reactions to the Jos Crisis

The Nigerian Federal Government and the Government of Plateau State, where Jos is located, have responded by setting up several commissions of inquiry, panels and committees to investigate the causes of the violence, to identify the persons responsible for the crimes, and to make recommendations to help prevent future violence.[17] These include:

- The Commission of Inquiry into the Riots of 12th April 1994 in Jos Metropolis (*Fiberesima* Commission);
- The Judicial Commission of Inquiry into the Civil Disturbances in Jos and its Environs, 2001 (*Niki Tobi* Commission);
- The Plateau Peace Conference (18 August–21 September 2004);

[13] Section 25(1) of the Constitution of the Federal Republic of Nigeria of 1999, provides for indigenship as condition for citizenship by birth if a person was born before independence, and Section 143 makes indigenship a condition for appointment as Minister of a State. See also Human Rights Watch 2010, p. 2, International Crisis Group 2012, p. 7.

[14] Krause 2011, p. 25.

[15] Solomon Lar Report 2010, p. 2.

[16] Ajibola Report 2009, p. 33.

[17] See Ajibola Report 2009; Fiberesima Report 2004; Niki Tobi Report 2002; and Solomon Lar Report 2010; as well as the Report of the Plateau Peace Conference 2004.

- The Commission of Inquiry into the Unrest of 28 November 2008 in Jos North Local Government Area of Plateau State (*Ajibola* Commission); and
- The Presidential Advisory Committee on Jos Crisis, 2010 (*Solomon Lar* Advisory Committee).

However, these bodies have also ascribed the ownership and indigenship of Jos to the *Berom*, *Anaguta*, and *Afizere* ethnic groups only, excluding the *Hausa/Fulani* groups.[18] This discriminatory attitude has fuelled the fire of the conflict.

Another response by the Federal Government was the deployment of the Special Task Force[19] to step in whenever there was another outbreak of violence. However, it is evident that these measures have not succeeded in putting an end to the conflict.[20] To the contrary, it has been reported that state forces have also committed crimes against the population.[21]

With regard to prosecution, the Office of the Attorney General of the Federation charged more than 600 persons in connection with the violence that occurred in Jos in January 2010. Of these, 74 were convicted by the Federal High Court for terrorism under Section 15(2) of the Economic and Financial Crimes Act,[22] conspiracy and unlawful possession of firearms under the Firearms Act. Seventeen appealed the judgment but the Court of Appeal upheld the decision of the lower court. More than 100 accused were discharged and acquitted for lack of sufficient evidence. The remaining cases are still on-going.[23]

Although the Nigerian authorities have expended at least some effort to bring to book the perpetrators of the crisis, it has to be noted that no prosecutions have been initiated by the Federal Prosecutors in respect of the numerous violent attacks committed in Jos subsequent to 2010. Sporadically, persons have been tried before the Plateau State High Court in respect of the Jos violence by State Prosecutors for crimes such as murder or causing grievous hurt. However, in these trials grave atrocities committed on a large scale in the protracted Jos crisis did not play a role. Hence, the main perpetrators have still largely not been brought to justice. Therefore, there remain urgent demands from part of the population and NGOs for more to be done in this regard.[24] *Human Rights Watch*, for example, in 2013 came to the conclusion that "[w]ith the exception of a series of successful prosecutions by the

[18] Solomon Lar Report 2010, p. 2.

[19] The Special Task Force is composed of the best trained units in the Nigerian security forces, to which the Central Government has entrusted the task of restoring law and order in Jos and parts of Northern Nigeria. It has been present in Jos since 2010.

[20] See for the statements on the need of the international community to act with regard to the Jos crisis: Nigerian Coalition of the International Criminal Court, Newsletter, vol. 2, 2011, 22.

[21] Amnesty International 2013, p. 197; International Crisis Group 2012, pp. 21 et seq.; Office of the Prosecutor 2013, p. 19.

[22] See Act No. 1, 2004.

[23] These figures are based on information supplied by the Office of the Director of Public Prosecution of Nigeria (letter dated 4 November 2013, Ref: SGF/PS/NHRC/180/T).

[24] See Human Rights Watch 2010a, pp. 2 et seq.; International Crisis Group 2012, p. 21.

federal authorities, following the 2010 violence in Plateau State, those responsible for organizing or carrying out these killings have not been brought to justice".[25]

It came, therefore, as no surprise that the issue of whether international crimes have been committed in Jos was brought to the attention of the Prosecutor of the International Criminal Court by a coalition of NGOs in Nigeria.[26] Nigeria ratified the Rome Statute on 27 September 2001, although it is yet to domesticate it. Consequently, the International Criminal Court has complementary jurisdiction over international crimes committed in Nigeria after 1 July 2002. The situation is currently under preliminary observation by the Office of the Prosecutor.[27] However, the investigation is not restricted to the Jos crisis but extends to other violent incidents which have occurred in the country.

9.3 Legal Analysis of the Violence in Jos

In its reports on the situation in Nigeria published thus far, the Office of the Prosecutor of the International Criminal Court came to the conclusion that there is a reasonable basis to believe that crimes under international law were committed in Jos, but considering only acts of *Boko Haram* as possible crimes under the jurisdiction of the International Criminal Court.[28] However, the Prosecutor also stressed that the investigations were still at an early stage and that the current view might change in the light of new evidence emerging. The following sections seek to analyze, on the basis of the facts available, whether the violent attacks in Jos, including those not committed by *Boko Haram*, can be considered crimes under international law.[29]

9.3.1 Genocide

9.3.1.1 Protected Groups

As the groups involved in the violence in Jos can be distinguished by ethnicity and religion, one may ask legitimately whether the attacks committed against the members of certain groups amount to genocide.[30] Protected groups under

---

[25] Human Rights Watch 2013, p. 2.

[26] On the submission of the Jos situation to the International Criminal Court, see International Coalition for the Responsibility to Protect 2010.

[27] See Office of the Prosecutor 2013.

[28] Office of the Prosecutor 2013, pp. 20, 22 et seq.

[29] In determining this, the violence committed before the entering into force of the ICC Statute (1 July 2002) shall be excluded from the discussion.

[30] The Office of the Prosecutor, however, does not seem to consider this crime. At least the Office of the Prosecutor does not mention the crime of genocide in its reports which have so far been published.

international criminal law are national, ethnic, racial or religious groups as they are stable groups, membership of which is involuntary and permanent.[31] Emphasis is placed on the protection of the group's existence because an individual is attacked on the basis of his or her membership of the group.

The victims in the Jos conflict, who are Jos indigenes and settlers from other States, as well as the *Hausas/Fulanis*, are members of recognized ethnic groups in Nigeria. They can be classified equally by religion into Christians and Muslims, thereby fulfilling the definitional requirement of a positive group. However, the targeted groups in the Jos crisis consist of various ethnic groups, so that a clear identification of the victims as a single group under attack is impossible. As stated above, not only the indigenes of Jos but also settler groups such as the *Igbos*, *Yorubas* and *Urhobos* were subject to attacks. The *Hausa/Fulani* are, strictly speaking, two distinct ethnic groups. The fact that the victims in the Jos crisis stem from a range of different ethnic groups leads to the question whether, in a case where a number of different ethnic groups are involved in a violent conflict, an attack by one group on another may amount to genocide.

In this regard, it is accepted widely that a negative definition of a target group, that is, any group other than the group perpetrating the attack, is not acceptable.[32] As was held by the Yugoslavia Tribunal in the *Stakić* case,[33] a group consisting of all groups which the perpetrator does not consider to be a part of his or her own defined group cannot constitute a protected group in terms of the crime of genocide. The Tribunal stated that, unlike positive groups, "negatively defined groups have no unique distinguishing characteristics that could be destroyed".[34]

In the Jos situation one could argue, especially since the involvement of *Boko Haram*, that there are indeed two religious factions constituting two distinct groups of Christians and Muslims who are trying to eliminate each other. However, the fact that the *Hausa/Fulani* Muslims often have included the indigene Muslims and other Muslim settlers in their attacks on Christians[35] has blurred the distinction between Muslim and Christian groups.

Despite these general arguments against the existence of a protected group, an analysis on a case-by-case basis shows that some incidents indeed allow for the presumption that certain groups were attacked on the basis of their ethnicity and religion. One can mention, for instance, the attack by *Fulani* herdsmen on the village of Dogo Nahauwa. This attack was carried out on 7 March 2010 and resulted in the death of more than 300 persons; it virtually wiped out the entire village.[36] It was reported that the victims were targeted on the basis of their

---

31 *Prosecutor v. Jelisić*, Judgment, 14 December 1999, para 69; Cassese 2008, p. 130.

32 See e.g. Schabas 2009, p. 131, Werle 2009, marg no 707.

33 *Prosecutor v. Stakić*, Judgment, 22 March 2006, paras 16–28.

34 *Prosecutor v. Stakić*, Judgment, 22 March 2006, para 23. See also Cryer et al. 2010, p. 213.

35 See Ajibola Report 2009. The indigenes have allegedly also killed fellow indigenes of the same ethnicity because of their faith see Human Rights Watch 2005, p. 10.

36 See Human Rights Watch 2010b, pp. 1 et seq.

ethnicity (*Beroms*) as well as their Christian faith.[37] Therefore, they constituted a protected group which may be an object of genocide.

9.3.1.2 Genocidal Intent

Although there have been incidents in the Jos crisis in which the *actus reus* of genocide was fulfilled, in these cases the existence of specific intent is questionable. For genocidal intent the perpetrator must have aimed for the destruction of the group in whole or in part.[38]

In general, the Jos killings have been largely retaliatory. The indigenes, in particular, often have been provoked into violence by their people being killed by *Hausa/Fulani* Muslims. In addition, the killings were perpetrated with a desire to gain dominance over the opposing group. Therefore, the indigenes intended primarily to *expel* the *Hausa/Fulanis* from the Jos area rather than to *exterminate* them. This is evident in the several attempts to displace the rival groups forcibly from their communities by burning their houses and cattle during outbreaks of violence and chasing them out of their villages. Similarly, violent attacks by the *Hausa/Fulanis* have been motivated largely by revenge and envy, and they followed the same pattern.[39] In this regard, what the 2004 UN Commission of Inquiry into the Darfur Situation stated is valid also for the Jos situation:

> [T]he policy of attacking, killing and forcibly displacing members of some tribes does not evince a specific intent to annihilate, in whole or in part, a group distinguished on racial, ethnic, national or religious grounds. Rather, it would seem that those who planned and organized attacks on villages pursued the intent to drive the victims from their homes, primarily for purposes of counter-insurgency warfare.[40]

Hence, the killings that have taken place in the Jos crisis can be described generally as cases of (attempted) "ethnic cleansing", which has been defined as "a purposeful policy designed by one ethnic group to remove by violent and terror-inspiring means the civilian population of another ethnic or religious group from certain geographic areas".[41]

The question remains whether, in cases like the raid of the Dogo Nahauwa village in which the *actus reus* of genocide was fulfilled, the motivation of the perpetrators was different and had, indeed, the character of genocidal intent. It is

37 Kalu 2011; Duffield 2010.

38 Werle 2009, marg no 760.

39 See Higazi 2011, p. 29.

40 International Commission of Inquiry on Darfur 2005, para 518.

41 Commission of Experts to Investigate Violations of International Humanitarian Law in the Former Yugoslavia 1992, para 130. See also May, 2005, p. 117. The International Court of Justice also distinguished between killing with intent to remove a group from a region and killing with intent to destroy the group in whole or in part, holding that the former constitutes "ethnic cleansing", Bosnia and Herzegovina v. Srebrenica and Montenegro, Judgment, 26 February 2007, pp. 43–240, para 190.

accepted generally that a case of "ethnic cleansing" (which is, in fact, not a legal term) in certain constellations can amount to genocide.[42] However, in the Jos situation there is no evidence that the motivation of the perpetrators might have changed during the crisis, even when it became more deadly and escalated. On the contrary, it has been said that the attack on the Dogo Nahauwa village was driven by "retaliation for the killing of *Fulani* men, women, and children and their cattle in Beron areas in January 2010" as well as by "pre-existing grievances".[43]

9.3.1.3 Conclusion

The acts committed during the Jos crisis do not amount to genocide. This conclusion is supported by the fact that the opposing groups lived together and tolerated one another for periods of peace which occurred between the violence. Therefore, the situation in Jos differs considerably from other ethnic conflicts where genocide has been proved. For example, in Rwanda there was no instance in which both groups lived and related together, then killed one another only to live in peace for a while before resuming the killings.

9.3.2 *Crimes Against Humanity*

As regards crimes against humanity, the main questions center on the issues whether there were "attacks" committed in Jos which have been "widespread" or "systematic" as well as pursuant to or in furtherance of a "State or organizational policy".

9.3.2.1 Attack

An "attack" requires the multiple commission of acts as mentioned in Article 7 of the ICC Statute.[44] It is out of question that acts committed during the Jos crisis fulfilled the requirements of Article 7. From the facts available, acts such as "murder", "extermination", "rape", "enforced disappearance" and "other inhumane acts"[45] were committed in many instances. However, one may ask whether the acts committed by a conflict party constituted only one "attack" that spread over several years or rather many single "attacks". In its report the Office of the

---

[42] See Cassese 2008, pp. 134 et seq.; Gaeta 2009, pp. 103 et seq.; Werle 2009, marg nos 741 et seq.

[43] Higazi 2011, p. 29.

[44] See also Cryer et al. 2010, p. 237; Werle 2009, marg no 801.

[45] Article 7(1)(a), (b), (g), (i), (k) of the ICC Statute.

Prosecutor, although not discussing the issue in detail, speaks of a number of different "attacks", considering as one attack, for example, the bombing of a Christian church or the raid of a village.[46] This view is reasonable. As there have been longer peaceful periods between the violent outbreaks, it would be difficult (although not impossible) to establish that there was only one single attack upon each ethnic or religious group during the Jos crisis.

9.3.2.2 The Nature of the Attacks

A crucial threshold for crimes against humanity is that the "attack on a civilian population", according to Article 7(2)(a) of the ICC Statute, must be "widespread or systematic". The ICC Statute defines an attack as the "multiple commissions of any of the individual acts pursuant to a State or organisational policy to commit such an attack". "Widespread", on the one hand, refers to "the large scale nature of the attack, which should be massive, frequent, carried out collectively with considerable seriousness and directed against a multiplicity of victims".[47] It may also be determined by its spread over a large geographical area.[48] A "systematic" attack is, on the other hand, an organized attack following a regular pattern in execution of a common plan.[49]

If "widespread" is measured quantitatively, the recurrent attacks in Jos since 2002 were certainly widespread in terms of the number of victims: rural fighting which took place between 2002 and 2004 claimed the lives of about 2,000 people; further attacks resulted in the deaths of at least 800 people in 2004, some 781 in 2008, and more than 1,000 in 2010.[50] However, the violence can be regarded also as being "widespread" in that it often covered an extensive geographical area. Militia groups from *Hausa/Fulani* and the different indigenes groups reportedly attacked and destroyed in excess of 100 villages by 2004.[51] The attacks in 2008 began in the Ali Kazaure area of Jos North and soon spread to fourteen other locations in the city.[52] In January 2010 places such as Kuru Jenta, Sabon Gida

[46] Office of the Prosecutor of the ICC 2013, pp. 14 et seq.

[47] *Prosecutor v. Bemba Gombo*, Decision pursuant to Article 61(7)(a) and (b) of the Rome Statute, 10 June 2008, para 84. See also the ICTR in *Prosecutor v Akayesu*, Judgment, 2 September 1998, para 96.

[48] See Werle 2009, marg no 804.

[49] See Werle 2009, marg no 805. See also *Prosecutor v. Kordić and Ĉerkez*, Judgment, 17 December 2004, para 94; *Prosecutor v. Blagojević and Jokić*, Judgment, 17 January 2005, para 545.

[50] See Krause 2011, pp. 38 et seq.; Higazi 2011, p. 23.

[51] Krause 2011, p. 36.

[52] The names of these places affected by the violence are Rikkos, Tina Junction, Dogon Dutse, Congo Russia, Zolol Junction, Nassarawa, Bauchi Ring Road, Bauchi Road, Kwararafa Area, Zaria Road, Katako, Rock Haven, GadaBiyu and Tudun Wada. See Ajibola Report 2009, pp. 17, 33. For a map of the areas affected by the violence, see Krause 2011, p. 15.

Kanar, Gero, Timtim and others in Jos were destroyed almost completely; March 2010 saw the destruction of the villages of Dogo Nahauwa, Zot and Ratsat in Jos South and the killing of virtually all the villagers.[53] In 2013 clashes still occurred in various communities in Plateau State.[54]

As regards the "systematic" character of the attacks, one may have reference to their organized manner. The perpetrators were, according to *Higazi*, "generally small, highly mobile, well-armed groups with excellent local knowledge and familiarity with the bush".[55] They were said to have employed weapons such as "AK-47s, machine guns and sub-machine guns, G3 rifles, Mark 4 rifles, single- and double-barrel shotguns, pistols, obsolete firearms ('Dane guns'), and locally made guns".[56] In a report on the attack by *Hausa/Fulami* Muslims on the village of Dogo Nahauwa by *Human Rights Watch*, eye witnesses were quoted as testifying that the attackers "were dressed in camouflage like fake soldiers" with their "heads wrapped up in cloths". It is reported that the men came "with guns, ammunition, and machetes" at 3 am, surrounded the village and "started their operation simultaneously".[57] In the last several years, the nature of the attacks on the civilian population may be characterized as being more "systematic" than "widespread", as there were more selected reprisal killings of perceived members or supporters of rival groups on both sides, that is, organized attacks by *Hausa/Fulani* Muslims on Christians and *vice versa*.[58]

In its assessment, the Office of the Prosecutor has not questioned the "widespread" character of the attacks in the inter-communal violence, but has been somewhat hesitant to consider the violence in Jos as "systematic". However, in the end the Office of the Prosecutor did acknowledge that some of the attacks "have been well-coordinated and systematic in nature".[59]

The series of bomb attacks by *Boko Haram* in Jos has been, without a doubt, "widespread". The group has committed hundreds of attacks in more than 12 States in North and Central Nigeria, causing the death of more than 1,000 victims.[60] However, it seems justified to classify the attacks also as "systematic", as they were certainly well-planned and carried out in an organized manner.[61] For instance, in an attack in July 2012, in which a Senator was killed, the perpetrators were said to have been dressed in military uniform, wearing bullet-proof jackets

[53] Duffield 2010; Higazi 2011, pp. 27 et seq.; Kalu 2011; Human Rights Watch 2010b, pp. 1 et seq.

[54] For details see Amnesty International 2013, p. 198.

[55] Higazi 2008, pp. 107, 110.

[56] Krause 2011, p. 36.

[57] Human Rights Watch 2010b, p. 4.

[58] Amnesty International 2013, p. 198.

[59] Office of the Prosecutor of the ICC 2013, p. 17.

[60] See Office of the Prosecutor of the ICC 2013, p. 22.

[61] The Office of the Prosecutor's report only refers to the "widespread" manner of *Boko Haram* attacks not mentioning the "systematic" requirement. At the same it neither puts into question that the attacks were "systematic".

and carrying very sophisticated weapons; they executed the massacre with precision and expertise.[62] In addition, the choice of targets of terrorist attacks shows that they were not random but tended to be organizations that did not embrace the Islamist view of the group. Attacks were directed mostly against churches, police stations, newspapers and schools.[63]

9.3.2.3 Policy

According to Article 7(2)(a) of the ICC Statute, the attack must also be committed "in furtherance of a State or organizational policy". The "policy element" does not require proof of an elaborate political program; its aim rather is to exclude cases of sporadic acts of violence.[64] The "policy" does not necessarily have to be explicitly pronounced; it may be inferred from the circumstances and from the manner in which the acts were committed.[65]

The organized and systematic nature of the attacks in Jos proves that there exists a strategy to use violence to eject the rival groups in the area.[66] The motive behind this, as was explained above, is revenge for earlier attacks;[67] in addition, the attacks were carried out with the goal of dominating the opposing group so as to gain economic and political control of the region.[68] Therefore, it seems justifiable to speak of the existence of a "policy" which is executed through the systematic killing, wounding and displacement of members of the other groups in order to secure the upper hand in the region. As has been reported, a network has been established in Jos for this purpose "which could be convened, mobilized and armed at short notice".[69]

The policy underlying the involvement of *Boko Haram* is even more obvious. With the religious differences in the region having fuelled the violence, *Boko Haram* is exploiting the Jos crisis to pursue its Islamist goals. As the Office of Prosecutor convincingly put it, the attacks of *Boko Haram* were "committed pursuant to the policy defined at the leadership level of *Boko Haram* aiming at establishing an Islamic system of government in Nigeria".[70]

---

[62] See Bello 2012.

[63] Amnesty International 2013, p. 196.

[64] See Cassese 2008, p. 98; Werle 2009, marg no 811.

[65] See Cassese 2008, p. 8; Cryer et al. 2010, p. 240; Werle 2009, marg no 812. *Prosecutor v. Tadić*, Judgment, 7 May 1997, para 653. This position was confirmed by the International Criminal Court in *Bemba*, para 81.

[66] The Office of the Prosecutor held that the systematic manner in which some of the attacks were carried out "could be a relevant indicative factor in establishing such a policy". See Office of the Prosecutor of the ICC 2013, p. 16.

[67] According to Higazi 2011, p. 29, e.g. the attack on the Dogo Nahauwa village was driven not only by retaliation but also by "pre-existing grievances".

[68] See Ajibola Report 2009, pp. 26–28, 92, 95, 132, 151.

[69] Human Rights Watch 2005, p. 6.

[70] Office of the Prosecutor of the ICC 2013, p. 22.

9.3.2.4 Organization

According to Article 7(2)(a) of the ICC Statute the attack must be "in furtherance of a *State or organizational* policy to commit such attack" (emphasis added). The crucial question here is whether the violence in Jos can be attributed to an "organization". Such organization could be identified among the *Hausa/Fulani* Muslims,[71] the various indigenous associations[72] and the *Boko Haram* group. However, such identification depends on the attributes of the element "organization". The interpretation of this element, which is neither defined in the ICC Statute nor in the Elements of Crimes, lately has been subject to controversy.

The ICC Pre-Trial Chamber II, in the case of *Muthaura and Kenyatta*, held that the "formal nature of a group and the level of its organization should not be the defining criterion" for the "organization", but rather "a distinction should be drawn on whether a group has the capability to perform acts which infringe on basic human values".[73] Hence, "organizations not linked to a State may, for the purposes of the Statute, elaborate and carry out a policy to commit an attack against a civilian population".[74] In concluding that, in the Kenya situation, the *Mungiki* constituted an "organization", the Chamber found that it was a hierarchically structured organization which had an effective system of ensuring compliance by the members with the rules and orders imposed by higher levels of command.[75] It highlighted the characteristics of a group which may constitute an organization under Article 7(2)(a) of the ICC Statute as follows:

> (i) whether the group is under a responsible command, or has an established hierarchy; (ii) whether the group possesses, in fact, the means to carry out a widespread or systematic attack against a civilian population; (iii) whether the group exercises control over part of the territory of a State; (iv) whether the group has criminal activities against the civilian population as a primary purpose; (v) whether the group articulates, explicitly or implicitly, an intention to attack a civilian population; (vi) whether the group is part of a larger group, which fulfils some or all of the above mentioned criteria.[76]

The Court, however, stressed that these requirements should not be understood as "a rigid legal definition", and they do not "need to be exhaustively fulfilled."[77]

---

[71] Constituting groups such as the *Jasawa* and the "*Miyetti* Cattle Rearers Associations".

[72] This includes the "Plateau Youth Council", the "*Afizere* Cultural and Community Development Association", the "*Anaguta* Development Association" and the "*Berom* Elders Council", see Niki Tobi Report 2002, pp. 15 et seq.

[73] Decision pursuant to Article 15 of the Rome Statute on the authorization of an investigation into the situation in the Republic of Kenya, 31 March 2010, para 90 (hereafter Kenya Authorisation Decision); *Prosecutor v. Muthaura, Kenyatta and Ali*, Decision on the confirmation of charges, 23 January 2012, para 112 (hereafter *Muthaura and others*).

[74] Kenya Authorisation Decision, para 92.

[75] *Muthaura and others*, para 186; Kenya Authorization Decision, para 90.

[76] *Prosecutor v. William Samoei Ruto and Joshua Arap Sang*, Decision on the confirmation of charges, 23 January 2012, para 185.

[77] Ibid.

A definition which accords with the decision, although being somewhat more straight-forward, has been elaborated by *Werle and Burghardt*. On the basis of the ordinary meaning of the word "organization", and taking into account the context as well as object and purposes of the Rome Statute, the authors come to the conclusion that an organization "describes an association of persons possessing structures that make it possible, beyond a single concrete situation, to coordinate actions purposefully and attribute actions to the organization".[78]

However, in his dissenting opinion to the Kenya Authorization Decision, Judge *Kaul* posited that only an organization that has the character of a State ("State-like") could qualify as an organization under Article 7(2)(a) of the ICC Statute.[79] He stressed that international crimes had to be distinguished from human rights infractions or ordinary domestic crimes since the Court's jurisdiction was limited to grave crimes which were of the most serious concern to the international community and threatened world peace and security.[80] He concluded that, from a historical perspective, a teleological interpretation of crimes against humanity meant that only a State or a "State-like" organization could commit the crime. A "State-like organization", according to him, has to be:

> (a) a collectivity of persons; (b) which was established and acts for a common purpose; (c) over a prolonged period of time; (d) which is under responsible command or adopted a certain degree of hierarchical structure, including, as a minimum, some kind of policy level; (e) with the capacity to impose the policy on its members and to sanction them; and (f) which has the capacity and means available to attack any civilian population on a large scale.[81]

However, it has been argued that neither the ordinary meaning of the word "organization" nor a teleological nor a systematic interpretation supported such a narrow approach; rather a violation of human rights could amount to a threat to peace, security and well-being of the world without the organization being regarded as "State-like". In addition, it has been argued that the narrow concept reflected a Eurocentric view which might have been suitable for international crimes committed in the first half of the 20th century but not for many of today's conflicts in which the main characters are groups that are not "State-like" but have the means to commit massive human rights violations.[82]

The Jos crisis is, indeed, a vivid example in support of the last mentioned argument. Here, to insist in *Kaul's* requirement of a "State or State-like organization" would exclude all the groups which originally took part in the conflict and

---

[78] Werle and Burghardt 2012, p. 1166.

[79] Dissenting Opinion by Judge *Hans-Peter Kaul* to Kenya Authorization Decision, paras 65–67. Affirmed in the decisions in the Kenya situation thereafter.

[80] He referred to Articles 1(1), 5(1) and to preambles 4 and 5 of the ICC Statute to support his position.

[81] Kenya Authorization Decision, Dissenting Opinion, para 51. According to *Kaul*, these qualities must be cumulative. See also in support of this opinion Kress 2010, p. 862.

[82] See Werle and Burghardt 2012, p. 1163, as well as Sadat 2013, pp. 369 et seq.

which are responsible for the atrocities in Jos (probably even *Boko Haram*). However, the crimes committed by the Nigerian State Forces that later entered in the conflict could be considered as possible crimes against humanity on this basis as their violent acts (e.g. torture or killings of alleged terrorists) could be attributed to the Nigerian State.[83] Of course, it would be laudable in principle for the Court to consider also crimes that can be attributed to the Nigerian State as possible crimes against humanity (which the Prosecutor did indeed consider in the latest report[84]). However, it would not be consonant with the principle that the International Criminal Court should investigate "the most serious crimes of concern to the international community" (Preamble of the ICC Statute) to restrict investigations in this way and to exclude the acts of the groups that have sparked the conflict and that are responsible for the most serious, as well as the majority, of the human violations in Jos.

9.3.2.5 "Organizations" in Jos

On the basis of the majority opinion in the Kenyan Authorization Decision, there is no doubt that in the Jos crisis *Boko Haram* can be regarded as an organization within the meaning of Article 7 of the ICC Statute. *Boko Haram* is a structured Islamist group which has proved that it has the capacity and control to execute heavy attacks on the civilian population. This was confirmed by the Office of the Prosecutor, which held in its preliminary report, that the group "possesses the means to carry out a widespread and/or systematic attack, and displays internal coordination and organizational control required to that end".[85]

Boko Haram, in fact, has been responsible for a smaller number of the victims in Jos in comparison with the inter-communal violence.[86] As regards organizations other than *Boko Haram*, the Office of the Prosecutor, in its preliminary investigation, arrived at the conclusion that "the available information is insufficient to establish whether the attacks on the civilian population [...] were isolated and/or spontaneous acts of violence, or were committed pursuant to a State or organizational policy". It referred in particular to a "lack of information on alleged perpetrators"[87] and relied, *inter alia*, upon a report of *Human Rights Watch* which

[83] The commission of a number of human rights violations by the Nigerian police and security forces, in their response to the violence, in particular to the attacks by *Boko Haram*, has been criticized strongly e.g. by Amnesty International 2013, p. 197, and Human Rights Watch 2013, pp. 3 et seq.

[84] Office of the Prosecutor of the ICC 2013, pp. 19 et seq.

[85] Office of the Prosecutor of the ICC 2013, p. 7.

[86] The center of the terrorist actions of this group is the North of the country rather than the Jos area. See Human Rights Watch 2013, p. 1. In addition, in instances in which *Boko Haram* had claimed responsibility for attacks, doubts remained whether these claims were really true. See International Crisis Group 2012, p. 13.

[87] Office of the Prosecutor of the ICC 2013, p. 18.

found that "there are no formal or clearly identifiable armed groups who maintain a visible presence in the periods between the fighting".[88]

This conclusion is not convincing, especially as the Prosecutor ignored further information in the *Human Rights Watch* report which, in fact, concluded that "the pattern of the larger attacks, in particular, indicates a high level of organization, forethought and planning"; it added that claims "by sympathizers of both sides that these attacks were spontaneous lack credibility".[89] However, *Human Rights Watch* concedes that it "has proved more difficult to confirm the identity of their political sponsors—the individuals who are paying and arming these young men to attack their opponents". In other words, that there are, indeed, different "organizations" present in Jos is undeniable (the report of the Office of the Prosecutor does not actually seem to question this either). It is rather the *identification* of the groups' leaders that has proved complicated. Therefore, to conclude, as the Office of the Prosecutor has done, that there is no "reasonable basis to believe that acts were committed in furtherance of or pursuant to an organizational policy" is fallacious.

In fact, it seems that some of the main qualities that an "organization" must fulfil, as indicated in the majority opinion in the Kenya Authorization Decision, are attributable to groups in Jos, qualifying them as organizations under this heading. The "*Jasawa* Development Association", for example, constitutes and controls the regional *Hausa/Fulani* Muslim population and is the major contending group in Jos. The association and its leadership have been mentioned in the reports of the commissions of inquiry set up in 1994, 2001 and 2008, which found them responsible for some of the crimes committed during the crisis and for instigating its members to attack Christians.[90] The association is under a command and has an established hierarchy, as well as a youth agency. In addition, the "*Miyetti* Cattle Rearers Association", an association of *Fulani* herdsmen with a structured leadership, can without a doubt be regarded as an "organization". It has been involved intimately in the violence, not only suffering tremendous losses of lives and cattle deaths, but also allegedly committing several attacks on the indigenes and Christians in Jos.[91]

It seems, therefore, not unlikely that a deeper investigation could identify the organizations behind the violence in Jos. One gets the impression that the Office of the Prosecutor has shied away from this route in Jos. Obviously, the Nigerian authorities are under an obligation here and, without a doubt, could identify the organizations behind the attacks more easily than the ICC Prosecutor. Therefore, it

---

88 Human Rights Watch 2005, p. 6; Office of the Prosecutor of the ICC 2013, p. 18.

89 Human Rights Watch 2005, p. 6.

90 See Ajibola Report 2009, p. 186; Fiberesima Report 2004, p. 26; Niki Tobi Report 2002, p. 108, para 4.94.

91 These were attacks between 2002 and 2004, the March 2010 slaughter in Dogo Nahauwa, and many more recent attacks. See the entry "Soldiers raid Fulani Settlement on the Plateau" in Beegeagle's Blog, 13 July 2012, available http://beegeagle.wordpress.com/2012/07/13/soldiers-raid-fulani-settlements-on-the-plateau-not-true-say-stf/.

is encouraging at least that the Office of the Prosecutor also stated that the "initial assessment may be revisited by the Office in the light of new facts or evidence that could enable the identification of specific leaders or organizations allegedly responsible for instigating such violence or the existence of an organizational policy".[92]

Another question is whether an ethnic group *itself* may constitute an organization within the meaning of Article 7 ICC Statute. This cannot be answered generally. Rather it will depend on the hierarchical structure and how members of the ethnic group in a given territory are organized, as well as on the degree of control the group has over its members. Most ethnic groups in Nigeria have a recognized leadership consisting of kings and chiefs. An example is the *Gbong-Gwom*, who is the paramount leader of the Jos indigenes. However, he has not been implicated in the reports on the violence. Some community leaders have been arrested in connection with attacks.[93] In cases in which such structure existed, the ethnic group may qualify as an organization according to Article 7 of the ICC Statute.

9.3.2.6 Conclusion

From the foregoing arguments and from the nature of the crimes committed in the Jos crisis, one may conclude that crimes against humanity were committed. This is true not only with regard to the attacks of *Boko Haram* but also with regard to other attacks perpetrated in the course of the inter-communal violence in Jos. With regard to the latter, the persons behind the attacks still have to be identified. However, the fact that the attacks were carried out "pursuant to an organizational policy" hardly can be contested.

9.3.3 War Crimes

It is also conceivable that the parties involved in the Jos crisis committed war crimes. *Boko Haram*, for instance, declared publicly that it is "at war with Christians". Although, from a legal point of view, it is not decisive how the belligerent parties describe their own conflict, it gives reason to analyze whether the violent acts in Jos may be regarded as part of an armed conflict. The consequence of a positive answer would be that certain attacks, especially those directed against the civilian population, would amount to war crimes.

---

[92] Office of the Prosecutor of the ICC 2013, p. 6.

[93] See Adinoyi, This Day Live, 26 April 2012, available at http://www.thisdaylive.com/articles/attacks-plateau-arrests-3-community-leaders/114565/.

However, the ICC Statute does not define an armed conflict. In the *Lubanga* Judgment, Trial Chamber I of the International Criminal Court relied upon the jurisdiction of the Yugoslavia Tribunal.[94] According to the ICTY Appeals Chamber, "an armed conflict exists whenever there is a resort to armed force between States or protracted armed violence between governmental authorities and organized armed groups or between such groups within a State".[95] As there are no foreign states involved in the Jos situation, it could only be an internal armed conflict to which Article 8(2)(c) and (e) of the ICC Statute is applicable. As regards the requirements for such a conflict, reference can be made to Article 1 of Additional Protocol II to the Geneva Convention of 12 August 1949 relating to the Protection of Victims of Non-International Armed Conflicts. According to this Article the Protocol is applicable only where a conflict takes place:

> in the territory of a High Contracting Party between its armed forces and dissident armed forces or other organized armed groups which, under responsible command, exercise such control over a part of its territory as to enable them carry out sustained and concerted military operations and to implement this Protocol.

However, in the Jos crisis the conflict has not involved much "sustained and concerted military operations" between the parties in conflict. Instead, the violence in Jos has taken the form of attacks and counter attacks on the civilian population of opposing groups by militias.[96] Often, victims were attacked at night and burned alive in their homes or places of refuge,[97] or were shot, butchered or stabbed. The only major instances of violent clashes between rival groups were witnessed in 2001 and 2008.[98]

With respect to the requirement of the use of force by the government against the insurgents who are organized as a military force in possession of part of the territory, the Special Task Force indeed is present in Plateau State to control the situation, ensure peace and confront the dissidents should the need arise. However, while the Nigerian army could have been forced to engage armed perpetrators in gun-battle during major attacks in a bid to curb the violence, there have not been any reported cases of confrontations between the attackers and the government. In addition, none of the rival groups has possession of any part of the territory.

Although it has been argued that these conditions are not indispensable in determining whether an armed conflict is being waged,[99] at least the existence of organized armed groups engaged in intense fighting is necessary.[100] As held, for instance, by the Rwanda Tribunal, "the term, armed conflict in itself suggests the

---

[94] See *Prosecutor v. Thomas Lubanga Dyilo*, Judgment pursuant to Article 74 of the Statute, 14 March 2012, paras 533 et seq.

[95] *Prosecutor v. Tadić*, Judgment, 7 May 1997, para 70.

[96] Krause 2011, pp. 38 et seq.

[97] Ajibola Report 2009, p. 131.

[98] Ibid., p. 33; Niki Tobi Report 2002, pp. 9 et seq.

[99] Dörmann 2003, pp. 386 et seq.

[100] Greenwood 2008, p. 48; Werle 2009, marg no 984.

existence of hostilities between armed forces organized to a greater or lesser extent".[101] In the Jos crisis, some of the attacks were indeed carried out, as has been described above, in an organized manner. However, it cannot be said that the groups that carried out the attacks were organized, as required, along military lines with a command structure.[102] Therefore, the report of the Prosecutor correctly comes to the conclusion that the violence in the central States of Nigeria fall under the category of "internal disturbances and tensions".[103]

9.4 Conclusion

This chapter has explored the complexity of the Jos crisis: struggle over ethnicity and land, retaliation, religious fanaticism, excessive use of violence by State Forces—all these are features of the conflict. Apart from the political task of curbing the outbreaks of violence, Nigeria faces the challenge of enforcing its prosecutorial efforts and, in this context, of disclosing which organizations are responsible for the attacks and who heads them. The chapter has shown that it is evident from the facts available that the attacks were, in fact, planned and perpetrated by organized groups which are investing many resources into achieving their objectives. Hence, there is good reason to believe that proper and sincere investigations will bring to light facts that are necessary to determine the responsible organizations and their leaders. A foundation has been laid already in the reports of the commissions of inquiry in which certain top echelons within the conflicting groups have been indicted or implicated in witnesses' testimony.[104] To focus exclusively on the *Boko Haram* attacks, as the ICC Prosecutor has done so far, seems to be the wrong way to deal with the lack of information. Especially questionable is the view of the Office of the Prosecutor that the *Boko Haram* attacks are "a context different from the inter-communal violence".[105]

There remains an urgent need to intensify the efforts to bring to book the leaders of the organizations responsible for the crimes committed in Jos. Here it is the Nigerian authorities who bear the primary obligation.

---

[101] See *Prosecutor v. Akayesu*, Judgment, 2 September 1998, para 620. On the organizational requirement see Cullen 2010, pp. 123 et seq.; La Haye 2008, p. 10; Moir 2002, pp. 36 et seq.

[102] See the requirement for an organized group by Moir 2002, p. 36. According to La Haye 2008, p. 10, other factors, e.g. the existence of headquarters or designated zones of operation, are also to be taken into account, which, however, in the Jos crisis do not exist either.

[103] Office of the Prosecutor 2013, p. 20.

[104] Niki Tobi Report 2002, p. 185. In addition, see the persons indicted in Ajibola Report 2009, pp. 187–257. Likely "organizations" have been identified above in this text.

[105] Office of the Prosecutor of the ICC 2013, p. 6.

References

Bello B (2012) Nigeria senator killed at mass burial after ethnic clash, Reuters, 8 July 2012. http://www.reuters.com/article/2012/07/08/us-nigeria-violence-idUSBRE8670J820120708

Cassese A (2008) International Criminal Law, 2nd edn. Oxford University Press, Oxford

Cryer R, Friman H, Robinson D, Wilmshurst E (2010) An introduction to International Criminal Law and Procedure, 2nd edn. Cambridge University Press, Cambridge

Cullen A (2010) The concept of non-international armed conflict in International Humanitarian Law. Cambridge University Press, Cambridge

Danfulani U (2006) The Jos Peace Conference and the indigene/settler question in Nigerian politics. Presentation paper, ASC Leiden/University of Josh. http://www.ascleiden.nl/Pdf/paper-Danfulani.pdf

Dörmann K (2003) Elements of war crimes under the Rome Statute of the International Criminal Court. Cambridge University Press, Cambridge

Duffield C (2010) Nigeria ethnic violence 'leaves hundreds dead', BBC News, 8 March 2010. http://news.bbc.co.uk/2/hi/africa/8555018.stm

Gaeta P (ed) (2009) The UN Genocide Convention. Oxford University Press, Oxford

Greenwood C (2008) Scope of application of Humanitarian Law. In: Fleck (ed), The handbook of Humanitarian Law in armed conflict, 2nd edn. Oxford University Press, Oxford, pp 44–79

Higazi A (2008) Social mobilization and collective violence: vigilantes and militias in the lowlands of Plateau State, Central Nigeria, Africa. J Int Afr Inst 78:107–135

Higazi A (2011) The Jos crisis: a recurrent Nigeria tragedy. Friedrich-Ebert-Stiftung Nigeria, Abuja

Kalu U (2011) A cycle of reprisals turns Jos into killing field, Vanguard, 31 December 2011. http://www.vanguardngr.com/2011/12/a-cycle-of-reprisals-turns-jos-into-killing-field

Krause J (2011) A deadly cycle: ethno-religious conflict in Jos, Plateau State, Nigeria, Small Arms Survey, Geneva

Kress C (2010) On the outer limits of crimes against humanity: the concept of organization within the policy requirement: some reflections on the March 2010 ICC Kenya decision. Leiden J Int Law 23:855–873

La Haye E (2008) War crimes in internal armed conflicts. Cambridge University Press, Cambridge

May L (2005) Crimes against humanity: A normative account. Cambridge University Press, Cambridge

Moir L (2002) The law of internal armed conflict. Cambridge University Press, Cambridge

Sadat LN (2013) Crimes against humanity in the modern age. Am J Int Law 107:334–377

Schabas W (2009) Genocide in International Law, 2nd edn. Cambridge University Press, Cambridge

Werle G (2009) Principles of International Criminal Law, 2nd edn. T.M.C. Asser Press, The Hague

Werle G, Burghardt B (2012) Do crimes against humanity require the participation of a state or a 'State-like' organization? J Int Crim Justice 10:1151–1170

Williams A (2013) Nigeria considers amnesty for over 2,000 deaths by terrorist group Boko Haram, PolicyMic, 19 April 2013. http://www.policymic.com/articles/36025/nigeria-considers-amnesty-for-over-2-000-deaths-by-terrorist-group-boko-haram

Cases

The Prosecutor v. Thomas Lubanga Dyilo, Judgment pursuant to Article 74 of the Statute, 14 March 2012, ICC-01/04-01/06-2842.

The Prosecutor v. Bemba Gombo, Decision pursuant to Article 61(7)(a) and (b) of the Rome Statute, 10 June 2008, ICC-01/05-01/08-15.

Decision pursuant to Art.15 of the Rome Statute on the authorization of an investigation into the situation in the Republic of Kenya, 31 March 2010, ICC-01/09-19.
The Prosecutor v. Muthaura, Kenyatta and Ali, Decision on the confirmation of charges, 23 January 2012, ICC-01/09-02/11-382.
The Prosecutor v. William Samoei Ruto and Joshua Arap Sang, Decision on the confirmation of charges, 23 January 2012, ICC-01/09-01/11-37.
The Prosecutor v. Tadić, Judgment, 7 May 1997, IT-94-1-T.
The Prosecutor v. Jelisić, Judgment, 14 December 1999, IT-95-10-T.
The Prosecutor v. Blagojević and Jokić, Judgment, 17 January 2005, IT-02-60-T.
The Prosecutor v. Kordić and Ĉerkez, Judgment, 17 December 2004, IT-95-14/2-A.
The Prosecutor v. Stakić, Judgment, 22 March 2006, IT-97-24-A.
The Prosecutor v Akayesu, Judgment, 2 September 1998, ICTR-96-4-T.
Bosnia and Herzegovina v. Srebrenica and Montenegro, Judgment, 26 February 2007, ICJ Reports 2007, pp 43-240.

Other Documents

Ajibola Report (2009) Report of the Commission of Inquiry into the Unrest of 28th November 2008 in Jos North Local Government area of Plateau State. http://www.r2knigeria.org/PDF/BolaAjibolaReportonJos.pdf.
Amnesty International (2013) Annual Country Report, pp 196–199.
Fiberesima Report (2004) Government of Nigeria's "Whitepaper on the Report of the Commission of Inquiry into the Riots of 12 April 1994 in Jos Metropolis". http://www.r2knigeria.org/PDF/FIBERESIMAWHITEPAPERREPORT.pdf.
Final Report of the Commission of Experts Established Pursuant to Security Council Resolution 780 to Investigate Violations of International Humanitarian Law in the Former Yugoslavia (1992), UN Doc. S/1994/674.
Human Rights Watch (2005) Revenge in the Name of Religion, The Cycle of Violence in Plateau and Kano State, May 2005, Vol. 17, No. 8 (A).
Human Rights Watch (2010a) Nigeria: Use Restraints in Curbing Jos Violence, 19 January 2010.
Human Rights Watch (2010b) Nigeria: Investigate Massacre, Step up Patrols, 8 March 2010.
Human Rights Watch (2011) Nigeria: New Wave of Violence Leaves 200 Dead, 27 January 2011.
Human Rights Watch (2013) Nigeria: UPR Submission March 2013, 17 October 2013.
International Coalition for the Responsibility to Protect (2010), NGO Communiqué of January 2010, Jos Crisis details Nigeria's failure to protect, 5 March 2010. http://responsibilitytoprotect.org/index.php/component/content/article/136-latest-news/2724-icrtop-new-educational-materials-global-centre-policy-brief-on-burmamyanmar-and-rtop-upcoming-events#Jos.
International Commission of Inquiry on Darfur (2005) Report to the United Nations Secretary-General (2005), Pursuant to Security Council Resolution 1564 of 18 September 2004, Geneva, 25 January 2005.
International Crisis Group (2012) Curbing Violence in Nigeria (1): The Jos Crisis, Africa Report No.196, 17 December 2012.
Niki Tobi Report (2002) White Paper on the Report of the Judicial Commission of Inquiry into the Civil Disturbances in Jos and its Environs. http://www.r2knigeria.org/PDF/NikkiTobbiReportWhitepaper.pdf.
Office of the Prosecutor of the ICC (2013) Situation in Nigeria, Article 5 Report, 5 August 2013.
Report of the Plateau Peace Conference (2004) Plateau State of Nigeria Gazette No. 2, 11 November 2004. http://www.r2knigeria.org/PDF/PlateauResolve.pdf.
Solomon Lar Report (2010) Report of the Presidential Advisory Committee on Jos Crisis Vol. II—Executive Summary. May 2010. http://www.r2knigeria.org/PDF/ExecutiveSummaryOfTheChiefSolomonLarPresidentialAdvisoryCommitteeOnTheJanuary2010JosCrisis.pdf.

Chapter 10
'On Behalf of Africa': Towards the Regionalization of Universal Jurisdiction?

Florian Jeßberger

Contents

10.1 Introduction

In November 2008, the then Rwandan Chief of Protocol and former major of the Rwandan Patriotic Front, *Rose Kabuye*, was arrested at Frankfurt International Airport. Two years prior to the arrest, the German authorities had executed an international arrest warrant issued by a French judge for *Kabuye's* alleged involvement in the assassination of former Rwandan President *Habyarimana* in a plane crash. This plane crash triggered the 1994 genocide in Rwanda. After *Kabuye* was arrested by the German authorities, she was transferred to France. There, a couple of months later, the charges against her were dropped. The '*Kabuye* affair' provoked harsh protests by the Rwandan government and led to serious tensions between France and Rwanda.[1]

[1] For more information on this affair, see Jalloh 2010, pp. 29–42; van der Wilt 2011, pp. 1061–1062; see also Beste et al. 2008.

F. Jeßberger (✉)
University of Hamburg, Hamburg, Germany
e-mail: Florian.jessberger@uni-hamburg.de

G. Werle et al. (eds.), *Africa and the International Criminal Court*,
International Criminal Justice Series 1, DOI 10.1007/978-94-6265-029-9_10

In February 2014, the Higher Regional Court of Frankfurt found the Rwandan *Onesphore Rwabukombe* guilty of aiding and abetting genocide and sentenced him to 14 years of imprisonment.[2] After a three year trial, the Court found that the former mayor of the Rwandan town of Kiziguro assisted in the killing of hundreds of Tutsi in 1994.[3] The judgment marked the preliminary end of a judicial tug of war which had kept German and Rwandan authorities busy for years. *Rwabukombe* had left for Germany in 2002 and was granted asylum in 2007. The same year, Rwanda's justice authorities issued an international arrest warrant against him and *Rwabukombe* was taken into custody by the German police. However, a German court dismissed the Rwandan extradition request and ordered his release.[4] The court based its ruling on a decision of the ICTR Trial Chamber where the referral of a case to the Republic of Rwanda was denied due to a lack of fair trial guarantees.[5] Afterwards, the German Federal Prosecutor General decided to prosecute *Rwabukombe* in Germany and indicted him in 2010 on charges of genocide and murder. *Rwabukombe's* conviction in February 2014 was based on a provision in German law which establishes universal jurisdiction for the crime of genocide.[6] In a first reaction, the Rwandan Ambassador to Germany expressed her gratitude to the German authorities and judiciary for taking over the difficult task of prosecuting *Rwabukombe*. The Ambassador also expressed her satisfaction that *génocidaires* present in Germany would not get away with it.[7] German observers commented on the trial and judgment much more critically,[8] pointing, inter alia, to the difficulties of finding reliable witnesses, and ultimately, raising the question whether there is any point at all in adjudicating offences committed thousands of kilometers away in German courts.

The two incidents, the '*Kabuye* affair' and the trial and conviction of *Onesphore Rwabukombe*, shed light on different but characteristic facets of the difficult and ambivalent relationship between Africa and Europe in the area of international criminal justice—a relationship which is not only determined by the prosecution (or non-prosecution) of 'African leaders' before European courts on the basis of

---

[2] Higher Regional Court (*Oberlandesgericht*) Frankfurt am Main, Judgment of 18 February 2014.

[3] For more information on this case, see Dehner 2014 and Johnson 2014; see also Kroker 2011.

[4] Higher Regional Court (*Oberlandesgericht*) Frankfurt am Main, Decision of 6 November 2008.

[5] *Prosecutor v. Munyakazi*, ICTR (TC), Decision of 28 May 2008; partly confirmed in *Prosecutor v. Munyakazi*, ICTR (AC), Decision of 8 October 2008. In the meantime, the ICTR as well as the European Court of Human Rights reassessed the conditions of criminal proceedings in Rwanda; today, suspects can be extradited or transferred to Rwanda, see *Prosecutor v. Uwinkindi*, ICTR (TC), Decision of 28 June 2011, paras 222–225; confirmed in *Prosecutor v. Uwinkindi*, ICTR (AC), Decision of 16 December 2011; see also *Ahorugeze v. Sweden*, ECHR, Judgment of 27 October 2011, paras 117–129.

[6] See Sections 220a and 6 No. 1 of the German Criminal Code in the applicable version (now, Sections 1 and 6 of the German Code of Crimes against International Law).

[7] See Dehner 2014.

[8] See, inter alia, Dehner 2014 and Johnson 2014 and the sources quoted there.

universal jurisdiction, but also, and perhaps even more so, by proceedings before the International Criminal Court, such as the cases against the Heads of State of Kenya and the Sudan respectively, *Kenyatta* and *Al Bashir*.

Against this background, this chapter will present some observations concerning the exercise of universal jurisdiction in an African context. To begin with, it will recapitulate, in a nutshell, a few key elements of the theory of universal jurisdiction. It will then try to identify and outline the 'African position' on universal jurisdiction. Subsequently, some observations concerning the use, the non-use, and the alleged "abuse" of universal jurisdiction shall be presented. Here, the chapter will distinguish the exercise of universal jurisdiction by African states and their courts on the one hand from the exercise of universal jurisdiction by non-African states against accused from Africa on the other. In the subsequent brief sections the chapter will indicate what the author thinks are the three latest trends in the exercise of universal jurisdiction including a novel mode of extraterritorial jurisdiction: 'regionalized' universal jurisdiction.

10.2 Different Kettle of Fish: Universal Jurisdiction and Related Issues

Surprisingly enough, a significant number of official statements addressing the prosecution of crimes under international law committed in Africa lack a nuanced understanding of the legal issues involved. Given this confusion, it may be useful to clarify what this chapter is concerned about: universal jurisdiction. This is not a modern concept. In fact, universal jurisdiction is much older than the enforcement of criminal law through international courts and tribunals; universal jurisdiction represents the most far-reaching form of (extraterritorial) jurisdiction.[9] Traditionally, the concept is based on the idea that certain acts which concern common interests of the community of states are eligible for prosecution and punishment by each of those states. Anyone of those states, the so-called third states, may then act as a trustee or agent for the international community.[10] It is safe to say today that international customary law allows for the exercise of universal jurisdiction over genocide, crimes against humanity and war crimes. These crimes are directed against the interests of the international community. Thus, not only the international community may defend itself with criminal sanctions against attacks on its elementary values, but also each individual state can—but is not obliged to—prosecute such crimes, regardless of where, by whom and against whom they have been committed.

It is less the validity of the principle as such, but the specific conditions of its exercise which are a matter of discussion. Major controversies concern the

---

[9] For more details, see Jeßberger 2009 and Werle and Jeßberger 2014, marg nos 212 et seq.

[10] On the theory of universal jurisdiction, see also Sammons 2003, pp. 125–137.

following questions: Is there any specific nexus required (other than the one established through the nature of the crime itself) linking the crime or the perpetrator to the prosecuting third state? In particular: Is the presence of the perpetrator in the forum state a prerequisite for prosecution and trial? And: Is the exercise of universal jurisdiction a mere subsidiary means of ensuring that there is no impunity? In other words: Should the territorial state and perhaps an international tribunal have priority? If so: Could or should the complementarity regime applicable under the ICC Statute be transferred to the horizontal level of the interstate relationship?[11] Who would then be competent to determine whether the state with priority has taken serious action? According to what criteria? To what extent, if at all, is the (expected) fairness of proceedings to be taken into account? And at what time should the priority principle be taken into consideration? Should it already bar investigations in a third state? While these issues are controversial indeed, it is submitted that it is possible to identify a position on the requirements of the exercise of universal jurisdiction to which a great majority of scholars and state officials, including those from Africa, could subscribe. Such a position would make the exercise of universal jurisdiction subject to the presence of the accused in the territory of the prosecuting state at least at (but not necessarily before) trial stage, and would give priority to the territorial state, as long as this state is willing and able to seriously investigate and prosecute.

As a legal concept, universal jurisdiction should not be mixed up with related issues of international criminal law, including: the International Criminal Court, the implementation of the Rome Statute into the domestic legal orders, extraterritorial jurisdiction, and the immunity of certain officials from foreign prosecution. Accordingly, in this chapter, the difficult relationship between the International Criminal Court and Africa will not be addressed.[12] Second, the issue of the incorporation of the Rome Statute into domestic legal orders shall not be addressed.[13] It is true not only that many states took the ratification of the Rome Statute as an opportunity to revise and adapt their domestic legislation, but also that this new legislation often implements or extends universal jurisdiction. Third, the prosecution of crimes under international law on bases other than universal jurisdiction shall not be addressed. This concerns territorial prosecutions but also other forms of extraterritorial jurisdiction such as jurisdiction based on the

[11] In determining whether a particular case is being or was investigated or prosecuted by a state and, therefore, whether proceedings before the International Criminal Court are generally inadmissible, the Court adopts a narrow approach and requires that the same person is investigated or prosecuted by the state's authorities for substantially the same conduct as he or she would be before the International Criminal Court ("same person, same conduct" test), see *Prosecutor v. Muthaura, Kenyatta and Hussein Ali*, ICC (AC), Judgment of 30 August 2011, paras 39–46; *Prosecutor v. Ruto, Kosgey and Sang*, ICC (AC), Judgment of 30 August 2011, paras 40–47.

[12] For discussion of this issue, see Ambos 2013; du Plessis et al. 2013; Magliveras and Naldi 2013. As is well known, the International Criminal Court in particular does not have universal jurisdiction—with the notable exception of Security Council referrals.

[13] On this topic, see Chap. 6 by *Kemp* in this book.

nationality of the offender or the victim. And finally, from a legal point of view it is useful to distinguish the ambit of domestic criminal law as a matter of substantive criminal law from the immunity of certain officials from prosecution by foreign courts.

10.3 Mixed Feelings: 'African Attitudes' Towards Universal Jurisdiction

What then are the 'African attitudes' towards universal jurisdiction? Needless to say: there is no such thing as a uniform position of Africa—different states have different positions, the official position may differ from the position of civil society and so on. However, the point of reference in the debate is usually the position as it has been voiced full-throated by the Heads of State and Government in the Assembly of the African Union.

In October 2013, on the occasion of an extraordinary summit held in Addis Ababa, the African Union once again reaffirmed its position on, what it called, "the abuse of the principle of universal jurisdiction".[14] Since 2008, the condemnation of the alleged "abuse" of universal jurisdiction has become a routine element of almost every AU meeting.[15] Then, triggered by criminal investigations against Rwandan officials in Spain on charges of genocide and crimes against humanity,[16] the Assembly had adopted the "Report of the Commission on the Abuse of the Principle of Universal Jurisdiction" and resolved that:

> The abuse of the principle of universal jurisdiction is a development that could endanger international law, order and security. The political nature and abuse of the principle of universal jurisdiction by judges from some non-African States against African leaders,

[14] Decision on Africa's Relationship with the International Criminal Court (ICC), AU Extraordinary Session, 2013 Addis Ababa, Ext/Assembly/AU/Dec. 1 (Oct. 2013), para 3. This Decision, as well as the Decisions referred to in the following footnotes, can be found in the Annex to this book.

[15] Decision on the Abuse of the Principle of Universal Jurisdiction, Doc.EX.CL/731(XXI), AU 19th session, 2012 Addis Ababa, Doc. Assembly/AU/Dec. 420 (XIX); Decision on the Abuse of the Principle of Universal Jurisdiction, Doc.EX.CL/640(XVIII), AU 16th session, 2011 Addis Ababa, Assembly/AU/ /Dec. 335 (XVI); Decision on the Abuse of the Principle of Universal Jurisdiction, Doc.EX.CL/606(XVII), AU 15th session, 2010 Kampala, Assembly/AU/Dec. 292 (XV); Decision on the Abuse of the Principle of Universal Jurisdiction, Doc.EX.CL/540(XVI), AU 14th session, 2010 Addis Ababa, Assembly/AU/Dec. 271 (XIV); Decision on the Abuse of the Principle of Universal Jurisdiction, Doc. Assembly/AU/11(XIII), AU 13th session, 2009 Sirte, Assembly/AU/Dec. 243 (XIII) Rev. 1; Decision on the Implementation of the Assembly Decision on the Abuse of the Principle of Universal Jurisdiction, DOC. Assembly/AU/3(XII), AU 12th session, 2009 Addis Ababa, Assembly/AU/Dec. 213 (XII).

[16] For a thorough discussion, see Commentator 2008.

> particularly Rwanda, is a clear violation of the sovereignty and territorial integrity of these States.[17]

This position has been, in more drastic words, endorsed by several heads or high ranking officials of individual states. For instance, the Rwandan Minister of Justice and Attorney General accused European judges of seeking to recolonialize Africa through a form of what he called a "neo-colonial judicial *coup d'etat*" under the guise of judicial independence and universal jurisdiction.[18]

Interestingly, or perhaps, irritatingly, the African Union, at the very same meeting in October 2013, encouraged its Member States to take full advantage of an "African Union Model National Law on Universal Jurisdiction over International Crimes"[19] in order to enact or strengthen their domestic legislation in this area. This Model Law, which has been drafted by a group of experts and government officials, is ambitious indeed and, surprisingly, by no way does it limit the reach of universal jurisdiction. According to Section 4(1) of the Model Law

> the court shall have jurisdiction to try any person charged with any crime prohibited under this law, regardless of whether such a crime is alleged to have been committed in the territory of the State or abroad and irrespective of the nationality of the victim, provided that such a person shall be within the territory of the State at the time of the commencement of the trial.

Furthermore, the Model Law provides for a hierarchy of jurisdictions by suggesting that priority should be given

> to the court of the State in whose territory the crime is alleged to have been committed, provided that the State is willing and able to prosecute.[20]

Remarkably, the Model Law extends this universal jurisdiction regime even beyond genocide, crimes against humanity and war crimes and includes piracy, trafficking in narcotics and terrorism.[21] Also, with regard to the immunity issue, the Model Law does not take a particularly restrictive position. Section 16 provides that

> Foreign State officials entitled to jurisdictional immunity under international law shall not be charged or prosecuted under this law [...].

---

[17] Decision on the Report of the Commission on the Abuse of the Principle of Universal Jurisdiction, Doc. Assembly/AU/14(XI), AU 11th session, 2008 Sharm El-Sheik, Assembly/AU/Dec. 199 (XI), para 5 (i–iii).

[18] For references to severe criticism expressed by the Rwandan government, see Commentator 2008, p. 1009 n. 39.

[19] African Union (Draft) Model National Law on Universal Jurisdiction over International Crimes, Meeting of Government Experts and Ministers of Justice/Attorneys General on Legal Matters, 7–15 May 2012, Addis Ababa, EXP/MIN/Legal/VI.

[20] Section 4(2) of the African Union (Draft) Model National Law on Universal Jurisdiction over International Crimes, Meeting of Government Experts and Ministers of Justice/Attorneys General on Legal Matters, 7–15 May 2012, Addis Ababa, EXP/MIN/Legal/VI.

[21] Sections 12, 13 and 14 of the African Union (Draft) Model National Law on Universal Jurisdiction over International Crimes, Meeting of Government Experts and Ministers of Justice/Attorneys General on Legal Matters, 7–15 May 2012, Addis Ababa, EXP/MIN/Legal/VI.

Reference to 'international law' is the traditional approach to immunity issues in the majority of jurisdictions around the world. The key question, however, is (and remains) to what extent, if any, international law allows for immunity from foreign prosecution of crimes under international law.[22] Many would suggest that there is broad agreement that even before national courts there is no such immunity except for the personal immunity which incumbent Heads of State and perhaps a small number of other high(est)-ranking state officials, such as Heads of Government, Foreign Ministers etc. enjoy.[23] However, the Model Law is silent on this point.

In addition to the rhetoric about the "abuse of universal jurisdiction" on the one hand and the Model Law on the other, there is a third element which may be consulted to understand the 'African position' on universal jurisdiction. In 2009, an ad hoc expert group jointly established by the African Union and the European Union and composed of lawyers from Algeria, Zambia, Tanzania, Italy, Belgium and Australia presented its "Report on the Principle of Universal Jurisdiction".[24] Perhaps surprisingly, this report again takes up quite a progressive stance. According to the Report, international law does not provide for any rule specifically restricting the exercise of universal jurisdiction—neither the presence requirement nor the subsidiarity principle is, the Report finds, part of universal jurisdiction under international law.[25] In fact, the Report approves of unrestricted universal jurisdiction for crimes under international law. As a matter of policy only, the report recommends to accord priority to territoriality as a basis of

[22] In the case of crimes under international law, immunity *ratione materiae* is inapplicable not only to trials before international courts, but also vis-à-vis state judiciaries. This is today anchored in customary international law, see Cassese 2002, pp. 870–874 (with numerous examples from state practice); Werle and Jeßberger 2014, marg no 721 et seq. On the more restrictive approach taken by the International Law Commission, see International Law Commission, Sixtieth session, Immunity of State Officials from Foreign Criminal Jurisdiction, Memorandum by the Secretariat, 31 March 2008, UN Doc. A/CN.4/596, para 189 ("uncertainty that still appears to surround this question"), and the Report by the Special Rapporteur RA Kolodkin concluding that "the arguments set out above demonstrate that the various rationales for exceptions to the immunity of officials from foreign criminal jurisdiction prove upon close scrutiny to be insufficiently convincing", International Law Commission, Sixty-second session, Second Report on Immunity of State Officials from Foreign Criminal Jurisdiction, 10 June 2010, UN Doc. A/CN.4/631, para 90. Immunity *ratione personae*, however, creates an obstacle to prosecution before domestic courts, at least as long as the respective person holds office, see *DR Congo v. Belgium*, ICJ, judgment of 14 February 2002 (Case Concerning the Arrest Warrant of 11 April 2000), para 56; Cassese 2002, pp. 865–866; Gaeta 2002, pp. 983–989.

[23] It is unsettled if other officials than acting Heads of State, Heads of Government, Foreign Ministers, and diplomats belong to the small set of persons entitled to immunity *ratione personae*. For discussion of this issue, see Akande and Shah 2010, pp. 820–825 (with further references); Cryer et al. 2010, p. 548; Sanger 2013, pp. 196–199.

[24] AU-EU Expert Report on the Principle of Universal Jurisdiction, paras 8-14. For detailed discussion of this report, see Geneuss 2009. Council of the EU, The AU-EU Expert Report on the Principle of Universal Jurisdiction, Doc. 8672/1/09 Rev. 1, 16 April 2009.

[25] AU-EU Expert Report on the Principle of Universal Jurisdiction, para 14. See also Geneuss 2009, pp. 955–959.

jurisdiction.[26] This Report has been endorsed by the AU Assembly when it "urged the EU and its member states to implement the recommendations of the AU-EU Joint ad hoc Expert group".[27]

In concluding this part of this chapter, the official (AU) 'African position' on universal jurisdiction may be characterized as follows: Despite concerns regarding the exercise of universal jurisdiction by some European countries—which are framed under the heading of "the abuse" of the principle—, the African Union does not reject the principle altogether. The Union explicitly endorses the view that universal jurisdiction is a principle of international law and stresses that it is an important tool in the fight against impunity. Regarding the requirements for the exercise of universal jurisdiction, the African Union has taken a progressive stance. After all, it seems that the main concern of 'African states' is to a lesser extent related to the principle of universal jurisdiction as such but rather to the supposed disregard of immunity of 'African leaders'. It should be noted however, that the implicit understanding of who qualifies as a 'leader' and, thus, qualifies for immunity from prosecution, is rather broad.[28]

10.4 The Use, the Non-use and the Abuse of Universal Jurisdiction

Let us now turn to the practical implementation and application of the principle of universal jurisdiction in an African context. Is there a point in the "abuse" argument?

First, the exercise of universal jurisdiction by courts and prosecutors in Africa shall be examined. A considerable number of African states have provided their courts with statutory universal jurisdiction—including, inter alia, Kenya, Uganda, Senegal and South Africa.[29] For instance, the South African Implementation of the Rome Statute of the International Criminal Court Act of 2002 provides that crimes committed outside South African territory are under the jurisdiction of South

[26] AU-EU Expert Report on the Principle of Universal Jurisdiction, R9.

[27] Decision on the Abuse of the Principle of Universal Jurisdiction, Doc.EX.CL/640(XVIII), AU 16th session, 2011 Addis Ababa, Assembly/AU/ /Dec. 335 (XVI), para 6; Decision on the Abuse of the Principle of Universal Jurisdiction, Doc. EX.CL/606(XVII), AU 15th session, 2010 Kampala, Assembly/AU/Dec. 292 (XV), para 8.

[28] See also Jalloh 2010, pp. 29–49.

[29] Section 8(c) of Kenya's International Crimes Act 2008; Article 669 of the Code of Criminal Procedure of Senegal; Section 18(d) of Uganda's International Criminal Court Act 2010; Section 4(3)(c) of South Africa's Implementation of the Rome Statute of the International Criminal Court Act 27 of 2002. See also AU-EU Expert Report on the Principle of Universal Jurisdiction, para 15–16.

African courts "if the perpetrator is a South African citizen or resident or if she' after the commission of the crime, is present in the territory of the Republic".[30]

However, this jurisdiction has been exercised only exceptionally. In 2009, the AU-EU expert group found that not a single African state was, in effect, exercising universal jurisdiction.[31] Meanwhile, we know of at least three cases. The most remarkable case is the prosecution and trial of former Chadian dictator *Hissène Habré* before a Senegalese tribunal. This case deserves closer scrutiny and will be discussed in detail below.[32] The two other cases concern proceedings pending before South African courts. The subject of these proceedings are alleged crimes committed by the former Madagascan President *Ravalomanana*, and acts of torture committed in Zimbabwe. The latter proceedings demonstrate once again how reluctant justice systems typically are to go after foreign officials. In March 2008, a human rights group—the Southern Africa Litigation Centre—asked the South African law enforcement authorities to initiate an investigation under the Implementation of the Rome Statute of the International Criminal Court Act of 2002 on the basis of the principle of universal jurisdiction. The request related to a case of alleged crimes against humanity involving mainly torture committed in Harare, Zimbabwe in March 2007. Then, the headquarters of the Zimbabwean opposition political party—the Movement of Democratic Change—was attacked by the Zimbabwean police. More than 100 people were arrested and some of them were taken into custody for a few days. In police custody, they were, inter alia, severely beaten and tortured through mock executions, waterboarding and electric shocks. According to information of the Southern Africa Litigation Centre, the raid was ordered by members of the *Mugabe* regime and the ruling party, the Zimbabwe African National Union—Patriotic Front (ZANU-PF). It is reported that the alleged perpetrators often visit South Africa on official or private occasions.[33] In June 2009, the South African investigating and prosecuting authorities decided not to open an investigation because it would lack the chance of success and could lead to diplomatic complications with Zimbabwe. The Southern Africa Litigation Centre challenged this decision and filed a complaint with the North Gauteng High Court in December 2009.[34] On 8 May 2012, the Court delivered a judgment in favor of the Centre[35]

---

[30] See also Chap. 6 by *Kemp* in this volume. For more information on the South African implementation of the Rome Statute, see Jeßberger and Powell 2001.

[31] AU-EU Expert Report on the Principle of Universal Jurisdiction, para 19.

[32] See also Chap. 8 by *Fall* in this book.

[33] Southern Africa Litigation Centre 2013, p. 70; Werle and Bornkamm 2013, pp. 660–661.

[34] Southern Africa Litigation Centre 2013, p. 71.

[35] *SALC and Another v. National Director for Public Prosecutions and Others, High Court of South Africa (North Gauteng High* Court), Judgment of 8 May 2012. For a more detailed discussion of this judgment, see Werle and Bornkamm 2013, pp. 665–673. See also Southern Africa Litigation Centre 2013, pp. 72–76.

which was confirmed by the Supreme Court of Appeal of South Africa[36] in November 2013.[37]

The Zimbabwe case is, however, a rare exception. The truth is that courts and prosecutors located in Africa do not prosecute and punish crimes under international law on the basis of universal jurisdiction—although their statutory law often explicitly allows for it. This corresponds to the generally rather poor record of African states with regard to the prosecution of international crimes.[38] With Rwanda being an exception,[39] only a handful of proceedings took place, inter alia, in the Democratic Republic of the Congo, Ethiopia, Uganda, Sierra Leone and, most recently, in Northern African Arab Spring states.[40]

Obviously, however, the "abuse" argument is based on the arbitrary application of universal jurisdiction by courts and prosecutors in Europe against accused persons from Africa.[41] Concerning legislation, universal jurisdiction is, in principle, available across Europe with regard to war crimes, genocide, and crimes against humanity.[42] Unlike in Africa, those statutes have been applied at least occasionally. Proceedings in Spain[43] and Belgium[44] between 1998 and 2008 received the most public attention. But courts in other European countries, too, did deal with universal jurisdiction cases, for instance in Austria, Denmark, Finland, France, Germany, the Netherlands, Norway, Sweden, Switzerland and the UK.[45]

---

[36] *National Commissioner of the South African Police Service and Another v. Southern African Human Rights Litigation Centre and Another*, Supreme Court of Appeal of South Africa, Judgment of 27 November 2013, paras 51–70. On both decisions see Chap. 6 by *Kemp* in this book.

[37] One of the immediate effects of the judgment of the North Gauteng High Court was the opening of criminal proceedings against the former Madagascan president *Marc Ravalomanana* who lives in exile in South Africa. In August 2012, the South African prosecuting authorities initiated an investigation against *Ravalomanana* who is allegedly responsible as a superior for crimes against humanity committed in Antananarivo in 2009. See Southern Africa Litigation Centre 2013, p. 76.

[38] Van der Wilt 2011, p. 1054 (he additionally mentions proceedings in Sierra Leone and Uganda).

[39] In Rwanda, tens of thousands of *génocidaires* have been tried by national courts and so-called *Gacaca* courts. However, the view on these mass proceedings is divided. In particular, the guarantee of fair trial rights to the suspects is questionable. See, e.g., Lahiri 2009; Sadat 2009, p. 556. See also Bornkamm 2012, and Chap. 7 by *Rugege* in this book.

[40] For further details and references, see van der Wilt 2011, pp. 1052–1053, in particular for the *Mengistu Haile Mariam* trial in Ethopia see Tiba 2007.

[41] See AU-EU Expert Report on the Principle of Universal Jurisdiction, para 26 (EU member states); Jalloh 2010, pp. 14–28; Langer 2011 (for the period of 1961 until June 2010); Reydams 2003, pp. 86–219; van der Wilt 2011, pp. 1055–1059.

[42] AU-EU Expert Report on the Principle of Universal Jurisdiction, para 23.

[43] See Langer 2011, pp. 32–41.

[44] Ibid., pp. 26–32.

[45] For details and further references see Werle and Jeßberger 2014, marg nos 344 et seq.; Langer 2011, p. 42 (Table 2). AU-EU Expert Report on the Principle of Universal Jurisdiction, para 26.

During the last 10 or 15 years, main 'targets'—numerically—of those proceedings were accused or suspects from Rwanda and Yugoslavia. Only exceptionally did investigations result in actual trial, save convictions. A majority of cases were dismissed for immunity reasons, by exercising prosecutorial discretion, or transferred to the ad hoc Tribunals. Based on a systematic analysis of available data, *Maximo Langer* identified 1.051 accused persons involved in complaints or cases considered by public authorities around the world—a majority in Europe or the rest of the Western world—or on their own motion. Of those, one third were suspected for crimes under Nazi-rule (here, for plausible reasons, *Langer* did not distinguish by nationality), 18 % former Yugoslavs, 12 % Argentineans, 8 % Rwandans, 5 % US-Americans, 4 % Israelis and 4 % Chinese.[46] Only 32 (3 %) of those 1.051 accused persons have been brought to trial. Of those 32 defendants who were brought to trial, three-quarters were Rwandans, former Yugoslavs or persons allegedly responsible for crimes under the Nazi-rule.[47] *Langer* convincingly concludes that universal jurisdiction cases have concentrated on what he calls "low cost defendants"—those for whom their states of nationality have not been willing to exercise their leverage and especially those on whose prosecution the international community has been in broad agreement.[48] Such accused persons may include accused persons from Africa, but a racial or geographic bias is not supported by the data.[49]

The findings of *Langer's* study are confirmed if one examines the individual countries. Let us take Germany as an example. Starting in the mid-1990s, the German Federal Prosecutor General led investigations against 177 accused persons for crimes, in particular genocide and war crimes, committed in former Yugoslavia. In four cases the accused were convicted.[50] Later, based on legislation which was introduced in 2002 and which provides for unrestricted universal jurisdiction, the German Federal Prosecutor General received more than 60 complaints.[51] All these complaints which concerned alleged crimes committed in Uzbekistan, Iraq, Guantanamo, China and the Middle East, were dismissed, mostly because the perpetrators were not present in Germany. These complaints concerned, inter alia, *Donald Rumsfeld*, *Henry Kissinger*, *Ariel Sharon*, *Jiang Zemin* and *Zakir Almatov*—but, this may be relevant in our context, no 'African leader'.

In 2003, the first complaint on the basis of the German Code of Crimes against International Law of 2002 that attracted public attention was filed against former Chinese President *Jiang Zemin* and other members of his government. This complaint regarding acts of persecution of *Falun Gong* practitioners, amounting to

---

[46] Langer 2011, p. 8 (Table 1).

[47] Ibid., p. 8 (Table 1).

[48] Ibid., p. 5.

[49] See also AU-EU Expert Report on the Principle of Universal Jurisdiction, para 40; Jalloh 2010, pp. 14–18.

[50] See Werle and Jeßberger 2014, marg nos 344 et seq. See also Reydams 2003, pp. 149–156.

[51] Langer 2011, pp. 14–15.

genocide and crimes against humanity, was dismissed by the Federal Prosecutor General in 2005. The Prosecutor argued, inter alia, that *Jiang* would enjoy immunity under international law. With regard to the other accused, the prosecutor based his decision particularly on their absence from German territory.[52] Another complaint was presented in 2005 against the Minister of Internal Affairs of Uzbekistan, *Zakir Almatov* and others, for their alleged responsibility for the massacre of Andijan as well as for systematic torture in Uzbek prisons. The Federal Prosecutor General again refused to open investigations because the accused were not present on German territory and they were not expected to enter the country.[53] What attracted the most public attention were the complaints against former US Secretary of Defence *Donald Rumsfeld* and other superiors of the military and civil staff of the United States as well as legal consultants of the US Government. These complaints were filed on the basis of allegations of maltreatments and torture committed in the Iraqi detention center Abu Ghraib and in Guantánamo Bay. Again, no official proceedings were instituted. The first complaint was filed in 2004 and dismissed in 2006, since—at least in the view of the German Federal Prosecutor General—the 'Abu Ghraib complex' has adequately been prosecuted by the US judiciary.[54] In 2006, a second complaint regarding the incidents in Abu Ghraib followed, as well as allegations of war crimes committed in Guantánamo Bay. According to the Federal Prosecutor General, this time the requirements of Section 153f of the German Code of Criminal Procedure were given so that he could exercise his discretion. Contrary to the arguments brought by the complainants, the Prosecutor opined that none of the alleged crimes was committed on German territory.[55] Besides, no suspect resided or was expected to reside in Germany. The Prosecutor clarified that the mere theoretical possibility of a presence on German territory would not suffice.[56] The Prosecutor based his decision to dispense with prosecuting the alleged crimes on the lack of a prospect of success of such an investigation.[57] In addition, he was of the view that an overstraining of the German law enforcement authorities, as well as forum shopping, should be prevented.[58]

In Germany, only two trials concerned accused persons from Africa. The first one was the trial of *Onesphore Rwabukombe*. As explained above, he was convicted for aiding and abetting genocide and sentenced to 14 years' imprisonment. Representatives of the Rwandan government applauded the judgement. The second trial is still ongoing. It is the trial against *Ignace Murwanashyaka*, the former

---

[52] Keller 2013, p. 147; Langer 2011, p. 14.

[53] See Amnesty International 2008, pp. 104–105. For detailed discussion of the Prosecutor's decision, see Zappalà 2006.

[54] Amnesty International 2008, pp. 103–104; Keller 2013, pp. 143–144.

[55] Keller 2013, p. 142. See also Amnesty International 2008, p. 104.

[56] Keller 2013, p. 143.

[57] Langer 2011, p. 15.

[58] Keller 2013, pp. 144–145.

president of the *Forces Democratiques de Liberation de Rwanda* and his Vice President *Musoni* on charges of war crimes and crimes against humanity committed in the Democratic Republic of Congo.[59] The Stuttgart Higher Regional Court (*Oberlandesgericht*) started to hear this case in 2011. Unlike the *Rwabukombe* trial, this trial is not based on universal jurisdiction. Since both accused of the Stuttgart trial had lived in Germany for 20 years and allegedly committed the crimes from German territory (using mobile phones and internet communication devices), the prosecution is based on territorial rather than extraterritorial jurisdiction.

10.5 Keeping It at Bay: The Decline of Universal Jurisdiction in Europe

Now, three trends will be indicated which have the potential to shape the exercise of universal jurisdiction in the coming years. The first trend which shall be mentioned is relatively well described.[60] After 10 years of enthusiasm and optimism about universal jurisdiction in Europe we now start to see disillusionment. As *David Luban* put it, "the honeymoon is over".[61] Universal jurisdiction in Europe, the heartland of the movement, is on the decline. Many states and judicial systems have by now realized that universal justice is costly, complicated and exhausting. The consequences are manifold. Prime examples are Belgium and Spain. Both cut back their laws on universal jurisdiction, and are thus no longer able to prosecute international crimes that have no direct connection to their territory or citizens. *Baltasar Garzón*, the judge who initiated the proceedings against *Pinochet* in the mid-1990s, and one of the most visible protagonists of a forceful system of international criminal justice, has been sidelined. In several countries, such as Germany, new and ambitious legislation has rarely been applied.

10.6 Striking Back: The Reversion of Universal Jurisdiction

The second 'trend', which has not yet developed to a real trend though, relates to what could be called the 'reversion' of universal jurisdiction. Universal jurisdiction is not a one-way road. Theoretically, it never was. Practically, some observers, as we have seen in particular observers from Africa, have suggested this: a North-South levy in the exercise of universal jurisdiction. And, yes, we have seen that

[59] For details see Keller 2013, pp. 148–151.

[60] See the contributions in Jeßberger and Geneuss 2013.

[61] Luban 2013, p. 505.

universal jurisdiction has been exercised primarily by European judges and prosecutors. Against this background it is remarkable indeed that in September 2013 an Argentinean judge issued international arrest warrants for four former Spanish police officials accused of torturing political prisoners under the *Franco* Regime in Spain. After attempts to initiate proceedings in Spain had failed due to the Spanish amnesty law of 1977, a number of victims supported by human rights organizations filed complaints in 2010 in Buenos Aires. Two of the four suspects have already died and the Spanish authorities seem unlikely to extradite the others. At least, they had to deliver their passports and are obliged to report regularly to the police. At the moment, the case is pending before the *Audiencia Nacional* that has to decide about the admissibility of the extradition. Here, it will probably be crucial if the amnesty law is valid.[62] This represents a perhaps novel development, since it is, to the author's knowledge, the first time that a judiciary of the 'global south' 'strikes back' and uses universal jurisdiction to go after perpetrators from Europe.

10.7 Keeping It Home: The Regionalization of Universal Jurisdiction

The third and perhaps most sustainable trend concerns a development which may be called the regionalization of universal jurisdiction. This is what finally happened in the *Habré* case: *Hissène Habré* ruled Chad from 1982 to 1990, when he was overthrown by the current President of Chad *Idriss Déby Itno*. During his dictatorship serious violations of human rights occurred.[63] The truth commission which was established after the fall of *Habré* stated in its report of 1992 that he and his government were responsible for about 40,000 murders of political opponents and established a regime of systematic torture.[64] In 1990, *Habré* went into exile to Senegal where he initially lived unmolested. In the aftermath of the arrest warrant decision against *Pinochet*, some of *Habré's* victims supported by human rights groups tried to initiate criminal proceedings against him in Senegal. At first, investigations were carried out, leading to an indictment and *Habré* was placed under house arrest.[65] However, the Senegalese *Court d'Appel* of Dakar held in July 2000 that criminal proceedings against *Habré* in Senegal are inadmissible because he committed his alleged deeds abroad and therefore Senegal lacked jurisdiction.[66]

[62] Hamilos 2013; Minder 2013.

[63] For more background information, see Brody 2006, pp. 278–281. See also Moghadam 2007–2008, pp. 495–496; Neldjingaye 2011, pp. 187–189. See also *Belgium v. Senegal*, ICJ Judgment of 20 July 2012 (Questions relating to the Obligation to Prosecute or Extradite), paras 15–41.

[64] See Brody 2006, p. 283.

[65] Ibid., pp. 286–287; Moghadam 2007–2008, pp. 497–499.

[66] République du Sénégal, Cour d'Appel de Dakar, Chambre d'accusation, Arret no. 135 du 4 juillet 2000. For a critical view on this decision, see Magliveras 2012, p. 3; see also Moghadam 2007–2008, pp. 501–503.

This decision was confirmed by the Senegalese *Court de Cassation* in March 2001.[67] Besides these efforts to initiate proceedings against *Habré* in the country of his residence, some victims addressed their complaints under the Belgian universal jurisdiction law to the Belgian law enforcement authorities, who then started investigations. In 2002, a Belgian investigating judge and other officials travelled to Chad and conducted investigations in situ.[68] Three years later, the Belgian authorities finally issued an international arrest warrant against *Habré* and filed an extradition request to Senegal. However, the Senegalese authorities refused to extradite *Habré*. The *Court d'Appel* of Dakar held that it did not have jurisdiction to rule on the extradition request.[69] Triggered by the Belgian engagement in the *Habré* case, Senegal reported the issue to the African Union which, in turn, set up a "Committee of Eminent African Jurists" to consider the possibilities of prosecuting *Habré*.[70] In a Decision of 2006 the AU Assembly mandated

> the Republic of Senegal to prosecute and ensure that *Hissène Habré* is tried, on behalf of Africa, by a competent Senegalese court with guarantees for fair trial.[71]

At about the same time, the Committee against Torture declared that Senegal is in breach of its obligations arising from the Convention against Torture and Other Cruel, Inhuman or Degrading Treatment or Punishment (Torture Convention) by failing to extradite or prosecute *Habré*.[72] In 2007, the Senegalese legislator amended its penal and constitutional law and allowed for the prosecution of international crimes even though they were committed abroad.[73] After a further period of standstill, in February 2009 Belgium referred the case to the International Court of Justice with the aim to compel Senegal to comply with its obligation to extradite or prosecute resulting from the Torture Convention.[74] In the meantime, *Habré* filed a complaint against his prosecution in Senegal to the Court of Justice of the Economic Community of the West African States. In November 2010, this court ruled that a prosecution of *Habré*, based on the amended Senegalese penal law would violate the principle of *nullum crimen sine lege* (the absolute

---

[67] République du Sénégal, Cour de Cassation, Première chamber statuant en matière pénale, Arret no. 14 du 20 mars 2001.

[68] Brody 2006, pp. 288–289.

[69] Magliveras 2012, p. 5 (with further references).

[70] Decision on the Hissene Habré Case and the African Union, Doc.Assembly/AU/8 (VI) Add.9, AU 6th session, 2006 Khartoum, Assembly/AU/Dec.103 (VI). See also Magliveras 2012, pp. 6–7.

[71] Decision on the Hissène Habré Case and the African Union, Assembly/AU/Dec.127(VII), August 2, 2006, Doc. Assembly/AU/3(VII), para 5(ii).

[72] UN Committee against Torture, *Communication No. 181/2001: Suleymane Guengueng and Others v. Senegal*, 19 May 2006.

[73] For thorough discussion, see Niang 2009. See also Adjovi 2013, p. 1021 (with further references); Magliveras 2012, pp. 9–11.

[74] See Magliveras 2012, pp. 12–13.

prohibition of the retroactivity of criminal law) but he could be prosecuted by an extraordinary or ad hoc Tribunal.[75]

After a governmental change in Senegal in March 2012 and the judgment of the International Court of Justice in July 2012 in favor of Belgium[76] an agreement between Senegal and the African Union[77] was concluded. According to this agreement which was signed in August 2012, special chambers were established within the existing Senegalese justice system—the so-called 'Extraordinary African Chambers' (EAC).[78]

Surprisingly, the African Union and Senegal established the Extraordinary African Chambers to prosecute a former Head of State with retroactive universal jurisdiction.[79] The Chambers differ from other hybrid courts in that they are established in a third state and exercise universal jurisdiction. Under Article 3(1) of the EAC Statute, the Chambers

> shall have the power to prosecute and try the person or persons most responsible for crimes and serious violations of international law, customary international law and international conventions ratified by Chad, committed in the territory of Chad during the period from 7 June 1982 to 1 December 1990.[80]

---

[75] *Habré v. Senegal*, Court of Justice of the Economic Community of States of Western Africa, 18 November 2010. For a critical assessment of this judgment, see Spiga 2011, pp. 16–22. See also Magliveras 2012, pp. 13–15; Neldjingaye 2011, pp. 190–191.

[76] The International Court of Justice held by majority that Senegal has breached its obligations under Articles 6(2) and 7(1) of the Torture Convention "by failing to make immediately a preliminary inquiry into the facts relating to the crimes allegedly committed by [...] Habré" and "by failing to submit the case to its competent authorities for the purpose of prosecution", see *Belgium v. Senegal*, ICJ, Judgment of 20 July 2012 (Questions relating to the Obligation to Prosecute or Extradite), para 122.

[77] International Legal Materials 2013, 1024–1027.

[78] The four different chambers established according to Article 2 of the EAC Statute are mainly composed of judges of Senegalese nationality but both the trial and the appeals chamber will be presided by a non-Senegalese judge from another African Union Member State. See Articles 11(3)(2) and (4)(2) of the Statute. On the structure of the Extraordinary African Chambers, see also Southern Africa Litigation Centre 2013, p. 88, and Chap. 8 by *Fall* in this book.

[79] In the meantime, the African Union even considered building special criminal chambers at the existing African Court of Justice and Human Rights to prosecute, inter alia, genocide, crimes against humanity and war crimes, see Draft Protocol on Amendments to the Protocol on the Statute of the African Court of Justice and Human Rights, Revisions up to Tuesday 15 May 2012, Meeting of Government Experts and Ministers of Justice/Attorneys General on Legal Matters, 7–11 and 14–15 May 2012, Addis Ababa, EXP/MIN/IV/Rev.7. The decision on the adoption of the amended protocol was postponed for further consideration. See Decision on the Protocol on Amendments to the Protocol on the Statute of the African Court of Justice and Human Rights, Doc. Assembly/AU/13(XIX)a, AU 19th session, 2012 Addis Ababa, Assembly/AU/Dec. 427 (XIX). See also Decision on Africa's Relationship with the International Criminal Court (ICC), AU Extraordinary Session, 2013 Addis Ababa, Ext/Assembly/AU/Dec. 1 (Oct. 2013), para 10(iv). For discussion, see Murungu 2011.

[80] The Chambers have jurisdiction *ratione materiae* with respect to genocide, crimes against humanity, war crimes and torture. These crimes are defined by Articles 5 to 8 of the EAC Statute. Besides international law and the Statute itself, the Chambers will apply Senegalese law in

In February 2013, the Extraordinary African Chambers were inaugurated and investigations started. *Habré* was charged with crimes against humanity, war crimes and torture and placed in custody in July 2013.[81] The trial is expected to start later in 2014.[82]

The '*Habré* saga' is a typical example of the stamina needed to actually trigger criminal proceedings involving crimes under international law: It took more than 20 years, required enormous external pressure—proceedings under universal jurisdiction in Belgium, involvement of the civil society, regional mechanisms, international mechanisms, including most notably the International Court of Justice—and was ultimately successful only because the political atmosphere in the countries involved was favorable for the trial to be held. At the same time, the *Habré* saga ended in uncharted waters. What makes the *Habré* trial a model? Perhaps the low cost, perhaps the regional if not local 'ownership'. Is this model compatible with the universal jurisdiction theory? Yes, it is submitted that it is, since it corresponds to the very logic of the concept of universal jurisdiction that a state, as a trustee can act 'on behalf' of a specific, not necessarily a global group of states.

10.8 Conclusion

Universal jurisdiction has been predominantly exercised in (Western) Europe (and some other Western countries). For a few years now there have been signs of a possible downtrend. There is no evidence of a racial or geographical bias in the selection of universal jurisdiction cases, be it on investigation or on trial stage. The majority of the accused have been Europeans (in this respect, universal jurisdiction practice differs from the International Criminal Court, but corresponds to the practice of international tribunals as a whole). Therefore, there is no basis to suggest an "abuse". There is, however, evidence that 'low-cost defendants' are disproportionally affected. Such defendants are 'low-cost' in terms of the political and enforcement resources their prosecutions require, which may be particularly so because there is a consensus in the international community to prosecute and punish specific groups of perpetrators. The group of low-cost defendants may also include Africans, in particular, Rwandans (given the worldwide consensus to prosecute and punish those responsible for the 1994 genocide). Interestingly,

(Footnote 80 continued)
particular the Code of Senegalese Criminal Procedure, Article 1(4) of the Agreement and Articles 16 and 17(1) of the Statute. According to Article 3(1) of the Agreement and Article 32 of the Statute, the Chambers will be financed "in accordance with the budget approved by the Donor's Round Table of 24 November 2010." Table ronde des donateurs pour le financement du process de Monsieur Hissène Habré, Dakar, le 24 novembre 2010, Document Final, p. 4. Thus, the costs will be bore, inter alia, by the EU (2 million Euro), the AU (1 million US Dollars), Chad (2 billion CFA francs or 3,743,000 US Dollars), Belgium (1 million Euro), and Germany (500,000 Euro).

[81] Adjovi 2013, p. 1020. See also Chap. 8 by *Fall* in this volume.

[82] Southern Africa Litigation Centre 2013, p. 88.

consensus on the international level triggers not only direct enforcement through international courts (the ad hoc tribunals, the International Criminal Court), but is also a key factor in the indirect enforcement of international criminal law.

Still, universal jurisdiction remains an exception.[83] Only a few persons were convicted worldwide. It would be unrealistic to argue that universal jurisdiction will hold a substantial share of the perpetrators of international crimes accountable. Rather, purposes other than conviction come to the fore when we discuss the role of third states: triggering prosecution in territorial states, collecting and providing evidence and so on. This is also why it is useful and necessary to discuss universal jurisdiction as part and parcel of the complex and multileveled system of international criminal justice. This system includes international courts, territorial states and third states exercising universal jurisdiction on behalf of the international community. With the Extraordinary African Chambers operating "on behalf of Africa" currently a novel intermediate level is about to be established, located between the national and the international levels on the basis of universal jurisdiction.

The regionalization of universal jurisdiction is an option, if it works. So far, the reports are promising. It may help to ensure the independence and legitimacy of the proceedings. It may insulate local judges to some degree against intimidation from their governments. It may enhance local 'ownership' and counter the 'jurisdictional imperialism' critique.[84] But more than that, it may also help to avoid or mitigate many of the practical problems that European courts exercising universal jurisdiction have experienced. Regionalized universal jurisdiction has, therefore, the power to address the problems of both cases mentioned in the introduction, the *Kabuye* incident—triggering harsh accusations of colonial justice—and the *Rwabukombe* conviction—giving reason to rethink the use and possibility of trials far away from the *locus delicti*. In this perspective, the *Habré* case may indeed open a new chapter in the story of Africa and universal jurisdiction.

Acknowledgments The valuable assistance of *Eva Bohle*, LLM (University of the Western Cape) in the preparation of this paper is gratefully acknowledged.

References

Adjovi R (2013) Introductory note to the Agreement on the Establishment of the Extraordinary African Chambers within the Senegalese judicial system between the Government of the Republic of Senegal and the African Union and the Statute of the Chambers. Int Leg Mater 52:1020–1023

Akande D, Shah S (2010) Immunities of state officials, international crimes, and foreign domestic courts. Eur J Int Law 21:815–852

[83] See also AU-EU Expert Report on the Principle of Universal Jurisdiction, paras 26, 40; Jalloh 2010, pp. 20–25.

[84] Moghadam 2007–2008, pp. 511–521.

Ambos K (2013) Expanding the focus of the, African Criminal Court'. In: Schabas WA, McDermott Y, Hayes N (eds) The Ashgate research companion to International Criminal Law. Ashgate, Farnham, pp 499–529
Amnesty International (2008) Germany, End impunity through universal jurisdiction. www.amnesty.de/files/2696_Univ_Jurisd_003Germany_final.pdf. (All internet sources in this chapter were accessed on 20 March 2014)
Beste R, Puhl J, Simons S (2008) Kigali v. Paris: shedding lights on the Rwandan genocide. http://www.spiegel.de/international/world/kigali-v-paris-shedding-light-on-the-rwandan-genocide-a-590967.html
Bornkamm PC (2012) Rwanda's Gacaca Courts between retribution and reparation. Oxford University Press, Oxford
Brody R (2006, reprinted 2008) The Prosecution of Hissène Habré: international accountability, national impunity. In: Roht Arriaza N, Mariezcurrena J (eds) Transitional justice in the twenty-first century, beyond truth versus justice. Cambridge University Press, Cambridge, pp 278–300
Cassese A (2002) When may senior state officials be tried for international crimes? some comments on the Congo v. Belgium Case. Eur J Int Law 13:853–875
Commentator (2008) The Spanish indictment of high-ranking Rwandan officials. J Int Crim Justice 6:1003–1011
Cryer R, Friman H, Robinson D, Wilmshurst E (2010) An introduction to International Criminal Law and Procedure, 2nd edn. Cambridge University Press, Cambridge
Dehner D (2014) 14 Jahre Haft wegen Beihilfe zum Völkermord in Ruanda. Der Tagesspiegel, 18 February 2014
du Plessis M, Maluwa T, O'Reilly A (2013) Africa and the International Criminal Court, Chatham House. www.chathamhouse.org/sites/default/files/public/Research/International%20Law/0713pp_iccafrica.pdf
Gaeta P (2002) Official capacity and immunities. In: Cassese A, Gaeta P, Jones JRWD (eds) The Rome Statute of the International Criminal Court: a commentary, vol I. Oxford University Press, Oxford, pp 975–1002
Geneuss J (2009) Fostering a better understanding of Universal jurisdiction, a comment on the AU-EU report on the principle of Universal jurisdiction. J Int Crim Justice 7:945–962
Hamilos P (2013) Argentina calls for extradition of Francoists over human rights abuses. http://www.theguardian.com/world/2013/sep/19/argentina-spain-franco-extraditions
Jalloh CC (2010) Universal jurisdiction, universal prescription? A preliminary assessment of the African Union perspective on universal jurisdiction. Crim Law Forum 21:1–65
Jeßberger F (2009) Universal jurisdiction. In: Cassese A (ed) The Oxford companion to International Criminal Justice. Oxford University Press, Oxford, pp 555–557
Jeßberger F, Geneuss J (eds) (2013) Recent setbacks for International Criminal Justice put into perspective. J Int Crim Justice 11:501–570
Jeßberger F, Powell C (2001) Prosecuting Pinochets in South Africa—implementing the Rome Statute of the International Criminal Court. S Afr J Crim Justice 14:344–362
Johnson D (2014) Ein grenzwertiges Urteil. Tageszeitung, 18 February 2014
Keller R (2013) Das Völkerstrafgesetzbuch in der praktischen Anwendung: Eine kritische Bestandsaufnahme. In: Jeßberger F, Geneuss J (eds) Zehn Jahre Völkerstrafgesetzbuch, Bilanz und Perspektiven eines "deutschen Völkerstrafrechts". Nomos, Baden-Baden. Stämpfli Verlag, Bern, pp 141–160
Kroker P (2011) Universal jurisdiction in Germany: the trial of *Onesphore R.* Before the Higher Regional Court of Frankfurt. Ger Yearb Int Law 54:671–687
Lahiri K (2009) Rwanda's 'Gacaca' courts: a possible model for local justice in international crime? Int Crim Law Rev 9:321–332
Langer M (2011) The diplomacy of Universal Jurisdiction, the role of political branches in the transnational prosecution of international crimes. AJIL 105:1–49
Luban D (2013) After the honeymoon: reflections on the current state of international criminal justice. J Int Crim Justice 11:505–515

Magliveras KD (2012) Fighting impunity unsuccessfully in Africa, The African Union and the Habré Case. www.academia.edu/1513605/African_Union_and_the_Case_of_Hissene_Habre.
Magliveras KD, Naldi GJ (2013) The International Criminal Court's involvement with Africa: evaluation of a fractious relationship. Nord J Int Law 82:417–446
Minder R (2013) Argentine judge seeks to put Franco officials on trial. http://www.nytimes.com/2013/10/01/world/europe/argentine-judge-seeks-to-put-franco-officials-on-trial.html
Moghadam T (2007–2008) Revitalizing universal jurisdiction: lessons from hybrid tribunals applied to the case of Hissène Habré. Columbia Hum Rights Law Rev 39:471–528
Murungu CB (2011) Towards a criminal chamber in the African Court of Justice and Human Rights. J Int Crim Justice 9:1067–1088
Neldjingaye K (2011) The trial of Hissène Habré in Senegal and its contribution to international criminal law. In: Murungu C, Biegon J (eds) Prosecuting international crimes in Africa. Pretoria Law University Press, Pretoria, pp 185–196
Niang M (2009) The Senegalese legal framework for the prosecution of international crimes. J Int Crim Justice 7:1947–1062
Reydams L (2003) Universal jurisdiction, international and municipal legal perspectives. Oxford University Press, Oxford
Sadat L (2009) Transjudicial dialogue and the Rwandan genocide: aspects of antagonism and complementarity. Leiden J Int Law 22:543–562
Sammons A (2003) The under-theorization of universal jurisdiction: implications for legitimacy on trials of war criminals by national courts. Berkeley J Int Law 21:111–143
Sanger A (2013) Immunity of state officials from the criminal jurisdiction of a foreign state. Int Comp Law Q 62:193–224
Southern Africa Litigation Centre (2013) Positive reinforcement: advocating for International Criminal Justice in Africa, Johannesburg
Spiga V (2011) Non-retroactivity of Criminal Law, a new chapter in the Hissène Habré saga. J Int Crim Justice 9:5–23
Tiba FK (2007) The *Mengistu* genocide trial in Ethiopia. J Int Crim Justice 5:513–528
Werle G, Jeßberger F (2014) Principles of International Criminal Law, 3rd edn. Oxford University Press, Oxford
Werle G, Bornkamm PC (2013) Torture in Zimbabwe under scrutiny in South Africa—the judgment of the North Gauteng High Court in SALC v. National Director of Public Prosecution. J Int Crim Justice 11:659–675
van der Wilt H (2011) Universal Jurisdiction under attack, an assessment of African Misgivings towards international criminal justice as administered by Western States. J Int Crim Justice 9:1043–1066
Zappalà S (2006) The German federal prosecutor's decision not to prosecute a former Uzbek minister, missed opportunity or prosecutorial wisdom. J Int Crim Justice 4:602–622

Cases

The Prosecutor v. Munyakazi, ICTR (TC), Decision of 28 May 2008, ICTR-97-36-R11*bis*
The Prosecutor v. Munyakazi, ICTR (AC), Decision of 8 October 2008, ICTR-97-36-R11*bis*
The Prosecutor v. Uwinkindi, ICTR (TC), Decision of 28 June 2011, ICTR-2001-75-R11*bis*
The Prosecutor v. Uwinkindi, ICTR (AC), Decision of 16 December 2011, ICTR-01-75-AR11*bis*
The Prosecutor v. Muthaura, Kenyatta and Hussein Ali, Judgment on the appeal of the Republic of Kenya against the decision of the Pre-Trial Chamber II of 30 May 2011 entitled "Decision on the application by the Government of Kenya challenging the admissibility of the case pursuant to Article 19(2)(b) of the Statute", ICC-01/09-02/11OA, 30 August 2011
The Prosecutor v. Ruto, Kosgey and Sang, Judgment on the appeal of the Republic of Kenya against the decision of the Pre-Trial Chamber II of 30 May 2011 entitled "Decision on the

application by the Government of Kenya challenging the admissibility of the case pursuant to Article 19(2)(b) of the Statute", ICC-01/09-01/11OA, 30 August 2011

DR Congo v. Belgium, ICJ, Judgment of 14 February 2002 (Case Concerning the Arrest Warrant of 11 April 2000), ICJ Reports 2002, pp 3 et seq

Belgium v. Senegal, ICJ, Judgment of 20 July 2012 (Questions Relating to the Obligation to Prosecute or Extradite), ICJ Reports 2012, pp 422 et seq

UN Committee against Torture, Communication No. 181/2001: *Suleymane Guengueng and Others v. Senegal*, 19 May 2006, UN Doc. CAT/C/36/D/181/2001

Ahorugeze v. Sweden, ECHR, Judgment of 27 October 2011 (Application No. 37075/09)

Habré v. Senegal, Court of Justice of the Economic Community of States of Western Africa, Decision No. ECW/CCJ/JUD/06/10, 18 November 2010 http://www.asser.nl/upload/documents/20120419T034816-Habre%20Ecowa%202010.pdf

Oberlandesgericht Frankfurt am Main, Decision of 6 November 2008, 2 Ausl A 175/07

Oberlandesgericht Frankfurt am Main, Judgment of 18 February 2014, 5-3 StE 4/10 - 4 - 3/10

SALC and Another v. National Director for Public Prosecutions and Others, High Court of South Africa (North Gauteng High Court), Judgment of 8 May 2012, Case No. 77150/09

National Commissioner of the South African Police Service and Another v. Southern African Human Rights Litigation Centre and Another, Supreme Court of Appeal of South Africa, Judgment of 27 November 2013, Case No. 485/2012

République du Sénégal, Cour d'Appel de Dakar, Chambre d'accusation, Arret no. 135 du 4 juillet 2000. http://www.hrw.org/legacy/french/themes/habre-decision.html

République du Sénégal, Cour de Cassation, Première chamber statuant en matière pénale, Arret no. 14 du 20 mars 2001. http://www.hrw.org/legacy/french/themes/habre-cour_de_cass.html

Part III
The African Union and the International Criminal Court

Chapter 11
Between Political Justice and Judicial Politics: Charting a Way Forward for the African Union and the International Criminal Court

Tim Murithi

Contents

11.1 Introduction

The International Criminal Court was established as a permanent independent institution to prosecute individuals who have orchestrated and executed the most serious crimes of international concern, including genocide, crimes against humanity and war crimes. The Rome Statute, which entered into force on 1 July 2002, is explicit on the role of the Court in exercising a criminal jurisdiction over perpetrators of these crimes. African countries were actively involved in the creation of the International Criminal Court and played a crucial role at the Rome conference when the Court's Statute was drafted and adopted. To date, Africa represents the largest regional grouping of countries within the ICC's Assembly of States Parties. While African countries were initially supportive of the

T. Murithi (✉)
Institute for Justice and Reconciliation, Cape Town, South Africa
e-mail: tmurithi@ijr.org.za

G. Werle et al. (eds.), *Africa and the International Criminal Court*,
International Criminal Justice Series 1, DOI 10.1007/978-94-6265-029-9_11

International Criminal Court the relationship degenerated in 2008 when President *Omar Al Bashir* of Sudan was indicted by the Court. Following this move the African Union, which is representative of virtually all countries on the continent, adopted a hostile posture towards the International Criminal Court. The African Union called for its Member States to implement a policy of non-cooperation with the Court, which remains the stated position of the continental body. This chapter will discuss the trajectory of Africa's relationship with the International Criminal Court and suggest that, even though both organizations share a mandate to address impunity, they are in fact engaged in practicing a variation of 'political justice' and 'judicial politics'. This chapter will then offer insights into the way forward for both organizations and assess how their differences can be addressed.

11.2 Africa and the Establishment of the International Criminal Court

The establishment of the International Criminal Court was the culmination of an evolution of international justice that can be traced back to the Nuremberg and Tokyo trials following the Second World War. The Rome conference which led to the signing of the statute establishing the Court, in July 1998, was a long and arduous affair of international negotiation and brinkmanship. The majority of countries represented at the Rome conference, including African countries, were of the view that it would be a positive development in global governance to operationalize an international criminal justice regime which would hold accountable individuals who commit gross atrocities and violations against human rights. Specifically, the Court has jurisdiction over war crimes, crimes against humanity and genocide; its jurisdiction over the crime of aggression will not become operative before 2017. The reality of the Rwandan genocide of 1994 also convinced many African governments of the need to support an international criminal justice regime which would confront impunity and persistence of mass human rights violations on the continent. African countries were therefore part of a wider campaign of support for the International Criminal Court.

The Court also had its opponents. At the 1998 Rome conference, 120 participants voted for the final draft of the Rome Statute, but 21 abstained and seven voted against. From its inception, "the Court faced a strong challenge from the United States, which first signed the Statute and then 'unsigned' it".[1] The failure of powerful countries, including Russia and China, proactively to support the Court and subject themselves to its criminal jurisdiction, immediately began to raise alarm bells about the reach and ultimately the efficacy of the Court. The concern was that the remit of the Court would be confined to the middle and weaker powers within the international system. The Statute required 60

[1] Sriram 2009, p. 315.

ratifications to come into force which were obtained in April 2002, paving the way for the launch of the International Criminal Court in July 2002. The African governments subsequently raised objections about the self-exclusion by powerful countries, underpinned by concerns about how the original noble intentions of the Court had become subverted by the political expediency of great power interests.

11.3 Interventions of the International Criminal Court and Perceptions in Africa

The Court's current prosecutorial interventions are exclusively in Africa: the Democratic Republic of the Congo, Central African Republic, Sudan (Darfur), Uganda (Northern), Libya, Côte d'Ivoire, Mali and Kenya. Through a combination of self-initiated interventions by the former Prosecutor, *Louis Moreno Ocampo*, as well as two UN Security Council referrals, and the submission by individual governments of situations to the Court, this Afro-centric focus has created a distorted perception, within the African continent, about the intention underlying the establishment of the Court. It is important to note that the cases in the Central African Republic, the Democratic Republic of the Congo and Uganda were self-referrals by the governments of these countries. There is sense in which 'political justice' is informing the cases currently before the International Criminal Court.

By examining each African case one might be able to formulate a rational explanation why all the current cases of the International Criminal Court are from Africa. The reality is that African countries voluntarily signed up to be subject to the jurisdiction of the Court, so some have questioned why they subsequently have criticized the Court for doing its work. One might even argue that it is impossible for a neutral observer, who critically analyzes the facts, to develop the perception that the International Criminal Court was established for the sole purpose of prosecuting cases from Africa. At the same time, one can conclude that there is a combination of domestic and international political interests behind the submission of, for the time being, only African cases and UN Security Council referrals to the International Criminal Court. Irrespective of the prism through which one chooses to assess the situation, there is a perception among several African governments that the Prosecutor has been selective in submitting cases to the ICC Pre-Trial Chambers. The selective justice in the Court's current prosecutions is seen as an injustice towards the African continent and a form of 'judicial politics'. War crimes are being committed across the world. Hence, it appears to African governments that the International Criminal Court is keen to pursue cases on their continent only, where the states are weak when compared to the diplomatic, economic and financial might of the US, the United Kingdom, Russia, and China. This has hit a diplomatic nerve within the African continent. According to some African officials, there is an entrenched injustice in the actions of this international criminal court whose primary function is to pursue justice for victims of gross violations. Proponents of the Court also have to engage in highly convoluted and incoherent arguments as to why there are no cases from outside of Africa.

The moral integrity of the International Criminal Court, therefore, has been called into question by a number of commentators and observers in Africa. The essential accusation is that cases are not being pursued on the basis of the universal demands of justice, but according to the political expedient of choosing cases that will not cause the Court and its main financial supporters any concerns. The ICC system and the Office of the Prosecutor have failed to answer this charge adequately. Ultimately, what is needed are actions to demonstrate that this Court is for all and not for the select and marginalized few. In the absence of a dialogue reinforced by a concrete action to demonstrate otherwise, the efficacy of the Court will continue to decline across the African continent.

11.4 The African Union's Rationale for Criticizing the International Criminal Court

It is often the case that individuals and leaders who have been accused of planning, financing, instigating and executing atrocities against citizens of another group, all in the name of civil war, can be investigated by the International Criminal Court if the country in question is a State Party or if the issue is referred to the Court by the United Nations Security Council. However, it is often the case also that these individuals and leaders are the very same people who are called upon to engage in a peace process that will lead to the signing of a peace agreement and ensure its implementation.[2]

In this regard, in the situation in Darfur, Sudan, the case of *Prosecutor v. Omar Al Bashir* proved to be controversial. The ICC Pre-Trial Chamber I has issued an arrest warrant for *Al Bashir* for genocide, crimes against humanity and war crimes. Meeting shortly after the Court's decision, the African Union Peace and Security Council issued a communiqué on 5 March 2009[3] which lamented that this decision came at a critical juncture in the ongoing process to promote lasting peace in Sudan.[4] Additionally, through its communiqué of 5 March 2010, the PSC requested the UN Security Council to exercise its powers under Article 16 of the Rome Statute to defer the indictment and arrest of *Al Bashir*. The PSC subsequently expressed its regret over the UN Security Council's failure to exercise its powers of deferral and effectively postpone any action of the International Criminal Court. Consequently, on 3 July 2009, at the 13th Annual Summit of the Assembly of Heads of State and Government held in Sirte, Libya, the African Union decided not to cooperate with the International Criminal Court in

---

[2] Meernik 2005.

[3] See Communiqué of 5 March 2009, PSC/PR/COMM (CLXXV).

[4] African Union 2009.

facilitating the arrest of *Al Bashir*. This decision led to a souring of relations between the Union and the Court.

The African Union was making the case for sequencing the prosecution by the Court due to the fragile peace in Darfur, but there were undoubtedly political reasons for such a request, since the arrest and arraignment of a sitting Head of State in Africa could set a precedent for a significant number of other leaders on the continent, who could potentially be subject to the criminal jurisdiction of the International Criminal Court for their own actions. Therefore, rallying behind *Al Bashir*, who was re-elected as the President of Sudan in April 2010, could be construed not only as a face-saving exercise but also one that seeks to prevent the Court from having such a remit in the administration of international justice on the continent. However, the African Union made the point that Sudan finds itself at a critical juncture of its peacemaking process in Darfur and *Al Bashir* is the key interlocutor with the armed militia and political parties. This argument clearly cannot be wished away or ignored.

The Prosecutor of the International Criminal Court so far has been faced with non-compliance from the Government of Sudan with regard to the arrest warrant for *Al Bashir*, and even other African countries have declined to arrest *Al Bashir* when he has travelled there, including Djibouti, Kenya and Chad. In this case, the prosecution is being delayed not because of the decision and discretion of the Court but because of the non-compliance of African countries and the international community in seeing through its request.[5]

In the majority of cases that the International Criminal Court is currently engaged in, the issue of prosecuting alleged perpetrators is problematic. As noted earlier, given the contentious reality that, more often than not, individuals who have been subject to the jurisdiction of the Court are also key interlocutors in ongoing peace processes, the Court currently is implicated in influencing the dynamics of peacebuilding in the countries in which prosecutions are pending or ongoing. Therefore, the International Criminal Court has the potential to disrupt in-country peacebuilding initiatives if its interventions are not sequenced appropriately.[6]

On 29 and 30 January 2012, the 18th Ordinary Session of the Assembly of AU Heads of State and Government, which was held in Addis Ababa, Ethiopia, reiterated its position not to cooperate with the International Criminal Court. It stipulated that all AU states had to abide by this decision and that failure to do so would invite sanctions from the Union. In particular, the decision urged "all member states to comply with AU Assembly Decisions on the warrants of arrest issued by the Court against President *Bashir* of the Sudan".[7] The African Union further requested its Member States to ensure that its request to defer the situations in Sudan, as well as Kenya, is considered by the UN Security Council.

---

[5] De Waal 2008, p. 31.

[6] De Waal 2008, p. 31.

[7] African Union 2012, para 8.

According to a number of African governments, a court that does not apply the law universally does not justify the label of a court.[8] This is particularly important if the jurisdiction of the Court does not apply to some Western countries that are actively engaged and operating in African conflict zones. What would happen if a citizen of these non-signatory states to the Rome Statute commits war crimes in Africa; who will administer international justice in those particular cases? Although pursuant to the territoriality principle the International Criminal Court would have jurisdiction over such crimes if committed on the territory of an African State Party to the ICC Statute, African leaders seem to be convinced that the Court would not take up the cases, the same way they seem to be convinced that the United Nations would not take any step. This glaring discrepancy undermines the evolving international justice regime and reverses gains made on constraining the self-serving agendas of powerful countries, particularly where their relations with weaker states are concerned.

The view in Africa is that if one demands accountability for African leaders then the same justice should be demanded also of Western, Russian and Chinese leaders, particularly in situations where there is the perception that these leaders have committed the most serious crimes of international concern.[9] In the absence of an over-arching system of global political administration or government, international criminal justice will always be subject to the political whims of individual nation-states.

The African Union has argued that the Rome Statute cannot override the immunity of state officials whose countries are not members of the Assembly of States Parties. The African Union intends to seek an advisory opinion from the International Court of Justice on the immunities of state officials within the rubric of international law.

11.5 Diverging African Opinions on the International Criminal Court

Following the 18th Ordinary Session of the Assembly of AU Heads of State and Government in Addis Ababa, where the African Union reiterated its position not to cooperate with the International Criminal Court, stipulating that all AU States had to abide by this decision and that failure to do so would invite sanctions from the Union, some African countries have expressed their reservations about the Union's position on the International Criminal Court. Botswana publicly disagreed with the AU's decision not to cooperate with the Court, quoting its international obligations under the Rome Statute. South Africa also has reiterated its commitment to

[8] Branch 2011, p. 213.

[9] Schabas 2010.

upholding its legal obligations as a State Party to the Rome Statute. However, while Botswana has been emphatic and unwavering in its support for the Court's actions, South Africa has played a more nuanced diplomatic game due to its key role within the African Union.

In January 2012, South Africa sought the appointment of *Nkosazana Dlamini-Zuma*, its former Foreign Minister, as the Chairperson of the African Union Commission indicating its desire to play a more assertive role within the Union. At the July 2012 AU Summit in Addis Ababa, *Dlamini-Zuma* was ultimately victorious with 37 member states voting for her as the new Chairperson of the Union's Commission. South Africa has adopted a cautious approach towards dealing directly with or raising the profile of the ICC's prosecutions, given its stated position to uphold its international commitment to the Rome Statute. South Africa, therefore, is caught between a rock and a hard place when it comes to the AU-ICC relationship. Given the appointment of *Dlamini-Zuma* as the Chairperson of the AU Commission, and her initial pronouncements on this issue, indications are that it more likely will side with the African Union rather than pursue the Court's agenda on its behalf across the continent. This ultimately does not augur well for the International Criminal Court, given South Africa's important regional role.

11.6 The Second Chief Prosecutor and the Prospects for the AU-ICC Relationship

In December 2011, the Assembly of States Parties appointed *Fatou Bensouda*, former Attorney-General and Minister of Justice of Gambia, as the consensus choice for the Office of the Prosecutor. *Bensouda* was a key member of the *Ocampo* team, as the Deputy Prosecutor in charge of the ICC Prosecutions Division, and it is unlikely that she will digress significantly from the parameters stipulated in the Rome Statute.

Ocampo was emphatic that he did not 'play politics', but it was all too obvious that he was more enthusiastic about initiating prosecutions in African cases only, not even undertaking preliminary investigations into alleged war crimes in Gaza, Sri Lanka and Chechnya, due to the politically sensitive nature of such actions. The Office of the Prosecutor has conducted preliminary investigations in Afghanistan, Georgia, Colombia, Honduras, Korea and Nigeria. However, in *Ocampo's* version of international justice these preliminary investigations took on an air of permanency. 'Permanent preliminary investigations' are essentially a technical way of avoiding launching prosecutions indefinitely.

The historical discrepancy in *Ocampo's* behavior and attitude towards non-African war crime situations was not lost on African leaders. In fact, this fuelled allegations that the ICC Prosecutor was implementing a thinly veiled pro-western agenda, even though he was emphatic in denying this. Critical scholars like *Adam Branch* have argued that there is no valid reason why *Ocampo* could not have instigated prosecutions in non-African countries during his tenure.[10] As a consequence, *Ocampo's* version of the execution of the Court's mandate was viewed with suspicion by some actors in Africa, as a form of 'judicial politics'. For example, *Ocampo's* indictment of six individuals with regard to the crimes against humanity committed during Kenya's post-electoral violence in 2007 and 2008 was used by some politicians as a campaigning tool in the presidential elections in 2013. Such politicians argued that *Ocampos's* selection of only six people was one of the ways in which the Court was used as a tool for political opportunists to dispose of opponents. The appointment of *Bensouda* as the Chief Prosecutor was a move calculated to appease the African members of the Assembly of States Parties. By appointing an African and former Minister of Justice of Gambia, the Assembly of States Parties is communicating the notion that it does not view the Court as advancing an anti-African agenda. An African at the helm of the prosecutorial arm of the Court supposedly will dispel any suspicions that the International Criminal Court is a neo-colonial instrument for disciplining the untamed and still barbaric African landscape.

Bensouda, however, has a mammoth task, since the trust that has been broken between the African Union and the International Criminal Court still needs to be mended. She will need to initiate dialogue with the African Union leadership. Two years after assuming the office, she has not managed yet to distance herself from the confrontational relationship between the Court and the African Union that developed during the *Ocampo* regime. *Bensouda* still has a significant amount of work to do to communicate effectively and directly to African constituencies, governments and civil society and utilize them to convey the objectives and the mandate of the Court. As of 2014, *Bensouda* has convened a series of direct talks with *Dlamini-Zuma*, the Chairperson of the AU Commission. However, this has not translated into a rapprochement between the two organizations.

On Darfur, Bensouda's hands effectively are tied by the stand-off between the African Union and the UN Security Council. The UN Security Council, to date, has declined to issue a formal communication to the African Union on its request for the *Al Bashir* indictment to be deferred. Some members of the UN Security Council have stated informally that the African Union should take the 'hint' and consider the Council's 'silence' as a form of communication. Such dismissive attitudes do not augur well for a mutually acceptable resolution of the impasse between the African Union and the UN Security Council, which in effect also drag in the International Criminal Court and make it appear complicit in not responding to the African Union's request. It is submitted that a good indication that *Bensouda* is serious about opening dialogue with the African Union will be the establishment of a fully operational ICC office in Addis Ababa, the headquarters of the African Union, to serve as liaison office and means for the Court regularly to engage the Union as an interlocutor in its own backyard.

[10] Branch 2011.

11.7 Charting a Way Forward for the African Union and the International Criminal Court

The African Union constantly "reiterates its commitment to fight impunity in conformity with the provisions of Article 4(h) of the Constitutive Act of the African Union".[11] According to officials of the African Union, the body takes exception to being constrained by how other international actors choose to fight impunity on the African continent. This sentiment is not unique to Africa. There is no other region of the world which is subject to the prosecutorial interventions of the International Criminal Court, so it is not possible to gauge the reasonableness of the AU's stance comparatively. All inter-governmental organizations undoubtedly would want to determine how their member states engage with issues relating to transitional justice, peacebuilding, democratic governance and the rule of law, without feeling that there is an overbearing and paternalistic entity in effect stipulating how the continent should be going about doing so.

It is an understatement to note that the relationship between the African Union and the International Criminal Court has commenced badly. Indeed, one could not imagine a worse start. Both organizations share a convergence of mandates to address impunity and to ensure accountability for violations, atrocities and harm done in the past. The organizations diverge in that the African Union is a political organization and the International Criminal Court is an international judicial organization. In this divergence lies the key to how the two organizations go about "addressing impunity and ensuring accountability for past violations, atrocities and harm done". The African Union, by its very nature, will gravitate first to a political solution and approach to dealing with the past, which places an emphasis on peacemaking and political reconciliation. The International Criminal Court, by contrast, will tend to pursue international prosecutions, because this is written into its DNA, the Rome Statute. On paper it would appear that the two approaches may never converge.

Yet, in terms of charting a way forward, there is scope for the African Union to become more nuanced in the situations in which it would side with and support ICC interventions to promote accountability for past violations. Conversely, the International Criminal Court essentially has to acknowledge and communicate that it is aware that it is operating in an international political milieu and that on occasion it would have to craft or sequence its prosecutions to enable political reconciliation processes to run their course. This will require the ICC system to step down from the artificial pedestal on which *Ocampo* has placed it, asserting that it does not play politics, when in fact it appeared that everything that it did was tainted politically. In effect, the International Criminal Court will need to embrace the political lessons of its past transgressions and omissions, and acknowledge openly that, in the absence of a world government, it works in an inherently

[11] African Union 2000.

unrestrained international political system. *Bensouda* and her team will need to reframe the Court's orientation in this regard. This will not require re-opening the Rome Statute to further engineering and potential dismemberment. *Bensouda* can communicate her intentions by issuing Policy Papers of the Office of the Prosecutor on how the Court will order its activities to enable peacemaking to proceed and how her administration intends to go about rectifying and remedying the misperceptions that persist across Africa.

There potentially could be cases in the future in which the African Union would countenance allowing the International Criminal Court to do what it was designed to do; with the proviso that given its nature as a political organization, the Union leadership would be reluctant to expose its membership to a precedent in which one amongst its ranks is prosecuted by the Court. This is, of course, an unpalatable position to take for human rights activists and advocates of prosecuting those who commit egregious atrocities. Specifically, this would be a contravention of the principles of human rights, which would have to be sacrificed at the altar of political pragmatism. There is clearly merit in the position of the human rights organizations. However, in the real world the International Criminal Court has already demonstrated that it is prepared to play politics by failing to pursue certain prosecutions or encouraging the UN Security Council to pursue cases without fear or favor, such as Syria, Gaza, Sri Lanka, Iraq, and Afghanistan where international crimes may have been committed.

Indeed, both the African Union and the International Criminal Court, both which in fact have been practicing a variant of 'political justice' and 'judicial politics', need to reorient their stances. The African Union would need to move away from its exclusively political posture towards embracing international jurisprudence and the limited interventions by the International Criminal Court. Conversely, the Court needs to move away from its unilateral prosecutorial fundamentalism and recognize that there might be a need to arrange its interventions in order to give political reconciliation an opportunity to stabilize a country.

This strategy for repairing the embattled relationship between the African Union and the International Criminal Court would seem to be an unacceptable compromise by some actors on both sides of the spectrum. Their preference would be for their organizations to stick to their ideological guns. In fact, this scenario is playing itself out already. The African Union is undertaking an assessment of how the mandate of its continental institution, the African Court on Human and Peoples' Rights, can be expanded to establish a continental jurisdiction for war crimes, crimes against humanity and genocide.[12] The idea behind this move is essentially to establish a Pan-African Criminal Court with the same mandate as the International Criminal Court, and thereby prosecute all future cases which fall under its jurisdiction on the continent. The AU's criminal court would in essence be seeking to circumventing all future ICC interventions on the African continent. Whether this would lead to African States Parties withdrawing from the Rome Statute is not

[12] African Union 2013, para 10(iv).

yet clear. Furthermore, while the Rome Statute makes provisions for complementarity with national jurisdictions, it does not have similar provisions for continental jurisdictions, so there is no guarantee that a Pan-African Criminal Court would be recognized by the International Criminal Court. However, whether the African Union succeeds in establishing a continental jurisdiction is beside the point; the key issue is that the continental body views its relationship with the International Criminal Court as having deteriorated to such a point that it is exploring actively how to make the Court's presence in Africa an irrelevancy in the future. International organizations such as the League of Nations have folded when their members effectively ignored their mandates. Will the International Criminal Court suffer the same fate in Africa? The response to this question cannot be given for years to come, but it compels us to acknowledge that there is an urgent case to chart a different path for the relationship between the African Union and the International Criminal Court.

On 12 October 2013, an Extraordinary Session of the Assembly of Heads of State and Government of the African Union was convened in Addis Ababa, Ethiopia, to discuss Africa's relationship with the International Criminal Court. The African Union issued a series of decisions, including the need to "safeguard the constitutional order, stability and integrity of member states" by ensuring that "no charges shall be commenced or continued before any International Court or Tribunal against any serving AU Head of State or Government or anybody acting or entitled to act in such a capacity during their term of office".[13] Furthermore, the AU Heads of State called for suspension of the trials of *Kenyatta* and *Ruto* until they have completed their terms of office. In a controversial move, the AU Assembly also stipulated "that any AU member state that wishes to refer a case to the ICC may inform and seek the advice of the African Union".[14] In a direct challenge to a case before the International Criminal Court, the AU Assembly decided "that President *Uhuru Kenyatta* will not appear before the ICC until such time as the concerns raised by the AU and its member states have been adequately addressed by the UN Security Council and the ICC".[15]

Some analysts have argued that this series of decisions signified the African Union consolidating and entrenching its position with regard to the International Criminal Court. The notion that an AU Member State has to inform and seek the advice of the Union if it wishes to refer a case to the International Criminal Court has been criticized for its overt politicization of what should be impartial legal processes.

On 15 November 2013, at the 7,060th Meeting of the UN Security Council, a Resolution seeking to request the International Criminal Court, under Chapter VII of the UN Charter, to defer the investigation and prosecution of President *Kenyatta* and Deputy President *Ruto* for 12 months, in accordance with Article 16 of the

[13] African Union 2013, para 10(i).

[14] African Union 2013, para 10(viii).

[15] African Union 2013, para 10(xi).

Rome Statute, failed to win a majority. In terms of the vote, seven members voted in favor and eight members abstained, which prevented the securing of a mandatory nine votes and no veto to pass the resolution.

On 22 November 2013, there were early indications that the International Criminal Court is open to addressing the concerns of African countries when the 12th Session of the Assembly of States Parties to the Rome Statute of the International Court convened a special segment, at the request of the African Union, on the theme of "Indictment of Sitting Heads of State and Government and its Consequences on Peace and Stability and Reconciliation". The speakers included the AU Legal Counsel, *Djenaba Diarra*, and the Kenyan Attorney General, *Githu Muigai*. *Diarra* commended the Assembly of States Parties for convening the debate and then went on to reiterate her organization's concern about the failure of the International Criminal Court to undertake prosecutions outside Africa, as well as the impact of international criminal proceedings upon efforts to promote peace and stabilize regions. *Muigai* argued that immunities for sitting Heads of State already exist in domestic jurisdictions and that it would be anachronistic not to recognize and implement them at the international level.

11.8 African Civil Society and the International Criminal Court

African civil society does not have a common view as regards the role of the International Criminal Court on the continent. There are several schools of thought among civil society and the wider public. There are those who view the Court as a necessary palliative to the gross impunity which has wreaked havoc with the lives of African citizens. There is a critical view that the International Criminal Court is not a panacea to cure Africa of all of its ills and rid it of its criminal elite. The pro-ICC civil society camp views the Court as confronting and subverting attempts by African leaders and governments to circumvent accountability for past atrocities. It argues that the domestic legal systems are incapable of dealing with the most serious crimes of international concern, and therefore, the Rome Statute's jurisdiction has to be operationalized. The ICC-skeptics question whether justice meted out in The Hague ultimately will bring about any genuine change on the ground, if there is no political will to do so. They argue that even though African legal systems may not be able to live up to some illusionary 'international standard of the administration of justice', there is no reason to sub-contract the judicial process to a remote and aloof Court in The Hague. They further argue that the Court's exclusive focus on African cases during its first 10 years of operation is tantamount to judicial imperialism and a neo-colonial encroachment into national jurisdictions.

On 26 January 2011, approximately 30 civil society organizations from about 20 African countries wrote collectively to African members of the ICC Assembly of States Parties urging them to support the Court. Even though these civil society initiatives are receiving scant attention from the African Union and the majority of African states, they can contribute towards encouraging a more constructive dialogue between the Union and the Court. Ultimately, the matter will be resolved at the level of governments due to the state-centric nature of international relations.

11.9 Strategies for Repairing the AU-ICC Relationship

As to concrete initiatives to repair the relationship between the African Union and the International Criminal Court, the Court needs to reconsider its attitude towards the African Union. In particular, the ICC system, including the Office of the Prosecutor, Registrar and Assembly of States Parties, ought to improve its outreach to and active engagement with African civil society. This could be achieved through meetings across the African continent as well as by adopting a more welcoming and accommodative approach to AU representatives when they come to engage with the International Criminal Court at The Hague. The Court's Chief Prosecutor, *Fatou Bensouda*, needs to appoint a senior political adviser to act as a liaison with political organizations such as the African Union. This might assist with efforts to accredit the International Criminal Court to the AU headquarters in Addis Ababa. Also, *Bensouda* should issue a series of OTP Policy Papers on sequencing the administration of justice to enable the promotion of peacebuilding, particularly in countries that still are affected by war.

As far as the African Union is concerned, it can also adopt a range of initiatives to contribute towards repairing the inter-organizational relationship. In particular, the African Union needs to assess how and when the International Criminal Court can function as its partner in terms of addressing the violation of human rights on the continent. The African Union can engage in a dialogue with the Court and utilize the presence of African countries in the ICC Assembly of States Parties to communicate its views to the Court system. Further, the African Union can work more closely with civil society in relation to policy analysis, victim support, documentation, awareness raising, advocacy and lobbying on issues pertaining to international criminal justice. African civil society should adopt a balanced view when analyzing the impact of the Court's interventions on peace building processes on the continent. This will require a posture of constructive criticism towards the International Criminal Court, rather than the blind and uncritical support that some civil society actors are displaying towards the Court.

11.10 Conclusion

The International Criminal Court is a court of last resort and not a court of first instance. Ideally, national criminal jurisdiction should take precedence in efforts to address impunity. While the Preamble to the Rome Statute recognizes "that such grave crimes threaten the peace, security and well-being of the world",[16] it does not elaborate how the Court will contribute towards advancing "peace" in the broader sense, beyond ensuring that the perpetrators of these crimes are punished. In Africa, the activities of the International Criminal Court have focused on exercising its criminal jurisdiction without engaging in the wider issue of how its actions contribute towards consolidating peace.

The Court's relationship with Africa and, in particular, with the African Union deteriorated following the arrest warrant issued for President *Al Bashir* of Sudan. The AU's policy of non-cooperation with the International Criminal Court is undermining the prospects for the development of international justice, particularly on the African continent. The refusal by some countries to place themselves under the jurisdiction of the Rome Statute means, according to African governments, that the International Criminal Court will fall short of being a genuinely international court. Some African governments view this limited and restricted mandate as undermining the principles of international justice. The former ICC Prosecutor has indicated in private that he cannot apply the same remit of justice to cases in Chechnya, Iraq and Afghanistan because this would be difficult politically. African countries have argued that this approach amounts to there being one law for the powerful and another law for the weak, and selectivity in the administration of international justice.

There is an urgent need to chart a different way forward for the relationship between the African Union and the International Criminal Court. Both organizations need to recognize that while they are fulfilling different functions—delivering justice in the case of the International Criminal Court, and looking out for the interests of African governments in case of the African Union—they need to find a way to ensure that the administration of justice complements efforts to promote political reconciliation.

In a contest between the implementation of international justice and the securing of political interests of African countries, continued tension between the two organizations will not augur well for improving the relationship. The UN Security Council also has an important role to play to communicate formally with the African Union on issues that have been raised in the Council relating to Sudan and Kenya. Ultimately, the UN Security Council is integral to charting a way forward for the African Union and International Criminal Court, which charting will have to be predicated on addressing the perceptions of political justice and judicial politics which persist.

[16] ICC Statute, Preamble.

References

African Union (2000) Constitutive Act of the African Union

African Union (2009) Peace and Security Council, statement on the ICC arrest warrant against the President of the Republic of Sudan, Omar Al Bashir. PSC/PR/COMM.(CLXXV), 5 March

African Union (2012) Decisions, resolutions and declarations of the assembly of the union, eighteenth ordinary session of the assembly of heads of state and government. Assembly/Au/Dec.397(XVIII), 29–30 January, Addis Ababa, Ethiopia

African Union (2013) Decisions and declarations of the assembly of the union, extraordinary session of the assembly of heads of state and government. Ext/Assembly/AU/Dec.1–2, 12 October 2013

Branch A (2011) Displacing human rights: war and intervention in Northern Uganda. Oxford University Press, Oxford

De Waal A (2008) Darfur, the court and Khartoum: the politics of state non-cooperations. In: Waddell N, Clark P (eds) Courting conflict? Justice, peace and the ICC in Africa. Royal African Society, London, pp 29–35

Meernik J (2005) Justice and peace? How the International Criminal Tribunal affects societal peace in Bosnia. J Peace Res 42(3):271–289

Schabas W (2010) The International Criminal Court. In: Black D, Williams P (eds) The international politics of mass atrocities: the case of Darfur. Routledge, London, pp 134–153

Sriram CL (2009) The ICC Africa experiment: the Central African Republic, Darfur, Northern Uganda and the Democratic Republic of the Congo. In: Sriram CL, Pillay S (eds) Peace versus justice? The dilemma of transitional justice in Africa. University of Kwa-Zulu Natal Press, Scotsville, p 315

Chapter 12
Africa, the United Nations Security Council and the International Criminal Court: The Question of Deferrals

Juliet Okoth

Contents

12.1 Introduction

Africa's current relationship with the International Criminal Court has deteriorated considerably. Africa seems to have turned from being the Court's greatest supporter to one of the Court's biggest opponents.[1] All situations presently before the International Criminal Court relate to Africa.[2] One would think of this as being something good given the continent's long history of atrocities being committed but in respect of which none or very few perpetrators have been held accountable. Instead, the Court has been branded, at least by African leaders, as an enemy of the African people. One issue that has put the continent's leaders at crossroads with not only the Court but also the UN Security Council is the question of deferring cases under Article 16 of the ICC Statute. This is reflected in the bitter statements

[1] African States played a central role in negotiating and accelerating the entry into force of the Rome Statute that establishes the International Criminal Court. See Jalloh et al. 2011, pp. 13–15.
[2] The situations are in: Uganda, Democratic Republic of the Congo, Darfur/Sudan, Central African Republic, Kenya, Libya, Cote d'Ivoire, and Mali.

J. Okoth (✉)
University of Nairobi, Nairobi, Kenya
e-mail: julietokoth@gmail.com

G. Werle et al. (eds.), *Africa and the International Criminal Court*,
International Criminal Justice Series 1, DOI 10.1007/978-94-6265-029-9_12

that followed the most recent failed attempt to defer cases before the International Criminal Court in respect to the Kenyan situation. Kenya's Ministry of Foreign Affairs sharply criticized this outcome and accused certain important members of the Security Council of abdicating global leadership and humiliating the African continent and its leadership.[3]

The African Union has been discontent for a while now with the UN Security Council's manner of handling its requests for deferrals. This discontentment was first triggered by the failure of the Security Council to consider the African Union's request to defer proceedings in respect of *Al Bashir*, the President of Sudan.[4] This calls for a closer look into whether Africa's contention with the way the issue of deferrals has so far been handled is genuine or rather an attempt to prevent justice for the many victims of international crimes on the continent.

This chapter will begin by giving a chronology of the events that have contributed to the AU's dissatisfaction with the use of Article 16 of the Rome Statute. It then looks at the legal framework of Article 16, giving a brief background of its drafting history and its rationale. It will then look into the practice that has been grounded by the law in Article 16 and finally give an analysis of the merits of the AU's contention on the use of this Article.

12.2 Genesis of the Problem

In 2005 the UN Security Council adopted Resolution 1593 which referred the Darfur conflict to the International Criminal Court for investigation.[5] This resulted in the summoning of, among others, the President of Sudan, *Al Bashir*, and subsequently the issuance of two warrants for his arrest in relation to the crimes of genocide and crimes against humanity committed in the Darfur region.[6] This course of events did not please both the government of Sudan and the African Union. The African Union was of the view that the ICC process would jeopardize the delicate peace process that it was spearheading in respect of the Darfur conflict. The African Union thus requested the UN Security Council to suspend the ICC process in respect of the Darfur conflict, using its powers under Article 16 of the ICC Statute.[7] The UN Security Council has consistently failed to act on this request. In response to the UN Security Council's failure to consider its request,

---

[3] Kenyan Ministry of Foreign Affairs (2013).

[4] Assembly of the African Union, Decision on the Meeting of African States Parties to the Rome Statute of the International Criminal Court (ICC), Assembly/AU/Dec.245 (XIII), Sirte, July 3, 2009.

[5] S.C. Res. 1593, 31 March 2005, 5158th mtg., U.N. Doc. S/RES/1593 (2005).

[6] *Prosecutor v. Omar Hassan Ahmed Al Bashir*, first warrant of arrest issued on 4 March 2009, second warrant of arrest issued on 12 July 2010.

[7] African Union Peace and Security Council communiqué, PSC/PR/COMM.(CLXXV), 5 March 2009.

the African Union directed all its Member States not to cooperate with the International Criminal Court in the arrest and surrender of *Al Bashir*, citing Article 98 of the ICC Statute as the legal basis of its decision.[8] As a result, several African states, even States Parties to the Rome Statute of the International Criminal Court, have hosted *Al Bashir* thus failing to execute the Court's request for arrest and surrender.[9] The consequence of this was the AU's proposal seeking to amend Article 16 to allow the UN General Assembly to decide on the question of deferrals should the UN Security Council turn down the proposal.[10] This proposal did not, however, materialize and the African Union seems to have since stopped pursuing the issue.

On 15 February 2011, demonstrations against the administration of the late *Muammar Gaddafi* broke out in Libya. In an attempt to quell these demonstrations state hardware was used, resulting into the deaths of several civilians. This situation prompted the UN Security Council, under its mandate of maintaining peace and security, to unanimously adopt Resolution 1970 which referred the situation in Libya to the International Criminal Court.[11] This resulted in, among others, a warrant of arrest issued against the then Head of State *Gaddafi*.[12] Once again the concerns of the African Union in the *Al Bashir* case were raised with regard to the *Gaddafi* case. The African Union was deeply concerned that *Gaddafi's* warrant of arrest undermined its efforts in facilitating negotiations that would lead to a peaceful solution. The African Union took a similar position to the one in the case of *Al Bashir* and decided not to cooperate with the International Criminal Court, noting that the warrant of arrest "seriously complicates the efforts aimed at finding a negotiated political solution to the crisis in Libya".[13] The African Union, in its decision, also requested the "UN Security Council to activate the provisions of Article 16 of the Rome Statute with a view to deferring the ICC process on Libya, in the interest of justice as well as peace in the country".[14] This request was never considered and eventually the *Gaddafi* regime was overthrown.

On 12 October 2013, Kenya rallied the rest of Africa to support its bid to defer the cases before the International Criminal Court in respect to its President *Uhuru*

---

[8] Assembly of the African Union, Decision on the Meeting of African States Parties to the Rome Statute of the International Criminal Court (ICC), Assembly/AU/Dec.245 (XIII), Sirte, July 3, 2009, paras 9–10.

[9] Among the nations that *Al Bashir* has visited are Kenya and Chad which are States Parties to the ICC Statute.

[10] For a detailed discussion on the proposal see Jalloh et al. 2011, pp. 5–50.

[11] S.C. Res. 1970, 26 February 2011, 6491st mtg., U.N. Doc. S/RES/1970 (2011).

[12] Situation in Libya, Warrant of Arrest for Muammar Mohammed Abu Minyar Gaddafi, 27 June 2011.

[13] African Union Assembly, Decision on the implementation of the assembly decisions on the International Criminal Court, Assembly/AU/Dec. 366 (XVII), Doc.EX.CL/670 (XIX), 30 June–1 July 2011, para 6.

[14] Ibid.

Kenyatta, and his deputy, *William Ruto*.[15] The two are charged before the Court with crimes against humanity that were allegedly committed during the post-election violence that occurred in Kenya after the contested 2007 presidential elections.[16] The AU's main concern in this case was that the continued prosecution of the President and his deputy undermined the sovereignty, stability and peace of the people of Kenya, and that it also compromises their ability to spearhead the fight against terrorism in the East African region.[17] The UN Security Council failed to adopt a draft resolution to defer these proceedings.[18] Although this was the first time the issue was formally considered by the UN Security Council, Kenya had previously made unsuccessful attempts to have the Court's jurisdiction deferred in respect of cases relating to its citizens.[19] The failure to adopt the resolution for a deferral elicited sharp criticism from the African representatives. The Kenyan representative, while expressing his disappointment, stated that the Security Council is "[...] no institutional destination for serving complex and fluid international security and political problems".[20] The sentiments of the Kenyan representative were followed by a letter from the Kenyan Ministry of Foreign Affairs which accused certain members of the Security Council who held veto powers of not appreciating issues concerning peace and security.[21] The Ministry criticized the Security Council for failing to take note of the African Union Resolution, which emphasized that no sitting Head of State or Government should appear before the International Criminal Court.

The above chronology of events gives the background to the AU's dissatisfaction with the manner in which the UN Security Council has dealt with the question of deferrals. The African Union considers Article 16 of the ICC Statute as essential, especially when the question of peace is at stake. The AU's request for a deferral in the Sudan situation was motivated by its concerns that the arrest warrant against *Al Bashir* would have a negative impact on the peace process in Sudan. Similar sentiments were expressed by the African Union in reference to the conflict in Libya and the arrest warrant issued against *Gaddafi*. In the Kenya situation, the concern was that the continued prosecution of a Head of State and his Deputy undermined Kenya's capability to carry out its constitutional mandate and to deal with serious issues relating to peace and security in the region. The AU's

---

[15] African Union Assembly, Decision on Africa's relationship with the International Criminal Court (ICC), Ext/Assembly/AU/Dec. 1, October 2013.

[16] See *Prosecutor v. William Samoei Ruto and Joshua Arap Sang*; *Prosecutor v. Uhuru Muigai Kenyatta*.

[17] African Union Assembly, Decision on Africa's relationship with the International Criminal Court (ICC), Ext/Assembly/AU/Dec. 1, October 2013.

[18] UNSC, 7060th Meeting, S/PV.7060 "Peace and security in Africa", 15 Nov 2013.

[19] See Security Council Report, "Chronology of Events, Kenya". Other attempts had been in April 2011 and May 2013. In both instances council members had advised Kenya that its requests would be best pursued before the International Criminal Court itself.

[20] UNSC, 7060th Meeting, S/PV.7060 "Peace and security in Africa", 15 Nov 2013.

[21] Kenyan Ministry of Foreign Affairs (2013).

requests on the use of Article 16 show its preference for the adoption of a political solution where the question of peace prevails over the question of justice. This position was confirmed during its 21st ordinary session when the African Union reaffirmed that "the search for justice should be pursued in a way that does not impede or jeopardize efforts aimed at promoting lasting peace".[22] Although the question of peace has always been cited in AU's requests for deferrals, an issue that has greatly displeased it is the prosecution of its leaders before the International Criminal Court, and this, perhaps, to a great extent informed its motive for the requests for deferrals.[23] This motive could be deciphered from the decision made on its extraordinary session in October 2013, when the African Union reiterated its "concern on the politicization and misuse of indictments against African Union leaders". [24] The African Union has thus lamented the failure of the UN Security Council to use Article 16 for purposes that suit African leaders. This makes it important to look into the merits of the AU's expectations in light of the law that informs Article 16 of the Rome Statute.

12.3 The Legal Foundation of Deferrals

Article 16 of the ICC Statute allows the UN Security Council, through a resolution under Chapter VII of the UN Charter, to suspend an ICC investigation or prosecution for a renewable period of 12 months. Article 16 specifically provides:

> No investigation or prosecution may be commenced or proceeded with under this Statute for a period of 12 months after the Security Council, in a resolution adopted under Chapter VII of the Charter of the United Nations, has requested the Court to that effect, that request may be renewed by the Council under the same conditions.

The UN Security Council is authorized under Chapter VII of its Charter to take measures to maintain or restore international peace and security in the case where it has been established that there is a threat to the peace, breach of peace or act of aggression. Thus Article 16 provides an instance in which the UN Security Council may interfere with the work of the Court if it considers the Court's intervention as threatening peace and security.

During the drafting of the ICC Statute negotiations on Article 16 was among the most contentious issues.[25] There was a great concern that the Article would allow the UN Security Council to interfere with the independent functioning of the

---

[22] African Union Assembly, Decision on International Jurisdiction, Justice and the International Criminal Court, Doc. Assembly/AU/13 (XXI), 26–27 May 2013, para 4.

[23] Tladi 2009, p. 61.

[24] See African Union Assembly, Decision on Africa's relationship with the International Criminal Court (ICC), Ext/Assembly/AU/Dec. 1, October 2013, para 4.

[25] Jalloh et al. 2011, p. 15; Abass 2005, p. 269.

Court.[26] The initial draft of the Article automatically prevented the Court from taking action in a situation that was being dealt with by the Security Council under the Chapter VII of the UN Charter, unless the UN Security Council decided otherwise. The draft Article stated:

> No prosecution may be commenced under this Statute from a situation which is being dealt with by the Security Council as a threat to or a breach of the peace or an act of aggression under Chapter VII of the Charter, unless the Security Council otherwise decides.[27]

One concern raised with this draft was that it made the Court's intervention inferior to the Security Council's responsibility to maintain peace and security.[28] Another challenge that the draft proposal presented was the possibility of the Security Council dealing with a matter indefinitely, thus preventing any intervention from the Court.[29] There was need to adopt a proposal that checked the extent to which the Security Council could interfere with the independent functioning of the Court. This led to further negotiations that eventually culminated in the final draft that now forms the wording of Article 16.[30]

When considering a matter under Article 16, the Security Council is called to perform a balancing act between the issues of peace and justice, which makes this Article inherently very controversial.[31] Nonetheless, Article 16 clearly articulates that the only situation that would justify a deferral must be one that poses a threat to peace and security.

12.4 A False Start?

On 12 July 2002 the UN Security Council adopted Resolution 1422.[32] This Resolution exempted from the ICC jurisdiction personnel from states that are not party to the ICC Statute and that are involved in an operation authorized by the UN Security Council for a period of 12 months. The United States had prompted this Resolution with the sole motive of protecting its troops participating in UN operations from the possibility of being prosecuted before the Court.[33] The Resolution was made by the Security Council acting under Chapter VII of the UN Charter and invoking Article 16 of the ICC Statute. It partly stated:

---

[26] Kim 2011, p. 178; Abass 2005, p. 269.

[27] Draft Statute for an International Criminal Court, Report of the International Law Commission, UN GAOR, Supp. No. 10, UN Doc. A/49/10, Article 23 (3).

[28] Neuner 2012, p. 299; Jalloh et al. 2011, p. 16.

[29] Neuner 2012, p. 300; Kim 2011, p. 179.

[30] Kim 2011, pp. 179–180; Abass 2005, pp. 269–271.

[31] Krzan 2009, p. 77.

[32] S.C. Res. 1422, U.N. SCOR, 57th Sess., 4572d mtg., U.N. Doc. S/RES/1422 (2002).

[33] Jalloh et al. 2011, p. 17; Krzan 2009, p. 80; Jain 2005, p. 240; Zappala 2003, p. 117.

> Requests, consistent with the provisions of Article 16 of the Rome Statute, that the ICC, if a case arises involving current or former officials or personnel from a contributing State not a Party to the Rome Statute over acts or omissions relating to a United Nations established or authorized operation, shall for a twelve-month period starting 1 July 2002 not commence or proceed with investigation or prosecution of any such case, unless the Security Council decides otherwise.[34]

On 12 June 2003 this Resolution was renewed through resolution 1487, extending the same *status quo* for a further 12 months.[35] Resolutions 1422 and 1487 were not popular with the proponents of the Court and fuelled the controversy around the question as to what extent the UN Security Council should influence the work of the International Criminal Court.[36] The tension arising from this debate led to the withdrawal by the United States of a further attempt to renew Resolution 1487 and instead the more controversial Resolution 1497 was adopted.[37] This Resolution provided that states contributing troops for the UN operation in Liberia would have exclusive jurisdiction for crimes committed by their troops unless that jurisdiction is expressly waived. Resolution 1497 thus expressly shut out the possibility of an ICC intervention and also locked out the possibility of other third states, who may otherwise have jurisdiction for crimes committed against their nationals or in their territory, from exercising jurisdiction.[38]

The opponents of Resolutions 1422 and 1487 argued that they discriminated against officials from States Parties of the International Criminal Court. They further contended that they attempted to modify the Rome Statute indirectly without seeking an amendment, and that they were vehemently opposed to the clauses that seemed to imply that the Resolutions would be automatically renewable, regardless of whether the circumstances that led to the initial deferral had changed.[39] The next Security Council Resolutions that cited Article 16 are Resolutions 1593 and 1970 that referred the Darfur and the Libya situation respectively to the International Criminal Court.[40] The Resolutions, although recalling the particulars of Article 16, did not specifically indicate what part of the Resolutions Article 16 would apply to. It can only be presumed that in light of Resolutions 1422 and 1487, Article 16 was cited in reference to Para 6 of both Resolutions, in which the Security Council decided to exempt officials from non-States Parties from the jurisdiction of the International Criminal Court (this

[34] U.N. Doc. S/RES/1422 (2002), para 1.

[35] S.C. Res. 1487, U.N. SCOR, 58th Sess., 4772d mtg., U.N. DOC. S/RES/1487 (2003).

[36] Jalloh et al. 2011, p. 17; Abass 2005, p. 272.

[37] S.C. Res. 1497, U.N. SCOR, 58th Sess., 4803d mtg., U.N. Doc. S/RES/1497 (2003).

[38] For further analysis on Resolution 1497, see Abass 2005, pp. 263–297; Jain 2005, pp. 239–254.

[39] Jalloh et al. 2011, p. 17; Abass 2005, p. 272.

[40] U.N. Doc. S/RES/1593 (2005), preamble para 2; U.N. Doc. S/RES/1970 (2011), Preamble para 12.

exemption did not apply to officials from the Sudan and Libya), and instead to give exclusive jurisdiction to the contributing states.[41]

Both Resolutions 1422 and 1487 made reference to Article 16 of the ICC Statute. The legality of these Resolutions has been the subject of much debate.[42] A deferral under Article 16 requires that the criteria set out in it are met. There has to be a threat to international peace and security under Chapter VII of the UN Charter, and any deferral adopted is for a renewable period of 12 months. The circumstances under which these Resolutions were made could not be characterized as situations that threatened international peace and security. Article 16 was intended to operate once the Court is seized of a situation, that is once the ICC prosecutor starts investigations or after an individual has been charged before the Court, marking the beginning of prosecution.[43] Resolutions 1422 and 1487 instead used Article 16 to preemptively grant immunity under the ICC Statute to troops belonging to states not party to the International Criminal Court.[44] It is difficult to see how the hypothetical future possibility of the International Criminal Court carrying out investigations or prosecuting a peace keeper from a country not party to the Court would threaten the peace and security of the country.[45]

In the case of Resolutions 1593 (Darfur situation) and 1970 (Libya situation),[46] Para 6 effectively terminates the jurisdiction of the International Criminal Court. Article 16 was only intended to suspend the Court's jurisdiction for a renewable period of 12 months. It is also questionable that preventing the Court from exercising jurisdiction as envisaged by these Resolutions can be considered to restore international peace and justice. This makes it difficult to support the legal basis of Para 6 of both Resolutions under Article 16 of the ICC Statute.[47]

Resolutions 1422, 1487, 1593 and 1970 show that the initial applications of Article 16 by the Security Council were inconsistent with the express wording and original purpose of this Article. The *travaux preparatoires* of Article 16 and the sentiments of the states that opposed Resolutions 1422 and 1487 reveal that the understanding of most states at the time of adopting Article 16 was that the power of the Security Council to defer investigations or prosecutions would be used only in exceptional cases where there was a threat to peace and security and for a limited period of time.[48] In this respect the Security Council abused its power under Article 16, thus undermining the credibility of the Court.

---

[41] Jalloh et al. 2011, p. 20.

[42] See Kim 2011, pp. 180–186; Abass 2005, pp. 271–273; Jain 2005, pp. 239–254.

[43] Kim 2011, p. 182.

[44] Kim 2011, pp. 180-181.

[45] Jain 2005, p. 302.

[46] Both Resolutions can be found in the Annex to this volume.

[47] Cf. Jain 2005, pp. 244–245.

[48] Jalloh et al. 2011, pp. 18–21.

12.5 The AU Deferral Requests: An Analysis of Their Merits Under Article 16

The AU's contention with the UN Security Council, the International Criminal Court and the use of Article 16 has been with the failure to adopt its request to defer proceedings relating in particular to its Heads of State. When the African Union forwarded the request of deferral of proceedings in respect of *Al Bashir*, it contended that this was essential to facilitate the negotiation of a peace deal in the Darfur crisis. The same reasoning was given for the deferral request in the situation of Libya when arrest warrants were issued against *Gaddafi*. The reasoning of the African Union in the two situations was that the demands of peace dictated that the prosecution of the two leaders be set aside. The demands of the African Union cannot be considered as far-fetched because this very reasoning informed the inclusion of Article 16 in the Rome Statute. When the Security Council is of the view that the needs of peace dictate that the question of justice be set aside at least temporarily, Article 16 allows for a deferral to be adopted if it would be the best solution in the circumstances.

The challenge perhaps with the Darfur and Libya crisis was that both situations were referred to the International Criminal Court by the Security Council under Article 13 (b) of the Rome Statute. Such referrals are made only if the situation in question is considered to be a threat to peace and security under Chapter VII of the UN Charter.[49] In such circumstances, it would be difficult to envisage a situation that has been referred to the Court by the Security Council as qualifying for deferral under Article 16.[50] A deferral request under such instances would require proof that the Court's interventions has further contributed to a deterioration of the situation, which can almost be an impossible task. The African Union failed to show that the ICC intervention in Darfur and Libya in fact constituted a threat to peace and that the suspension of the ICC process would effectively contribute to restoration of peace. By referring both situations in Darfur and Libya to the International Criminal Court, the Security Council confirmed that issues of peace and justice can be pursued simultaneously. A humanitarian crisis still looms in the Darfur region but in the meanwhile the Government of Sudan has set up courts in the region to prosecute perpetrators of international crimes.[51] Although no high profile person has been prosecuted by these courts, particularly those being pursued by the International Criminal Court, there is an attempt to hold some perpetrators accountable and this process can most likely be attributable to the ICC

---

[49] Article 13(b) ICC Statute allows the Court to exercise its jurisdiction in respect of international crimes if a situation in which one or more of such crimes appears to have been committed is referred to the Prosecutor by the Security Council acting under Chapter VII of the Charter of the United Nations.

[50] Tladi 2009, p. 68.

[51] The latest report from the UN indicates that the security situation in Darfur over the course of 2013 deteriorated and remains volatile, see UN News Centre 2014.

intervention.[52] The crisis in Libya culminated in a regime change and the death of its former leader *Muammar Gaddafi*.[53]

In the case of Kenya, the AU's view was that the ICC proceedings undermined the capabilities of the recently elected President and his Deputy in performing their constitutional duties, and as such, they also undermined the sovereignty of the people of Kenya. To satisfy the peace and security requirement, Kenya and the African Union asserted that there was the problem of terrorism that plagued the country and the East Africa region, and the President's and Deputy's role in fighting terrorism were being compromised by the cases before the International Criminal Court. The question that arises here is whether the Security Council can invoke Article 16, citing the official capacity of the accused person. This argument is not supported by the threat to peace and security criteria set out in Article 16. The argument can also not be supported by virtue of Article 27(2) of the ICC Statute which overrides the immunity of state officials. The President of Kenya and his deputy had long been indicted by the International Criminal Court before they decided to seek the highest elective offices of the land. They were fully aware of the charges and their implications should they win the presidential elections.[54] The attempt thereafter to seek suspension of the proceedings can only be interpreted as ill-motivated. If the Security Council had adopted a deferral resolution founded on this ground, it would not only contradict the purpose of Article 16, but would also set a dangerous precedent. This would encourage any suspected perpetrators who are before the International Criminal Court to seek elective office, and thereafter frustrate the ICC proceedings through the deferral process hence, encourage impunity.

Another interesting dimension emerged in the request for a deferral in the Kenya situation. Kenya is a country that has been seriously affected by the crime of terrorism.[55] This problem has since been heightened since Kenya joined in the war against *Al Shaabab*, a terrorist group based in Somalia.[56] This dimension was introduced by Kenya in its request for deferral following the *Al Shaabab's* most recent attack in the country.[57] The problem that then emerges is whether the

---

52 Sterling 2006.

53 The circumstances that led to the overthrow of *Gaddafi's* regime, and eventually to his death, were criticized as an opportunistic construction of UNSC Res 1973 (2011), which introduced active measures, including no-fly zone, by the NATO to engineer a regime change. See Mbeki (2012).

54 During one of the presidential election debates *Uhuru Kenyatta* was asked how he would be able to govern the country with his case pending before the International Criminal Court. He clearly indicated that this was a personal challenge that would not affect his duties as the President of Kenya.

55 East African Centre for Law and Justice 2013.

56 Blanchard 2013.

57 On 21 September 2013, unknown gunmen attacked the Westgate shopping mall in Nairobi, causing the death of at least 72 people and over 200 casualties. The *Al Shabaab* terrorist group claimed responsibility for the attack.

question of threat to peace and security under Article 16 must relate directly to the situation that led to the Court's intervention, or may as be extended to any other situation of peace and security. The situation of Kenya before the International Criminal Court relates to the post-2007 election violence. At the time of the deferral request there was no indication that the violence that occurred in Kenya in 2007–2008 threatened to reoccur. In fact, there is no evidence that since the Court has intervened there has been an increased threat to peace and security in the country. The peaceful presidential elections in 2013 can mostly be attributed to the ICC process. An assessment of the *travaux preparatoires* of Article 16 shows that its drafters could not have intended that the question of peace and security be extended to situations that do not relate directly to the question of justice before the International Criminal Court. This may be debatable, but it is difficult to cite the terrorism threat in Kenya as a reason that would justify an Article 16 intervention in the proceedings against its leaders.

The AU's main problem with the International Criminal Court began when the Court started to initiate proceedings against the AU Heads of State. The African Union contends that the Rome Statute cannot override the personal immunity of a serving Head of State.[58] Article 27(2) makes official capacity irrelevant in the Court's exercise of its jurisdiction. Thus the question of immunity cannot be raised to oppose the ICC proceedings. This applies especially to States Parties such as Kenya. As for non-State parties like Sudan and Libya, a referral by the Security Council to the International Criminal Court makes them subject to the provisions of the ICC Statute, making Article 27 also applicable to them.[59]

The issue of deferral under Article 16 also has a temporal aspect. A deferral is valid for only 12 months and although renewable, such renewal cannot be automatic. At the time of the request for a renewal it must be shown that the circumstances that led to the deferral still prevail. This means that the ICC process cannot be suspended indefinitely. The AU's requests for deferral in respect of Kenya and Sudan have taken issue with proceedings in the International Criminal Court against constitutionally elected Heads of State. The implication of this is that if any deferral would be adopted on account of an accused's official capacity, it would have to take into account the elective term of such official. In the case of Kenya an electoral cycle is every five years, therefore, any deferral would have to last for this period, and in case the President would be re-elected a further five years.[60] Such a deferral would clearly contravene the express terms of Article 16.

---

[58] See African Union Assembly, Decision on Africa's relationship with the International Criminal Court (ICC), Ext/Assembly/AU/Dec. 1, October 2013, para 10, where the AU decided, "[t]hat to safeguard the constitutional order, stability and integrity of Member States, no charges shall be commenced or continued before any International Court or Tribunal against any serving Head of State or Government or anybody acting or entitled to act in such capacity during their term of office".

[59] Ciampi 2008, p. 895.

[60] The Constitution of Kenya allows for a two-term presidency, Section 142 of the Constitution of Kenya, 2010.

Article 16 allows political considerations to be measured against the question of justice. A deferral under Article 16 can have serious consequences for a situation before the Court. It can interfere with the collection and preservation of evidence, complicate the protection of witnesses, affect the right of the accused to a fair and expeditious trial, and also affect the rights of the victims.[61] Thus when considering a request for a deferral, its potential consequences need to be taken into account. It is necessary that any request should be for the sole purpose of enhancing peace and security and not to shield certain individuals and encourage impunity by derailing judicial proceedings.

Assessing the general practice on Article 16, the AU's assertion that the UN Security Council applies double standards on questions of international criminal justice perhaps has merit in light of the initial deferral requests, which granted immunity from the ICC jurisdiction to troops of states not party to the ICC Statute. Comparing these earlier Resolutions to the AU's requests for deferral, the AU situations would in fact make better cases for the application of Article 16. This practice by the UN Security Council unfortunately justifies the sentiments of the Rwandan representative, following the recent failed attempt to adopt a deferral request in the case of Kenya, when he stated that international mechanisms only serve the interests of a few select and that Article 16 was never intended to be used by an African State.[62]

The cases that the African Union have presented for deferral indicate a motive to shield its leaders from humiliation by being subjected to international justice mechanisms as opposed to genuine situations that would merit an Article 16 intervention. The Security Council, when exercising its powers under the ICC Statute, should do so with the purpose of supporting the Court in its goal of ending impunity. The standard adopted by the UN Security Council in rejecting AU requests for deferral should be the standard in all future situations. It would avoid political interference in the working of the International Criminal Court, thus enhancing its independence and credibility.

12.6 Conclusion

The instances in which the UN Security Council has used its power under Article 16 have proved to be controversial. Reconciling the interests of peace and security on the one hand and the interests of justice and the fight against impunity on the other is a delicate and complicated task. Article 16 of the Rome Statute is one tool that attempts to achieve this reconciliation. A deferral of prosecutions or investigations under Article 16 should not simply be there for the asking. It is necessary that any request for a deferral meets the conditions provided for in Article 16.

[61] Neuner 2012, p. 306; Kim 2011, pp. 200–209.

[62] UNSC, 7060th Meeting, S/PV.7060 "Peace and security in Africa", 15 November 2013.

A convincing case for deferral must be made clearly, indicating to what extent the ICC intervention affects the interests of peace and security. It is also important to take into account the far reaching consequences that a deferral may have in the ICC process as regards the collection and preservation of evidence and the rights of the victims and the accused. Any deferral adopted as a result must be for 12 months only, and any further attempts to renew must clearly show that conditions that justified the deferral in the first place still prevail. Deferrals should not be made with the aim of shielding certain individuals from prosecution.

Although the African Union is dissatisfied with the UN Security Council and its manner of handling its requests under Article 16, the reasons it has presented for deferral for the various cases have not been very convincing. When the Security Council refers a matter to the International Criminal Court on the ground that it is a threat to world peace and security, it must be convinced that the ICC intervention is necessary to facilitate the peace process. To suspend this process again under the ICC Statute would need very compelling reasons. A strong case would have to be made out to show that the ICC process has otherwise become complicated, making the peace process impossible. Article 16 should not be allowed to give perpetrators of international crimes the opportunity to foster impunity by threatening violence in exchange for immunity, under the guise of pursuing peace and political stability. The AU's calls for deferrals have been politically motivated, being attempts to secure immunity for high ranking state officials. Under the ICC official capacity is irrelevant when the person is suspected of having committed international crimes. Article 16 cannot, therefore, be used to pursue immunity for Heads of State. A deferral because of official capacity would set a dangerous precedent. It would encourage future suspects who are before the International Criminal Court, and who are most likely to be high-profile political figures in their respective countries, to vie for elective posts, thus making it difficult for their cases before the Court to proceed.

The AU's requests for deferral have not been at variance with the initial application of Article 16, where the UN Security Council preemptively granted certain officials, from non-States Parties to the International Criminal Court, immunity from the ICC jurisdiction. The practice initially adopted by the UN Security Council on deferrals was clearly inconsistent with the purpose of Article 16. Unfortunately, when looking at the practice on deferrals one would be justified to say that the principle of fair and equal application of the law has not been observed, which provides sound reasons for the AU's concerns that the UN Security Council applies double standards. This practice seriously undermines the credibility and authority of the Court. By rejecting the AU requests for deferral, the UN Security Council has clearly set up a high threshold to satisfy the threat to peace and security criteria under Article 16. This represents the correct direction that the Security Council should take when looking into Article 16. Any power exercised under Article 16 should be to support the goal of the Court to end impunity. The AU's calls for deferral should be to pursue the concerns for peace genuinely and not to shield its Heads of State from prosecution by the International Criminal Court.

References

Abass A (2005) The competence of the Security Council to terminate the jurisdiction of the International Criminal Court. Texas Int Law J 40:263–298

Blanchard LP (2013) The September 2013 terrorist attack in Kenya: In Brief. November 2013. Congressional Research Service

Ciampi A (2008) The proceedings against President Al Bashir and the prospects of their suspension under Article 16 ICC Statute. J Int Crim Justice 6:885–897

Jain N (2005) A separate law for peacekeepers: the clash between the Security Council and the International Criminal Court. Eur J Int Law 16:239–254

Jalloh CC, Akande D, du Plessis M (2011) Assessing the African Union concerns about Article 16 of the Rome Statute of the International Criminal Court. Afr J Legal Stud 4:5–50

Kim S (2011) Maintaining the independence of the International Criminal Court: the legal and procedural implications of an Article 16 deferral request. Agenda Int 18:175–212

Krzan B (2009) The relationship between the International Criminal Court and the Security Council. Pol Yearb Int Law 29:65–84

Mbeki T (2012) Reflections on peacemaking, state sovereignty and democratic governance in Africa. www.thabombekifoundation.org.za/Pages/Dullah-Omar-Eighth-Memorial-Lecture-By-The-Tmf-Patron.aspx

Neuner M (2012) The Security Council and the ICC: assessing the first ten years of coexistence. N Engl J Int Compar Law 18:283–310

Sterling F (2006), No justice for Darfur in local courts, June 8, 2006, Global Policy Forum

Tladi D (2009) The African Union and the International Criminal Court: the battle for the soul of international law. S Afr Yearb Int Law 34:57–69

Zappala S (2003) The reaction of the US to the entry into force of the ICC Statute: comments on UN SC resolution 1422 and Article 98 agreements. J Int Crim Justice 1:114–134

Cases

The Prosecutor v. Omar Hassan Ahmed Al Bashir, first warrant of arrest issued on 4 March 2009, second warrant of arrest issued on 12 July 2010, ICC-02/05-01/09.

The Prosecutor v. William Samoei Ruto and Joshua Arap Sang, ICC-01/09-01/11.

The Prosecutor v. Uhuru Muigai Kenyatta, ICC-01/09-02/11.

Other Documents

Situation in Libya, Warrant of Arrest for Muammar Mohammed Abu Minyar Gaddafi, 27 June 2011, ICC-01/11.

African Union Peace and Security Council communiqué, PSC/PR/COMM. (CLXXV), 5 March 2009.

East African Centre for Law and Justice 2013, "Terrorism in Kenya", October 2013. http://eaclj.org/general/23-general-feature-articles/156-terrorism-in-kenya.html.

Kenyan Ministry of Foreign Affairs (2013), Full Statement by the Ministry of Foreign Affairs, Kenya, on the Negative UN Security Council Vote. http://whereiskenya.com/full-statement-ministry-foreign-affairs-kenya-negative-un-security-council-vote/

Security Council Resolution 1422, U.N. SCOR, 57th Sess., 4572d mtg., U.N. Doc. S/RES/1422 (2002).

Security Council Resolution 1487, U.N. SCOR, 58th Sess., 4772d mtg., U.N. DOC. S/RES/1487 (2003).

Security Council Resolution 1497, U.N. SCOR, 58th Sess., 4803d mtg., U.N. Doc. S/RES/1497 (2003).
Security Council Resolution 1593, 31 March 2005, 5158th mtg., U.N. Doc. S/RES/1593 (2005).
Security Council Resolution 1970, 26 February 2011, 6491st mtg., U.N. Doc. S/RES/1970 (2011).
Security Council, 7060th Meeting, S/PV.7060 "Peace and security in Africa", 15 Nov 2013.
Security Council Report, "Chronology of Events, Kenya". http://www.securitycouncilreport.org/chronology/kenya.php.
UN News Centre 2014, Amid deteriorating conditions in Darfur, UN Official urges all parties to join peace effort, 23 January 2014. http://www.un.org/apps/news/story.asp/story.asp?NewsID=46991&Cr=darfur&Cr1=.

Chapter 13
A Strained Relationship: Reflections on the African Union's Stand Towards the International Criminal Court from the Kenyan Experience

Sosteness Francis Materu

Contents

13.1 Introduction

This chapter is a commentary on the current 'hostile' attitude adopted by the African Union towards the International Criminal Court. The chapter focuses mainly on two aspects: First, it comments on the African Union's 'common positions' on the Court regarding the prosecution of African serving Heads of State, Kenya being the main point of reference here. Second, also using the Kenyan experience, it analyzes how

S.F. Materu (✉)
University of Dar Es Salaam, Dar Es Salaam, Tanzania
e-mail: osakisos@yahoo.com

G. Werle et al. (eds.), *Africa and the International Criminal Court*,
International Criminal Justice Series 1, DOI 10.1007/978-94-6265-029-9_13

the International Criminal Court is perceived in Africa by mainly two groups: the political elite and the ordinary citizens, including victims of the atrocities investigated by the Court. Kenya is refered to for two main reasons. Kenya is a State Party to the ICC Statute, which means it has direct treaty obligations with regard to the Court. Then, both the President and Deputy President of Kenya are currently undergoing trial before the International Criminal Court, a fact which has stirred the most recent attitude of the African Union towards the Court.

The chapter finally reveals that although the AU Assembly brings together Heads of State of almost all African countries, the current views of the Assembly about the International Criminal Court do not necessarily represent the views of the African people in general. Consequently, any assertion that 'Africa is against the International Criminal Court' is shown to be flawed. It will also be contended that the Court remains a relevant institution for Africans, especially the victims of serious human rights violations, despite any flaws or limitations which may be associated with the Court's current legal framework.

13.2 Contextualizing the Problem

There are now three popular facts about Africa and the International Criminal Court. First, African states strongly supported the establishment of the Court. Second, so far, five African states have out of their own invited the Court to prosecute crimes committed on their respective territories. Third, African states make up the largest regional grouping represented at the Court. But as various scholars and commentators rightly indicate,[1] the relationship between the African Union and the International Criminal Court is now strained. Such a relationship started turning 'sour' when the Court indicted *Omar Al Bashir*, the incumbent Sudanese President. The issuance of an arrest warrant against *Muammar Gaddafi*, the former Libyan leader, would have worsened the relationship had he not met with his untimely death before appearing before the Court. But currently it is obvious that the situation has become worse following the Court's indictment of *Uhuru Kenyatta* and *William Ruto*, Kenya's President and Deputy President, respectively, who had already been indicted by the Court before they were elected to office.

Whereas in the case of Sudan and Libya the Court's jurisdiction was triggered by the United Nations Security Council,[2] the Court's jurisdiction in respect of Kenya was invoked *proprio motu* by the ICC Prosecutor.[3] Prior to the indictments

---

[1] See, e.g., Jalloh 2012, p. 203 et seq; Villa-Vicencio 2011, pp. 38–41; Mills 2012, p. 404 et seq; Hansen 2013; Cote 2012, pp. 411–412; Murithi 2012, pp. 4–9; and Murithi 2013.

[2] Article 13(b) of the ICC Statute, read together with UN Charter, Chapter VII, Article 39.

[3] Articles 13(c) and 15 of the ICC Statute. See also Bergsmo and Pejic 2008, pp. 581–593.

resulting from these three particular referrals, the International Criminal Court had already started exercising jurisdiction over cases arising from other referrals made by three other African states, namely the Democratic Republic of the Congo,[4] the Central African Republic,[5] and Uganda.[6] Besides, the International Criminal Court is currently also exercising jurisdiction over cases arising from two other African countries, namely Mali (self-referral)[7] and Côte d'Ivoire (resulting from a voluntary acceptance of Court's jurisdiction by a non-State Party).[8] Both States referred their respective situations to the International Criminal Court in the face of the strained AU-ICC relationship.

By and large, it is the indictment of African politicians who are still in power which has influenced the African Union to adopt various Decisions and 'common positions' expressing 'hostility' with the Court.[9] In addition, various pronouncements by some of the AU leaders have branded the International Criminal Court as a racist, neo-colonial and biased institution that is only targeting Africa and its leaders in particular.

What is also worth mentioning is the fact that the African Union has not, so far, adopted any common position (be it in favor or against the Court) in respect of cases arising from the self-referrals or indictments of 'ordinary' Africans. Two things are noteworthy here: First, the African Union has raised concerns about ICC indictments only when they touch the African political leaders in power or their allies, but not when such indictments are against their political opponents (or rebels), such as *Thomas Lubanga, Germain Katanga, Mathieu Ngudjolo Chui, Joseph Kony and Jean Pierre Bemba.* Second, the indictments complained about have all resulted from either Security Council referrals (Libya and Sudan) or *proprio motu* investigations of the ICC Prosecutor (Kenya).

---

4 International Criminal Court, Press Release 2004.

5 International Criminal Court, Press Release 2005.

6 International Criminal Court, Press Release 2004.

7 See Referral letter by the government of Mali http://www.icc-cpi.int/NR/rdonlyres/A245A47F-BFD1-45B6-891C-3BCB5B173F57/0/ReferralLetterMali130712.pdf. (All internet sources in this chapter were accessed on 24 March 2014).

8 See Article 12(3) of the ICC Statute; and the Letter reconfirming the acceptance of the ICC jurisdiction http://www.icc-cpi.int/NR/rdonlyres/498E8FEB-7A72-4005-A209-C14BA374804F/0/ReconCPI.pdf.

9 See, e.g., the following specific decisions and declarations of the AU Assembly on the International Criminal Court as adopted in its various Sessions Ext/Assembly/AU/Dec.1(Oct.2013), Extraordinary Ordinary Session, 12 October 2013; Assembly/AU/Dec.397(XVIII)—Doc.EX.CL/710(XX), 18th Ordinary Session, 29–30 January 2012; Assembly/AU/Dec.366(XVII)—Doc. EX.CL/670(XIX), 17th Ordinary Session 30 June–1 July 2011; Assembly/AU/Dec.334(XVI)—Doc. EX.CL/639(XVIII) 16th Ordinary Session 30–31 January 2011; and Assembly/AU/Dec.245(XIII) Rev.1—Doc. Assembly/AU/13 (XIII) 3, 13th Ordinary Session, 1–3 July 2009. The Decisions can be found in the Annex to this book.

13.3 Regional Positions Versus Obligations of States Towards the International Criminal Court

13.3.1 Regional Common Positions on the International Criminal Court

Common regional positions on various matters are not uncommon, neither are they confined to the African Union as a regional bloc. In fact, the AU's common positions are contemplated under its Constitutive Act, one of whose main objective is that the African Union shall "promote and defend African common positions on issues of interest to the continent and its peoples".[10] One of the earliest such positions as regards the International Criminal Court was adopted in 1998 by the Council of Ministers of the then Organization of African Unity, urging its Member States not only to support but also to participate in the ongoing processes towards creating and making the Court operational.[11] Like the African Union, the European Union has similarly adopted various common positions with regard to the International Criminal Court. One of them that was adopted on 16 June 2003[12] repealed and replaced an earlier position originally adopted in 2001 and amended in June 2002.[13]

All the common positions adopted so far by the European Union have leaned towards strengthening the Court. The European Union has stressed its objective "to support the effective functioning of the Court and to advance universal support for it by promoting the widest possible participation in the Rome Statute".[14] To achieve this objective, the EU's common positions have not only insisted on ratification and implementation of the ICC Statute, but also on the need to extend the moral and financial support to the International Criminal Court.[15] Consistent with its above-mentioned objectives, the European Union adopted yet another common position in 2002, specifically rejecting USA's bilateral agreements with other States.[16] These agreements were (and still are) intended to shield US citizens from arrest and surrender to the International Criminal Court for prosecution.[17] The fact that all EU Members are signatories to the ICC Statute is a symbolic gesture which may lend more legitimacy to EU's 'common' positions. This is not the case with the African Union.

---

[10] See Constitutive Act of the African Union of 11 July 2000, Article 3(d).

[11] See Decision CM/Dec.399 (LXVII), 67th Ordinary Session of OAU's Council of Ministers Addis Ababa, 25–28 February 1998.

[12] See EU Council Common Position 2003/444/CFSP of 16 June 2003.

[13] See EU Council Common Position 2002/474/CFS amending Common Position 2001/443/CFSP.

[14] EU Council Common Position 2003/444/CFSP, Article 1(2).

[15] EU Council Common Position 2003/444/CFSP, Articles 2 and 3.

[16] See Coalition of the International Criminal Court 2002.

[17] See Coalition of the International Criminal Court 2002. For more information see Bantekas 2012, pp. 439–440.; Hafner 2005, p. 323 et seq.; Benzing 2004, pp. 181–236.

Contrary to the central objective of EU's positions, which is to have a strong and functioning International Criminal Court, the Decisions adopted by the African Union, especially after the Court started its work, are implicitly aimed at weakening rather than strengthening the Court. More concerning is the fact that such Decisions include those which have expressly asked African Union Member States, *regardless of whether they are parties or non-parties to the ICC Statute,* not to cooperate with the Court.[18] A question that arises is this: Does the African Union care about the treaty obligations that some of its Member States have voluntarily incurred under the ICC Statute? Only 33 out of 54 (61 %) of African countries have ratified the Statute.[19] This means that, as the African Union adopts Decisions purportedly entailing African 'common positions' on the International Criminal Court, 39 % of the AU Members who associate themselves with such Decisions are not States Parties to the Court. Through its Decisions, the African Union turns a blind eye to the fact that the obligations of these two groups of African states with regard to the International Criminal Court differ, and that different consequences may flow from the relationship between them and the Court.

13.3.2 Obligations of African States Parties to the International Criminal Court

There are crucial points which must be clearly highlighted before going further. Pursuant to the complementarity principle under which the International Criminal Court operates,[20] and as far as the African continent is concerned, the Court has a direct relationship with only the 33 African States that have ratified the ICC Statute. With regard to such States, an obligation arises pursuant to the principle of *pacta sunt servanda* according to which states parties to an international treaty (e.g. the ICC Statute) are required to perform their obligations under the respective treaty in good faith i.e. in a manner that does not defeat but promote the objectives of the treaty.[21] As far as the remaining 21 African non States Parties to the ICC Statute are concerned, a relationship that arises with the Court is only to the extent contemplated under Articles 13(c) and 12(3) of the ICC Statute, that is to say: (i) when the International Criminal Court is exercising jurisdiction over situations referred to it by the United Nations Security Council; or (ii) when such a State lodges a declaration to accept the jurisdiction of the Court with respect to the specific crime in question. According to Article 13(c) above, the Security Council,

---

[18] See, for example, AU Decision Assembly/AU/Dec.245(XIII) Rev.1, 3 July 2009, Article 10.

[19] See ICC Statute ratification status at https://treaties.un.org/pages/ViewDetails.aspx?src=TREATY&mtdsg_no=XVIII-10&chapter=18&lang=en.

[20] See ICC Statute, Article 1.

[21] See Vienna Convention on the Law of Treaties of 1969 (VCLT), Article 26.

acting under Chapter VII of the UN Charter, is empowered to refer a case or situation in any State to the International Criminal Court, whether or not that State is party to the ICC Statute, if the Security Council deems it fit for purposes of restoring or maintaining peace and security. In such a scenario, every State is bound to cooperate with the Court when requested, despite the general rule that a treaty cannot create obligations or rights for a third state unless such a state expressly consents in writing.[22] In this case, any State's defiance towards the Court's orders or requests (whether or not such State is party to the Statute) is arguably tantamount to defying orders of the Security Council under the UN Charter, and consequently, sanctions can be imposed by the Security Council on the defiant state.[23]

Apart from the relationship between states and the International Criminal Court as explained above, the ICC Statute does not contemplate a relationship between the Court and regional groupings as such. However, this is not to say that common positions articulated by such regional groupings regarding how their Member States should relate with or act towards the International Criminal Court may not have any impact whatsoever on how some of those states may actually behave towards the Court. Rather, it is to argue that such common positions should not aim at making states which are members to such regional groupings and at the same time are parties to the ICC Statute to disregard their obligations under the Statute, which obligations such states incurred voluntarily, exercising their sovereignty.

From the foregoing it follows that AU Decisions and Declarations purporting to 'instruct' or 'encourage' its members, including those 33 States which have voluntarily ratified the ICC Statute, to behave defiantly towards the Court are unjustifiable. As already stated, the African Union has the mandate under its Constitutive Act to adopt common positions, including on the International Criminal Court. But before acting on instructions entailed in such decisions, it is important for the African States Parties to the ICC Statute to individually weigh them against their obligations under the ICC Statute. It is important for these States to evaluate if the respective AU Decisions impose obligations which are in conflict with State Parties' obligations under the ICC Statute. Specifically, such States must consider whether by implementing AU Decisions they may end up breaching their obligations under the ICC Statute; or whether by not implementing such Decisions they will be breaching their obligations under the AU Constitutive Act. If conflicting obligations arise in this respect, then such States could seek a solution, *inter alia*, under international law. But we find no such conflict here for the following reasons:

Most of the issues raised by the African Union in its Decisions are political in nature, save for a few which are purely legal or are on the border of law and politics. The most important and relevant legal issue that has featured more

---

[22] See VCLT, Articles 34 and 35.

[23] See Akande 2009, pp. 342–338; Fletcher and Ohlin 2006, pp. 428–433.

prominently is the argument that the Court's indictment of African leaders violates a customary law principle that grants immunity from prosecution to the serving Heads of State and Government of Kenya and Sudan. But this argument is not as significant or convincing as the African Union would like it to be, and even the issue of immunity which it raises does not give rise to any conflict that could put African States Parties to the Statute in a dilemma with regard to the implementation of their obligations under the ICC Statute and those under the AU's Constitutive Act.

The main reason for this argument lies at the heart of Article 27 of the ICC Statute. This provision explicitly states that as far as the crimes in the ICC Statute are concerned, the official capacity of a suspect is not a bar to prosecution; and that any immunity that a national or international law may provide to such a person on the basis of his or her official capacity is not a bar to prosecution by the International Criminal Court. This makes the AU's arguments on immunity of Kenya's Head and Deputy Head of State unsustainable for two reasons. First, Kenya's voluntary ratification of the ICC Statute was an unequivocal waiver of immunity to serving Heads of State as far as the core crimes under the Statute are concerned. This deprives the African Union of any justification whatsoever for protesting against the enforcement of this clear exception to the general rule which Kenya, as a sovereign state, has not only endorsed, but also enshrined in its own Constitution. The Kenyan Constitution provides explicitly that although "the President or a person performing the functions of that office" enjoys a general protection against legal proceedings "during their tenure in office", such immunity "shall not extend to a crime for which the President may be prosecuted under any treaty to which Kenya is party and which prohibits such immunity".[24]

Second the AU had earlier acknowledged the existence and validity of the waiver of immunity under Article 27 of the ICC Statute. The African Union noted that such a waiver could be valid provided it is applied only to states which have ratified the ICC Statute. The only thing that the African Union strongly contested and flawed is an extension of such waiver to a third state like Sudan, which is not party to the ICC Statute.[25] But even as regards third states, it must be mentioned that the AU's argument above is correct only to the extent that the International Criminal Court is *not* acting on referrals made by the Security Council. The reason is that a mere referral of a situation or case involving a serving Head of State of a third state (e.g. Sudan) to the Court is tantamount to extending the applicability of Article 27(2) (and the entire ICC Statute) to that state by the Security Council.[26] And since the UN Charter, under which the Security Council acts in such a scenario, is the supreme treaty, then the ICC Statute as a whole becomes

---

[24] Constitution of Kenya of 2010, Articles 143(1) and (4).

[25] AU Press Release No. 002/2012, 9 January 2012, p. 2.

[26] See Chap. 3 in this volume by *Trendafilova* (under Section 3.3.3., Head of State Immunity and Security Council Referrals).

applicable to that third state as if such state were party to the Statute.[27] As regards ICC States Parties, the AU's argument in its press release of 9 January 2012 cited above stated the correct position. Interestingly, the AU's correct position of the law as regards the applicability of the waiver of official capacity changed later when *Kenyatta* and *Ruto* were elected as Kenya's President and Deputy President, respectively. The African Union now argues that such immunity *cannot be waived,* even where the state in question is party to the ICC Statute.

Despite the AU's Decision of 12 October 2013, categorically instructing Kenya's President and Deputy President not to continue attending their trials before the Court, the Deputy President, whose trial had commenced, continued to appear before the Court, while Kenya continued to invoke other legal means within the legal framework of the ICC Statute to address its demands and concerns. Similarly, despite the AU's calls for non-cooperation with the International Criminal Court, several African countries which are parties to the Statute, specifically Botswana and Malawi under the new President *Joyce Banda*, expressly refused to act in a manner that would result in a breach of their obligations under the ICC Statute.[28] In addition, on 31 January 2014, barely two months after the AU's most recent hostile Decision against the International Criminal Court, the parliamentarians from four Francophone African States Parties to the ICC Statute, namely Mali, Guinea, Senegal and Côte d'Ivoire, met with the President of the Assembly of States Parties to the ICC Statute and made statements supporting "the ongoing judicial work of the International Criminal Court throughout Africa".[29] All this shows that these individual States Parties to the ICC Statute have realized that AU's instructions on how they should behave towards the Court are flawed in principle.

At another level, the African Union presents an alternative argument: It argues that the International Criminal Court should defer the cases against Kenya's President and Deputy President until such a time that they are no longer serving in their current capacities.[30] This proposal must be dismissed. Apart from not being contemplated under Article 27 explained above, such a view has both implicit and explicit implications on justice for the victims. Despite the fact that hitherto six years have already lapsed since the alleged crimes were committed in Kenya, the AU's argument would further mean that the Court has to defer the Kenyan cases until 2017 or 2023. This is because the first term of the *Kenyatta-Ruto* presidency ends in 2017, and assuming they are re-elected (as they are eligible), their second and final term will end in 2023. By the time the cases resume, it is clear that the evidence will have greatly been affected—witnesses will have probably died or their memories will have faded. In short, therefore, embedded in the AU's argument is an implicit motive to shield the suspects. From the point of view of the victims, it suffices to say that justice delayed is justice denied.

---

[27] See Blommestijn and Ryngaert 2010, pp. 432–436.

[28] Murithi 2012, p. 6.

[29] See ICC, Press Release 2014.

[30] AU, Decision Ext/Assembly/AU/Dec.1(Oct.2013), Article 10(ii).

13.3.3 The AU's Shift of Attention from Victims to Perpetrators

The last thing to highlight in this section is that since the Court's interventions started in Africa, no serious Decision has ever been adopted by the African Union with regard, for example, to mitigating the suffering of the internally displaced persons or generally, the victims or even with regard to measures to ensure or assist the situation countries to address criminal accountability at the domestic level. Thus, whereas the focus of the International Criminal Court is to punish the perpetrators and at least bring some justice to the victims, the position currently held by the African Union in relation to the ICC activities in Africa diverts the attention (protection) from where it should be to where it should not be—from the victims to the perpetrators of heinous crimes in Africa, specifically when such perpetrators happen to be part of the African ruling elite.

13.4 How Is the International Criminal Court Perceived in Africa? The Kenyan Experience[31]

13.4.1 Introduction

Following Kenya's 2007/2008 post-election violence, serious atrocities were committed, including 1,200 murders, 3,000 rapes, 350,000 incidents of forceful removals, 3,561 incidents of grievous bodily injuries, 117,216 incidents of destruction of properties and 41,000 cases of destruction of houses.[32] Following Kenya's failure to institute domestic proceedings against the alleged perpetrators, the ICC Prosecutor's *proprio motu* intervention was invoked pursuant to an earlier agreement.[33] Subsequently, the International Criminal Court indicted six Kenyans for crimes against humanity committed during the violence.[34] Among those indicted were *Uhuru Kenyatta* and *William Ruto* who were later elected Kenya's President and Deputy President, respectively.

[31] On the Kenya Situation before the International Criminal Court see Materu SF, The Post-Election Violence in Kenya: Domestic and International legal Responses (forthcoming book).

[32] See Republic of Kenya, Report of the Commission of Inquiry into Post-Election Violence (CIPEV), 2008, pp. 345–352. See also Kenya National Commission on Human Rights (KNCHR) 2008.

[33] See CIPEV Report, p. 473.

[34] See Decision on the Prosecutor's application for summonses to appear for Francis Kirimi Muthaura, Uhuru Muigai Kenyatta and Mohammed Hussein Ali, 8 March 2011; and Decision on the Prosecutor's application for summons to appear for William Samoei Ruto, Henry Kiprono Kosgey and Joshua Arap Sang.

The question of how the Court is perceived in Kenya did not arise prior to the ICC intervention; it only arose subsequently. Various groups have, at different times, expressed different opinions in relation to the on-going ICC process. Such opinions differ according to the group. For example, politicians as opposed to ordinary citizens, including civil society; (alleged) perpetrators or their allies as opposed to the victims of the crimes; believers in justice as opposed to perpetuators of impunity, etc.

13.4.2 The Political Elite

Before the International Criminal Court intervened in Kenya there had been a domestic agreement that a special tribunal would be formed to prosecute the perpetrators of the alleged crimes against humanity.[35] The political elite, specifically the Members of Parliament, became immediately divided when efforts were being undertaken to implement this recommendation. A small group of Members of Parliament genuinely favored a domestic special tribunal, but many others were against it and preferred the 'The Hague option', i.e. the ICC route to criminal accountability. Those who favored the ICC route were also divided into two groups, although each group had a different motive. The first and small group believed that Kenya's judicial institutions were too weak to render impartial justice as they could easily be manipulated by those with "vested interests". Thus, for this group, the International Criminal Court was perceived as an impartial and neutral institution when compared to the domestic courts, including even a special tribunal, which could be manipulated easily.[36] The second and bigger group of Members of Parliament who favored the ICC route did so solely for political reasons. They perceived the Court as a 'remote threat' as they seem to have hoped that it would involve a protracted procedure that would delay criminal accountability.[37] Until then the ICC Prosecutor had not named any suspects yet.

Thus, those who expected to use the International Criminal Court to settle scores against political opponents also played a political card. Interestingly, *Uhuru Kenyatta*, who was then Deputy Prime Minister doubling as Finance Minister, and *William Ruto*, Member of Parliament and former Education Minister, were among those who urged the Court to intervene immediately, not knowing that they themselves would be arraigned before it.[38] *Ruto,* for example, argued that instead of wasting time on a special tribunal, the names of suspects should be handed over to the International Criminal Court "so that proper investigations can start".[39]

[35] See CIPEV Report, p. 472.

[36] International Crisis Group 2012, p. 6.

[37] Cf. Asaala 2012, p. 131; International Crisis Group 2012, pp. 6–7.

[38] See The Star, 12 March 2011; International Crisis Group 2012, p. 6.

[39] The Daily Nation, 21 February 2009.

Apparently, *Ruto, Kenyatta* and their allies hoped to use the Court to indirectly settle scores against *Raila Odinga,* their political rival. They seem to have hoped that *Odinga*, who was a presidential candidate in the 2007 election, would be among those to be indicted by the Court. However, later, *Ruto* and *Kenyatta* were named as suspects, and *Odinga* not. Thenceforth the duo and their political allies changed the tone of their original stand with a view to keeping the International Criminal Court away.[40]

When *Kenyatta* and *Ruto* indicated their intention to contest for presidency in the 2013 elections, a group of financially powerful political elite started criss-crossing the country trying to persuade ordinary citizens to believe that their 'sons' were being indicted by a "white man's court", and that such an indictment was a "neo-colonialist ploy […] taking them back to before independence".[41] The same group described the International Criminal Court as an "imperialist imposition" dangerous to Kenya's sovereignty and as "a Western colonial institution that is bent on re-colonizing Africa".[42] And on 12 October 2013, six months after being elected, as Kenya's President, *Kenyatta* claimed before African Heads of State and Government that "Western powers are the key drivers of the ICC", since the EU funds 70 % of the Court's budget; and that "the threat of prosecution" by this Court is being used as a tool to make "pliant states execute policies favorable to these [Western] countries".[43]

13.4.3 Civil Society and Ordinary Citizens

The views of ordinary Kenyans about the ICC process in Kenya differ significantly from those of the political elite. Soon after the violence, the emerging debate had two themes: (i) the role and competence of the national judicial system to prosecute the perpetrators of the violence; and (ii) and the role of the International Criminal Court in the breaking of the 'culture of impunity' which had been entrenched in Kenya with respect to crimes involving the political class. Both the Kenyan Catholic Church and prominent scholars believed that the ICC route was the only hope to true justice, because it was by far more competent and impartial when compared to the local judicial organs..[44]

Independent surveys indicated that the majority of Kenya's general public, including the victims of the violence, perceived the International Criminal Court as

[40] International Crisis Group 2012, p. 7; The Daily Nation, 26 March 2011.

[41] See Drakard 2011.

[42] See Jalloh 2010.

[43] See Daily Standard, 13 October 2013.

[44] The Daily Nation, 19 July 2009. See also Musila 2009, p. 456. For a detailed discussion on the independence of judges and lawyers as well as on allegations and investigations into corruption of judges in Kenya, see Mbote and Akech 2011, pp. 99–115.

the most trustworthy, independent and reliable forum to try the perpetrators.[45] Periodic survey reports were published by South Consulting, an independent research firm which continuously monitored the situation on behalf of the AU Panel of Prominent Personalities which mediated in the conflict. The April 2011 survey confirmed that there was a "clear disconnect" between ordinary Kenyans and the politicians as regards how the International Criminal Court was perceived in Kenya.[46] It concluded that while the political elite had "a common interest in opposing accountability and other measures to end impunity [...] there [was] a strong public mood against impunity",[47] with most ordinary citizens perceiving the Court as "the only concrete action to hold powerful people [i.e. politicians] accountable for [the] post-election violence".[48] Similarly, the January 2012 survey found, *inter alia*, that victims of the post-election violence had a strong perception that "the Kenyan government [would] unlikely conduct genuine investigations and prosecute the suspects" at the domestic level.[49] In view of this, a victim in one of the internally displaced persons' camps believed that

> the ICC is the only option left to fight impunity in Kenya because the [domestic] institutions and the politicians have failed. Ocampo [...] must not fail. If he does, that will be the end of Kenya because there will be nothing left to fear anymore.[50]

13.4.4 *Quantifying the Perception*

The surveys show that by April 2011 the support for the International Criminal Court in Kenya by the general public was 78 % nationally,[51] although it fluctuated

---

[45] Alai and Mue 2011, p. 1232. For example, the survey conducted by Infotrack Research & Consulting in November 2009 showed that the public support was 62 % for the ICC trials and 2 % for trials under the proposed Special Tribunal. See Alai and Mue 2010. In September 2010, a poll by Synovate indicated that despite the judicial and legal reforms planned domestically, the public support for accountability measures was as follows: trial at the International Criminal Court (54 %), local trials (22 %), granting of amnesty (22 %). See Reuters 27 September 2010. From another poll published by Synovate in April 2011, the results were: ICC trials (61 %) and a special tribunal (24 %). See The Africa Review, 5 April 2010.

[46] Kenya National Dialogue and Reconciliation Monitoring Project 2011, p. 25, para 60.

[47] Kenya National Dialogue and Reconciliation Monitoring Project 2011, p. VI, para 9.

[48] Kenya National Dialogue and Reconciliation Monitoring Project 2011, p. 8, para 26.

[49] Kenya National Dialogue and Reconciliation Monitoring Project, January 2012, p. 52, para 133, and p. 57, para 142.

[50] As quoted *verbatim* in Kenya National Dialogue and Reconciliation Monitoring Project 2011, p. 25, para 59. See also International Center for Transitional Justice 2011, pp. 51–54.

[51] Kenya National Dialogue and Reconciliation Monitoring Project 2011, p. 9, para 27. See also p. 12, para 34, showing that in March 2011, the confidence was at 72 %.

between 60 and 82 % at the provincial level.[52] Throughout the year 2012, surveys, including the one conducted in January 2012 (towards ICC Decisions on confirmation of charges against the Kenyan suspects), found that the public support for the Court was still above 50 %.[53] The most recent survey conducted by *Ipsos Synovate* in November 2013, immediately after AU's Extraordinary Summit which purported to instruct President *Kenyatta* and Deputy President *Ruto* not to attend their ICC trials,[54] still found that, generally, 67 % of the ordinary citizens wanted President *Kenyatta* to continue attending his trial at the International Criminal Court regardless of his official status.[55]

However, there is another trend established by the surveys which is worth noting. This trend indicates that after the names of the six suspects were revealed, and also after the charges against four of the six suspects were confirmed,[56] the support for the International Criminal Court amongst their ethnic communities started declining.[57] This is evident in the February 2013 survey which indicated that although generally, the support for the Court in Kenya was at 66 % national wide, it only remained strongest in five provinces, namely Nyanza, Nairobi, Western, North Eastern and Coastal provinces (from where not a single ICC suspect came). It remained lowest in the Central province and in Rift Valley, from where the suspects hailed.[58] It was this new dimension—gradual ethnicization of the ICC process at the domestic level—that prompted the controversial KAMATUSA ethnic association (bringing together the Kalenjin, Maasai, Turkana and Samburu ethnic groups) to even claim that it was "the entire Kalenjin community [which] was on trial at the International Criminal Court by virtue of *Ruto* being a suspect".[59] Apparently, the perception here was, or still is, not necessarily that the accusations against *Ruto,* who is currently a *de facto* Kalenjin leader, are false or baseless. Rather, the perception was, and still is, that the Court is practicing "selective justice" by only 'targeting' *Ruto* and not "other known suspects" (ostensibly from other ethnic communities) who could have also been charged.[60]

---

[52] In December 2010, confidence in the International Criminal Court per province was: North Eastern (82 %), Western and Nyanza (75 %), Eastern (74 %), Rift Valley (60 %). See Kenya National Dialogue and Reconciliation Monitoring Project 2011, pp. 9–12, paras 28–33.

[53] Kenya National Dialogue and Reconciliation Monitoring Project January 2012, p. 51, para 132; see also Second Review Report, May 2012, paras 52–60 (indicating, at para 56, that by May 2012, up to 58 % of Kenyans were happy about the work of the International Criminal Court in Kenya).

[54] See Ext/Assembly/AU/Dec.1 (Oct.2013), para 10(ix).

[55] The Daily Nation, 14 November 2013.

[56] See *Prosecutor v. Francis Kirimi Muthaura, Uhuru Muigai Kenyatta and Mohammed Hussein Ali*, Decision on the confirmation of charges, 23 January 2012; *Prosecutor v. William Samoei Ruto, Henry Kiprono Kosgey and Joshua Arap Sang*, Decision on the confirmation of charges, 23 January 2012.

[57] Kenya National Dialogue and Reconciliation Monitoring Project, January 2012, p. 57, para 142.

[58] Kenya National Dialogue and Reconciliation Monitoring Project 2003, para 75.

[59] The Star, 3 April 2012.

[60] See Kenya National Dialogue and Reconciliation Monitoring Project, January 2012, p. 53, para 134; Human Rights Watch 2013, p. 5.

13.5 Evaluation

One can discern from the discussion above that the AU's views about the International Criminal Court are not necessarily the 'common' views of all African states, neither do they embody 'the African perception' about the Court; they do not necessarily represent the views of all individual African states or citizens. In addition, the Kenyan experience demonstrates that various groups—political, ethnical, religious, etc.—within a country may have varying opinions about the Court, one of the main determinant factors being how the Court has actually impacted or is likely to impact on the group in question. Naturally, those who are or are likely to be *negatively* affected by the International Criminal Court must be against the Court. It can be contended that a *section* of the African ruling political class falls squarely under this category.

It is common knowledge that the African continent has a long history of, among other things, serious deficiencies as regards good governance and the rule of law. It has also been engulfed in massive corruption and undemocratic practices which are orchestrated, for the most part, by the ruling political elite. As a consequence, this group has always had the ability and tendency of manipulating local judicial institutions so as to avoid criminal accountability in respect of crimes they commit. They would even try to do the same with the International Criminal Court. One finds no better evidence of this assertion than the AU's letter dated 10 September 2013 to the ICC Presidency purporting to explain AU's 'expectations' regarding how the International Criminal Court should make judicial rulings on issues relating to the cases against Kenya's President and Deputy President.[61] Notably, it is this group of the ruling political elite which supports the Court—or at least remains indifferent—whenever it is clear to them that the Court could be used to settle scores against political opponents in Africa. This, as shown above, is evident in the manner in which the majority of the Kenyan political elite behaved initially when the ICC process started. It is also evident in the self-referrals that have emanated from the Continent so far.

For example, Uganda goes down in history, being the first country to have made a voluntary referral of crimes committed on its territory to the International Criminal Court. When this referral was being made, the ruling elite viewed the Court as a part of the solution to the rebellion in Uganda as regards investigating the crimes of the Lord's Resistance Army, a rebel group operating in the northern part of the country.[62] But since the Court started indicting part of the African ruling political elite (in other countries)—apparently, a clear message that even the crimes allegedly committed by the government forces[63] could be investigated—the President of Uganda has come out as one of the main critics of the Court,

[61] See ICC Press Release 2013.

[62] See ICC Press Release 2004.

[63] See Human Rights Watch 2011, pp. 22–29.

describing it as a "shallow" and "biased" court that "mishandle[s] complex African issues".[64]

Thus, by indicting a section of the African ruling class, including now serving Heads of State, the International Criminal Court has become an imminent threat not only to the part of the ruling class actually indicted, but also to their peers who, judging from the way they govern their countries, some of them could be described as 'potential clients' of the Court. The fear of the Court arises from the fact that, by its very nature, it targets those who are "most responsible" for the serious crimes (planners, sponsors and instigators), who, more often than not, will involve politicians or their allies. It is, therefore, not surprising that members of this group, represented by the AU Assembly, have now developed a phobia for the Court, and are adopting a hostile attitude to frustrate its course.

But there is another group comprising the victims of crime who are ordinary Africans. From this group, and by using the Kenyan experience, a completely different conclusion can be reached. To them the International Criminal Court remains a credible Court—a ray of hope that promises not only to address impunity but also to deter people from committing crimes in the future. To this group, the Court is still relevant as a judicial institution and enjoys overwhelming support, as currently there is no 'African alternative' to it.[65] It is, therefore, the interests of this group—the quest for justice and an end to impunity for serious crimes in Africa—that should be given more weight. However, it is unfortunate that the views and needs of this particular group, which comprises the majority of Africans, are not taken seriously by the small but powerful group of the political elite represented by the AU leaders. This is perhaps the reason why there is no 'common position', resolution or an 'extra-ordinary' meeting held by the AU leaders with the view to designing concrete steps or measures for serious domestic prosecutions of the alleged crimes committed in Kenya or in any of the situation countries. In addition, there have never been any concrete and serious efforts by the African Union to help Kenya address the plight of the internally displaced persons who remain in camps six years after the post-election violence.

13.6 Conclusion and Recommendations

The achievement of the dream to establish and operationalize the International Criminal Court remains a breakthrough in the fight against impunity for serious crimes of concern to Africa and to the international community as a whole. But a successful fight against impunity cannot be realized by the International Criminal

[64] See 'Statement by H.E. Yoweri Kaguta Museveni President of the Republic of Uganda at the 68th United Nations General Assembly' http://www.statehouse.go.ug/media/speeches/2013/09/25/statement-he-yoweri-kaguta-museveni-president-republic-uganda-68th-united-.

[65] Cf. Allison 2012, pp. 25–28.

Court alone; it requires concerted efforts of other stake holders, including the African Union and African countries in particular. The recent antagonistic attitude taken by the African Union towards the Court is retrogressive in this regard and should not be allowed take us back to the Cold War era in which international criminal justice remained stagnant owing to political mistrust.[66]

Admittedly, the current legal framework under which the International Criminal Court operates is not without flaws or limitations. This is shown by the fact that not all the concerns raised by the African Union lack some validity.[67] But such flaws or anomalies should not be attributed to or blamed on the Court. Instead, any emerging concerns should be directed to the Assembly of ICC States Parties, the political body with the mandate to amend the Statute and address the concerns. At all times, the sanctity and independence of the Court as a judicial institution must be respected and maintained not only by the Court itself but also by all other stake holders. The fact of the matter remains that the International Criminal Court is a creature of a treaty which was politically adopted amidst many controversies and contestations, some of which are bound to re-emerge. But despite this fact, the Court itself is not a political body. It is a judicial institution which must always act as such by remaining focused on and confined to its mandate as defined in its Statute. As it has recently informed the African Union about this very fact,[68] and commendably so, the Court must not succumb to the political pressure surrounding it, but must always remain alive to the fact that such pressure will always exist.

References

Akande D (2009) The legal nature of security council referrals to the ICC and its impact on Al Bashir's immunities. J Int Crim Justice 7:333–352

Alai C, Mue N (2010) Kenya: impact of the Rome Statute and the International Criminal Court. ICTJ briefing: the Rome Statute review conference June 2010, Kampala. http://ictj.org/sites/default/files/ICTJ-Kenya-ICC-Impact-2010-English.pdf

Alai C, Mue N (2011) Complementarity and the impact of the Rome Statute and the International Criminal Court in Kenya. In: Stahn C, El Zeidy M (eds) The International Criminal Court and complementarity: from theory to practice, vol II. Cambridge University Press, New York

Allison S (2012) Is there an African alternative to the International Criminal Court? Afr Fact J Good Gov Afr 5:25–28

Asaala EO (2012) The International Criminal Court factor on transitional justice in Kenya'. In: Ambos K, Maunganidze OA (eds) Power and prosecution: challenges and opportunities for international criminal justice in Sub-Saharan Africa. Universitätsverlag, Göttingen, pp 119–143

Bantekas I (2012) International Criminal Law, 4th edn. Hart Publishing, Portland

---

[66] See Werle 2009, p. 15.

[67] See, e.g., Chap. 12 by *Okoth* in this book on the abuse and politicization by the Security Council of the mandate under Article 16 of the ICC Statute.

[68] See ICC letter to the African Union dated 13 September 2013, Ref. 2013/PRESS/00295-4/VPT/MH attached to ICC Press Release, ICC-CPI-20130920-PR943.

Benzing M (2004) U.S bilateral non-surrender agreements and article 98 of the Statute of the International Criminal Court: an exercise in the law of treaties. Max Planck UNYB 8:181–236
Bergsmo M, Pejic J (2008) Article 15: prosecutor. In: Triffterer O (ed) Commentary on the Rome Statute of the International Criminal Court. Verlag C.H. Beck, München
Blommestijn M, Ryngaert C (2010) Exploring the obligations for states to act upon the ICC's arrest warrant for Omar Al-Bashir: a legal conflict between the duty to arrest and the customary status of head of state immunity. Z Int Strafrechtsdogmatik 5:428–444
Cote L (2012) Independence and impartiality. In: Reydams L, Wouters J, Ryngaert C (eds) International prosecutors. Oxford University Press, Oxford
Drakard M (2011) International Criminal Court investigation of Kenyans is perceived as mixed blessing. The cutting edge 11 April 2011. http://www.thecuttingedgenews.com/index.php?article=51772&pageid=13&pagename=Analysis
Fletcher GP, Ohlin JD (2006) The ICC: two courts in one? J Int Crim Justice 4:428–433
Hafner G (2005) An attempt to explain the position of the USA towards the ICC. J Int Justice 3:323–332
Hansen TO (2013) Africa and the International Criminal Court. In: Murithi T (ed) Africa's international relations: a handbook. Routledge, London
Jalloh C (2010) Kenyan parliament endorses ruto motion calling for withdrawal from ICC statute. International Criminal Law in ferment blog. http://iclferment.blogspot.com/2010/12/kenyan-parliament-endorses-ruto-motion.html
Jalloh C (2012) Africa and the International Criminal Court: collision course or cooperation? N C Cent Law Rev 34:203–229
Mbote PK, Akech M (2011) Kenya: justice sector and the rule of law. The Open Society Initiative for Eastern Africa, Nairobi
Mills K (2012) "Bashir is Dividing Us": Africa and the International Criminal Court. Hum Rights Q 34:404–447
Murithi T (2012) Africa's relationship with the ICC: a need for restoration? Perspectives: Polit Anal Comment Afr 2012:4–9
Murithi T (2013) The African Union and the International Criminal Court: an embattled relationship? Institute for Justice and Reconciliation, Policy Brief No. 8, March 2013. http://ijr.org.za/publications/pb10.php
Musila G (2009) Options for transitional justice in Kenya: autonomy and the challenge of external prescriptions. Int J Transitional Justice 3:445–464
Villa-Vicencio C (2011) The ICC in Africa. Thinker 26:38–41
Werle G (2009) Principles of International Criminal Law, 2nd edn. T.M. Asser Press, The Hague

Cases

Prosecutor v. Francis Kirimi Muthaura, Uhuru Muigai Kenyatta and Mohammed Hussein Ali, Decision on the confirmation of charges, 23 January 2012, ICC-01/09-02/11-382-Red.
Prosecutor v. William Samoei Ruto, Henry Kiprono Kosgey and Joshua Arap Sang, Decision on the confirmation of charges, 23 January 2012, ICC-01/09-01/11-373.
Decision on the Prosecutor's application for summonses to appear for Francis Kirimi Muthaura, Uhuru Muigai Kenyatta and Mohammed Hussein Ali, 8 March 2011, ICC-01/09-02/11-01.
Decision on the Prosecutor's application for summons to appear for William Samoei Ruto, Henry Kiprono Kosgey and Joshua Arap Sang, 8 March 2011, ICC-01/09-01/11-01.

Other Documents

Coalition of the International Criminal Court (2002), EU Council Approves Common Position Rejecting US Bilateral Agreements. http://www.iccnow.org/documents/09.30.02EUAdoptsCP.pdf.

European Union (2003) Council Common Position 2003/444/CFSP of 16 June 2003 on the International Criminal Court. Official Journal of the European Union. http://consilium.europa.eu/uedocs/cmsUpload/l_15020030618en00670069.pdf.

European Union (2002) Council Common Position of 20 June 2002 Amending Common Position 2001/443/CFSP on the International Criminal Court (2002/474/CFSP). Official Journal of European Communities. http://www.consilium.europa.eu/uedocs/cmsUpload/ICC25EN.pdf.

Human Rights Watch (2013) Perceptions and Realities: Kenya and the International Criminal Court. http://www.hrw.org/sites/default/files/related_material/Perceptions%20and%20Realities%20-%20Updated%20November%202013.pdf.

Human Rights Watch (2011) Unfinished Business: Closing Gaps in the Selection of ICC Cases 1-56432-810-4, September 2011. http://www.hrw.org/sites/default/files/reports/icc0911webwcover.pdf.

International Center for Transitional Justice (2011) "To Live as Other Kenyans Do": A Study of the Reparative Demands of Kenyan Victims of Human Rights Violations', July 2011. http://www.ictj.org/sites/default/files/ICTJ-Kenya-Reparations-Demands-2011-English.pdf.

International Criminal Court, Press Release (2004) President of Uganda refers situation concerning the Lord's Resistance Army (LRA) to the ICC, ICC-20040129-44.

International Criminal Court, Press Release (2004) Prosecutor receives referral of the situation in the Democratic Republic of Congo, ICC-OTP-20040419-50.

International Criminal Court, Press Release (2005) ICC Prosecutor receives referral concerning Central African Republic), ICC-OTP-20050107-86.

International Criminal Court, Press Release (2014), President of the Assembly welcomes continued commitment to the International Criminal Court from politicians from Francophone African States, ICC-ASP-20140210-PR981.

International Crisis Group (2012) Impact of the ICC Proceedings. Africa Briefing No. 84, 9 January 2012. http://www.crisisgroup.org//media/Files/africa/horn-of-africa/kenya/B084%20Kenya%20-%20Impact%20of%20the%20ICC%20Proceedings.pdf.

Kenya National Commission on Human Rights (2008), On the Brink of the Precipice: A Human Rights Account of Kenya's Post-2007 Election Violence, Nairobi.

Kenya National Dialogue and Reconciliation Monitoring Project (2011), Draft Review Report, April 2011 http://www.dialoguekenya.org/docs/April2011KNDRReport.pdf.

Kenya National Dialogue and Reconciliation Monitoring Project (2012), First Draft Review Report January 2012 http://www.dialoguekenya.org/docs/KNDRFinal Report January 2012.pdf.

Kenya National Dialogue and Reconciliation Monitoring Project (2013), Kenya's 2013 General Election: A Review of Preparedness http://www.dialoguekenya.org/Monitoring/(February%202013)%204TH%20Review%20Report%20on%20Electoral%20Preparedness.pdf.

Organization of African Unity, Decision CM/Dec.399 (LXVII) adopted at the Sixty Seventh Ordinary Session of OAU's Council of Ministers, 25–28 February 1998, Addis Ababa, Ethiopia.

Republic of Kenya, Report of the Commission of Inquiry into Post-Election Violence (CIPEV), 15 October 2008. Government Printer, Nairobi.

Annex 1
Africa and the International Criminal Court—Recommendations

Introduction

From 22 to 23 November 2013, the South African-German Centre for Transnational Criminal Justice held an international conference in Cape Town, South Africa, under the theme "Africa and the International Criminal Court". The two-day conference was well attended by representatives of the International Criminal Court, practitioners from various African countries and legal scholars.

Also among the conference participants were students, as well as alumni and alumnae of the South African-German Centre for Transnational Criminal Justice, a collaborative project between the University of the Western Cape and Humboldt-Universität zu Berlin and funded by the German Academic Exchange Service. The conference discussions and debates exposed the participants to practical issues bearing governance and justice in Africa.

In order to foster the practical, academic and political discourse on the International Criminal Court and Africa, the students and alumni of the centre (see at the bottom of this Annex) made the following key observations and recommendations.

Regarding Politics in Relation to the Prosecution of African Leaders

- The argument that the International Criminal Court is "targeting" African leaders is delicately intertwined with the politics of perception. This perception is compounded when viewed in the context of Africa's history, its colonization, and its experience with racism and economic exploitation.
- While the norms that underpin the establishment of the International Criminal Court are universally accepted, the fact that certain powerful countries such as China, Russia and the United States of America are not ICC Member States poses a challenge for the credibility of the International Criminal Court.

G. Werle et al. (eds.), *Africa and the International Criminal Court*,
International Criminal Justice Series 1, DOI 10.1007/978-94-6265-029-9

This credibility is further undermined by the influential and decisive powers wielded by these countries in decisions taken by the UN Security Council either to refer situations to the Court or defer cases over which the Court has started to exercise jurisdiction.

- There is a serious need to reform the UN Security Council and to reflect on its relationship with the International Criminal Court so as to avoid perceptions of bias and double standards.
- There are dense political issues surrounding the prosecution of African leaders, including Heads of State, by the International Criminal Court. The politics surrounding the prosecution of African leaders are not unique in nature, as politics and the pursuit of justice have always been inseparable since the commencement of international criminal prosecutions following World War II, the Yugoslavian conflict and the Rwandan genocide.
- While politics are a reality and must not influence the pursuit of justice negatively, the power of political influence must not be underestimated and may be an important factor in determining the sequencing of peace and justice. The virtually sole focus on punitive justice in post-conflict states tends to draw attention to the perpetrators and drowns out the voice of the victims clamoring justice. A broader approach and understanding of justice must be adopted. Therefore, while the International Criminal Court will remain an important tool to achieving legal justice, alternative approaches for achieving restorative, social and economic justice remain vital.
- The criticisms by certain African leaders and the African Union against the International Criminal Court, *inter alia*, as a cherry-pick, racist or Western Court, do not hold water. The International Criminal Court and its establishing Statute may have gaps, but arguing that the Court is "witch-hunting" African leaders is misleading. Such opinion is not shared by the victims of horrendous atrocities and the broad masses in Africa who not only continue to support the International Criminal Court but also depend on the Court to serve as a watchdog to prevent egregious human rights violations and to end the cycle of impunity on the Continent. African leaders and the African Union should address any challenges they have with the Court, using formal mechanisms and in a manner that will strengthen and not weaken the Court. Most importantly, the AU leaders need to join efforts to prevent conflicts, stop human rights violations, and combat impunity in Africa. They need to redouble their efforts at ensuring the inviolability of the person. They have to ensure that perpetrators are brought to book, and that genuine justice is dispensed by truly independent African mechanisms. This will, in turn, end the interventions by the International Criminal Court or third states.

The Contest of Immunity for Serving Heads of State and the Duty to Prosecute Crimes Under International Law

- It should be kept in mind that it is settled under international law, and complemented by the jurisprudence of international criminal institutions, that the duty to prosecute crimes under international law stands above the immunity of serving Heads of State.
- This duty is recognized by African States and overtly acknowledged in the drafting of the Rome Statute. It is also reflected in various instruments and Decisions of the African Union. The about-turn in this understanding, as reflected in the Decision of the Extraordinary Summit of the African Union of November 2013, will serve only to perpetuate impunity on the Continent.

Possible Complements to the International Criminal Court in the Pursuit of Criminal Justice

- It is vitally important to establish and to sustain justice as a broader concept in Africa. The lessons learnt from the Rwandan *Gacaca* courts are indispensible in this regard. African societies need, however, to choose an acceptable alternative justice mechanism. The impartiality of such bodies has to be guaranteed.
- The domestic options should not create a hideout for powerful suspects who can influence the make-up of these institutions. The carefully worded Rome Statute, as far as the checks for prosecuting under the domestic justice systems are concerned, are instructive, as they bear on considerations of a State's genuine willingness and ability to fight impunity.
- While the Rome Statute makes specific reference to the principle of complementarity in relation to national courts, a purposive interpretation of the principle can include regional courts. In assessing the admissibility of a case before the Court, it is important to consider whether any action, if any, has been taken not only in the national courts of the State, but also at regional courts.

*

Judith Christabella Aceng (Uganda), *Seada Adem* (Ethiopia), *Deborah Adeyemo* (Nigeria), *Tangu Banda* (Zambia), *Noela Barasa* (Kenya), *Philippa Bogere* (Uganda), *Chiwala Chipeta* (Malawi), *Daniel Daka* (Malawi), *Francis Dusabe* (Rwanda), *Etienne Dusabeyezu* (Rwanda), *Saba Gebremeskel* (Ethiopia), *Arnold Gesase* (Tanzania), *Envar Hartnick* (South Africa), *Joshua Kabwe* (Zambia), *Sylvester Kalembera* (Malawi), *Nelly Kamunde* (Kenya), *Florian Kling* (Germany), *Selemani Kinyunyu* (Tanzania), *Alayna Lewendal* (South Africa), *Olwethu Majola* (South Africa), *Zainabu Mango* (Tanzania), *Sosteness Materu* (Tanzania), *Awamu Mbagwa* (Tanzania), *Angela Mudukuti* (Zimbabwe),

Olivia Kaguliro Mulerwa (Uganda), *Viola Muthoni* (Kenya), *Windell Nortje* (South Africa), *Juliet Okoth* (Kenya), *Deborah Orina* (Kenya), *Julian Rindler* (Germany), *Fatuma Mninde Silungwe* (Malawi), *Cassandra Soko* (Zambia), *Priscilla Tamale* (Uganda), *Marshet Tessema* (Ethiopia), *Franziska Tolksdorf* (Germany), *Tumaini Wafula* (Kenya), *Charity Wibabara* (Rwanda), *Caroline Wilson* (South Africa), *Marian Yankson* (Ghana), *Gamaliel Zimba* (Zambia)

Annex 2
African Union Decisions Regarding the Enforcement of International Criminal Law in Africa

G. Werle et al. (eds.), *Africa and the International Criminal Court*,
International Criminal Justice Series 1, DOI 10.1007/978-94-6265-029-9

1. Assembly of the African Union
Tenth Ordinary Session
31 January–2 February 2008
Addis Ababa, Ethiopia

Assembly/AU/Dec.177 (X)

Decision on the Activities of the Peace and Security Council of the African Union and the State of Peace and Security in Africa

The Assembly:

1. TAKES NOTE of the Report on the activities of the Peace and Security Council (PSC) and the state of peace and security in Africa;
2. WELCOMES the efforts deployed to promote peace, security and stability in Africa, as well as the progress made in this regard. The Assembly ENCOURAGES all the parties concerned to redouble their efforts to consolidate the gains realized thus far, and REQUESTS the Commission to continue to support the ongoing processes and mobilize the international community assistance in this respect;
3. EXPRESSES ITS SATISFACTION with the ongoing efforts to consolidate peace and stability in the Democratic Republic of Congo (DRC), including the signing by the concerned parties of an Act of Commitment aimed at restoring peace and stability in Eastern DRC and speeding up the national reconciliation process, following the Conference on Peace, Security and Development on the North and South Kivu Provinces, held in Goma, from 6 to 23 January 2008, and URGES the parties to scrupulously honour their commitments, including those pertaining to disarmament of armed groups operating in the East of DRC;
4. NOTES WITH SATISFACTION the encouraging developments in Côte d'Ivoire, since the signing of the Ouagadougou Political Agreement and the progress made in its implementation, and CALLS UPON the parties to redouble their efforts so as to speed up the implementation of the Agreements that have been signed, in order to pave the way for the holding of presidential elections not later than the first half of 2008;
5. WELCOMES the resolution of the institutional crisis in Burundi with the establishment of a Government in line with the Constitution, following the political dialogue initiated by the President of the Republic with the political opposition parties in August 2007. At the same time, the Assembly EXPRESSES ITS CONCERN over the lengthy delays and difficulties faced in the implementation of the Comprehensive Ceasefire Agreement of 7 September 2006. The Assembly ENCOURAGES the Mediator to pursue his efforts and REQUESTS the Regional Initiative to remain actively seized of the peace process in Burundi;
6. WELCOMES the progress made regarding post-conflit reconstruction in Liberia and REQUESTS the Member States, the United Nations and bilateral and multilateral partners to continue to extend all the necessary support;

7. TAKES NOTE of the efforts deployed to re-launch the peace process in Darfur, particularly the opening of the Sirte peace talks on 27 October 2007. The Assembly REAFFIRMS its support to the joint efforts being exerted by the AU and the United Nations, especially through their respective Special Envoys, with a view to commencing substantive discussions on the pending issues, and URGES all the parties concerned to provide the necessary cooperation;
8. WELCOMES the launching of the African Union/United Nations hybrid operation in Darfur (UNAMID) and the transfer of authority which took place on 31 December 2007, ENCOURAGES the AU Commission and the UN Secretariat to pursue their efforts towards the early deployment of UNAMID, FURTHER ENCOURAGES the Government of the Sudan to continue to cooperate with the AU and the United Nations towards the early completion of the deployment of the Mission and the smooth conduct of its operations, and REQUESTS the AU, the UN and the Government of Sudan to continue to cooperate closely in order to create conditions conducive for the successful execution of UNAMID mandate. The Conference COMMENDS the African Union Mission in the Sudan (AMIS) and its personnel for the remarkable work accomplished in Darfur despite the numerous difficulties the Mission had to grapple with;
9. WELCOMES the measures taken by the parties to the Comprehensive Peace Agreement (CPA) in the Sudan to overcome the difficulties encountered in its implementation and URGES them to pursue their efforts to ensure the full implementation of the Agreement in letter and spirit;
10. EXPRESSES ITS SERIOUS CONCERN at the lack of progress in resolving the crisis in the Comorian Island of Anjouan, particularly the restoration of the Union Government authority in Anjouan. The Assembly FULLY SUPPORTS the efforts deployed by the AU in pursuance of the pertinent decisions of the PSC with a view to restoring State authority in Anjouan and put a definite end to the crisis arising from the attitude of the illegal authorities of Anjouan;
11. EXPRESSES ITS CONCERN over the persistent tension between the Sudan and Chad, CALLS ON the two Governments to exercise restraint and do everything possible to defuse the current tension and contribute to the restoration of normalcy along their common border and WELCOMES the efforts being deployed by Libya to assist the two countries;
12. NOTES WITH SATISFACTION the on-going efforts aimed at consolidating peace and reconciliation in the Central African Republic (CAR), including the holding of an inclusive political dialogue, and ENCOURAGES all the parties concerned to participate in the dialogue in a constructive spirit. The Assembly UNDERSCORES the work accomplished by the Multinational Force of the Economic and Monetary Community of Central Africa (CEMAC) and TAKES NOTE of the decision of the Summit of the Economic Community of Central African States (ECCAS), held in Brazzaville on 30 October 2007, to transfer the CEMAC Multinational Force (FOMUC) from CEMAC to ECCAS;

13. REITERATES ITS DEEP CONCERN at the continued impasse in the Ethiopia Eritrea peace process and at its implications for peace, security and stability in the region at large, EMPHASIZES the need for more sustained and coordinated efforts to help the parties overcome the current impasse in the peace process, including the demarcation of their common border, and normalize their relations, and EXPRESSES THE READINESS of the African Union to assist Eritrea and Ethiopia in this endeavour;
14. EXPRESSES DEEP CONCERN at the post-electoral violence and tension in Kenya and at its social, humanitarian and economic consequences, as well as at its implications for peace and stability in Kenya and the region as a whole ONCE AGAIN CALLS ON all the parties to exercise restraint, refrain from acts of violence and from any other act that could further complicate the situation, as well as prevail on their supporters to put an immediate end to the violence, and speedily resolve the crisis and the electoral dispute within the established legal framework;
15. WELCOMES the efforts made by the current Chair of the AU, John Kufuor, the Chair of the East African Community (EAC), Yoweri Museveni, and by other leaders and organisations both within and outside the region, to assist in resolving the crisis in Kenya. The Assembly REQUESTS the Kenyan parties to extend full cooperation to the mediation efforts being conducted by the group of eminent African elders led by former UN Secretary-General, Kofi Annan;
16. REQUESTS the PSC to pursue its efforts aimed at promoting peace, security and stability in the continent, with special attention to conflict prevention, and, whenever necessary, to be involved in all situations likely to pose a threat to peace and security in the continent;
17. RECALLS decision Assembly/AU/Dec. 145 (VIII) adopted by the Assembly at its 8th ordinary session held in January 2007, calling upon the United Nations to examine, within the context of Chapter VIII of the Charter of the United Nations, the possibility of funding, through assessed contributions, peace keeping operations undertaken by the AU or under its authority, with the consent of the United Nations, and WELCOMES the steps taken by the AU Commission and Member States in pursuance of this decision;
18. LOOKS FORWARD to the report that will be submitted by the United Nations Secretary-General on the relationship between the United Nations and regional organisations, in particular the African Union, in the maintenance of international peace and security, as provided for by Security Council Presidential Statement of 28 March 2007. The Assembly WELCOMES the REQUESTS the Security Council to consider this report with the view to achieving concrete results in further strengthen cooperation between the AU and the UN. In this regard, the Assembly REQUESTS the offer of South Africa to avail its presidency of the United Nations Security Council in April 2008 to discuss the report of the United Nations Secretary General, and REQUESTS the Security Council to consider this report with the view to achieving concrete results in further strengthen cooperation between the AU

and the UN. In this regard, the Assembly REQUESTS the United Nations Security Council to collaborate with, and invite, the AU PSC during the consideration of this report;

19. TAKES NOTE of the report of the international workshop on security sector reform (SSR) in Cape Town, South Africa, on 7–8 November 2007, and ENCOURAGES the Commission to develop a comprehensive AU Policy Framework on SSR, within the context of the Policy Framework on conflict Reconstruction and Development adopted by the Executive Council in Banjul, in June 2006.

**2. Assembly of the African Union
Tenth Ordinary Session
31 January–2 February 2008
Addis Ababa, Ethiopia**

Assembly/AU/Dec.187 (X)

Decision on the Situation in Kenya Following the Presidential Election of 27 December 2007

The Assembly:

1. EXPRESSES ITS DEEP CONCERN at the prevailing situation and its humanitarian consequences, as well as at its implications for peace and stability in Kenya and the region as a whole;
2. STRONGLY DEPLORES the loss of lives and CONDEMNS the gross violations of human rights that occurred in the past weeks;
3. STRESSES the need for all those involved in these violations to be held accountable and, to this end, CALLS for an in-depth investigation with a view to identifying those responsible and bringing them to justice;
4. CALLS on all the parties to exercise restraint, refrain from acts of violence, as well as prevail on their supporters to put an immediate end to the violence;
5. STRONGLY URGES the parties to commit themselves to a peaceful solution to the current crisis through dialogue and in conformity with the rule of law;
6. WELCOMES the visit undertaken by the former Chairman of the African Union, President John Kufuor, to Nairobi, from 8 to 10 January 2008, as well as the efforts deployed by President Yoweri Museveni, in his capacity as the Chairperson of the East African Community (EAC), and by other leaders of the region;
7. STRESSES the need for the parties to extend full cooperation to the mediation efforts undertaken by the group of eminent African elders led by Mr. Kofi Annan, former Secretary-General of the United Nations, and comprising Mr. Benjamin Mkapa and Mrs. Graca Machel, established as a follow-up to the visit of the former Chairperson of the AU. The Assembly WELCOMES the agreement on the ending of violence and the pursuit of dialogue, reached by the parties on 1st February 2008, and URGES them to build on this encouraging development to find a lasting solution to the current crisis. The Assembly COMMENDS Mr. Kofi Annan and the members of his team for the results achieved so far and ENCOURAGES them to pursue their efforts;
8. STRESSES the need to initiate a collective reflection on the challenges linked to the tension and disputes that often characterize electoral processes in Africa, including the strengthening of the African capacity at national, regional and continental levels to observe and monitor elections.

3. Assembly of the African Union
Eleventh Ordinary Session
30 June–1 July 2008
Sharm El-Sheikh, Egypt

Assembly/AU/ Dec.199(XI)

Decision on the Report of the Commission on the Abuse of the Principle of Universal Jurisdiction

The Assembly:

1. TAKES NOTE of the Report of the Commission on the abuse of the Principle of Universal Jurisdiction pursuant to the recommendation of the Ministers of Justice/Attorneys General in Addis Ababa, Ethiopia on 18 April 2008;
2. RECALLS the Johannesburg Declaration of the Pan-African Parliament dated 15 May 2008;
3. RECOGNIZING that universal jurisdiction is a principle of International Law whose purpose is to ensure that individuals who commit grave offences such as war crimes and crimes against humanity do not do so with impunity and are brought to justice, which is in line with Article 4(h) of the Constitutive Act of the African Union;
4. NOTING the Brazzaville statement by the Inter-ministerial Committee of the International Conference on the Great Lakes Region dated 22 May 2008;
5. RESOLVE as follows:

   (I) The abuse of the Principle of Universal Jurisdiction is a development that could endanger International law, order and security;
   (II) The political nature and abuse of the principle of universal jurisdiction by judges from some non-African States against African leaders, particularly Rwanda, is a clear violation of the sovereignty and territorial integrity of these States;
   (III) The abuse and misuse of indictments against African leaders have a destabilizing effect that will negatively impact on the political, social and economic development of States and their ability to conduct international relations;
   (IV) Those warrants shall not be executed in African Union Member States;
   (V) There is need for establishment of an international regulatory body with competence to review and/or handle complaints or appeals arising out of abuse of the principle of universal jurisdiction by individual States.

4. Assembly of the African Union
Twelfth Ordinary Session
1–3 February 2009
Addis Ababa, Ethiopia

Assembly/AU/Dec.213(XII)

Decision on the Implementation of the Assembly Decision on the Abuse of the Principle of Universal Jurisdiction

The Assembly:

1. TAKES NOTE of the Progress Report of the Commission on the Implementation of the Assembly Decision Assembly/AU/ Dec.199(XI) adopted by the Assembly in Sharm El-Sheikh, Egypt, in July 2008 on the Abuse of the Principle of Universal Jurisdiction;
2. ALSO TAKES NOTE of the work of the African Union–European Union (AU–EU) Technical Ad-hoc Expert Group set up by the Eleventh AU–EU Ministerial Troika with the mandate to clarify the respective understanding on the African and EU side on the principle of universal jurisdiction;
3. REITERATES its commitment to fighting impunity in conformity with the provisions of Article 4(h) of the Constitutive Act of the African Union;
4. EXPRESSES its regret that in spite of its previous Summit decision calling for a moratorium and whilst the African Union (AU) and the European Union (EU) were already in discussion to find a durable solution to this issue, a warrant of arrest was executed against Mrs Rose Kabuye, Chief of Protocol to the President of the Republic of Rwanda, thereby creating tension between the AU and the EU;
5. UNDERSCORES that the African Union speaking with one voice, is the appropriate collective response to counter the exercise of power by strong states over weak states;
6. REITERATES its appeal to all United Nations (UN) Member States, in particular the EU States, to suspend the execution of warrants issued by individual European States until all the legal and political issues have been exhaustively discussed between the AU, the EU and the UN;
7. REQUESTS the Chairperson of the African Union to follow up on this matter with a view to ensuring that it is exhaustively discussed at the level of the UN Security Council and the UN General Assembly;
8. URGES the AU and EU Commissions to extend the necessary support to the Joint Technical Ad-hoc Expert Group;
9. REQUESTS the Commission, in consultation with the African Commission on Human and Peoples' Rights, and the African Court on Human and Peoples' Rights, to examine the implications of the Court being empowered to try international crimes such as genocide, crimes against humanity and war crimes, and report thereon to the Assembly in 2010 Assembly/AU/Dec.213(XII)
10. ALSO REQUESTS the Commission to follow up on this matter with a view to ensuring that a definitive solution to this problem is reached and to report to the next ordinary session of the Assembly through the Executive Council in July 2009.

5. Assembly of the African Union
Twelfth Ordinary Session
1–3 February 2009
Addis Ababa, Ethiopia

Assembly/AU/Dec.221(XII)

Decision on the Application by the International Criminal Court (ICC) Prosecutor for the Indictment of the President of the Republic of the Sudan

The Assembly:

1. EXPRESSES ITS DEEP CONCERN at the indictment made by the Prosecutor of the International Criminal Court (ICC) against the President of the Republic of The Sudan, H.E. Mr. Omar Hassan Ahmed El Bashir;
2. CAUTIONS that, in view of the delicate nature of the peace processes underway in The Sudan, approval of this application would seriously undermine the ongoing efforts aimed at facilitating the early resolution of the conflict in Darfur;
3. ENDORSES the Communiqué issued by the Peace and Security Council (PSC) of the African Union (AU) at its 142nd meeting, held on 21 July 2008, and URGES the United Nations Security Council, in accordance with the provisions of Article 16 of the Rome Statute of the ICC, and as requested by the PSC at its above-mentioned meeting, to defer the process initiated by the ICC.
4. REQUESTS the Commission to implement this Decision by sending a high-level delegation from the African Union for necessary contacts with the UN Security Council;
5. FURTHER REQUESTS the Commission to convene as early as possible, a meeting of the African countries that are parties to the Rome Statute on the establishment of the International Criminal Court (ICC) to exchange views on the work of the ICC in relation to Africa, in particular in the light of the processes initiated against African personalities, and to submit recommendations thereon taking into account all relevant elements;
6. REITERATES AU's unflinching commitment to combating impunity and promoting democracy, the rule of law and good governance throughout the entire Continent, in conformity with its Constitutive Act;
7. CONDEMNS the gross violations of human rights in Darfur, and URGES that the perpetrators be apprehended and brought to justice, and SUPPORTS the decision by the PSC to establish a High-Level Panel of Eminent Personalities under the chairmanship of former President of the Republic of South Africa, H.E. Mr. Thabo Mbeki, to examine the situation in depth, and to submit recommendations on how best the issues of accountability and combating impunity, on the one hand, and reconciliation and healing, on the other, could be effectively and comprehensively addressed;

8. NOTES the steps taken by the Republic of The Sudan to address human rights violations in Darfur, and REITERATES the call by various AU Organs for the Government of The Sudan to take immediate and concrete steps to investigate and bring the perpetrators to justice, and to take advantage of the availability of qualified lawyers to be seconded by the AU and the League of Arab States, and in this regard CALLS UPON all parties to scrupulously respect the values and principles of human rights.

6. Assembly of the African Union
Twelfth Ordinary Session
1–3 February 2009
Addis Ababa, Ethiopia

Assembly/AU/Dec.240(XII)
Decision on the Hissène Habré Case
The Assembly:

1. RECALLS its Decision Assembly/AU/Dec.127(VII) taken in Banjul, the Gambia, in July 2006 mandating the Republic of Senegal "to prosecute and ensure that Hissène Habré is tried, on behalf of Africa, by a competent Senegalese court with guarantees for fair trail";
2. REITERATES its commendation of the Government of the Republic of Senegal for having taken constitutional, legal and regulatory measures to carry out the mandate;
3. TAKES NOTE that despite the establishment of the budget for the case by the European Union, which offered to be partner, together with the Government of the Republic of Senegal, the resources needed for the prosecution are not yet available;
4. CONSIDERS that the final budget of the case should be prepared and adopted by the African Union, in conjunction with the Government of the Republic of Senegal and the European Union;
5. CALLS ON all Member States of the African Union, the European Union and partner countries and institutions to make their contributions to the budget of the case by paying these contributions directly to the African Union Commission;
6. REQUESTS the Commission to report on the status of execution of this Decision to the 13th Assembly of the African Union.

7. Assembly of the African Union
Thirteenth Ordinary Session
1–3 July 2009
Sirte, Great Socialist People's
Libyan Arab Jamahiriya

Assembly/AU/Dec.243(XIII) Rev.1
Decision on the Abuse of the Principle of Universal Jurisdiction
Doc. Assembly/AU/11(XIII)
The Assembly:

1. TAKES NOTE of the Progress Report of the Commission on the Implementation of Decision Assembly/AU/Dec.199(XI) adopted by the Assembly in Sharm El-Sheikh, Egypt in July 2008 as well as Decision Assembly/AU/Dec.213 (XII) on the Abuse of the Principle of Universal Jurisdiction adopted in Addis Ababa, Ethiopia in February 2009;
2. ENDORSES the recommendations of the Executive Council;
3. REITERATES its appeal to the Chairperson of the African Union to follow-up on this matter with a view to ensuring that it is exhaustively discussed at the level of the United Nations Security Council and the General Assembly, as well as the European Union;
4. REITRATES its previous positions articulated in Decisions Assembly/ Dec.199(XI) and Assembly/Dec.213(XII) adopted in Sharm El Sheikh and Addis Ababa in July 2008 and February 2009 respectively to the effect that there has been blatant abuse of the Principle of Universal Jurisdiction particularly by some non-African States and EXPRESSES its deep concern that indictments have continued to be issued in some European States against African leaders and personalities. To this end, it CALLS FOR immediate termination of all pending indictments;
5. FURTHER REITERATES its conviction on the need for an international regulatory body with competence to review and/or handle complaints or appeals arising out of abuse of the Principle of Universal Jurisdiction by individual States;
6. CALLS UPON all concerned States to respect International Law and particularly the immunity of state officials when applying the Principle of Universal Jurisdiction;
7. EXPRESSES APPRECIATION to the Chairperson of the African Union and the Chairperson of the Commission for efforts made so far towards ensuring that this matter is exhaustively discussed at the level of the United Nations General Assembly and with the European Union, respectively;
8. REQUESTS the Commission to follow up on this matter and to report to the Assembly on progress made in the implementation of this Decision, in January/ February 2010.

8. Assembly of the African Union
Thirteenth Ordinary Session
1–3 July 2009
Sirte, Great Socialist People's
Libyan Arab Jamahiriya

Assembly/AU/Dec.245(XIII) Rev.1

Decision on the Meeting of African States Parties to the Rome Statute of the International Criminal Court (ICC)

Doc. Assembly/AU/13(XIII)

The Assembly:

1. TAKES NOTE of the recommendations of the Executive Council on the Meeting of the African States Parties to the Rome Statute of the International Criminal Court (ICC);
2. EXPRESSES ITS DEEP CONCERN at the indictment issued by the Pre-Trial Chamber of the ICC against President Omar Hassan Ahmed El Bashir of the Republic of The Sudan;
3. NOTES WITH GRAVE CONCERN the unfortunate consequences that the indictment has had on the delicate peace processes underway in The Sudan and the fact that it continues to undermine the ongoing efforts aimed at facilitating the early resolution of the conflict in Darfur;
4. REITERATES the unflinching commitment of Member States to combating impunity and promoting democracy, rule of law and good governance throughout the continent, in conformity with the Constitutive Act of the African Union;
5. REQUESTS the Commission to ensure the early implementation of Decision Assembly/Dec.213(XII), adopted in February 2009 mandating the Commission, in consultation with the African Commission on Human and Peoples' Rights and the African Court on Human and Peoples' Rights to examine the implications of the Court being empowered to try serious crimes of international concern such as genocide, crimes against humanity and war crimes, which would be complementary to national jurisdiction and processes for fighting impunity;
6. ENCOURAGES Member States to initiate programmes of cooperation and capacity building to enhance the capacity of legal personnel in their respective countries regarding the drafting and safety of model legislation dealing with serious crimes of international concern, training of members of the police and the judiciary, and the strengthening of cooperation amongst judicial and investigative agencies;
7. FURTHER TAKES NOTE that any party affected by the indictment has the right of legal recourse to the processes provided for in the Rome Statute regarding the appeal process and the issue of immunity;

8. REQUESTS the Commission to convene a preparatory meeting of African States Parties at expert and ministerial levels (Foreign Affairs and Justice) but open to other Member States at the end of 2009 to prepare fully for the Review Conference of States Parties scheduled for Kampala, Uganda in May 2010, to address among others, the following issues:
   (I) Article 13 of the Rome Statute granting power to the UN Security Council to refer cases to the ICC;
   (II) Article 16 of the Rome Statute granting power to the UN Security Council to defer cases for one (1) year;
   (III) Procedures of the ICC;
   (IV) Clarification on the Immunities of officials whose States are not party to the Statute;
   (V) Comparative analysis of the implications of the practical application of Articles 27 and 98 of the Rome Statute;
   (VI) The possibility of obtaining regional inputs in the process of assessing the evidence collected and in determining whether or not to proceed with prosecution; particularly against senior state officials; and
   (VII) Any other areas of concern to African States Parties.
9. DEEPLY REGRETS that the request by the African Union to the UN Security Council to defer the proceedings initiated against President Bashir of The Sudan in accordance with Article 16 of the Rome Statute of the ICC, has neither been heard nor acted upon, and in this regard, REITERATES ITS REQUEST to the UN Security Council;
10. DECIDES that in view of the fact that the request by the African Union has never been acted upon, the AU Member States shall not cooperate pursuant to the provisions of Article 98 of the Rome Statute of the ICC relating to immunities, for the arrest and surrender of President Omar El Bashir of The Sudan;
11. EXPRESSES CONCERN OVER the conduct of the ICC Prosecutor and FURTHER DECIDES that the preparatory meeting of African States Parties to the Rome Statute of the ICC scheduled for late 2009 should prepare, inter alia, guidelines and a code of conduct for exercise of discretionary powers by the ICC Prosecutor relating particularly to the powers of the prosecutor to initiate cases at his own discretion under Article 15 of the Rome Statute;
12. UNDERSCORES that the African Union and its Member States reserve the right to take any further decisions or measures that may be deemed necessary in order to preserve and safeguard the dignity, sovereignty and integrity of the continent;
13. FINALLY REQUESTS the Commission to follow-up on the implementation of this Decision and submit a report to the next Ordinary Session of the Assembly through the Executive Council in January/February 2010 and in this regard AUTHORIZES expenditure for necessary actions from arrears of contributions.

9. Assembly of the African Union
Thirteenth Ordinary Session
1–3 July 2009
Sirte, Great Socialist People's
Libyan Arab Jamahiriya

Assembly/AU/Dec.246(XIII)
Decision on the Hissène Habré Case
Doc. Assembly/AU/12 (XIII) Rev.1
The Assembly,

1. TAKES NOTE of the Progress Report of the Commission on the Implementation of Assembly Decision Assembly/AU/Dec.240(XII) adopted by the Assembly in Addis Ababa, Ethiopia, in February 2009 on the Hissène Habré Case;
2. ALSO TAKES NOTE of the final estimated budget for the trial;
3. EXPRESSES its regret that in spite of its previous Assembly decision calling on all Member States of the African Union (AU) to make voluntary contributions to the budget of the Hissène Habré case, there has been no positive reactions from Member States;
4. REITERATES its appeal to all Member States to contribute to the budget of the trial and extend the necessary support to the Government of Senegal in the execution of the AU mandate to prosecute and try Hissène Habré;
5. DECIDES that the AU should make a token contribution to the budget of the trial for a sum to be determined following consultations between the Commission and the Permanent Representatives Committee (PRC);
6. REQUESTS the Government of Senegal and the Commission in collaboration with the Partners, particularly the European Union to consider the possibility of organizing a donors' conference as soon as possible;
7. INVITES all partner countries and institutions to support this process and participate in the Donors Round Table that will be organized in this regard in Dakar, Senegal during the last quarter of 2009;
8. REQUESTS the Commission to closely monitor the implementation of this Decision and to report to the next ordinary session of the Assembly in February 2010; and in this regard, AUTHORIZES expenditure for necessary actions from arrears of contributions.

10. Assembly of the African Union
Fourteenth Ordinary Session
31 January–2 February 2010
Addis Ababa, Ethiopia

Decision on the Report of the Second Meeting of States Parties to the Rome Statute on the International Criminal Court (ICC)

DOC. Assembly/AU/8(XIV)

The Assembly,

1. TAKES NOTE of the Report of the Ministerial Preparatory Meeting on the Rome Statute of the International Criminal Court (ICC) held in Addis Ababa, Ethiopia on 6 November 2009 in conformity with Decision Assembly/AU/Dec.245(XIII) adopted in Sirte, Great Libyan Arab Jamahiraya, in July 2009, to prepare for the Review Conference of States Parties scheduled for Kampala, Uganda in May-June 2010;
2. ENDORSES the recommendations contained therein, and in particular the following:
   - (I) Proposal for amendment to Article 16 of the Rome Statute;
   - (II) Proposal for retention of Article 13 as is;
   - (III) Procedural issues: Guidelines for the exercise of prosecutorial discretion by the ICC Prosecutor;
   - (IV) Immunities of Officials whose States are not parties to the Rome Statute: the relationship between articles 27 and 98; and
   - (V) Proposals regarding the crime of aggression.
3. REITERATES its commitment to fight impunity in conformity with the provisions of Article 4(h) of the Constitutive Act of the African Union;
4. ALSO TAKES NOTE of the Report of the Commission on the 8th Assembly of States Parties of the ICC (ASP) held in The Hague, Netherlands from 16 to 26 November 2009 and the outcome of the ASP meeting.
5. WELCOMES the submission by the Republic of South Africa, on behalf of the African States Parties to the Rome Statute of the ICC of a proposal which consisted of an amendment to Article 16 of the Rome Statute in order to allow the United Nations (UN) General Assembly to defer cases for one (1) year in cases where the UN Security Council would have failed to take a decision within a specified time frame.
6. UNDERSCORES the need for African States Parties to speak with one voice to ensure that the interests of Africa are safeguarded;
7. WELCOMES Resolution ICC-ASP/8/Res.6 on the Review Conference that establishes a Working Group of the ASP for the purpose of considering, as from its Ninth Session, amendments to the Rome Statute including among others the proposal for amendment to Article 16 of the Rome Statute together with the proposals from other States Parties or group of States Parties;
8. TAKES NOTE of the fact that the other proposals made by the Second Meeting of the African States Parties to the Rome Statute will not be

considered during the Review Conference and REQUESTS accordingly, the African States Parties to raise the issue of the immunities of Officials whose States are not parties to the Rome Statute (the relationship between articles 27 and 98 under the topic "Cooperation" at the level of the Working Group of New York of the Bureau of ASP as well as during the stocktaking exercise of the Review Conference;

9. ALSO TAKES NOTE of the fact that there was no debate on the crime of aggression during the 8th ASP;
10. DEEPLY REGRETS that the request by the African Union to the UN Security Council to defer the proceedings initiated against President Bashir of The Sudan in accordance with Article 16 of the Rome Statute of ICC on deferral of cases by the UN Security Council, has not been acted upon, and in this regard, REITERATES its request to the UN Security Council;
11. URGES the African States Parties to the Rome Statute to follow-up on the concerns raised by Member States;
12. TAKES NOTE of the Review Conference of States Parties to the International Criminal Court scheduled to be held in Kampala, Uganda from 31 May to 11 June 2010, and CALLS UPON African Member States Parties to attend and effectively participate in the Conference;
13. REQUESTS the African Group in New York and the African Members of the Bureau of ASP, to follow-up on the implementation of this Decision in collaboration with the Commission and to ensure that the concerns raised by the Assembly of the Union and its Member States are properly addressed through consultations with other Regional Groups with a view to finding a durable solution and to report to the Assembly through the Commission on actions taken;
14. ALSO REQUESTS the Commission to follow-up on the implementation of this Decision and to report to the next Ordinary Session of the Assembly through the Executive Council in July 2010.

11. Assembly of the African Union
Fourteenth Ordinary Session
31 January–2 February 2010
Addis Ababa, Ethiopia
Decision on the Abuse of the Principle of Universal Jurisdiction
Doc. EX.CL/540(XVI)
The Assembly:

1. TAKES NOTE of the recommendations of the Executive Council on the Progress
Report of the Commission on the Implementation of Decision Assembly/AU/Dec.243 (XIII) adopted in Sirte, Great Libyan Arab Jamahiriya in July 2009;
2. ALSO TAKES NOTE of United Nations General Assembly (UNGA) Resolution A/RES/64/L117 on the Scope and Application of the Principle of Universal Jurisdiction adopted on 16 December 2009 by the United Nations (UN) General Assembly and INVITES all Member States to submit to the UN Secretary General, before 30 April 2010, information and observations on the scope and application of the principle of universal jurisdiction, including information on the relevant applicable international treaties, their domestic legal rules and judicial practice;
3. REITERATES its previous positions articulated in decisions Assembly/Dec.199(XI), Assembly/Dec.213(XII) and Assembly/Dec.243 (XIII) adopted in Sharm el Sheikh, Addis Ababa and Sirte in July 2008, February 2009 and July 2009 respectively to the effect that there has been blatant abuse of the Principle of Universal Jurisdiction particularly by some non-African States and REITERATES its call for immediate termination of all pending indictments;
4. FURTHER REITERATES its commitment to fight impunity in conformity with the provisions of Article 4(h) of the Constitutive Act of the African Union;
5. URGES the European Union (EU) and its Member States to extend the necessary cooperation to the African Union to facilitate the search for a durable solution to the abuse of the Principle of Universal Jurisdiction;
6. ALSO REITERATES its conviction of the need for an international regulatory body with competence to review and/or handle complaints or appeals arising out of abuse of the Principle of Universal Jurisdiction by individual States;
7. CALLS UPON all concerned States, particularly European States, to respect international law and particularly the immunity of state officials when applying the Principle of Universal Jurisdiction; Assembly/AU/Dec.271(XIV)
8. EXPRESSES APPRECIATION to the Chairperson of the African Union and the Chairperson of the Commission for efforts made so far towards ensuring that this matter is exhaustively discussed at the level of the United Nations;

9. URGES Member States affected by the abuse of the Principle of Universal Jurisdiction by non-African States to respond to the request made by the Chairperson of the Union and to communicate to the Commission the list and details of pending cases in non-African States against African personalities;
10. REQUESTS the African Group in New York to follow-up on the implementation of this Decision in collaboration with the Commission and to ensure that the concerns raised by the African Union and its Member States are properly addressed with a view to finding a durable solution and to report to the Assembly through the Commission on actions taken;
11. ALSO REQUESTS the Commission to follow-up on this matter with a view to ensuring that a definitive solution to this problem is reached and to report to the next Ordinary Session of the Assembly through the Executive Council in July 2010

12. Assembly of the African Union
Fifteenth Ordinary Session
25–27 July 2010
Kampala, Uganda
Decision on the Abuse of the Principle of Universal Jurisdiction
Doc. EX.CL/606(XVII)
The Assembly:

1. TAKES NOTE of the Progress Report of the Commission on the Implementation of Decision Assembly/AU/Dec.271 (XIV) adopted in Addis Ababa, Ethiopia in February 2010;
2. REITERATES its commitment to fight impunity in conformity with the provisions of Article 4(h) of the Constitutive Act of the African Union;
3. ALSO REITERATES its conviction that there has been blatant abuse of the Principle of Universal Jurisdiction, particularly in some non African States and CALLS for immediate termination of all pending indictments;
4. FURTHER REITERATES its conviction on the need for an international regulatory body with competence to review and/or handle complaints or appeals arising out of the abuse of the Principle of Universal Jurisdiction by individual States;
5. REQUESTS the Commission to finalise the study on the implications of empowering the African Court on Human and Peoples' Rights to try international crimes such as genocide, crimes against humanity and war crimes and report to the next Ordinary Session of the Assembly through the Executive Council in January/February 2011;
6. CALLS ON all concerned States to respect International Law and particularly the immunity of state officials when applying the Principle of Universal Jurisdiction;
7. URGES the European Union (EU) and its Member States to extend the necessary cooperation to the African Union (AU) to facilitate the search for a durable solution to the abuse of the Principle of Universal Jurisdiction;
8. ALSO URGES the EU and its Member States to implement the recommendations of the AU–EU Joint ad-hoc Expert group;
9. EXPRESSES APPRECIATION to the Chairperson of the AU and the Chairperson of the AU Commission for efforts made so far towards ensuring that this matter is exhaustively discussed at the level of the United Nations;
10. UNDERSCORES the need for African States Parties to speak with one voice to ensure that the interests of Africa are safeguarded during the forthcoming negotiations on the Principle of Universal Jurisdiction at the level of the United Nations; Assembly/AU/Dec.292(XV)
11. REQUESTS the African Group in New York to follow-up on the implementation of this Decision in collaboration with the Commission and to ensure that the concerns raised by the AU and its Member States regarding the Abuse of the Principle of Universal Jurisdiction by some non African States are properly addressed at the Level of the United Nations with a view to

finding a durable solution and to submit a report thereon to the Assembly through the Executive Council on actions taken;

12. ALSO REQUESTS the Commission to follow-up on the implementation of this Decision and to report to the next Ordinary Session of the Assembly through the Executive Council in January 2011.

13. Assembly of the African Union
Fifteenth Ordinary Session
25–27 July 2010
Kampala, Uganda

Decision on the Progress Report of the Commission on the Implementation of Decision Assembly/AU/DEC.270(XIV) On The Second Ministerial Meeting on the Rome Statute of the International Criminal Court (ICC)

Doc. Assembly/AU/10(XV)

The Assembly:

1. TAKES NOTE of the Progress Report of the Commission on the Implementation of Decision Assembly/AU/Dec.270 (XIV) adopted by the Fourteenth Ordinary Session of the Assembly held in Addis Ababa, Ethiopia, on the Second Ministerial Meeting on the Rome Statute of the International Criminal Court (ICC) and all comments and observations made by Member States and ENDORSES the recommendations contained therein;
2. REITERATES its commitment to fight impunity in conformity with the provisions of Article 4(h) of the Constitutive Act of the African Union;
3. RECALLS the African Union (AU) position expressed through the Decision Assembly/AU/Dec.270(XIV);
4. EXPRESSES its disappointment that the United Nations Security Council (UNSC) has not acted upon the request by the African Union to defer the proceedings initiated against President Omar Hassan El-Bashir of the Republic of The Sudan in accordance with Article 16 of the Rome Statute of ICC which allows the UNSC to defer cases for one (1) year and REITERATES its request in this regard;
5. REITERATES its Decision that AU Member States shall not cooperate with the ICC in the arrest and surrender of President El-Bashir of The Sudan;
6. REQUESTS Member States to balance, where applicable, their obligations to the AU with their obligations to the ICC;
7. URGES all Member States to speak with one voice to ensure that the proposed amendment to Article 16 of the Rome Statute which would allow the UN General Assembly to take over the power of the UNSC to defer cases for one (1) year in cases where the UNSC has failed to take a decision within a specified timeframe;
8. DECIDES to reject for now, the request by ICC to open a Liais on Officer to the AU in Addis Ababa, Ethiopia and REQUESTS the Commission to inform the ICC accordingly; Assembly/AU/Dec.296(XV)
9. EXPRESSES CONCERN over the conduct of the ICC prosecutor, Mr. Moreno Ocampo who has been making egregiously unacceptable, rude and condescending statements on the case of President Omar HassanEl-Bashir of The Sudan and other situations in Africa;
10. REQUESTS the Commission to report regularly on the implementation of this decision

14. Assembly of the African Union
Fifteenth Ordinary Session
25–27 July 2010
Kampala, Uganda
Decision on the Hissène Habré Case
Doc. Assembly/AU/11(XV)
The Assembly:

1. TAKES NOTE of the Progress Report of the Commission on the Implementation of Decision Assembly/AU/Dec.240(XII) adopted in Addis Ababa, Ethiopia, in February 2010 on the Hissène Habré case;
2. REITERATES its commitment to fight impunity in conformity with the provisions of Article 4(h) of the Constitutive Act of the African Union;
3. REITERATES its appeal to all Member States to contribute to the budget of the trial and extend the necessary support to the Government of Senegal in the execution of the African Union mandate to prosecute and try Hissène Habré;
4. REQUESTS the Government of Senegal, the Commission and Partners, particularly the European Union to continue consultations with the view to the holding of the Donors Round Table;
5. INVITES all partner countries and institutions to attend the Donors Round Table that will be organized in this regard in Dakar, Senegal in November 2010;
6. REQUESTS the Commission to monitor the implementation of this decision and to report to the next Ordinary Session of the Assembly through the Executive Council in January 2011.

15. Assembly of the Union
Sixteenth Ordinary Session
30–31 January 2011
Addis Ababa, Ethiopia

Decision on the Implementation of the Decisions on the International Criminal Court Doc. EX.CL/639(XVIII)

The Assembly:

1. TAKES NOTE of the Progress Report of the Commission on the Implementation of ecision Assembly/AU/Dec.296 (XV) adopted in Kampala, Uganda on 27 July 2010;
2. REITERATES its commitment to fight impunity in conformity with the provisions of Article 4(h) of the Constitutive Act of the African Union;
3. DEEPLY REGRETS that the request by the African Union (AU) to the United Nations (UN) Security Council to defer the proceedings initiated against President Bashir of The Sudan, in accordance with Article 16 of the Rome Statute of ICC on deferral of cases by the UN Security Council, has not been acted upon, and in this regard, REITERATES its request to the UN Security Council; and REQUESTS the African members of the UN Security Council to place the matter on its agenda of the Council;
4. ALSO DEEPLY REGRETS the Decisions no.: ICC-02/05-01 of the Pre-trial Chamber I of the ICC dated 27 August 2010 informing the UN Security Council and the Assembly of the States Parties to the Rome Statute (ASP) about the visit of President Omar El-Bashir of the Sudan to the Republic of Chad and the Republic of Kenya on 21st July and 27th August 2010 respectively;
5. DECIDES that by receiving President Bashir, the Republic of Chad and the Republic of Kenya were implementing various AU Assembly Decisions on the warrant of arrest issued by ICC against President Bashir as well as acting in pursuit of peace and stability in their respective regions;
6. SUPPORTS AND ENDORSES Kenya's request for a deferral of the ICC investigations and prosecutions in relation to the 2008 post election violence under Article 16 of the Rome Statute to allow for a National Mechanism to investigate and prosecute the cases under a reformed Judiciary provided for in the new constitutional dispensation, in line with the principle of complementarity, and in this regard REQUESTS the UN Security Council to accede to this request in support of the ongoing peace building and national reconciliation processes, in order to prevent the resumption of conflict and violence; and REQUESTS the African members of the UN Security Council to place the matter on the agenda of the Council;
7. TAKES NOTE of the outcome of the Ninth Assembly of States Parties to the Rome Statute of the International Criminal Court (ICC) regarding the consideration of the proposed amendment to Article 16 of the Rome Statute;
8. ALSO TAKES NOTE of the Decision of the Ninth ASP-ICC to hold informal consultations on the proposed amendments to the Rome Statute in the context

of a Working Group before its Tenth Session scheduled in December 2011 and CALLS UPON all African States Parties to the Rome Statute of the ICC that have not yet done so to co-sponsor the proposal for the amendment to Article 16 of the Rome Statute and indicate such willingness to the UN Secretary General, the Depositary of the Rome Statute, with copy to the AU Commission;

9. UNDERSCORES the need for African States Parties to the Rome Statute of the ICC to speak with one voice during the forthcoming negotiations at the level of the New York and The Hague Working Groups respectively and REQUESTS the Group of African States Parties in New York to ensure that the proposal for amendment to Article 16 of the Rome Statute is properly addressed during the forthcoming negotiations and to report to the Assembly through the Commission. In addition, they should ensure that the position of the ICC Prosecutor goes to an African during the forthcoming elections for Prosecutor scheduled for December 2011;
10. REQUESTS the Commission to follow-up on this matter and to report regularly on the implementation of the various Assembly decisions on ICC.

**16. Assembly of the African Union
Sixteenth Ordinary Session
30–31 January 2011
Addis Ababa, Ethiopia**

Assembly/AU/Dec.335(XVI)
Decision on the Abuse of the Principle of Universal Jurisdiction
Doc. EX.CL/640(XVIII)
The Assembly:

1. TAKES NOTE of the Progress Report of the Commission on the Implementation of Decision Assembly/AU/Dec.292 (XV) adopted in Kampala, Uganda, in July 2010;
2. REITERATES its commitment to fight impunity in conformity with the provisions of Article 4(h) of the Constitutive Act of the African Union;
3. FURTHER REITERATES its conviction on the need for an international regulatory body with competence to review and/or handle complaints or appeals arising out of the abuse of the Principle of Universal Jurisdiction by individual States;
4. CALLS UPON all concerned States to respect international law and particularly the immunity of state officials when applying the Principle of Universal Jurisdiction;
5. URGES the European Union (EU) and its Member States to extend the necessary cooperation to the African Union (AU) to facilitate the search for a durable solution to the abuse of the Principle of Universal Jurisdiction and REQUESTS the Commission to inform the EU accordingly;
6. ALSO URGES the EU and its Member States to implement the recommendations of the AU–EU Joint ad-hoc Expert group;
7. TAKES NOTE of Resolution A/RES/65/33 on the Scope and Application of the Principle of Universal Jurisdiction adopted on 6 December 2010 by the 65th United Nations General Assembly (UNGA) and INVITES all Member States that have not done so to submit to the UN Secretary General, before 30 April 2011, information and observations on the scope and application of the Principle of Universal Jurisdiction, including information on the relevant applicable international treaties, their domestic legal rules and judicial practice;
8. INVITES Member States affected by the abuse of the Principle of Universal Jurisdiction by non-African States to respond to the request made by the Chairperson of the Union and to communicate to the Commission the list and details of pending cases in non African States against African personalities;
9. REQUESTS Member States to apply the principle of reciprocity on countries that have instituted proceedings against African State Officials and to extend mutual legal assistance to each other in the process of investigation and prosecution of such cases;

10. UNDERSCORES the need for Member States to speak with one voice during the forthcoming negotiations at level of the United Nations and REQUESTS the African Group in New York under the coordination of the Members of the Bureau of the Assembly at the level of the said group to ensure that the concerns raised by the AU and its Member States regarding the abuse of the Principle of Universal Jurisdiction by some non African States are properly addressed at the Level of UN with a view to finding a durable solution and to report to the Assembly, through the Commission, on actions taken during the forthcoming negotiations at the level of the United Nations;
11. ALSO REQUESTS the Commission to follow-up on this matter and to report regularly on the implementation of this Decision.

17. Assembly of the African Union
Sixteenth Ordinary Session
30–31 January 2011
Addis Ababa, Ethiopia

Assembly/AU/Dec.340(XVI)
Decision on the Hissène Habré Case
Doc. Assembly/AU/9(XVI)
The Assembly:

1. TAKES NOTE of the Progress Report of the Commission on the Implementation of Decision Assembly/AU/Dec.297 (XV) on the Hissène Habré Case, adopted in Kampala, Uganda, on 27 July 2010;
2. REITERATES ALSO its previous Decisions on the Hissène Habré case adopted in July 2006, in February and July 2009, in February and July 2010 respectively;
3. CONFIRMS the mandate given by the African Union (AU) to Senegal to try Hissène Habré considering the continued readiness of Senegal to try him;
4. ALSO REITERATES its commitment to fight impunity in conformity with the provisions of Article 4(h) of the Constitutive Act of the African Union;
5. ENDORSES the recommendation of the Committee of the Permanent Representatives (PRC) for an amount of US$ one (1) million as AU contribution to the budget of the trial and AUTHORISES expenditure from arrears of contributions;
6. WELCOMES the conclusions of the Donors Round Table for the funding of the Hissène Habré trial, held in Dakar, Senegal on 24 November 2010;
7. REQUESTS the Commission in collaboration with the Government of Senegal, Chad, and Partner countries and institutions to continue with their consultations with the view to mobilizing the pledges made during the Donors Round Table;
8. CALLS ON Member States, all partner countries and relevant institutions to disburse within a reasonable time the funds pledged at the Donors Round Table held on 24 November 2010 for the funding of the Hissène Habré trial in Senegal;
9. REQUESTS the Commission to undertake consultations with the Government of Senegal in order to finalise the modalities for the expeditious trial of Hissène Habré through a special tribunal with an international character consistent with the Economic Community of West African States (ECOWAS) Court of Justice Decision;
10. FURTHER REQUESTS the Commission to follow-up and to report on the implementation of this Decision in June 2011.

18. Assembly of the African Union
Seventeenth Ordinary Session
30 June–1 July 2011
Malabo, Equatorial Guinea

Assembly/AU/Dec.366(XVII)
Decision on the Implementation of the Assembly Decisions on the International Criminal Court
Doc. EX.CL/670(XIX)
The Assembly:

1. TAKES NOTE of the Progress Report of the Commission on the Implementation of Decision Assembly/AU/Dec.296 (XV) adopted by the Fifteenth Ordinary Session of the Assembly in Kampala, Uganda on 31 July 2010;
2. REITERATES its commitment to fight impunity in conformity with the provisions of Article 4(h) of the Constitutive Act of the African Union;
3. STRESSES the need to pursue all efforts and explore ways and means of ensuring that the request by the African Union (AU) to the United Nations (UN) Security Council to defer the proceedings initiated against President Bashir of The Sudan, in accordance with Article 16 of the Rome Statute of International Criminal Court (ICC) on deferral of cases by the UN Security Council, be acted upon, and in this regard, REITERATES its request to the UN Security Council; and REQUESTS the African members of the UN Security Council to place the matter on the agenda of the Council;
4. ALSO STRESSES the need to pursue all efforts in ensuring that the request by the AU to the UN Security Council to defer the investigations and prosecutions in relation to the 2008 post-election violence in Kenya under Article 16 of the Rome Statute be acted upon to allow for a National Mechanism to investigate and prosecute the cases under a reformed Judiciary provided for in the new constitutional dispensation, in line with the principle of complementarity;
5. REAFFIRMS that by receiving President Bashir, the Republic of Chad, Kenya, and Djibouti were discharging their obligations under Article 23 of the Constitutive Act of the African Union and Article 98 of the Rome Statute as well as acting in pursuit of peace and stability in their respective regions;
6. EXPRESSES DEEP CONCERN at the manner in which the ICC Prosecutor handles the situation in Libya which was referred to the ICC by the UN Security Council through Resolution 1970 (2011). The Assembly NOTES that the warrant of arrest issued by the Pre-Trial Chamber concerning Colonel Qadhafi, seriously complicates the efforts aimed at finding a negotiated political solution to the crisis in Libya, which will also address, in a mutually-reinforcing way, issues relating to impunity and reconciliation. In this regard, the Assembly DECIDES that Member States shall not cooperate in the execution of the arrest warrant, and REQUESTS the UN Security Council to activate the provisions of Article 16 of the Rome Statute with a view to

deferring the ICC process on Libya, in the interest of Justice as well as peace in the country;
7. REQUESTS the Group of African States Parties in New York and in the Hague as well as the African Members of the UN Security Council to closely follow-up on the implementation of the Assembly's Decisions on ICC;
8. ALSO REQUESTS the Commission in collaboration with the Permanent Representatives' Committee to reflect on how best Africa's interests can be fully defended and protected in the international judicial system, and to actively pursue the implementation of the Assembly's Decisions on the African Court of Justice and Human and People' Rights being empowered to try serious international crimes committed on African soil;
9. REQUESTS the Commission to follow-up on this matter and to report regularly on the implementation of the various Assembly decisions on ICC.

19. Assembly of the African Union
Seventeenth Ordinary Session
30 June–1 July 2011
Malabo, Equatorial Guinea

Assembly/AU/Dec.371(XVII)
Decision on the Hissène Habré Case
Doc. Assembly/AU/8(XVII)
The Assembly:

1. TAKES NOTE of the Progress Report of the Commission on the Implementation of Assembly Decisions on the Hissène Habré case;
2. REITERATES its commitment to fight impunity in conformity with the provisions of Articles 4(h) and (o) of the Constitutive Act of the African Union;
3. REITERATES its decision in January 2011 confirming the mandate given to Senegal to try Hissène Habré on behalf of Africa and URGES Senegal to carry out its legal responsibility in accordance with the United Nations Convention against Torture the decision of the United Nations (UN) Committee against Torture as well as the said mandate to put Hissène Habré on trial expeditiously or extradite him to any other country willing to put him on trial;
4. CALLS ON other Member States, Parties to the United Nations Convention against Torture willing to try Hissène Habré to notify the Commission of their willingness to do so and to take necessary measures to put Hissène Habré on trial;
5. REQUESTS the Commission to closely monitor the implementation of this Decision and to report to the next ordinary session of the Assembly in January 2012.

**20. Assembly of the African Union
Eighteenth Ordinary Session
29–30 January 2012
Addis Ababa, Ethiopia**

Assembly/AU/Dec.397(XVIII)

Decision on the Progress Report of the Commission on the Implementation of the Assembly Decisions on the International Criminal Court (ICC)

Doc. EX.CL/710(XX)

The Assembly:

1. TAKES NOTE of the Progress Report of the Commission on the implementation of Assembly Decisions on the International Criminal Court (ICC);
2. REITERATES its commitment to fight impunity in conformity with the provisions of Article 4(h) and (o) of the Constitutive Act of the African Union;
3. STRESSES the need to explore ways and means to ensure that the request by the African Union (AU) to the United Nations (UN) Security Council to defer the proceedings initiated against President Bashir of The Sudan in accordance with Article 16 of the Rome Statute of ICC on deferral of cases by the UN Security Council, be acted upon and, in this regard, REITERATES its request to the UN Security Council and REQUESTS African members of the UN Security Council to place the matter on the agenda of the Council;
4. RECOGNISES the efforts by African Members of the UN Security Council to initiate dialogue and discussions on the issue of placing AU's request for deferral under Article 16 of the Rome Statute, both with regard to The Sudan and Kenya on the UN Security Council agenda and ENCOURAGES African non-Permanent Members of the UN Security Council to pursue their efforts in this regard;
5. REQUESTS the Group of African States Parties to the Rome Statute in New York and in the Hague as well as African Members of the United Nations Security Council to scrupulously follow-up on the implementation of Assembly Decisions on the ICC in collaboration with the Commission to ensure that African proposals and concerns are properly considered by the UN Security Council and the Assembly of States Parties to the Rome Statute;
6. REAFFIRMS its understanding that Article 98(1) was included in the Rome Statute establishing the ICC out of recognition that the Statute is not capable of removing an immunity which international law grants to the officials of States that are not parties to the Rome Statute, and by referring the situation in Darfur to the ICC, the UN Security Council intended that the Rome Statute would be applicable, including Article 98;
7. ALSO REAFFIRMS that by receiving President Bashir, the Republic of Malawi, like Djibouti, Chad and Kenya before her, were implementing various AU Assembly Decisions on non-cooperation with the ICC on the arrest and surrender of President Omar Hassan Al Bashir of The Sudan;

8. URGES all Member States to comply with Assembly Decisions on the warrants of arrest issued by the ICC against President Bashir of The Sudan pursuant to Article 23(2) of the Constitutive Act and Article 98 of the Rome Statute of the ICC;
9. REGRETS that the AU's endorsement of two (2) persons as sole African candidates for the post of judge of the ICC was not respected by some Member States and REQUESTS that this situation, as it repeats itself in several other instances, be considered by the Commission together with the Permanent Representatives' Committee with a view to identifying ways and means of addressing it, in order to find a durable solution that will strengthen the African Common Positions and endorsements, and make appropriate recommendations to the Executive Council;
10. REQUESTS the Commission to consider seeking an advisory opinion from the International Court of Justice regarding the immunities of State Officials under international law;
11. ALSO REQUESTS the Commission to place the Progress Report of the Commission on the implementation of Assembly Decisions on the ICC on the agenda of the forthcoming Meeting of Ministers of Justice and Attorneys General for additional input;
12. FURTHER REQUESTS the Commission to report on regular basis on the implementation of this Decision to the Executive Council.

21. Assembly of the African Union Eighteenth Ordinary Session 29–30 January 2012 Addis Ababa, Ethiopia

Assembly/AU/Dec.401(XVIII)
Decision on the Hissène Habré Case
Doc. Assembly/AU/12(XVIII)
The Assembly:

1. TAKES NOTE of the Progress Report of the Commission on the Implementation of the Assembly Decisions on the Hissène Habré case;
2. ALSO TAKES NOTE of the willingness of the Republic of Rwanda to handle the trial of Hissène Habré;
3. REITERATES its commitment to fight impunity in conformity with the provisions of Article 4(h) of the Constitutive Act of the African Union;
4. TAKES NOTE that the Appeal Court of Senegal, has not yet pronounced itself on the request for extradition of Hissène Habré to Belgium;
5. REQUESTS the Commission to continue consultations with partner countries and institutions and the Republic of Senegal and subsequently with the Republic of Rwanda with a view to ensuring the expeditious trial of Hissène Habré and to consider the practical modalities as well as the legal and financial implications of the trial;
6. REQUESTS the Commission to closely monitor the implementation of this Decision and report accordingly to the next Ordinary Session of the Assembly in June 2012.

22. Assembly of the African Union
Nineteenth Ordinary Session
15–16 July 2012
Addis Ababa, Ethiopia

Assembly/AU/Dec.419(XIX)
Decision on the Implementation of the Decisions on the International Criminal Court (ICC)
Doc. EX.CL/731(XXI)
The Assembly:

1. TAKES NOTE of the Report of the meeting of Ministers of Justice and/or Attorneys General held in Addis Ababa, Ethiopia on 14 and 15 May 2012 and the recommendations contained therein;
2. REITERATES its commitment to fight impunity in conformity with the provisions of Article 4(h) and 4 (o) of the Constitutive Act of the African Union and UNDERSCORES the importance of putting the interests of victims at the centre of all actions in sustaining the fight against impunity;
3. ENDORSES the recommendation of the Meeting of Ministers of Justice/ Attorneys General to approach the International Court of Justice (ICJ), through the United Nations General Assembly (UNAG), for seeking an advisory opinion on the question of immunities, under international law, of Heads of State and senior state officials from States that are not Parties to the Rome Statute of ICC and this regard, REQUESTS the Commission to undertake further study on the advisability and implications of seeking such advisory opinion from ICJ and to report thereon to the Executive Council;
4. REITERATES its request to the United Nations Security Council (UNSC) for deferral of the proceedings against President Omar al Bashir of the Sudan and those issued in the Kenyan situation;
5. URGES African State Parties to the Rome Statute to implement Decision Assembly/AU/Dec.296 (XV) adopted by the Fifteenth Ordinary Session in Kampala, Uganda in July 2010 which requested Member States to balance, where applicable, their obligations to the African Union (AU) with their obligations to ICC;
6. ENDORSES Libya's request to put on trial in Libya its own citizens charged with committing international crimes;
7. ENCOURAGES, for effective reliance on Article 98 of the Rome Statute, African State Parties to the Rome Statute of ICC and African non-State Parties to consider concluding bilateral agreements on the immunities of their Senior State officials;
8. URGES African States Parties to the Rome Statute to enhance African representation on the Bench of the ICC in order to ensure that Africa contributes optimally to the evolution of the Court's jurisprudence and in this context, Member States shall in the future respect the decisions of the AU endorsing candidatures to international institutions;

9. REQUESTS the AU Chairperson, the Permanent Representatives Committee (PRC) and the African Groups in New York and in The Hague to promote and support the African common position on ICC;
10. ALSO REQUESTS the Commission, the African Commission on Human and Peoples' Rights and the African Court on Human and Peoples' Rights to publicize, within the continent, what it has done towards the protection of civilians in situations where international crimes have been perpetrated;
11. WELCOMES the steps taken by the Commission to follow up on various Assembly Decisions on the Abuse of the principle of Universal Jurisdiction by some non-African States, in particular the elaboration of a Model National Law on Universal Jurisdiction over International Crimes and ENCOURAGES Member States to fully take advantage of this Model National Law in order to expeditiously enact or strengthen their National Laws in this area;
12. REQUESTS the Commission to follow-up on this matter and to report regularly on the implementation of the various Assembly decisions on ICC.

23. Assembly of the African Union
Nineteenth Ordinary Session
15–16 July 2012
Addis Ababa, Ethiopia

Assembly/AU/Dec.420(XIX)
Decision on the Abuse of the Principle of Universal Jurisdiction
Doc. EX.CL/731(XXI)
The Assembly:

1. TAKES NOTE of the Report of the meeting of Ministers of Justice and/or Attorneys General held in Addis Ababa, Ethiopia on 14 and 15 May 2012 and the recommendations contained therein;
2. URGES Member States to participate actively in the upcoming discussions and negotiations on the scope and application of the principle of Universal Jurisdiction at the level of the Sixth Committee of the United Nations General Assembly (UNGA) during the sixty-seventh session of UNGA schedule for the last quarter of 2012;
3. INVITES Member States which have not yet done so, to submit their observations and information on the scope and application of Universal Jurisdiction to the UN Secretary General should UNGA through a Resolution make a similar request in the future;
4. URGES Member States through the African Group in New York to strongly put forth the concerns expressed on the abuse of the principle of Universal Jurisdiction by some non-African States as indicated in the various relevant Decisions of the Assembly;
5. ALSO URGES Member States to use the principle of reciprocity to defend themselves against the abuse of the principle of Universal Jurisdiction;
6. REITERATES its Decision Assembly/AU/Dec.199(XI) on the Abuse of the principle of Universal Jurisdiction which requested that the warrants of arrest issued on the basis of the abuse of the Principle of Universal Jurisdiction shall not be executed in any Member State;
7. REQUESTS the Commission, on behalf of the Assembly, to send an official communication to the European Commission, requesting the latter to transmit the AU concerns and request the Government of Spain to comply with the Laws of Spain with respect to the arrest warrants issued against Rwandan Leaders on the basis of the application of the principle of Universal jurisdiction and ALSO REQUESTS the AU Chairperson to send a similar request directly to the Prime Minister of Spain;
8. ALSO REQUESTS the Commission to follow-up on this matter and to report regularly on the implementation of the various Assembly decisions on the abuse application of Universal Jurisdiction.

24. Assembly of the African Union
Nineteenth Ordinary Session
15–16 July 2012
Addis Ababa, Ethiopia

Assembly/AU/Dec.427(XIX)

Decision on the Protocol on Amendments to the Protocol on the Statute of the African Court of Justice and Human Rights

Doc. Assembly/AU/13(XIX)a

The Assembly:

1. TAKES NOTE of the recommendation of the Executive Council on the draft Protocol on Amendments to the Protocol on the Statute of the African Court of Justice and Human Rights;
2. REQUESTS the Commission in collaboration with the African Court on Human and Peoples' Rights to prepare a study on the financial and structural implications resulting from the expansion of the jurisdiction of the African Court on Human and Peoples' Rights and submit the study along with the Draft Protocol on Amendments to the Protocol to the Statute of the African Court of Justice and Human Rights for consideration by the policy organs at the next summit slated for January 2013;
3. STRESSES the need for the AU to adopt a definition of the crime of unconstitutional change of government and, in this regard, request the Commission in collaboration with the AU Commission on International Law and the African Court on Human and Peoples' Rights to submit this definition for consideration by the policy organs at the next Summit to be held in January 2013.

25. Assembly of the African Union Twenty-First Ordinary Session 26–27 May 2013 Addis Ababa, Ethiopia

Assembly/AU/Dec.482(XXI)

Decision on International Jurisdiction, Justice and the International Criminal Court (ICC)

Doc. Assembly/AU/13(XXI)

The Assembly:

1. TAKES NOTE of the presentation made by the Republic of Uganda, on behalf of the Eastern African Region, on International Jurisdiction, International Justice and the International Criminal Court, as well as the recommendations made by the Executive Council;
2. REITERATES the African Union's unflinching commitment to combating impunity and promoting democracy, the rule of law and good governance throughout the entire continent, in conformity with its Constitutive Act;
3. DEEPLY REGRETS that the request by the African Union (AU) to the United Nations (UN) Security Council to defer the proceedings initiated against President Omar Al Bashir of The Sudan and Senior State Official of Kenya, in accordance with Article 16 of the Rome Statute of the International Criminal Court (ICC) on deferral of cases by the UN Security Council, has not been acted upon; REAFFIRMS that Member States such as the Republic of Chad that had welcomed President Omar Al Bashir of The Sudan did so in conformity with the decisions of the Assembly and therefore, should not be penalized;
4. FURTHER REAFFIRMS its previous Decisions on the activities of the ICC in Africa, adopted in January and July 2009, January and July 2010, January and July 2011, January and July 2012 respectively, in which it expressed its strong conviction that the search for justice should be pursued in a way that does not impede or jeopardize efforts aimed at promoting lasting peace and reiterated AU's concern with the misuse of indictments against African leaders;
5. STRESSES the need for international justice to be conducted in a transparent and fair manner, in order to avoid any perception of double standard, in conformity with the principles of international law, and EXPRESSES CONCERN at the threat that the indictment of H.E Uhuru Muigai Kenyatta and H.E William Samoei Ruto, the President and Deputy-President of the Republic of Kenya respectively, may pose to the on-going efforts in the promotion of peace, national healing and reconciliation, as well as the rule of law and stability, not only in Kenya, but also in the Region;
6. RECALLS that, pursuant to the principle of complementarity enshrined in the Rome Statute of the ICC, Kenya has primary jurisdiction over the investigations and prosecutions of crimes in relation to the 2007 post-election violence, in this regard, DEEPLY REGRETS the Decisions of the Pre-trial Chamber II and the appeals Chamber of the ICC on the admissibility of the

cases dated 30 May and 30 August 2011 respectively, which denied the right of Kenya to prosecute and try alleged perpetrators of crimes committed on its territory in relation to the 2007 post-election violence;

7. SUPPORTS AND ENDORSES the Eastern Africa Region's request for a referral of the ICC investigations and prosecutions in relation to the 2007 post-election violence in Kenya, in line with the principle of complementarity, to allow for a National Mechanism to investigate and prosecute the cases under a reformed Judiciary provided for in the new constitutional dispensation, in support of the on- going peace building and national reconciliation processes, in order to prevent the resumption of conflict and violence in Kenya;
8. REQUESTS the African Union Commission, in collaboration with the African Union Commission on International Law (AUCIL), to organize, with the participation of Member States, all the relevant Organs of the African Union and other relevant Stakeholders, a brainstorming session, as part of the 50th Anniversary discussion on the broad areas of International Criminal Justice System, Peace, Justice and Reconciliation as well as the impact/actions of the ICC in Africa, in order not only to inform the ICC process, but also to seek ways of strengthening African mechanisms to deal with African challenges and problems;
9. ALSO REQUESTS the African Union Commission to follow-up on this matter and to report regularly on the implementation of the various Assembly decisions on the ICC.

26. Assembly of the African Union
Extraordinary Session of the Assembly of the African Union
12 October 2013
Addis Ababa, Ethiopia
Ext/Assembly/AU/Dec.1(Oct.2013)
Decision on Africa's Relationship with the International Criminal Court (ICC)
The Assembly:

1. TAKES NOTE of the Progress Report of the Commission on the Implementation of Decision Assembly/AU/Dec.482(XXI) on the International Jurisdiction, International Justice and the International Criminal Court (ICC) and the Presentation made by the Republic of Kenya as well as the recommendations of the Executive Council thereon;
2. REITERATES, in accordance with the Constitutive Act of the African Union (AU), the AU 's unflinching commitment to fight impunity, promote human rights and democracy, and the rule of law and good governance in the continent;
3. REAFFIRMS its previous Decisions on the abuse of the principles of Universal Jurisdiction adopted in Sharm El Sheikh in July 2008 as well as the activities of the ICC in Africa, adopted in January and July 2009, January and July 2010, January and July 2011, January and July 2012, and May 2013 wherein it expressed its strong conviction that the search for justice should be pursued in a way that does not impede or jeopardize efforts aimed at promoting lasting peace;
4. REITERATES AU's concern on the politicization and misuse of indictments against African leaders by ICC as well as at the unprecedented indictments of and proceedings against the sitting President and Deputy President of Kenya in light of the recent developments in that country;
5. UNDERSCORES that this is the first time that a sitting Head of State and his deputy are being tried in an international court and STRESSES the gravity of this situation which could undermine the sovereignty, stability, and peace in that country and in other Member States as well as reconciliation and reconstruction and the normal functioning of constitutional institutions;
6. RECOGNIZES that Kenya is a frontline state in the fight against terrorism at regional, continental and international levels and, in this regard, STRESSES the threat that this menace poses to the region in particular and the continent in general, and the proceedings initiated against the President and the Deputy President of the Republic of Kenya will distract and prevent them from fulfilling their constitutional responsibilities, including national and regional security affairs;
7. RECALLS that following the 2007 Post Election Violence (PEV), the mediation process in Kenya was initiated by AU which led to the enactment of the National Accord and Reconciliation Act and the Agreement establishing the coalition government, and EXPRESSES concern that the ongoing process before the ICC may pose a threat to the full implementation of the National

Accord of 2008 and prevent the process of addressing the challenges leading to the post-election violence;

8. EXPRESSES its deep appreciation for the full cooperation that the President and Deputy President of Kenya have demonstrated to the ICC process and CALLS UPON the ICC to show the same level of cooperation in the process;
9. REAFFIRMS the principles deriving from national laws and international customary law by which sitting Heads of State and other senior state officials are granted immunities during their tenure of office;
10. NOW DECIDES:

    (i) That to safeguard the constitutional order, stability and, integrity of Member States, no charges shall be commenced or continued before any International Court or Tribunal against any serving AU Head of State or Government or anybody acting or entitled to act in such capacity during their term of office;
    (ii) That the trials of President Uhuru Kenyatta and Deputy President William Samoei Ruto, who are the current serving leaders of the Republic of Kenya, should be suspended until they complete their terms of office;
    (iii) To set up a Contact Group of the Executive Council to be led by the Chairperson of the Council, composed of five (5) Members (one (1) per region) to undertake consultations with the Members of the United Nations Security Council (UNSC), in particular, its five (5) Permanent Members with a view to engaging with the UNSC on all concerns of the AU on its relationship with the ICC, including the deferral of the Kenyan and the Sudan cases in order to obtain their feedback before the beginning of the trial on 12 November, 2013;
    (iv) To fast track the process of expanding the mandate of the African Court on Human and Peoples' Rights (AfCHPR) to try international crimes, such as genocide, crimes against humanity and war crimes;
    (v) That the Commission expedites the process of expansion of AfCHPR to deal with international crimes in accordance with the relevant decision of the Policy Organs and INVITES Member States to support this process;
    (vi) That African States Parties propose relevant amendments to the Rome Statute, in accordance with Article 121 of the Statute;
    (vii) To request African States Parties to the Rome Statute of the ICC, in particular the Members of the Bureau of the Assembly of States Parties to inscribe on the agenda of the forthcoming sessions of the ASP the issue of indictment of African sitting Heads of State and Government by the ICC and its consequences on peace, stability and reconciliation in African Union Member States;
    (viii) That any AU Member State that wishes to refer a case to the ICC may inform and seek the advice of the African Union;

(ix) That Kenya should send a letter to the United Nations Security Council requesting for deferral, in conformity with Article 16 of the Rome Statute, of the proceedings against the President and Deputy President of Kenya that would be endorsed by all African States Parties;

(x) Pursuant to this Decision, to request the ICC to postpone the trial of President Uhuru Kenyatta, scheduled for 12 November 2013 and suspend the proceedings against Deputy President William Samoei Ruto until such time as the UN Security Council considers the request by Kenya, supported by the AU, for deferral;

(xi) That President Uhuru Kenyatta will not appear before the ICC until such time as the concerns raised by the AU and its Member States have been adequately addressed by the UN Security Council and the ICC;

(xii) To convene, an Extraordinary Session, towards the end of November 2013, to review the progress made in the implementation of this Decision of the AU Assembly (Ext/Assembly/AU/Dec.1(Oct. 2013)).

11. FINALLY REQUESTS the Commission to report on the implementation of this Decision to the next Ordinary Session of the Assembly in January 2014.

27. Assembly of the African Union
Twenty-Second Ordinary Session
30–31 January 2014
Addis Ababa, Ethiopia

Assembly/AU/Dec.493 (XXII)

Decision on the Progress Report of the Commission on the Implementation of the Decisions on the International Criminal Court

The Assembly:

1. TAKES NOTE of the Progress Report of the Commission on the implementation of the Assembly Decisions on the International Criminal Court (ICC) and ENDORSES the recommendations contained therein;
2. REITERATES the unflinching commitment of the African Union and its Member States to combating impunity and promoting democracy, the rule of law and good governance throughout the entire continent, in conformity with the Constitutive Act of the African Union;
3. COMMENDS Member States which are parties to the Rome Statute of ICC for the unity of action demonstrated at the last Assembly of States Parties in the Hague in November 2013;
4. THANKS the Member State of the United Nations Security Council that supported the request of Kenya and the African Union to defer the proceedings initiated by the ICC against the President and Deputy President of the Republic of Kenya in accordance with Article 16 of the Rome Statute of ICC;
5. ALSO THANKS members of the Contact Group and the African Group in New York for their action in support of the African request;
6. EXPRESSES its deep disappointment that the request by Kenya supported by AU, to the United Nations (UN) Security Council to defer the proceedings initiated against the President and Deputy President of the Republic of Kenya in accordance with Article 16 of the Rome Statute of ICC on deferral of cases by the UN Security Council, has not yield the positive result expected;
7. ALSO EXPRESSES its deep disappointment that the request by the African Union to the UN Security Council to defer the proceedings initiated against the President of the Republic of The Sudan in accordance with Article 16 of the Rome Statute of ICC on deferral of cases by the UN Security Council, has not been acted upon to date;
8. STRESSES the need for the UN Security Council to reserve a timely and appropriate response to requests made by the AU on deferral in accordance with Article 16 of the Rome Statute under Chapter VII of the UN Charter so as to avoid the sense of lack of consideration of a whole continent;
9. DECIDES that the African Union and its Member States, in particular the African States Parties to the Rome Statute, reserve the right to take any further decisions or measures that may be necessary in order to preserve and Assembly/AU/Dec.493(XXII) safeguard peace, security and stability, as well as the dignity, sovereignty and integrity of the continent;

10. TAKES NOTE of the outcome of the 12th Session of the Assembly of States Parties (ASP) of the Rome Statute to the ICC and WELCOMES the inclusion on its agenda of a Special Segment on "Indictment of Sitting Heads of State and Government and its Consequences on Peace and Stability and Reconciliation" and the amendments to Rule 134 of the Rules of Procedure and Evidence of the ICC;
11. ALSO TAKES NOTE of the Decision of the 12th ASP inviting its Working Group on amendments to continue its consideration of amendments to the Rome Statute submitted prior to the Review Conference and those submitted following the decision by the Extraordinary Summit of the African Union held on 12 October 2013 and CALLS UPON all African States Parties to support the proposed amendment to Articles 16 and 27 of the Rome Statute;
12. DECIDES that:

    (i) African States Parties should comply with African Union Decisions on ICC and continue to speak with one voice to ensure that the African proposals for amendments to Articles 16 and 27 of the Rome Statute of the ICC are considered by the ASP working Group on amendments as well as by the forthcoming sessions of the Assembly of States Parties (ASP) to the Rome Statute;
    (ii) There is an imperative need for all Member States to ensure that they adhere and articulate commonly agreed positions in line with their obligations under the Constitutive Act of the African Union;
    (iii) The Group of African States Parties in New York and the African Members of the Bureau of ASP should follow-up on the implementation of various Decisions of the Assembly on ICC, in collaboration with the commission and ensure that the African proposals and concerns are properly considered/addressed by the ASP and report to the Assembly through the Commission on actions taken regularly;

13. RECALLS its decision aimed at extending the jurisdiction of the African Court of Justice and Human Rights to hear international crimes in the Continent and REQUESTS the Commission in collaboration with all stakeholders to speed up the process with a view to reporting thereon to the Assembly in June 2014;
14. REQUESTS the Commission to present a report on new developments in the issue, which is important to Africa, at its 24th Ordinary Session in January 2015.

Annex 3
United Nations Security Council Decisions Regarding the Enforcement of International Criminal Law in Africa

G. Werle et al. (eds.), *Africa and the International Criminal Court*,
International Criminal Justice Series 1, DOI 10.1007/978-94-6265-029-9

1. United Nations
Security Council
Resolution 1422 (2002)
(S/RES/1422)
Adopted by the Security Council at its 4572nd meeting, on 12 July 2002

The Security Council,

Taking note of the entry into force on 1 July 2002, of the Statute of the International Criminal Court (ICC), done at Rome 17 July 1998 (the Rome Statute),

Emphasizing the importance to international peace and security of United Nations operations,

Noting that not all States are parties to the Rome Statute,

Noting that States Parties to the Rome Statute have chosen to accept its jurisdiction in accordance with the Statute and in particular the principle of complementarity,

Noting that States not Party to the Rome Statute will continue to fulfill their responsibilities in their national jurisdictions in relation to international crimes,

Determining that operations established or authorized by the United Nations Security Council are deployed to maintain or restore international peace and security,

Determining further that it is in the interests of international peace and security to facilitate Member States' ability to contribute to operations established or authorized by the United Nations Security Council,

Acting under Chapter VII of the Charter of the United Nations,

1. Requests, consistent with the provisions of Article 16 of the Rome Statute, that the ICC, if a case arises involving current or former officials or personnel from a contributing State not a Party to the Rome Statute over acts or omissions relating to a United Nations established or authorized operation, shall for a twelve-month period starting 1 July 2002 not commence or proceed with investigation or prosecution of any such case, unless the Security Council decides otherwise;
2. Expresses the intention to renew the request in paragraph 1 under the same conditions each 1 July for further 12-month periods for as long as may be necessary;
3. Decides that Member States shall take no action inconsistent with paragraph 1 and with their international obligations;
4. Decides to remain seized of the matter.

2. United Nations
Security Council
Resolution 1487 (2003)
(S/RES/1487)
Adopted by the Security Council at its 4772nd meeting, on 12 June 2003

The Security Council,

Taking note of the entry into force on 1 July 2002, of the Statute of the International Criminal Court (ICC), done at Rome 17 July 1998 (the Rome Statute),

Emphasizing the importance to international peace and security of United Nations operations,

Noting that not all States are parties to the Rome Statute,

Noting that States Parties to the Rome Statute have chosen to accept its jurisdiction in accordance with the Statute and in particular the principle of complementarity,

Noting that States not Party to the Rome Statute will continue to fulfill their responsibilities in their national jurisdictions in relation to international crimes,

Determining that operations established or authorized by the United Nations Security Council are deployed to maintain or restore international peace and security,

Determining further that it is in the interests of international peace and security to facilitate Member States' ability to contribute to operations established or authorized by the United Nations Security Council,

Acting under Chapter VII of the Charter of the United Nations,

1. Requests, consistent with the provisions of Article 16 of the Rome Statute, that the ICC, if a case arises involving current or former officials or personnel from a contributing State not a Party to the Rome Statute over acts or omissions relating to a United Nations established or authorized operation, shall for a 12-month period starting 1 July 2003 not commence or proceed with investigation or prosecution of any such case, unless the Security Council decides otherwise;
2. Expresses the intention to renew the request in paragraph 1 under the same conditions each 1 July for further 12-month periods for as long as may be necessary;
3. Decides that Member States shall take no action inconsistent with paragraph 1 and with their international obligations;
4. Decides to remain seized of the matter.

3. United Nations
Security Council
Resolution 1593 (2005)
(S/RES/1593)
Adopted by the Security Council at its 5158th meeting, on 31 March 2005

The Security Council,

Taking note of the report of the International Commission of Inquiry on violations of international humanitarian law and human rights law in Darfur (S/2005/60),

Recalling article 16 of the Rome Statute under which no investigation or prosecution may be commenced or proceeded with by the International Criminal Court for a period of 12 months after a Security Council request to that effect,

Also recalling articles 75 and 79 of the Rome Statute and encouraging States to contribute to the ICC Trust Fund for Victims,

Taking note of the existence of agreements referred to in Article 98-2 of the Rome Statute,

Determining that the situation in Sudan continues to constitute a threat to international peace and security, acting under Chapter VII of the Charter of the United Nations,

1. Decides to refer the situation in Darfur since 1 July 2002 to the Prosecutor of the International Criminal Court;
2. Decides that the Government of Sudan and all other parties to the conflict in Darfur, shall cooperate fully with and provide any necessary assistance to the Court and the Prosecutor pursuant to this resolution and, while recognizing that States not party to the Rome Statute have no obligation under the Statute, urges all States and concerned regional and other international organizations to cooperate fully;
3. Invites the Court and the African Union to discuss practical arrangements that will facilitate the work of the Prosecutor and of the Court, including the possibility of conducting proceedings in the region, which would contribute to regional efforts in the fight against impunity;
4. Also encourages the Court, as appropriate and in accordance with the Rome Statute, to support international cooperation with domestic efforts to promote the rule of law, protect human rights and combat impunity in Darfur;

4. United Nations
Security Council
Resolution 1970 (2011)
(S/RES/1970)
Adopted by the Security Council at its 6491st meeting, on 26 February 2011

The Security Council,

Expressing grave concern at the situation in the Libyan Arab Jamahiriya and condemning the violence and use of force against civilians,

Deploring the gross and systematic violation of human rights, including the repression of peaceful demonstrators, expressing deep concern at the deaths of civilians, and rejecting unequivocally the incitement to hostility and violence against the civilian population made from the highest level of the Libyan government,

Welcoming the condemnation by the Arab League, the African Union, and the Secretary General of the Organization of the Islamic Conference of the serious violations of human rights and international humanitarian law that are being committed in the Libyan Arab Jamahiriya,

Taking note of the letter to the President of the Security Council from the Permanent Representative of the Libyan Arab Jamahiriya dated 26 February 2011,

Welcoming the Human Rights Council resolution A/HRC/S-15/2 of 25 February 2011, including the decision to urgently dispatch an independent international commission of inquiry to investigate all alleged violations of international human rights law in the Libyan Arab Jamahiriya, to establish the facts and circumstances of such violations and of the crimes perpetrated, and where possible identify those responsible,

Considering that the widespread and systematic attacks currently taking place in the Libyan Arab Jamahiriya against the civilian population may amount to crimes against humanity,

Expressing concern at the plight of refugees forced to flee the violence in the Libyan Arab Jamahiriya,

Expressing concern also at the reports of shortages of medical supplies to treat the wounded,

Recalling the Libyan authorities' responsibility to protect its population,

Underlining the need to respect the freedoms of peaceful assembly and of expression, including freedom of the media,

Stressing the need to hold to account those responsible for attacks, including by forces under their control, on civilians,

Recalling article 16 of the Rome Statute under which no investigation or prosecution may be commenced or proceeded with by the International Criminal Court for a period of 12 months after a Security Council request to that effect,

Expressing concern for the safety of foreign nationals and their rights in the Libyan Arab Jamahiriya,

Reaffirming its strong commitment to the sovereignty, independence, territorial integrity and national unity of the Libyan Arab Jamahiriya,

Mindful of its primary responsibility for the maintenance of international peace and security, under the Charter of the United Nations,

Acting under Chapter VII of the Charter of the United Nations, and taking measures under its Article 41,

1. Demands an immediate end to the violence and calls for steps to fulfil the legitimate demands of the population;
2. Urges the Libyan authorities to:

   (a) Act with the utmost restraint, respect human rights and international humanitarian law, and allow immediate
   (b) access for international human rights monitors;
   (c) Ensure the safety of all foreign nationals and their assets and facilitate the departure of those wishing to leave the country;
   (d) Ensure the safe passage of humanitarian and medical supplies, and humanitarian agencies and workers, into the country; and
   (e) Immediately lift restrictions on all forms of media;

3. Requests all Member States, to the extent possible, to cooperate in the evacuation of those foreign nationals wishing to leave the country;

ICC referral

4. Decides to refer the situation in the Libyan Arab Jamahiriya since 15 February 2011 to the Prosecutor of the International Criminal Court;
5. Decides that the Libyan authorities shall cooperate fully with and provide any necessary assistance to the Court and the Prosecutor pursuant to this resolution and, while recognizing that States not party to the Rome Statute have no obligation under the Statute, urges all States and concerned regional and other international organizations to cooperate fully with the Court and the Prosecutor;
6. Decides that nationals, current or former officials or personnel from a State outside the Libyan Arab Jamahiriya which is not a party to the Rome Statute of the International Criminal Court shall be subject to the exclusive jurisdiction of that State for all alleged acts or omissions arising out of or related to operations in the Libyan Arab Jamahiriya established or authorized by the Council, unless such exclusive jurisdiction has been expressly waived by the State;
7. Invites the Prosecutor to address the Security Council within two months of the adoption of this resolution and every six months thereafter on actions taken pursuant to this resolution;
8. Recognizes that none of the expenses incurred in connection with the referral, including expenses related to investigations or prosecutions in connection with that referral, shall be borne by the United Nations and that such costs shall be borne by the parties to the Rome Statute and those States that wish to contribute voluntarily;

Arms embargo

9. Decides that all Member States shall immediately take the necessary measures to prevent the direct or indirect supply, sale or transfer to the Libyan Arab Jamahiriya, from or through their territories or by their nationals, or using their flag vessels or aircraft, of arms and related materiel of all types, including weapons and ammunition, military vehicles and equipment, paramilitary equipment, and spare parts for the aforementioned, and technical assistance, training, financial or other assistance, related to military activities or the provision, maintenance or use of any arms and related materiel, including the provision of armed mercenary personnel whether or not originating in their territories, and decides further that this measure shall not apply to

    (a) Supplies of non-lethal military equipment intended solely for humanitarian or protective use, and related technical assistance or training, as approved in advance by the Committee established pursuant to paragraph 24 below;
    (b) Protective clothing, including flak jackets and military helmets, temporarily exported to the Libyan Arab Jamahiriya by United Nations personnel, representatives of the media and humanitarian and development works and associated personnel, for their personal use only; or
    (c) Other sales or supply of arms and related materiel, or provision of assistance or personnel, as approved in advance by the Committee;

10. Decides that the Libyan Arab Jamahiriya shall cease the export of all arms and related materiel and that all Member States shall prohibit the procurement of such items from the Libyan Arab Jamahiriya by their nationals, or using their flagged vessels or aircraft, and whether or not originating in the territory of the Libyan Arab Jamahiriya;
11. Calls upon all States, in particular States neighboring the Libyan Arab Jamahiriya, to inspect, in accordance with their national authorities and legislation and consistent with international law, in particular the law of the sea and relevant international civil aviation agreements, all cargo to and from the Libyan Arab Jamahiriya, in their territory, including seaports and airports, if the State concerned has information that provides reasonable grounds to believe the cargo contains items the supply, sale, transfer, or export of which is prohibited by paragraphs 9 or 10 of this resolution for the purpose of ensuring strict implementation of those provisions;
12. Decides to authorize all Member States to, and that all Member States shall, upon discovery of items prohibited by paragraph 9 or 10 of this resolution, seize and dispose (such as through destruction, rendering inoperable, storage or transferring to a State other than the originating or destination States for disposal) items the supply, sale, transfer or export of which is prohibited by paragraph 9 or 10 of this resolution and decides further that all Member States shall cooperate in such efforts;

13. Requires any Member State when it undertakes an inspection pursuant to paragraph 11 above, to submit promptly an initial written report to the Committee containing, in particular, explanation of the grounds for the inspections, the results of such inspections, and whether or not cooperation was provided, and, if prohibited items for transfer are found, further requires such Member States to submit to the Committee, at a later stage, a subsequent written report containing relevant details on the inspection, seizure, and disposal, and relevant details of the transfer, including a description of the items, their origin and intended destination, if this information is not in the initial report;
14. Encourages Member States to take steps to strongly discourage their nationals from travelling to the Libyan Arab Jamahiriya to participate in activities on behalf of the Libyan authorities that could reasonably contribute to the violation of human rights;

Travel ban

15. Decides that all Member States shall take the necessary measures to prevent the entry into or transit through their territories of individuals listed in Annex I of this resolution or designated by the Committee established pursuant to paragraph 24 below, provided that nothing in this paragraph shall oblige a State to refuse its own nationals entry into its territory;
16. Decides that the measures imposed by paragraph 15 above shall not apply:

    (a) Where the Committee determines on a case-by-case basis that such travel is justified on the grounds of humanitarian need, including religious obligation;
    (b) Where entry or transit is necessary for the fulfillment of a judicial process;
    (c) Where the Committee determines on a case-by-case basis that an exemption would further the objectives of peace and national reconciliation in the Libyan Arab Jamahiriya and stability in the region; or
    (d) Where a State determines on a case-by-case basis that such entry or transit is required to advance peace and stability in the Libyan Arab Jamahiriya and the States subsequently notifies the Committee within forty-eight hours after making such a determination;

Asset freeze

17. Decides that all Member States shall freeze without delay all funds, other financial assets and economic resources which are on their territories, which are owned or controlled, directly or indirectly, by the individuals or entities listed in Annex II of this resolution or designated by the Committee established pursuant to paragraph 24 below, or by individuals or entities acting on their behalf or at their direction, or by entities owned or controlled by them, and decides further that all Member States shall ensure that any funds,

financial assets or economic resources are prevented from being made available by their nationals or by any individuals or entities within their territories, to or for the benefit of the individuals or entities listed in Annex II of this resolution or individuals designated by the Committee;

18. Expresses its intention to ensure that assets frozen pursuant to paragraph 17 shall at a later stage be made available to and for the benefit of the people of the Libyan Arab Jamahiriya;
19. Decides that the measures imposed by paragraph 17 above do not apply to funds, other financial assets or economic resources that have been determined by relevant Member States:

    (a) To be necessary for basic expenses, including payment for foodstuffs, rent or mortgage, medicines and medical treatment, taxes, insurance premiums, and public utility charges or exclusively for payment of reasonable professional fees and reimbursement of incurred expenses associated with the provision of legal services in accordance with national laws, or fees or service charges, in accordance with national laws, for routine holding or maintenance of frozen funds, other financial assets and economic resources, after notification by the relevant State to the Committee of the intention to authorize, where appropriate, access to such funds, other financial assets or economic resources and in the absence of a negative decision by the Committee within five working days of such notification;
    (b) To be necessary for extraordinary expenses, provided that such determination has been notified by the relevant State or Member States to the Committee and has been approved by the Committee; or
    (c) To be the subject of a judicial, administrative or arbitral lien or judgment, in which case the funds, other financial assets and economic resources may be used to satisfy that lien or judgment provided that the lien or judgment was entered into prior to the date of the present resolution, is not for the benefit of a person or entity designated pursuant to paragraph 17 above, and has been notified by the relevant State or Member States to the Committee;

20. Decides that Member States may permit the addition to the accounts frozen pursuant to the provisions of paragraph 17 above of interests or other earnings due on those accounts or payments due under contracts, agreements or obligations that arose prior to the date on which those accounts became subject to the provisions of this resolution, provided that any such interest, other earnings and payments continue to be subject to these provisions and are frozen;
21. Decides that the measures in paragraph 17 above shall not prevent a designated person or entity from making payment due under a contract entered into prior to the listing of such a person or entity, provided that the relevant States have determined that the payment is not directly or indirectly received by a person or entity designated pursuant to paragraph 17 above, and after

notification by the relevant States to the Committee of the intention to make or receive such payments or to authorize, where appropriate, the unfreezing of funds, other financial assets or economic resources for this purpose, 10 working days prior to such authorization;

Designation criteria

22. Decides that the measures contained in paragraphs 15 and 17 shall apply to the individuals and entities designated by the Committee, pursuant to paragraph 24 (b) and (c), respectively;

    (a) Involved in or complicit in ordering, controlling, or otherwise directing, the commission of serious human rights abuses against persons in the Libyan Arab Jamahiriya, including by being involved in or complicit in planning, commanding, ordering or conducting attacks, in violation of international law, including aerial bombardments, on civilian populations and facilities; or
    (b) Acting for or on behalf of or at the direction of individuals or entities identified in subparagraph (a).

23. Strongly encourages Member States to submit to the Committee names of individuals who meet the criteria set out in paragraph 22 above;

New Sanctions Committee

24. Decides to establish, in accordance with rule 28 of its provisional rules of procedure, a Committee of the Security Council consisting of all the members of the Council (herein "the Committee"), to undertake to following tasks:

    (a) To monitor implementation of the measures imposed in paragraphs 9, 10, 15, and 17;
    (b) To designate those individuals subject to the measures imposed by paragraphs 15 and to consider requests for exemptions in accordance with paragraph 16 above;
    (c) To designate those individuals subject to the measures imposed by paragraph 17 above and to consider requests for exemptions in accordance with paragraphs 19 and 20 above;
    (d) To establish such guidelines as may be necessary to facilitate the implementation of the measures imposed above;
    (e) To report within thirty days to the Security Council on its work for the first report and thereafter to report as deemed necessary by the Committee;
    (f) To encourage a dialogue between the Committee and interested Member States, in particular those in the region, including by inviting representatives of such States to meet with the Committee to discuss implementation of the measures;

(g) To seek from all States whatever information it may consider useful regarding the actions taken by them to implement effectively the measures imposed above;
(h) To examine and take appropriate action on information regarding alleged violations or non-compliance with the measures contained in this resolution;

25. Calls upon all Member States to report to the Committee within 120 days of the adoption of this resolution on the steps they have taken with a view to implementing effectively paragraphs 9, 10, 15 and 17 above;

Humanitarian assistance

26. Calls upon all Member States, working together and acting in cooperation with the Secretary General, to facilitate and support the return of humanitarian agencies and make available humanitarian and related assistance in the Libyan Arab Jamahiriya, and requests the States concerned to keep the Security Council regularly informed on the progress of actions undertaken pursuant to this paragraph, and expresses its readiness to consider taking additional appropriate measures, as necessary, to achieve this;

Commitment to review

27. Affirms that it shall keep the Libyan authorities' actions under continuous review and that it shall be prepared to review the appropriateness of the measures contained in this resolution, including the strengthening, modification, suspension or lifting of the measures, as may be needed at any time in light of the Libyan authorities' compliance with relevant provisions of this resolution;
28. Decides to remain actively seized of the matter.

Annex I: Travel ban

1. Al-Baghdadi, Dr Abdulqader Mohammed
Passport number: B010574. Date of birth: 01/07/1950.
Head of the Liaison Office of the Revolutionary Committees. Revolutionary Committees involved in violence against demonstrators.
2. Dibri, Abdulqader Yusef
Date of birth: 1946. Place of birth: Houn, Libya.
Head of Muammar Qadhafi's personal security. Responsibility for regime security. History of directing violence against dissidents.
3. Dorda, Abu Zayd Umar
Director, External Security Organisation. Regime loyalist. Head of external intelligence agency.
4. Jabir, Major General Abu Bakr Yunis
Date of birth: 1952. Place of birth: Jalo, Libya.
Defence Minister. Overall responsibility for actions of armed forces.
5. Matuq, Matuq Mohammed

Date of birth: 1956. Place of birth: Khoms.
Secretary for Utilities. Senior member of regime. Involvement with Revolutionary Committees. Past history of involvement in suppression of dissent and violence.

6. Qadhaf Al-dam, Sayyid Mohammed
   Date of birth: 1948. Place of birth: Sirte, Libya.
   Cousin of Muammar Qadhafi. In the 1980s, Sayyid was involved in the dissident assassination campaign and allegedly responsible for several deaths in Europe. He is also thought to have been involved in arms procurement.
7. Qadhafi, Aisha Muammar
   Date of birth: 1978. Place of birth: Tripoli, Libya.
   Daughter of Muammar Qadhafi. Closeness of association with regime.
8. Qadhafi, Hannibal Muammar
   Passport number: B/002210. Date of birth: 20/09/1975. Place of birth: Tripoli, Libya. Son of Muammar Qadhafi. Closeness of association with regime.
9. Qadhafi, Khamis Muammar
   Date of birth: 1978. Place of birth: Tripoli, Libya.
   Son of Muammar Qadhafi. Closeness of association with regime. Command of military units involved in repression of demonstrations.
10. Qadhafi, Mohammed Muammar
    Date of birth: 1970. Place of birth: Tripoli, Libya.
    Son of Muammar Qadhafi. Closeness of association with regime.
11. Qadhafi, Muammar Mohammed Abu Minyar
    Date of birth: 1942. Place of birth: Sirte, Libya.
    Leader of the Revolution, Supreme Commander of Armed Forces. Responsibility for ordering repression of demonstrations, human rights abuses.
12. Qadhafi, Mutassim
    Date of birth: 1976. Place of birth: Tripoli, Libya.
    National Security Adviser. Son of Muammar Qadhafi. Closeness of association with regime.
13. Qadhafi, Saadi
    Passport number: 014797. Date of birth: 25/05/1973. Place of birth: Tripoli, Libya.
    Commander Special Forces. Son of Muammar Qadhafi. Closeness of association with regime. Command of military units involved in repression of demonstrations.
14. Qadhafi, Saif al-Arab
    Date of birth: 1982. Place of birth: Tripoli, Libya.
    Son of Muammar Qadhafi. Closeness of association with regime.
15. Qadhafi, Saif al-Islam
    Passport number: B014995. Date of birth: 25/06/1972. Place of birth: Tripoli, Libya.

Director, Qadhafi Foundation. Son of Muammar Qadhafi. Closeness of association with regime. Inflammatory public statements encouraging violence against demonstrators.

16. Al-Senussi, Colonel Abdullah
    Date of birth: 1949. Place of birth: Sudan.
    Director Military Intelligence. Military Intelligence involvement in suppression of demonstrations. Past history includes suspicion of involvement in Abu Selim prison massacre. Convicted in absentia for bombing of UTA flight. Brother -in-law of Muammar Qadhafi.

Annex II: Asset Freeze

1. Qadhafi, Aisha Muammar
   Date of birth: 1978. Place of birth: Tripoli, Libya.
   Daughter of Muammar Qadhafi. Closeness of association with regime.
2. Qadhafi, Hannibal Muammar
   Passport number: B/002210. Date of birth: 20/09/1975. Place of birth: Tripoli, Libya.
   Son of Muammar Qadhafi. Closeness of association with regime.
3. Qadhafi, Khamis Muammar
   Date of birth: 1978. Place of birth: Tripoli, Libya.
   Son of Muammar Qadhafi. Closeness of association with regime. Command of military units involved in repression of demonstrations.
4. Qadhafi, Muammar Mohammed Abu Minyar
   Date of birth: 1942. Place of birth: Sirte, Libya.
   Leader of the Revolution, Supreme Commander of Armed Forces. Responsibility for ordering repression of demonstrations, human rights abuses.
5. Qadhafi, Mutassim
   Date of birth: 1976. Place of birth: Tripoli, Libya.
   National Security Adviser. Son of Muammar Qadhafi. Closeness of association with regime.
6. Qadhafi, Saif al-Islam
   Passport number: B014995. Date of birth: 25/06/1972. Place of birth: Tripoli, Libya.
   Director, Qadhafi Foundation. Son of Muammar Qadhafi. Closeness of association with regime. Inflammatory public statements encouraging violence against demonstrators.

5. United Nations
Security Council
7060th Meeting (AM)
15 November 2013
Security Council Resolution Seeking Deferral of Kenyan Leaders' Trial Fails to Win (Adoption, with 7 Voting in Favour, 8 Abstaining)

An almost evenly divided Security Council, lacking the requisite nine affirmative votes, today failed to adopt a resolution seeking a one-year delay in International Criminal Court proceedings against the President and Deputy President of Kenya.

Seven Council members voted in favor of the text (Azerbaijan, China, Morocco, Pakistan, Russian Federation, Rwanda, Togo), none voted against, and 8 abstained (Argentina, Australia, France, Guatemala, Luxembourg, Republic of Korea, United Kingdom, United States). The draft was, therefore, not adopted.

Had it passed, the Council would have requested the International Criminal Court, under Chapter VII of the United Nations Charter, to defer the investigation and prosecution of President Uhuru Muigai Kenyatta and Deputy President William Samoei Ruto for 12 months, in accordance with Article 16 of the Rome Statute, which established the Court. By other terms, the Council would have decided that Member States would take no action inconsistent with their international obligations.

Following today's action, delegates explained the differences of opinion reflected in their respective actions.

The representative of the United States said the Assembly of States Parties to the Rome Statute, which oversaw the Court's administration, would meet next week to help address outstanding issues. Since the Court and the Assembly were the proper venues for addressing the concerns of Kenya and the African Union, the United States had abstained rather than voting against the draft resolution.

France's representative said the vote had been unnecessary when the Council was in the midst of consultations with African States. The United Kingdom's representative stressed that the sponsors had failed to establish the Charter VII threshold beyond which the Court's proceedings against the Kenyan leaders would pose a threat to international peace and security.

Guatemala's representative said it was offensive to suggest that those who had not voted in favor of the draft were somehow against Africa. However, today's vote had erected a "barrier of distrust". That some countries had submitted a draft resolution in full knowledge that it would not be adopted did not accord with the goal of promoting Council unity, he emphasized. Today's exercise had left a balance of losers, he said, adding that the vote was detrimental to the African Union, which perceived its proposal as having been rejected; to the Court, whose aspiration for universal membership was under assault; and to the Council, which now appeared divided.

The Russian Federation's representative said African countries had presented compelling arguments at a critical time for Kenya, whose military was playing a key role in Somalia. Their request did not undermine the integrity of the Rome Statute, and there had been no attempt to turn them against the Court. The application of Article 16 would have increased the credibility of the international system of justice among African countries, showing its readiness to address "complicated and ambiguous" situations, he said.

Council President Liu Jieyi (China), speaking in his national capacity, said Africa's request was a matter of interest to the entire continent. It was well grounded and based on the principles of the Charter.

Pakistan's representative said Kenya's case rested on sound, solid strategic, political and legal grounds, adding that its logic was compelling. From a strictly legal standpoint, the principle of complementarity must respect national jurisdiction, he said, noting that the functioning of the offices of the President and Deputy President was under question. A provision on deferral was already available in the Rome Statute, he pointed out.

Rwanda's representative emphasized that the Council was indeed the proper place to discuss today's issue, and expressed his delegation's deep disappointment at what had transpired. "Let it be written in history that the Council failed Kenya and Africa on this issue", he stressed. Today's vote undermined the principle of sovereign equality and confirmed the long-held view that international mechanisms were manipulated to serve select interests. Article 16 had never been meant to be used by an African State; it appeared to be a tool used by Western Powers to "protect their own", he added.

The representative of Ethiopia spoke in that country's capacity as current Chair of the African Union, stressing that the Rome Statute's Article 16 gave the Council authority to defer cases under the Court's remit for 12 months. The African request could not be rejected on legitimate grounds, and abstention under the circumstances amounted to rejection, he added.

Kenya's representative noted that some Council members had chosen to tie the denial of the African Union's request to a paranoid fear of imaginary possible future abuse of Article 16. "Indeed, our understanding is now clear. The Security Council is no institutional destination for solving complex and fluid international security and political problems", he said, adding that the Rome Statute had failed its first crucial test.

Also speaking today were representatives of Luxembourg, Argentina, Morocco, Azerbaijan, Australia, Republic of Korea and Togo.

The meeting began at 10:15 a.m. and ended at 12:00 p.m.

Background

As the Security Council considered peace and security in Africa this morning, members had before them identical letters dated 21 October 2013 (document S/2013/624), from the Permanent Representative of Kenya and addressed to the Secretary-General and the President of the Security Council. They outline that delegation's request that the Council defer investigations or prosecution by the International Criminal Court on cases relating to the situation in Kenya. The

Council was expected to vote on a draft resolution to that effect.

Action

By a vote of 7 in favor (Azerbaijan, China, Morocco, Pakistan, Russian Federation, Rwanda, Togo) to none against, with 8 abstentions (Argentina, Australia, France, Guatemala, Luxembourg, Republic of Korea, United Kingdom, United States), the Council did not pass draft resolution 2125 (2013).

Statements

GERT ROSENTHAL (Guatemala) said his delegation's abstention was a source of great sadness, as his Government had dedicated much time and effort to encouraging more constructive engagement between the Council and the International Criminal Court. Noting that one was a legal body and the other a political one, he said both were united by a mission to fight impunity and demand accountability from perpetrators of mass atrocities. However, today's vote had erected a "barrier of distrust" between them. That some countries had submitted a draft resolution in full knowledge that it would not be adopted did not accord with the goal of promoting Council unity, he emphasized, pointing out that a divided Council was on display without justification. Today's exercise had left a balance of losers, he said, adding: "All of us lost something". The vote was detrimental to the African Union, which perceived its proposal as having been rejected; to the Court, whose aspiration for universal membership was under assault; and to the Council, which now appeared divided. Efforts to build a fruitful partnership between the Council and the African Union had been compromised. "Sometimes we sacrifice justice to achieve peace", he said, rejecting the suggestion that not voting in favor of the resolution was an expression of ill will towards the African Union.

SYLVIE LUCAS (Luxembourg) recalled that the Council had met with the African Union Contact Group two weeks ago, to discuss the regional bloc's question about the situation of the President of Kenya. At that time, Luxembourg had hoped for solutions that were in the interests of all concerned parties, but unfortunately, that opportunity had not arisen. She said her delegation did not support today's text because recourse to Article 16 was not necessary or applicable in the case before the Council. There were other means available to allow Kenya to deal with its affairs, including cooperation with the Court. Moreover, the Court had taken steps to ensure that the President and Deputy President of Kenya would be available to deal with affairs of State, thereby taking their concerns into account. The second available means was the twelfth session of the Assembly of States Parties in The Hague, which would hold a special meeting on counts filed against Heads of State, she said. That was the appropriate body to address those counts. Continuing the proceedings did not threaten regional peace and security, she said, stressing that Luxembourg was open to continuing dialogue to address the concerns of both Kenya and the African Union.

MARÍA CRISTINA PERCEVAL (Argentina) said her delegation had abstained because it was the Council's duty to interpret strictly whether the trial posed a threat to international peace and security, and Argentina did not think it did. The Council was being seen as protecting the law of the jungle. In keeping with its voluntary submission to the Court's jurisdiction, Argentina strove for universal jurisdiction in the fight against impunity, she said. While understanding the motives of the draft's sponsors, as well as acknowledging Kenya's decision to cooperate with the Court, Argentina noted that the Assembly of States Parties was working on amending the rules of procedure. Historical awareness and collective fate pushed the countries of the South to avoid dead ends, she said. However, the rights of victims could not be forgotten or the subject of indifference; they deserved truth, justice and reconciliation.

MASOOD KHAN (Pakistan) said that, while his country was not a member of the Court, it recognized the obligations of members, and noted that the African Union had unanimously requested a deferral. That had produced a tension between those seeking justice and those seeking to promote peace and security. Kenya had made its case on sound, solid strategic, political and legal grounds, he said, adding that its logic was compelling. Kenya and the African Union were fully conscious of the complexity of the case and its repercussions for the region. From a strictly legal standpoint, the principle of complementary must respect national jurisdiction, he said, noting that the functioning of the offices of President and Deputy President was under question. A provision on deferral was already available in the Rome Statute, and could justifiably be applied to reconcile the tensions, he noted. The same considerations that had allowed a four-month deferral could have provided the basis for a longer one, he said, adding that his country had therefore supported the draft resolution. While it could not be adopted, however, Pakistan hoped that dialogue aimed at reaching a pragmatic solution would continue in the interests of the Council, the African Union and the International Criminal Court.

VITALY CHURKIN (Russian Federation) said his delegation had supported the draft resolution, but unfortunately, the Council had been unable to adopt it. African countries had presented compelling arguments at a critical time for Kenya, whose military was playing a key role in Somalia. The democratically elected President and Deputy President should have the possibility of being in their country, with their people, to carry out their tasks, he emphasized. The request by African States did not undermine the integrity of the Rome Statute, and there had been no attempt to turn them against the Court. The application of Article 16 would have increased the credibility of the international system of justice among African countries, showing its readiness to address "complicated and ambiguous" situations, he said, underlining his Government's commitment to combating impunity for the gravest violations of international law.

MARK LYALL GRANT (United Kingdom) said his Government understood the desire for the President and Deputy President of Kenya to fulfill their constitutional responsibilities, but that must be done at the Court and at the Assembly of States Parties, which would meet in five days. Part of that meeting would focus on addressing the African Union's concerns, with a number of amendments on "presence through video technology" already having been tabled. On 31 October, the start of President Kenyatta's trial had been pushed back to 2014, which demonstrated a constructive and legally proper response to the concerns raised. Noting that the Court was one of last resort, he said that, of the eight cases before it, five had been initiated at the request of African States parties. The question before the Council was whether continuing the Court's proceedings constituted a threat in itself. It did not, he emphasized, adding that the United Kingdom's abstention did not change its commitment to peace and security across Africa. However, it was disappointing that the draft resolution had been put to a vote that had highlighted disagreements in the Council. The United Kingdom would continue to engage in addressing the African Union's concerns, through the Assembly of States Parties, he said.

GÉRARD ARAUD (France) said the vote had been unnecessary at a time when the Council was in constant engagement with the African Union. The disagreement was not over the shared goal of allowing Kenyan leaders to pursue the obligations of their office, but over the means to achieve that. Other alternatives could have been pursued in the pursuit of common goals, as Kenyan lawyers and the Court had already demonstrated in recent proceedings, he said. Next week's meeting in The Hague would draw upon those alternatives, but today's effort had been a hasty one that could only widen divisions, he cautioned, emphasizing that dialogue must continue beyond that difficult episode. As an active partner in Africa, France had expended resources and lives on the continent, and would continue to work with Kenya as well as the African Union to address their concerns and uphold the obligations of the Rome Statute.

ABDERRAZZAK LAASSEL (Morocco) expressed regret over the absence of consensus, pointing out that the meeting between Council members and African Union representatives had brought the substance of the draft resolution to the fore. Kenya had made progress domestically in bolstering justice and reconciliation under the two elected leaders, he said, adding that they had demonstrated an untiring commitment to fighting terrorism while promoting regional and international security and stability. African States had produced a constructive basis for discussions that could no longer proceed.

SAMANTHA POWER (United States) said she had abstained because Kenya's concerns were best addressed in the Court and in the Assembly of States Parties. That position was consistent with the view that the United States had shared with the Contact Group at the end of October. Families affected by the 2007/2008 post-election violence had waited five years for a judicial "weighing" of the events, and it was incumbent upon everyone to support the pursuit of justice against those who had committed crimes against humanity, she emphasized. The United States shared the horror of the Westgate Mall attack and was mindful of the importance of such issues to the African Union. Noting that the Court had never tried a sitting Head of State, or a person who might act in that capacity, she said the Assembly of States Parties, which oversaw the Court's administration, would meet next week to help address outstanding issues. Because those were the proper venues for addressing such issues, the United States had abstained rather than voting against the draft resolution, she said, adding that her country valued its friendship with Kenya and would continue to work alongside it in combating terror and promoting human rights and justice, among other issues.

AGSHIN MEHDIYEV (Azerbaijan) said that, while his country was not a party to the Rome Statute, it believed that accountability contributed to the maintenance of international peace and security. Azerbaijan's vote in favour of the draft resolution was based on its understanding that Kenya and the wider region faced complex security challenges. The judicial proceedings against its senior officials would obstruct the functioning of State institutions and threaten efforts to promote peace and security in the region, he warned, adding that the request for deferral could not be considered a measure of impunity. Kenya had shown its commitment to fighting impunity, and both its President and Deputy President had cooperated fully with the Court process, he pointed out. Its Government had worked to restore stability since the political crisis, and was able to handle such judicial issues, he said, adding that for those reasons, Azerbaijan supported the deferral of the Court's proceedings.

GARY QUINLAN (Australia), expressing regret over the vote's outcome, said no one had emerged a winner. Australia recognized the case made by the draft's sponsors, but was also focused on the obligations of the international community under the Rome Statute. The threshold of threat to international peace and security had not been met in Kenya's case, he said, adding that alternative ways to proceed were available. Kenya and the Court were already working to address many of the country's concerns, and Australia would do everything it could to ensure that its President and Deputy President would be able to fulfil their obligations. At the same time, Australia hoped for understanding of the Court's obligations.

JOON OH (Republic of Korea) said his delegation's thorough deliberations with other Council members as well as representatives of the African Union had helped him better understanding the challenges involved. In the Republic of Korea's view, the African Union's concern was genuine and legitimate, but International Criminal Court issues were best addressed not in the Council, but in the Assembly of States Parties in The Hague, he said, emphasizing the importance of not setting a precedent wherein the Council stepped in the way of the Court's proceedings.

KODJO MENAN (Togo) expressed regret that the Council had not adopted the draft resolution, as requested by the African Union, adding that his delegation also regretted the Council's division over a "very significant" issue for Africa. Hopefully, the decision would not "sow the seeds of doubt" about the importance of partnership between the Council and the regional body, he said, adding that the growing number of Council agenda issues concerning Africa meant there was much work to be done.

EUGÈNE-RICHARD GASANA (Rwanda) emphasized that the Council was indeed the proper place to discuss today's issue. While Africa did not want confrontation, terrorism was the most serious threat to international peace and security, and Kenya's President and Deputy President were at the forefront in fighting it, he said, emphasizing that they should be respected, supported and empowered, not undermined. Rwanda was deeply disappointed at what had transpired, despite Africa's proactive efforts to engage the Council in a legitimate process, in the interest of international peace and security. "Let it be written in history that the Council failed Kenya and Africa on this issue," he stressed. Today's vote undermined the principle of sovereign equal and confirmed the long-held view that international mechanisms were manipulated to serve select interests, he continued. Article 16 had never been meant to be used by an African State; it appeared to be a tool used by Western Powers to "protect their own". Some had not even signed up to the Rome Statute because they wished to protect their own nationals, he pointed out. African Heads of State and Government had proposed a solution to the Kenyan issues, but Western Powers had an alternative solution in mind—interaction with the Court and the Assembly of States Parties.

LIU JIEYI (China), Council President, spoke in his national capacity, saying that he had voted in favour of the draft resolution. Kenya had been playing a long-standing role in the fight against terrorism and in bolstering peace and security in Africa, and its request was therefore a matter of interest to the entire continent. It was a matter of common sense to help the country's popularly elected leaders focus on upholding their mandate. International law should respect that mandate as well as the principle of complementarity and the sovereignty of nations, he emphasized. The request of the African countries was well grounded and based on the principles of the Charter. They sought respect for the two popularly elected leaders, he said, stressing that the Council should have heeded it and responded appropriately. China would continue to support the aspirations of African countries, he added.

MACHARIA KAMAU (Kenya) said Africa had come to the Council in the belief that the 15-member body was in command of its own reality and the master of its mandate. However, Africa had learned that despite the Council's own recognition of the recent terror attacks in Nairobi as threatening to international peace and security, that recognition counted for little in the Council when Article 16 was under consideration. The request for a 12-month deferral was not political pressure but the law, of which Africa wanted both the spirit and letter applied because it believed that the Rome Statute was as much the continent's own as anybody's. But reason and the law had been "thrown out the window". Fear and distrust and been allowed to prevail, he said, adding that Africa was disappointed.

Noting that some Council members had chosen to tie the denial of the request to a paranoid fear of imaginary possible future abuse of Article 16, he said today's turn of circumstances was simply sad, absurd and confounding. To certain Council members, the supposed fear of treading on legal niceties was clearly much more important than the need to promote international solidarity, peace and security, or the importance of helping to maintain stability in a nation, or region, under the threat of terror, he emphasized. "Indeed, our understanding is now clear. The Security Council is no institutional destination for solving complex and fluid international security and political problems", he said. "For Africa, the message is that we need only stay within the African family to solve unusual and complex political problems, working within the African Union to seek solutions to the challenges that we face".

He went on to underline that the Council belonged as much to Africa as to any other region. However, "our engagement here has been met with derision, suspicion, impatience and even irritation". That was wrong, unfair, sad and tragic, he said, adding that it was an indictment of the state of international relations at the dawn of the twenty-first century. The Rome Statute had failed its first crucial test. Nevertheless, Kenya was grateful for the recognition it had received from all Member States of the African continent and their leaders, as well as from the Russian Federation, Pakistan, Azerbaijan and China within the Security Council. For Africans, their business in the Council was done but the matter was not closed, he cautioned. The Council had removed itself from being part of an amicable solution and had thereby done irreparable damage to the Rome Statute and its future furtherance.

TEKEDA ALEMU (Ethiopia), speaking in his country's capacity as current Chair of the African Union, expressed his profound appreciation to those Council members who felt that African Heads of State and Government knew what was best for their continent and supported the deferral request. The African case had been made by the Contact Group, which had tried to convince the Council that the matter was not simply a Kenyan one, but an African one that had caused great concern for regional peace and security. It had emphasized that distracting the Kenyan leaders from their obligations would represent a grave threat to peace and security. What Africa had requested was within the law, he emphasized, explaining that Article 16 of the Rome Statute gave the Security Council the authority to defer cases under the Court's remit for 12 months.

He went on to stress that the Commander-in-Chief of the Kenyan Defence Forces ought to be given support, rather than be distracted by a body whose track record on African matters did not inspire confidence. The African request could not be rejected on legitimate grounds, and under the circumstances, abstention amounted to rejection, he said. The African Union did not allow sovereignty to be used as a shield for impunity, and for African leaders not to be trusted—which was what today's decision expressed—highlighted the challenge they faced in upholding international cooperation. African countries could thrive through partnerships, as had been seen in Somalia, Sudan-South Sudan and Mali, he said, pointing out, however, that today's response to the deferral request would lead many to conclude that Council members had difficulty seeing Africa exercise ownership over its policies and strategies for peace.

Index

G. Werle et al. (eds.), *Africa and the International Criminal Court*,
International Criminal Justice Series 1, DOI 10.1007/978-94-6265-029-9

FSC
www.fsc.org
MIX
Papier aus verantwortungsvollen Quellen
Paper from responsible sources
FSC® C105338

If you have any concerns about our products,
you can contact us on
ProductSafety@springernature.com

In case Publisher is established outside the EU,
the EU authorized representative is:
Springer Nature Customer Service Center GmbH
Europaplatz 3, 69115 Heidelberg, Germany

Printed by Libri Plureos GmbH
in Hamburg, Germany